MW00387540

A YOUNG GENERAL
AND THE FALL OF RICHMOND

A YOUNG GENERAL AND THE FALL OF RICHMOND

The Life and Career of Godfrey Weitzel

G. WILLIAM QUATMAN

OHIO UNIVERSITY PRESS • ATHENS

E
467.1
.W455
Q38
2015

Ohio University Press, Athens, Ohio 45701
ohioswallow.com
© 2015 by Ohio University Press
All rights reserved

To obtain permission to quote, reprint, or otherwise reproduce or distribute
material from Ohio University Press publications, please contact our rights
and permissions department at (740) 593-1154 or (740) 593-4536 (fax).

Cover photo: Major General Godfrey Weitzel. (Photo by Mathew Brady;
Library of Congress, Prints and Photographs Division, Reproduction
No. LC-DIG-cwpb-07632 DLC; retouching by Cristin Quatman-Euston.)

Printed in the United States of America
Ohio University Press books are printed on acid-free paper. ♾ ™

PBK: 20 19 18 17 16 15 5 4 3 2
HC: 20 19 18 17 16 15 5 4 3 2 1

Library of Congress Cataloging-in-Publication Data

Quatman, G. William, 1958–
  A young general and the fall of Richmond : the life and career of Godfrey Weitzel /
G. William Quatman.
     pages cm
  Includes bibliographical references and index.
  ISBN 0-8214-2141-7 (hc) — ISBN 0-8214-2142-5 (pb) — ISBN 0-8214-4516-2 (pdf)
  1. Weitzel, G. (Godfrey), 1835–1884. 2. Generals—United States—Biography. 3. United
States—History—Civil War, 1861–1865—Biography. 4. United States—History—Civil War,
1861–1865—Campaigns. I. Title.
  E467.1.W455 Q38 2014
  355.0092—dc23
  [B]
                                                                      2014042209

For Juney and Evie

At Eight in the Morning

At Eight in the morning
Brave Weitzel so true
Marched into the town
With his Heroes in Blue

SONG and CHORUS

BY

J. E. HAYNES.

CHICAGO
Published by H. M. HIGGINS 117 Randolph St.

Entered according to Act of Congress 1865 by H. M. Higgins in the Clerks Office of the Dist Court of the North Dist of Ill.

M. 1640
H

At eight in the morning, brave Weitzel so true
Marched into the town with his heroes in blue,
The slave that oppression had bound with her chain,
Went forward our laws and our rights to maintain;
O'erpowerd by the tyrant who reigned in his might,
Deprived of their freedom, forbidden their rights,
Ground down by oppression, shut out from the light,
For years they had dwelt in the darkness of night.

—Charles Haynes, "At Eight in the Morning"

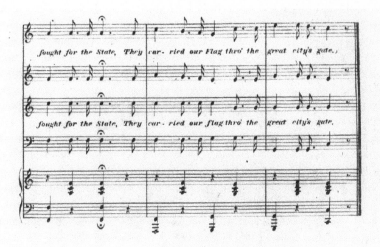

2.

At eight in the morning brave Weitzel so true
Marched into the town with his heroes in blue,
The slave that oppression had bound with her chain,
Went forward our laws and our rights to maintain;
O'erpowerd by the tyrant who reigned in his might,
Deprived of their freedom, forbidden their rights,
Ground down by oppression, shut out from the light,
For years they had dwelt in the darkness of night.

3.

Long years the poor African grovelled in dust,
Yet patiently waiting in God he did trust;
The Savior hath blessed him and given him light,
He's fought for his Country, his God, and the Right.
And now he rejoices his trials are o'er,
The lash of the tyrant shall scourge him no more,
Our armies have conquered and won the great fight,
Our legions have crushed the proud foe in his might.

At eight in the morning.

Contents

Illustrations

Figures

Prologue

An exhausted Abraham Lincoln was followed through the dusty streets of Richmond by a crowd of former slaves singing his praises and in a great state of excitement, all trying to get a look at "Father Abraham."[1] It was Tuesday, April 4, 1865, and smoke billowed from burning buildings a few blocks away. Cinders were still hot from the raging fire set by retreating Confederate soldiers so that the Union Army would not reap the spoils of war. Through the haze that choked many in the procession, the president finally stopped after his two-mile hike from the landing on the James River. He stared in wonder at the elegant three-story gray stucco mansion on the corner of Twelfth and Clay, the house formerly occupied by Jefferson Davis. Another crowd of Richmond residents was gathered out front of the Confederate White House, anxious to get a firsthand look at the Union's president. Ironically, some mistook Lincoln for Southern president Davis, who had caught the Danville train out of town only a day ago. There were shouts of "*Hang him! Hang him!*"[2]

As the tall man in a black frock coat and top hat climbed the steps to the front door, his twelve-year old son, Tad by his side, a Federal officer called for silence. He then introduced Abraham Lincoln, "the president of the United States." Wild cheering broke out at the confirmation that, indeed, Lincoln had arrived in the rebel capital, just one day after the city had fallen to black Union troops led by Major General Godfrey Weitzel. President Lincoln acknowledged the hearty cheers, then turned and bowed, a mark of respect that electrified the gathering.[3]

A few blocks away, Godfrey Weitzel was working in his makeshift office at the Virginia statehouse when a Union soldier rushed in out of breath. "The president arrived early! He is waiting for you at the Davis mansion!" The words took Weitzel by surprise, as Mr. Lincoln was not expected for a few more hours. The Union general dismissed the messenger and, hurrying from his desk, jumped into a carriage that transported him as quickly as possible to meet the president.[4]

Rushing awkwardly into the parlor at the Confederate White House, General Weitzel made his apologies to Abraham Lincoln. After a few pleasantries, the weary president took a seat in the Davis presidential office and the two men got down to business. Weitzel relayed to President Lincoln that several prominent men of Richmond had asked for a meeting to discuss the state of affairs. The president listened patiently, though he showed "great nervousness of manner, running his hands frequently through his hair and moving to and fro" as he sat in Jefferson Davis's desk chair. After a few moments' thought, Lincoln told General Weitzel, "Well, say to them that I will entertain their propositions, with the condition that I shall have *one friend*, with the same liberty to them."[5]

Abraham Lincoln selected Godfrey Weitzel as his "one friend" to join him as an eyewitness and, perhaps, bodyguard during the meetings with the Southern representatives. Weitzel had also served as a guard four years earlier, during Lincoln's first inauguration, when Godfrey was a mere foot soldier. The pair spent the next two days in confidential negotiations with former U.S. Supreme Court justice John A. Campbell, now the assistant secretary of war for the Confederacy. President Lincoln and Judge Campbell devised a plan to end the great Civil War, a plan that would end the bloodshed of the past four years. Twenty-nine-year-old Godfrey Weitzel was the only Federal officer to witness these discussions.

When Lincoln departed Richmond to return upriver to Washington, D.C., he gave the young general instructions to carry out the peace plan. Weitzel was to issue permission for the members of the Virginia legislature to return at once to Richmond for the sole purpose of adopting one resolution: *Virginia would re-join the Union.* Robert E. Lee would have no reason to continue the battle, and the Army of Northern Virginia would lay down its arms. Peace would be restored with the stroke of a pen rather than the blast of a musket. The plan seemed so logical.

But all hell was about to break loose for Godfrey Weitzel, who found himself in the middle of a national controversy, accused of being a liar and a traitor! Lincoln would never have issued such orders, claimed Secretary of War Edwin Stanton. An assassin's bullet silenced Mr. Lincoln only a few days later, but not before he penned a confidential letter to Godfrey Weitzel. Would that letter save the young general from court-martial and from the scorn of the Northern press? The German immigrant held on to the president's letter; it was his only defense.

When Lee surrendered days later, and the U.S. president was murdered, radical Republicans pounced on Weitzel as a flunky who misunderstood Lincoln's intentions in Richmond. As punishment, perhaps, while other generals were mustered out and sent home to grand parades and glory, Godfrey Weitzel was shipped off with his all-black Army corps to the Texas-Mexican border to evict the French, who had occupied Mexico while the United States was distracted with its own civil war.

Who was this twenty-nine-year-old Union general, the person Lincoln trusted as his "one friend"? Godfrey Weitzel's story is one of the great untold stories of the Civil War. Like Forrest Gump, he was always in the right place at the right time. If not for a chance first assignment in New Orleans, fresh out of West Point, he might have never amounted to more than a first lieutenant, perhaps an engineer assigned to one of the lesser-known major generals. But one success led to another, and Godfrey Weitzel's mentors saw to it that he gained recognition and promotions, each one placing him in a key location or battle. Win or lose, he seemed to come out on top with another commendation, brevet, or promotion. His timing was impeccable, guided sometimes more by fate than by effort.

"Like Grant took Richmond," the expression goes, although Ulysses S. Grant never set foot in Richmond until after the end of the Civil War. No, it was not the short, bearded general from Galena, Illinois, who seized the Confederate capital, but a tall young officer from Winzeln, Germany, Godfrey Weitzel, who bravely led the all-black Twenty-Fifth Army Corps of Union troops into the burning city on April 3, 1865. No doubt about it, Grant's nine-month siege and his final assault on nearby Petersburg led to the evacuation of Richmond and Weitzel's unopposed entrance. But the Federal officer who officially accepted the surrender of the rebel capital was, in fact, Major General Godfrey Weitzel.

"A braver and stronger man doesn't live," said one Union officer of Godfrey Weitzel. He earned the respect of top commanders in both the blue and the gray—P. G. T. Beauregard, Robert E. Lee, David G. Farragut, David D. Porter, Benjamin F. Butler, Ulysses S. Grant, and President Abraham Lincoln—all of whom played a significant role in shaping Weitzel's career. Yet, for a man who was known by all these great names of American history, he is one of the least known of all the war's brigadiers, a mere footnote in a few books on the great domestic conflict.

Godfrey Weitzel's exceptional military career began at age fourteen when he was accepted into the Academy at West Point, New York (the standard required age was sixteen). Against all odds, the tall young plebe rose to the top of his class, catching the attention of Superintendent Robert E. Lee. His career wove an unlikely course under the tutelage of Pierre "Little Napoleon" Beauregard and Benjamin "the Beast" Butler, both of whom mentored and promoted the bright young engineer, recognizing his skills despite his youth.

After success in early battles along the bayous of Louisiana, Godfrey became a division commander. He at first rejected an offer to command all-black Union regiments, but reluctantly accepted under pressure from his superior officer, Major General Ben Butler. That assignment led to a death sentence from Jefferson Davis, the "black flag," which the Confederate president ordered against all commissioned officers under Butler's command. After a series of missions on the Mississippi and the Sabine Rivers, Godfrey faced off against both Beauregard and Lee in Virginia, achieving victories against the two Southern leaders at Drewry's Bluff and Fort Harrison. Ulysses S. Grant then selected Godfrey Weitzel to lead a land assault on Fort Fisher, the impenetrable rebel sand fortress guarding Wilmington. A planned Christmas Day attack in 1864 turned into an embarrassing loss, however, when weather and lack of coordination with the naval fleet trapped hundreds of Union

FIGURE O.I. Major General Godfrey Weitzel towered above his staff at six feet four inches tall. This photo was taken by Mathew Brady. (Weitzel is standing, left side of steps, hand in pocket). (Library of Congress, Prints and Photographs Division, Reference No. LC-DIG-ppmsca-34141.)

soldiers on the North Carolina beach during a winter storm. Sent back to Virginia, Godfrey Weitzel found himself knocking on the door to Richmond.

When the Confederates abandoned their capital city and set it ablaze, Weitzel led in his all-black Twenty-Fifty Army Corps. The irony of freed slaves wearing the Union blue and marching into the burning Confederate capital was apparent to everyone who witnessed the scene. Some of the most remarkable moments of Weitzel's career took place over the next few days inside the Davis mansion, which Godfrey occupied as his quarters. Matured by battle but worn down by politics, Godfrey Weitzel slipped into a quiet career in the Army Corps of Engineers in 1866 after honorable discharge from the Volunteer Army. He spent the next eighteen years designing and overseeing canals and locks, as well as mutiple lighthouses, on the Great Lakes. He reverted to his rank of major in the regular Army, dropping the title of major general of Volunteers.

When Godfrey Weitzel died in Philadelphia of typhoid fever in 1884, his body was shipped home to Cincinnati and given a hero's funeral. The Army later honored his contribution to the Union's success by naming a road and entry gate at Arlington Cemetery after him. His grave, however, in Spring Grove Cemetery in Cincinnati, is marked by a small slab in a modest family plot, overlooked for nearly 150 years by thousands who pass by, unaware of the hero buried there. Perhaps with the publication of his life story, Godfrey Weitzel will receive the proper attention he has thus far been denied.

Acknowledgments

I want to thank the following people and institutions for their assistance in research for this book: the staff of the Archives and Manuscripts Department of the Library of Virginia (Richmond); Ruth Ann Coski, Library Manager of the Museum of the Confederacy; M'Lissa Kesterman and Rick Kesterman of the Cincinnati Historical Society Library; Susan Lintelmann, Manuscripts Curator, West Point Military Academy Library; Siva M. Blake, Reference Archivist, the Williams Research Center at the Historic New Orleans Collection; the reference staff at Tulane University and the New Orleans Public Library; and Ray Flowers, Site Historian, Fort Fisher, North Carolina, for his hospitality. Thank you to Johanna Quatmann for translations of German newspaper articles. Also, to my good friends from the Civil War Roundtable of Kansas City who opened my eyes to the events and personalities of that great conflict, and who urged me on with my research and writing.

Thanks especially to my good friends and family members, Jim Lynch, Admiral Tom Lynch, Tom Kehoe, Dena Daniel, Mark Mohlner, and Mike Callahan, for proofreading and for wonderful suggestions. Also to my college chum, John Jennings, now of LaHulpe, Belguim, who edited this book from across the world.

Thank you to Gillian Berchowitz, Director of Ohio University Press, for her support and belief in bringing this story to print; to Andrew Capone and the townspeople of Donaldsonville, Louisiana, for the warm hospitality received and the wonderful gumbo served on my research trips there.

A final thank-you to my wife, Denise, who was my loyal traveling companion as we "chased Godfrey" along the country roads and earthworks of Virginia, the bayous of Louisiana, and into the stately cemetery at Arlington. She encouraged me as I saddled up with the general and rode along with him over the past decade's journey. And to my loving family who humored their father's obsession with the Civil War and listened to countless stories as if they were really interested. I am now mustered out of service and back to civilian life, thankful for the experience.

G. William Quatman

Eng.d by A.H Ritchie

G. Weitzel

Brig. Gen.l

U. S. Vols.

FIGURE 0.2. Major General Godfrey Weitzel. (Engraving by Alexander Hay Ritchie [1822–1895] based on Mathew Brady photograph, ca. 1865. From author's collection.)

CHAPTER 1

Over-the-Rhine

Damned Dutch Cowards

America was an immigrant nation in 1861, in large part first-generation immigrants. More than 1.3 million Germans had migrated to the United States prior to the start of the Civil War. While a considerable number, this was less than 5 percent of the nation's total white population, a clear minority. Most of these German immigrants spoke English poorly, if at all, resulting in discrimination against those in the U.S. Army with an accent or a German name. Some of these foreign recruits had trouble understanding their English-speaking commanding officers, or even fellow soldiers in their regiment. This led to confusion, distrust, and prejudice against Germans for fear of errors on the battlefield.

Sometimes German troops or officers were singled out by newspaper writers when their performance was poor or if their regiment suffered defeat. Such was the case after the Battle of Chancellorsville in May 1863 near the village of Spotsylvania Courthouse, Virginia. There, Stonewall Jackson decimated the Union's Eleventh Army Corps, composed of large numbers of German-speaking volunteers. The immigrant troops became the scapegoat for that Northern loss after more than four thousand of them were taken prisoner without firing a shot. Author Christian B. Keller wrote, "It is not an exaggeration to say that the North's German-born population never got over what happened in the Virginia wood in May 1863. Its repercussions shook them throughout the rest of the Civil War."[1]

German soldiers were labeled "damned Dutch cowards" and unjustly blamed for the loss. Especially after Chancellorsville, Germans in the Union Army fought against prejudice in addition to the enemy, the elements, and disease. "The German is a 'Dutch soldier' and as a 'Dutchman' he is, if not despised, disrespected, and not regarded or treated as an equal," said one German immigrant Union soldier.[2]

It was into this military culture that a young German named Gottfried Weitzel entered. Tall and gangly, younger by years than his peers at West Point, he had to fight against prejudice to prove himself as a soldier. Nicknamed "Dutch" by his classmates at the Military Academy, a boy with a name like "Weitzel" needed to excel academically and on the battlefield to gain respect.

Gottfried Weitzel

Born in Winzeln, Germany

Most official publications and biographies, including George Cullum's famous West Point biographies, and even Godfrey's obituary, list Weitzel's birthplace as Cincinnati, Ohio. "Born in and appointed from Ohio," he wrote to Captain Cullum on September 11, 1859, while Godfrey was an assistant professor at West Point.[3] Godfrey even convinced his West Point classmates that his parents were native Germans, but that he was born a month or so after they landed in America.[4] To the contrary, the boy named "Gottfried" was born more than four thousand miles away on November 1, 1835, in Winzeln, Germany. It was shortly after his birth that the Weitzel family immigrated to the United States.[5]

Perhaps his parents changed the spelling of his first name from "Gottfried" to "Godfrey," just as his father had morphed from "Ludwig" to "Lewis" upon his immigration. But it was Godfrey's own decision to continue the ruse after graduation and throughout his military career to avoid the discrimination many Germans felt during the war and postwar years.

Weitzel was a top West Pointer, well trained, and a model of precision and obedience to orders from his superiors. His German upbringing and American education fitted him perfectly for a military career that reached unimaginable heights. To appreciate his accomplishments, one has to understand the modest roots from which he rose.

The Weitzels from Winzeln

In the rural southwest of Germany, near the French border, sits the tiny village of Winzeln. The area is just north of the well-known city of Strasbourg and due east from Metz, the famous twentieth-century capital of the Lorraine region. Winzeln is part of the province known as Rhineland-Palatinate. After the French Revolution, the region belonged to France for about eight years, but it was never part of French Alsace. After 1806, the town of Winzeln became German territory and remains so today. Official town records contain the marriage certificate of Ludwig and Susanna Weitzel, in addition to their son Gottfreid's birth certificate.[6]

Ludwig Weitzel served in the German military before immigrating. He followed his bother Wilhelm, who came to America in about 1835. Godfrey's mother had a brother named "Gottfried," so it is no surprise that she and Ludwig named their firstborn son after him. When Susanna became pregnant again in Germany in 1837, the couple gathered their infant son along with their modest possessions and booked passage for the cross-Atlantic steamship voyage to America. There, Ludwig hoped to make his fortune and find a better life for him and his growing family. Like so many other emigrants from Germany, the Weitzels immediately settled in Cincinnati, Ohio, where thousands of other Bavarians had already made their homes.

Having preceded the main migration by ten to fifteen years, Ludwig Weitzel was already well established in Cincinnati when the flood of Germans poured into Ohio in the 1840s and 1850s. He made a very quick adjustment to his new homeland, changing his first name to the more American-sounding "Lewis" and opening his own business. A bright and tall man with political ties, he became a very well-respected citizen in the town's Tenth Ward, where he ran a grocery store with the help of his wife and two young sons, Gottfried and Lewis, Jr. The Tenth Ward contained the Germanic "Over-the-Rhine" neighborhood, bounded by Liberty Street to the north and Twelfth Street to the south, extending west to Central and east to Vine. The small family store at 405 Elm Street was profitable, and the Weitzels made a decent living. Their grocery store shared a block with carpenters, tailors, shoemakers, chairmakers, and a coffeehouse, all run by Germans with names like Bicker, Fager, Krug, and Tutlekofer.[7] Customers and friends began to notice the unusually tall boy, Gottfried, who liked to build forts in the snow and to play soldier—a foreshadowing of things to come.[8]

Prior to the mid-1850s, most German immigrants became loyal members of the Democratic Party, which welcomed foreigners and spoke out for their political rights. No exception, Lewis Weitzel became active in local politics as a strong Democrat. In 1853, Lewis was made a city commissioner, a position he held for three years. He also served on the local school board, chaired by Bellamy Storer, a lawyer and former U.S. congressman from Ohio.[9] This relationship with Representative Storer would pay off handsomely when a congressman was needed to sponsor young Gottfried's application to West Point.

Both Weitzel boys were educated in the Cincinnati public schools and attended the new "central" high school that opened in November 1847 in the basement of the German Lutheran Church on Walnut Street, below Ninth Street. Even as a high school student, Gottfried Weitzel was described as having "a mathematical head" with an exceptional aptitude for figures. The bright boy finished at the top of his class in all courses.

Appointment to West Point

Young Gottfried's academic prowess caught the attention of the school board president, ex-congressman Bellamy Storer, who encouraged the boy's father to make sure his son advanced his education. Storer even offered to pay for Gottfried's college tuition. But that gave way to an even better idea, one that changed Gottfried's life forever—apply to the U.S. Military Academy.

A West Point education was not only free of cost, but also the best education a young man could receive. President Andrew Jackson had called West Point "the best school in the world."[10] Even if Gottfried was technically too young, he was certainly smart enough, and people often mistook him to be much older, due to his maturity and height. With the persuasion of Congressman Storer, the Weitzels decided to make the appropriate contacts for sponsorship.

Since the 1820s, admission to West Point had been distributed through the secretary of war by admitting just one cadet from each congressional district, plus two "at large" cadets from every state, and another dozen or so which the president himself could appoint at his discretion.[11] Storer contacted freshman congressman David Tiernan Disney to find out if there was an opening in Ohio's First District. Since this was his former congressional district, Bellamy Storer still had clout in Ohio political circles. He recruited another German immigrant, former Ohio state senator Heinrich ("Henry") Roedter, to help out. Roedter was publisher and editor of two German-language newspapers that catered to the large immigrant population, the *Ohio Staatszeitung* and the *Democratische Tageblatt*. Roedter and Storer made an impressive team in Gottfried's corner to push through his West Point application.

Applying to the "Best School"

In 1850, admission criteria for the U.S. Military Academy required that the candidate be *more than sixteen* but less than twenty-one years of age, and an actual resident of the state and district from which he was appointed. The boy had to be at least five feet tall and "free from every disease or deformity which might, in any manner, interfere with the discharge of the various and arduous duties of an army officer."[12] Height was no problem, but being only fourteen at the time, Gottfried did not meet the first and foremost criterion of age. Whether Roedter and Storer were ignorant of his actual birth date or Lewis Weitzel fibbed about his unusually tall son's age, we do not know. However, the application process began in earnest in August 1850, two and one-half months before Gottfried's *fifteenth* birthday.

The process for appointing new cadets to West Point began each May when the superintendent of the Academy designated the professors of mathematics and ethics to oversee a free tutorial of the candidates. The provisional cadets had to travel to New York in June for instruction that was carried out by upperclassmen assigned the task by the two professors. It was August 1850 when Gottfried's application was submitted, too late for admission to the Academy's June tutorial class for the fall term. As a result, Storer and Roedter set their sights on an appointment for the fall term of 1851, when Gottfried was another year older—yet still less than sixteen.

With the support of two high-powered Cincinnati politicians, Gottfried was nearly assured of obtaining the appointment. "We are unanimous in recommending Mr. Gottfried Weitzel, a son of Mr. Lewis Weitzel of this place" for the vacant spot, Roedter wrote in his August 16, 1850, letter to Congressman Disney. Roedter confirmed that the boy was born in Germany, adding, "He is now considered the best scholar, and he was the first of every class he passed." Roedter fudged a bit about Gottfried's age, adding, "He is now *about sixteen years old*, well built, healthy constitution, and so well behaved that by his good conduct and progress in learning he enjoys the good will and respect of all connected with the common school system."[13] Hardly "about sixteen," the boy was only fourteen going on fifteen. Roedter closed by noting that the father could not provide for the education of his son by his own means.

Apparently moved by the letters, Representative Disney wrote a short note to newly appointed U.S. secretary of war Charles Magill Conrad on September 6, 1850, nominating Gottfried Weitzel for the vacancy from his congressional district.

In mid-September, an official letter arrived at the Weitzel family home in an envelope marked "Secretary of War." Lewis and Susanna anxiously opened the letter and beamed with delight. President Fillmore had conferred a conditional appointment of "cadet" on their *fourteen-year-old* son, Gottfried, at the United States Military Academy.

Preparations Begin

The letter of acceptance was accompanied by a list known at West Point as "the articles marked thus." Gottfried was to bring specified items from home to the Academy (sheets, pillowcases, etc.), plus cash in the amount of $60.95, to be deposited with the school's treasurer.[14] The letter advised that cadets would receive $24 per month, and that they would have no leave of absence for the first two years, and then only if the cadet's conduct justified it.[15] Only two problems existed—school had already begun at West Point for the fall semester of 1850 and, an even greater obstacle—Gottfried was too young.

Since classes had already started, there was no rush to accept the appointment. The Weitzel family took nearly two months to consider the offer before sending their official acceptance letter, perhaps advised to wait for Gottfried's *fifteenth* birthday on the first of November. On December 3, 1850, the family sent its letter of acceptance to Secretary Conrad, signed in a very flamboyant manner by "Godfried Weitzel."

The new "conditional" cadet was told to present himself at West Point sometime between the the first and the twentieth days of June 1851 for the preparation and examination. With six months to wait, Gottfried had plenty of time to prepare for his entrance exam. He got a job at Eggers & Company, a German-owned bookstore, paper, and stationery warehouse, just two blocks east of the Weitzel family grocery.[16]

Entrance standards were not high and required only that the candidate be in good physical condition and demonstrate basic proficiency in the "three R's" of reading, writing, and arithmetic. With such a low threshold for admission, nine out of ten nominated candidates were admitted to the Academy after examination. This left the task to the instructors and superintendent of weeding out those not fit for four years of rigorous physical and mental training to prepare for military service. More than a quarter of the boys admitted failed to graduate with their class due to academic or disciplinary deficiencies. Gottfried Weitzel could not let his family down. This was a once-in-a-lifetime opportunity, and many people had high expectations for him.

Politics and the "Compromise" of 1850

While Gottfried's thoughts were focused on the Military Academy, the seeds of dissension were being planted between Northern industrialists and Southern plantation owners. The autumn of 1850 was a time of great political turmoil for the entire nation, particularly on the issue of slavery. Representative Disney of Ohio and his fellow congressmen debated and passed the Fugitive Slave Act in September, mandating that any federal marshal who did not arrest an alleged runaway slave could be fined $1,000. Any colored person merely *suspected* of being a runaway slave could be arrested without a warrant and turned over to the person claiming to be the slave's owner on nothing more than his sworn testimony of ownership. The suspected slave was not entitled to a jury trial and could not testify on his or her behalf. The law also penalized any person aiding a runaway slave with imprisonment for up to six months plus a $1,000 fine "for each fugitive so lost."

A decade later, Abraham Lincoln's election raised the issue of slavery in America to the forefront of the public conscience. The subject would do much to change the nation in the next ten years and place Gottfried Weitzel at the very center of the conflict. His life would be forever different from what the teenage boy could have imagined.

CHAPTER 2

Welcome to West Point

The historic land known as "West Point" is located on the west bank of the Hudson River, about fifty miles north of New York City, where the river takes a sharp S-curve before heading south. Nestled in picturesque mountains, the campus of the United States Military Academy sits on a commanding plateau almost two hundred feet above the waterline. From this impressive site, the Hudson River flows down into Lower New York Bay and, eventually, dumps into the deep blue Atlantic. The view of the Hudson is dramatic, with sailboats dotting the horizon. On a clear day, the view from the Crow's Nest, a mountaintop some more than fourteen hundred feet above sea level, one can see West Point below and the town of Cold Spring, New York, to the north.[1] Charles Dickens said, "It could not stand on more appropriate ground, and any ground more beautiful can hardly be."[2]

The Best School in the World

During the Revolutionary War, General George Washington considered West Point to be the most important strategic position in America. In 1777, he ordered the commander of the Continental troops in that area to build defensive works and obstructions "as may be necessary to defend and secure the river against any future attempts of the enemy." To prevent attacks by British ships, local iron-workers were hired to fabricate a massive 50-ton iron chain, dubbed "General Washington's Watch Chain" by the Continental soldiers. Eight hundred wrought-iron links were forged, each two feet long and weighing about 125 pounds. When completed, the massive chain was floated out into the river on forty huge log rafts that stretched east across the width of the Hudson and anchored to Constitution Island to block the strategic waterway from a British invasion. Today, thirteen of the links are still preserved at Trophy Point on the grounds of West Point.[3]

In his message to Congress in 1793, President Washington recommended that a military academy be established on the wide plateau on the west bank of the Hudson. However, it was not until nine years later, during the administration of Thomas Jefferson, that Congress finally enacted a law for the formation of a military academy there. The law of March 1802 also specified that the corps of "engineers" would operate the school.[4]

In 1816, a formal four-year program was put in place, and Sylvanus Thayer was made superintendent of the school in 1817. For two years, Thayer studied the French system of military education at the famous L'École Polytechnique in Paris, and he used that program as a model. His vision was more of an engineering school than a military one, and he assembled a faculty that was dedicated to keeping it that way.[5] Today, Thayer Road and Thayer Hall on the Academy's campus honor his legacy.

Based on the governing body he observed in Paris, Thayer introduced the formation of an academic board to help plan curriculum and to conduct the semiannual examinations. This board was also responsible to rank the cadets in each class based on their academic performance and conduct, and to decide whether students found deficient based on their examinations should be permitted to continue as cadets or be dismissed.

Though technically a civilian, it was the secretary of war who officially presided over the military school. This duty fell to a Kentucky-native, Secretary Jefferson Davis, from March 1853 to March 1857. Davis was himself a graduate of the Academy (class of 1828) and, as secretary of war, he visited the campus and actively participated in decisions on military policy and curriculum.

Arriving at West Point, New York—June 1851

Back in Cincinnati, Gottfried packed up his required items and departed in early June of 1851 to begin the cross-country trip to New York. His family and other well-wishers accompanied him to the Public Landing in Cincinnati, whose docks were jammed with tall-stacked steamboats and paddle wheelers. Gottfried said good-bye to his parents and brother Lewis Jr., and climbed the ramp to a steamer that would take him up the Ohio River and far from his hometown.

New York City was bursting with immigrants from Ireland, Germany, and elsewhere. The tall buildings and busy streets were a far cry from even the busiest intersection in Cincinnati's Over-the-Rhine District. Gottfried was in awe as he made his way to the passenger docks on the Hudson River, with every sight and sound intriguing him. Finding his steamboat, he started the last leg of his fabulous trip, paying the fifty-cent fare for his ticket. The tall, awkward boy carrying a bundle of clothes, sheets, and other supplies must have caught the eye of other candidates who also boarded the same steamer for their trip fifty miles upriver to West Point. From the top deck of the Hudson River steamer, the candidates could command the best view of the river and the green mountains, hoping to catch the first glimpse of the flag flying high above the Military Academy. Busy steamers often raced each other up and down the Hudson as a thrill for the passengers. Perhaps this one did, too, to which the boys cheered with delight.

Standing anxiously at the railing, straining his eyes, Godfrey caught his first sight of the impressive school where he would spend the next four years of his young life. As he stepped foot from the boat to the dock, he left his civilian life behind and entered a totally different world.

A Harsh Reality Awaits

At the West Point steamship dock, Godfrey put his modest belongings on a horse-drawn cart, which he followed up the long hill to the forty-acre campus on the Plain some two hundred feet above. Mounting the hill, he saw older cadets already at drill or parade in their sharp uniforms, with instructors barking out commands: "Hep! Hep! Hep!" There was no time for gawking, however, as the candidates had to report to the adjunct's office immediately upon arrival.

The tall fifteen-year-old from Cincinnati wanted to blend in with his class-mates. In the adjunct's office, he signed the official register of cadets "Godfrey" Weitzel, then reported to the treasurer, who relieved the young boy of what cash he had remaining from his trip and his required deposit. As was Academy policy, cadets could not have money in their possession while on school grounds. This served to deter any temptation to sneak off campus to nearby towns to buy cigars or liquor, both of which were prohibited in cadet barracks. From that point on, the eager young candidates were stripped of any ego they might have brought with then, referred to only as an "animal" or "plebe"—the lowest of the low in the pecking order at the Point.[6]

Godfrey was sent from one place to another for the next hour or so and fi-nally assigned a room in one of the freshman barracks. There he was introduced to his roommates from the "Fourth Class," as the freshman cadets were known. The barracks were crowded, with four or five boys assigned to a room no larger than twelve feet by twelve feet, poorly ventilated and unheated other than by coal-burning grates. The rooms had no furniture other than a chair and bed for each boy, along with his trunk. No decorations were allowed, in keeping with strict military standards. Gaslights were not installed in the barracks until 1857, so rooms were lighted only by candles and whale-oil lamps.[7]

Cyrus Ballou Comstock

On June 3, 1851, about the same time Godfrey arrived, another candidate from Massachusetts showed up at West Point named Cyrus Ballou Comstock. Cyrus was the son of a farmer from West Wrentham, Massachusetts. Unlike the boyish fifteen-year-old from Cincinnati, Comstock was a mature twenty years and five months old when he entered the Academy that summer. Cyrus was assigned a room with seventeen-year-old James McNeill Whistler, son of George Whistler, a prominent railroad engineer and 1819 graduate of the Academy, who once taught drawing there. James was an odd student with a sharp wit who loved to sketch but was not much for academics. Young Whistler was known as "Curly" to his classmates due to his hairstyle. He was quite a contrast to Comstock's stoic personality and academic prowess. Whistler left his mark on the Academy in a series of sketches that depicted life as a cadet.[8]

The Life of a Plebe

Before lunch that first day (called "dinner" at the Academy), Godfrey experienced his first drill and march, followed by more drilling and marching after lunch to the prompts of a bugle and drum. The new candidates were not accustomed to such physical drilling, described by some as "horrid work."[9] That first day, the plebes presented themselves to the upperclassmen who had been chosen to train the boys on how to be soldiers. It was a rude awakening for these young men. George C. Strong recalled his first such introduction to the upperclassmen:

> I knocked at Lieutenant K.'s door. "Come in, Sir," and in I went.
> "I—was—directed—to come here and report to "—
> "Stand attention, Sir," fiercely cried the eldest of those who were present. "How dare you come into the presence of your superior officer in that grossly careless and unmilitary manner?"
> I thought my head was off, and of course didn't speak.
> "I'll have you imprisoned. Stand attention, Sir," (even louder than before,)   "heels-together-and-on-the-same-line—toes-equally-turned-out—little-fingers-on-the-seams-of-your-pantaloons—button-your-coat—draw-in-your-chin—throw-out-your-chest—cast-your-eyes-fifteen-paces-to-the-front—don't-you-let-me-see-you-wearing-a-standing-collar-again—and-stand-*steady*-Sir. You've evidently mistaken your profession, Sir. In any other service, or at the seat of war, Sir, you would have been shot, Sir, without trial, Sir, for such conduct, Sir."[10]

After a brief pause, the elder cadet barked out, "I am ready now, Sir, to receive your report, Sir . . . What is your name?"[11]

Strong received a strong reprimand at this first session because his knees were knocking each other violently and he did not "stand steady" in the presence of a superior officer. After receiving a similar welcoming, Godfrey Weitzel visited the quartermaster, where he obtained basic necessities including a bottle of ink, twelve sheets of letter paper, two pencils, a blanket, an arithmetic book, a slate, a bucket, a tin dipper, a tin washbasin, a lump of soap, a candlestick, and a tallow candle. The collection of supplies was tied up together by the quartermaster's clerk and a broom handle was inserted through a knot tied in the blanket.

Godfrey and his fellow plebes then shouldered their loads for a humbling march back to their barracks. The procession looked like a parade of hoboes in plain view of the cadets, faculty, and visitors. The older cadets took the opportunity to chide the new recruits with taunts such as "What do you think of military glory, Mr. Plebe? I s'pose your Pa and Ma think you're a young Napoleon." Acting like drillmasters, the cadets barked orders at the frightened teenagers: "Keep step, Sir:—one, two, three, four; one, two, three; one, one, one."[12] Welcome to West Point, young men.

Daily Routines of a New Cadet

The freshman barracks were divided into small apartments.[13] That first hot night in June 1851, as Godfrey went to sleep on a worn mattress on an old iron bed frame, the Army blanket smelled of rancid lanolin.[14] But he dare not complain, or risk being chided by an upperclassman as unfit for field duty, a whiner or *a*

FIGURE 2.1. *Merit Its Own Reward, or The Best Man Leads off the Squad.* (Sketched by James McNeill Whistler [1852]; Library of Congress, Prints and Photographs Division, Reproduction No. LC-USZC4-4571.)

dandy. The next morning Godfrey reported to a classroom for more tutoring in reading, writing, grammar, and mathematics. The beating of drums at 1:00 p.m. signaled that the boys were to report to the parade ground for dinner roll call, followed by an hour break to eat in silence in the dining hall, then some recreation time. After a quick and unpleasant meal, Godfrey reported to the parade ground where cadet drillmasters tried to teach the new arrivals some fundamental military skills. Dressed in their civilian clothes, the young boys marched in the hot summer sun, trying their best to impress their instructors. The motley crew tumbled over one another while receiving bitter rebukes from the drillmasters for their inattention.[15]

Entrance Examinations Begin

After weeks of tutoring and drilling, the candidates were ready for that moment of truth—the entry examinations. The boys were marched from their barracks into the library where the Academic Board was assembled and waiting, following in the French system of military training. The board was made up of Superintendent Henry Brewerton, plus the commandant of cadets and the heads of the various departments at the Academy. One by one, as their names were called, each candidate would stride to the middle of the room for questioning.

Once he passed the mathematics exam, Godfrey was taken to another room in the library where he was asked to read aloud from *The History of the United States*, followed by testing in yet another room on penmanship and grammar by the professor of ethics, Rev. William T. Sprole. After a few queries, the examination was completed and the boys were marched outside for drills and then back to their quarters.

At ten o'clock the next morning, Saturday, June 21, the freshmen were led to the hospital to answer a series of medical questions, followed by the physical exam. Godfrey was more than the requisite five feet in height, and he had good eyesight and teeth. The medical board of three doctors weighed, measured, and examined him, probing his young body and head for any skeletal or dental deformities.[16] The doctors felt Godfrey's limbs, examined his feet, thumped his chest, and examined his teeth. An eye examination consisted of each boy viewing a dime from a distance of fourteen feet and telling whether the coin was "heads" or "tails."[17]

Camping Out on the Plain

After finishing the entry examinations, Godfrey and his classmates were assigned to one of several "fourth-class" companies in order of height and marched up to the Plain where the cadet encampment was already in progress. The boys would spend the next two months in cramped quarters, three to a tent. A horizontal timber was suspended from the ridgepole of the tent and allowed the boys to hang their new uniforms. The small tent was finished off with a gun rack for muskets, a tin box for candles and gun-cleaning materials, a broom, a washbowl, a bucket and dipper, and a small mirror.[18] Though packed like sardines, the chance to camp out under the stars was a welcome relief from the smell and heat of the freshman barracks.

On Tuesday, June 24, the young plebes were marched down to the armory where they were issued their first muskets. Two days later they got fatigue jackets, forage caps, belts, cartridge boxes, and bayonets. The small tents were filling up fast with clothing, bedding, and a growing collection of military hardware. Drilling now with their uniforms and weapons, the boys started to feel like real soldiers. However, the weight of the muskets made the marching more difficult, and before long, the boys were rebuked by their drillmasters for dropping their guns.[19]

After a full day of drills, the candidates assembled for evening parade. Cadet Captain Jerome Napoleon Bonaparte called them to attention and then read from a long list the names of the candidates who had passed all the exams and were admitted as new cadets. "Allen, Averill, Bennett," he began. "Comstock!" The list went on for a full seventy-one names and time seemed to drag on. At last, Bonaparte got to the end of the list, "Webb, Weitzel, Wheeler, Whistler." Not all of the candidates had passed, failing either the physical or the academic examination or both. The tall and lanky German boy breathed a sigh of relief. "*Danke, Gott!*" Of the names read that day, less than half would be around for graduation in four years.

The Youngest Cadet

As Godfrey's first academic year began, the official roll was taken of boys ranging in age from sixteen to twenty years, with sixteen being the minimum required age for a cadet. The roll listed Godfrey Weitzel's age—when formally admitted to the Academy on July 1, 1851, at "16 years and 7 months."[20] However, with his birth date of November 1, 1835, he was just 15 years and 8 months of age when formally admitted, making him the youngest cadet in *the entire Academy* as classes began that fall term of 1851. Despite his youth, just as the cream rises to the top, so did the bright cadet Weitzel, who became the star of his class. Neither his youth nor his German heritage held him back.

Learning the Demerit System

In order to instill strict military training, the cadets lived by a rigid code of conduct that was enforced by the issuance of "demerits" for misbehaving, followed in some cases by punishment, such as loss of privileges, confinement, extra duty, and, in the most extreme cases, expulsion. Cadet "sentinels" checked the rooms to be sure the boys were not visiting during study hours. If a cadet was found absent from his quarters, he would be reported and receive a demerit. A code of regulations contained the dos and don'ts under six pages of Article 12, titled simply "Discipline," plus another four pages under a separate heading, "More Discipline." The cadets of all four classes were subjected to the same demerit system, which was then tied to each cadet's grade in conduct. The demerit system became the great equalizer among the classes, though the plebes were the easiest targets for code violations and racked them up in sometimes alarming numbers during their first year.

Eight categories of offenses varied by degree of seriousness. The lightest offenses rated two demerits, such as being late to roll call or dress code violations. The most severe offenses, which earned ten demerits, included mutinous conduct or unauthorized absence. Cadets with one hundred demerits were members of the informal "Century Club" and had to be careful, because two hundred demerits in any one calendar year would result in discharge from the Academy. The entire cadet body was subjected to humiliation in front of their peers each evening at parade as the cadet adjutant read off the demerits that had been issued that day. The adjutant had the undivided attention of all 225 cadets assembled as he barked out the day's infractions:

> STUART: collar not neatly put on at inspection;
> RUGGLES: laughing in ranks;
> WEITZEL: talking in ranks marching.[21]

The list went on and on each evening. Freshmen were reported for such minor infractions as hanging a hat on a hook instead of a peg; laughing in ranks; coat unbuttoned and hat off while on post as sentinel; shoes not properly blacked at inspection of guard detail; washbowl not inverted at morning inspection; marching at double-quick time without command; hair too long at morning inspection, and not neatly shaved at same; collar not neatly put on and belts dirty at inspection. As one nervous classmate of Godfrey's put it, the upper-classman were "strict as can be, and if a plebe is not very careful he will get severely skinned!"[22]

Godfrey's social nature and immaturity earned him eighteen more demerits during his first year, for such things as "talking in ranks (2); talking in ranks leaving Academy (2); whistling in hall of barracks during study hours (3); feet on window sill (1)," and the most severe, "visiting on sentinel's post (5)" and just plain "visiting (5)." In a two-week period in October–November 1851, Godfrey received an additional twelve demerits for "trifling in ranks at breakfast" and "continued trifling conduct in Mathematical Academy." He appealed to the commandant and the dozen demerits were reduced to four.[23]

After some adjustments to his record, Godfrey had accumulated only forty demerits for relatively minor infractions during his first year, about average for most cadets.

Academic Life for Cadet Weitzel

The method of instruction at West Point was primarily by "recitation," where the cadet was tested either orally, on paper, or at the blackboard and asked to remember accurately what he had read in a text. For each of the first two years at the Academy, every cadet attended recitation in mathematics for ninety minutes alone, six days a week. Based on the student's performance at recitation, professors would ask questions and then grade responses on a scale of zero to 3.0. A mark of 2.6 to 3.0 was deemed "Thorough" or "The Best," while grades from 0.1 to 1.9 were "Tolerable," "Bad," or "Very Incomplete." The "Worst" performance by a cadet during recitation earned a mark of zero. At the conclusion of each week's classes, the instructor reported the daily grades of his students to the superintendent, who, in turn, forwarded a consolidated monthly report to the chief of engineers, Joseph G. Totten. Totten would then send an extract of the grades home to each cadet's parents.

The cadets were formally examined twice during each school year, once in January and again in June, by the Academic Board, who met jointly with the Board of Visitors to conduct the testing. A student's performance on the January examination was used to determine his relative class standing for the prior fall term. The results of the June examination were tallied with the January scores to establish annual class rankings.

Plebe Year, 1851–1852

On Monday, September 8, 1851, following their first week of classes, the members of the Fourth Class marched from dinner to the parade ground and were subsequently ordered to "break ranks." What followed was the traditional mad rush of the eager boys across the ground to the library building, where the results of the first week's academic progress were posted. The cadets were curious to see how they had performed during recitation in the various subjects. Each week thereafter the same anticipation was present, but there were no mad rushes as the boys learned the pace of academic life at West Point, some dreading to read the results.

Among the top students that first week were Cyrus Comstock, Alexander Webb, and Godfrey Weitzel. There were times when classes were not always easy for Godfrey, such as the day after Thanksgiving, when he was asked to find equal roots of an equation. Though Comstock solved the problem quickly, his classmate from Cincinnati stumbled. "Weitzel up on an equation of 5° and did not do it," Comstock wrote.[24]

On Christmas Day of 1851, the boys were allowed to leave the mess hall when they pleased after supper at 6:00 p.m., and were thereafter allowed to visit wherever they chose on campus until taps. However, it seems that more than two dozen cadets from several classes strayed off campus, past the guard post manned by plebe Cyrus Comstock, a devout teetotaler. "Probably in the course of the day," Comstock recalled, "there have been thirty men almost dead drunk, and in the third and fourth classes, four fifths have drank today." He wrote in his diary, "It is disgusting." Among the rowdy cadets who sneaked off campus were the cadet captain Bonaparte and Adjutant Russell, who Cyrus said were "staggering around—beastly drunk."[25] Bonaparte risked being stripped of his position as an officer if he had been caught. But he got away with it, a feat that Godfrey Weitzel would perhaps recall in his senior year at the Point.

Superintendent Lee

Godfrey's first superintendent in June 1851 was Captain Henry Brewerton, an engineer and West Point graduate, nicknamed "Old Brew" by the cadets. But on September 1, 1852, as Godfrey Weitzel began his sophomore year, Brewerton was replaced by Colonel Robert E. Lee of Virginia. Colonel Lee had been a model cadet himself and served admirably as superintendent for just under three years.

Superintendent of the military school was not the most desirous position for an officer in the Corps of Engineers due to its low salary and its bureaucratic nature. The superintendent was responsible not only for the efficient management of the school but for the general welfare and conduct of all the enlisted men, officers, civilians, and their dependents who lived and worked there. Also among the superintendent's duties was maintaining discipline among the young cadets through the system of rules and demerits. Other officers handled the day-to-day punishments for minor infractions, but the superintendent was responsible for the most serious cases.

The superintendent's home was a large and roomy stone structure with a garden, stables, and pasture. Saturdays were a "half-holiday" for the cadets, and Superintendent Lee would invite a number of the young men to his home for tea or for supper, which was always a "good, substantial meal." Many of the boys were awkward and shy in the superintendent's home, until Colonel Lee would put them at ease with his "genial manner and pleasant ways."[26]

It was during these open-house events that new Superintendent Lee and young Cadet Weitzel became well acquainted, as Lee took a special interest in the top students in each class, often inviting them into his home for parties, receptions, or tea. Godfrey Weitzel was at the top of his class all four years and developed great respect for his superintendent. Their relationship would play an important role in the lives of Weitzel and the Lee family a decade later.

Benny Havens' Tavern

Drinking or possessing alcohol at the Academy were offenses that could result in dismissal of a cadet. Local civilians sometimes smuggled alcohol onto the campus via the river by landing at a secluded cove below the Plain under cover of darkness. Drummer boys from bands that played at Saturday night dances would sneak whiskey inside the gates and sell it to the cadets. Other boys were able to obtain liquor while on furlough and hide it from the authorities when they returned to campus.

Visiting off-campus taverns was likewise prohibited, although such cadets as Ulysses S. Grant, William T. Sherman, George C. Strong, Ambrose Burnside, Fitzhugh Lee, and George Custer all sneaked into town to visit the notorious Benny Havens' Tavern in nearby Buttermilk Falls, New York (now Highland Falls). Benny Havens was a lovable, good-hearted character with a quick wit who had sold whiskey and other spirits to West Point cadets for more than two decades. Cadet Edgar Allan Poe once called Mr. Havens "the only congenial soul in the entire God-forsaken place." The thrill of "running it"—as the boys called their escapes—induced many cadets to stray off campus to visit either girls or the local pubs, mostly Havens's pub.[27]

West Point authorities tried for decades to close down Benny Havens' Tavern, without success, and several generations of cadets enjoyed food, beer, and whiskey there. The tavern inspired the popular poem "Benny Haven's O!" which was known by every cadet who had drunk his share at the local pub.

"Fill 'er up," the boys would say as Benny came around with whiskey and ale. Havens would then tell stories about other cadets he had known over the years, followed by more singing and another round of drinks. Trips to local taverns were so popular over the years that any unauthorized absence from campus was a crime frequently associated with drinking.

First Year Over, at Last!

Under the four-year program at West Point, cadets studied practical engineering, philosophy, mathematics, chemistry, ethics, art, drawing, mineralogy, geology, infantry tactics, cavalry, artillery, fencing, riding, and French.[28] Each particular subject was given a three-digit weighted value, and the top student in each class earned the most total points, such as 200 or 300, depending on the particular class. The faculty weeded out those with little aptitude, and that first year eleven of Godfrey's freshman classmates were recommended for discharge to Secretary of War Davis.[29] Godfrey ranked fifth his first year in mathematics, but his youthful lack of attention earned him several demerits for being inattentive in the classroom.[30]

The annual general order of merit combined the scores from all of Godfrey's classes during the year. The German boy's low grade in French and a few demerits in conduct did not hurt his overall class standing, though, and at the end of his first year Godfrey Weitzel ranked ninth overall in his class that now had just sixty cadets.[31]

FIGURE 2.2. U.S. Military Academy *Song of the Graduates* (book cover). (Sketch by James McNeill Whistler [1852]; Art Institute of Chicago, Walter Stanton Brewster Collection of Whistleriana, 1933.281.)

Orders were posted the last day of May 1852 for the program of the annual examination to close out the academic year. The next day began with a traditional formal dress assembly on the parade grounds for the benefit and viewing pleasure of the Board of Visitors, who assisted in administering the final exams. The assembly was concluded with a fifteen-gun salute from the field battery, which marked the end of regular studies for the year. The boys took pride as they switched from their

FIGURE 2.3. *On Post in Camp.* (Four-piece series of sketches by James McNeill Whistler [1852].)

winter gray uniforms to the summer white, looking sharp and feeling like soldiers and gentlemen. But uniforms were not the only cause for celebration on this day. The freshman class that began its studies back in September was now officially the Third Class—thus shedding the humiliating label of "plebe." As one cadet recalled that day, "We never, as a class, felt such a sudden increase of pride and importance as now when our title was transferred to others and we were *plebes* no longer."[32]

The excitement of that day faded with the sunset as the cadets began studying for, and worrying about, the next two weeks of year-end examinations. Being nearly five years older than Godfrey—older than even many of the "upperclassmen"—cadet Cyrus Comstock was naturally more mature. This showed not only academically but in his *perfect* conduct scores. At the conclusion of their first year, Comstock locked in the top spot in the entire freshman class. Incredibly, Cyrus held the top score in three of his first four courses, mathematics, engineering, and conduct—where he scored an unblemished 100. Only a 94.2 in French kept him from a perfect freshman year.[33]

Cyrus Comstock was in a select group of only four total cadets out of the entire Academy that spring term of 1852 who had achieved a perfect record in conduct. Godfrey Weitzel placed in the respectable top quarter with his conduct rating of forty-sixth—ahead of even the superintendent's own son, Custis Lee.

Although Godfrey kept up the story that he was born in Ohio, his classmates nicknamed him "Dutch" due to his family's German roots and his fluency in that language.[34] Dutch Weitzel made it through his grueling first year with flying colors, holding his own quite well against his classmates, despite his relative youth.

CHAPTER 3

No Longer a Plebe

Two months of encampment ended on August 30, 1852, but a violent gale, with rain and lightning, prevented the traditional "illumination" and dropping of tents ceremony. The boys hunkered down for another semester of academic and military training. As Godfrey's standing in his class rose, Superintendent Robert E. Lee took note and invited him to entertainment at the Lee home. Godfrey spent many hours at the superintendent's residence, in the company of Colonel Lee and his family, including his nephew, Fitzhugh Lee, a rowdy cadet nicknamed "Fitz".

Second Year at the Point, 1852–1853

In September 1852, the sophomore cadets took up riding, a class that left many sore with chafing or even broken bones. Cyrus Comstock was so chafed from the saddle that his pants were thick with blood. "Seriously, I came near to killing myself," he wrote in his diary.[1] His saddle sores were so severe that he went to the hospital and was excused from riding class until he healed up. Even when he recovered, Cyrus chafed again during almost every outing on horseback.

Riding classes were the source not only of saddle sores but of embarrassment and humor, with many cadets being thrown from their mounts or becoming the victims of runaway animals. During cavalry drills the sophomore class took up jumping their horses. Once, when the boys were challenged to make three jumps, Godfrey Weitzel made a spectacle on his first two jumps, hanging half off his horse with only one leg in the saddle. The episode must have raised his German temper, as rival classmate Cyrus Comstock characterized Godfrey's riding style as "very ungraceful" and his attitude "unpleasant."[2]

In his third and final jump, despite "the most desperate and almost super-human attempts," Godfrey successfully cleared the hurdle, but slid off the horse's side while trotting off and fell into the dirt. "Poor fellow," Comstock wrote, "but the whole squad and [our instructor] too, laughed consumedly."[3] Due to his awkward start, "Dutch" Weitzel worked especially hard and eventually excelled in cavalry class. By the end of his senior year, Godfrey had become an assistant instructor in cavalry, finishing at the head of his class. That was quite an improvement from his sloppy start as a horseman.

Mathematics remained Godfrey's strong suit, and at the end of the fall term of 1852, Godfrey rose five notches, from ninth place to fourth out of just fifty-two cadets who now remained in his shrinking class.[4] However, he continued to struggle in French class, though he improved his dismal first-year finish of twenty-fourth place to sixteenth by midterm of the second year.[5] Surprisingly for the young man who would go on to design significant fortifications, locks and dams, and lighthouses, Godfrey's worst grades at West Point were in Professor Robert W. Weir's drawing class. Weir had taught at West Point for nearly twenty years, and he believed in having his students learn "by doing" and instead of lecturing. His students sketched human figures or landscapes as Weir strolled around, palette in hand, making corrections to their work.[6]

Godfrey was not much of an artist and ranked an embarrassing thirty-fourth place in Wier's class. He had improved only slightly, to twenty-fourth place, by the end of his second year.[7] A keen mind, yes, but he was no Whistler when it came to drawing. By contrast, classmate James "Curly" Whistler was an accomplished artist, but fell far behind in the all-important mathematics class to a dismal thirty-seventh place.[8] Young Whistler was eventually dismissed after erroneously calling silicon a gas—instead of an element. Coupled with 136 demerits in six months, the budding artist was found deficient in chemistry and was promptly dismissed from the Academy. "If silicon were a gas, I would have been a general one day," Whistler later told his friends.[9]

By the end of his sophomore year, Godfrey Weitzel had risen to third place overall in his rapidly shrinking class of now just forty-nine cadets. Cadet Weitzel was surpassed in rank by only two cadets, Cyrus B. Comstock and George H. Elliot.[10]

In April 1853, Godfrey began courses in surveying, a class that would pay benefits his entire career as a civil engineer, especially during the war. That same year, in Washington, D.C., on April 11, a forty-one-year-old lawyer from Alabama was sworn in as an associate justice of the U.S. Supreme Court. Justice John A. Campbell was one of the youngest persons ever appointed to the U.S. Supreme Court. Within the next ten years, this Southern jurist would come to play a key role on behalf of the Confederacy, attempting multiple times to act as a peacemaker between the North and the South. A different April several years later would find Judge Campbell and Godfrey Weitzel locked in private meetings with the president of the United States, trying to devise a plan to end a bloody civil war. But in the spring of 1853, Godfrey Weitzel was a virtually unknown cadet at West Point, focusing on his grades and military training. Some 235 miles away, John Campbell raised his hand to take an oath of office in the nation's capital. Fate would throw them together during one of the most historic weeks in our nation's history.

Junior Year, 1853–1854

Christmas of 1853 turned into a rowdy affair when, on December 24, a large number of the cadets "ran it" to the local taverns. Others drank in private on campus from stashed bottles and flasks. "There have not been so many drunken men before in 18 years," observed the campus caretaker. "There are scarcely half a dozen who were not drunk last night," an indignant Cyrus Comstock wrote of his classmates. "Averill and Elliott were crazy," he added. "Thank heaven that I do not drink."[11]

It was during Godfrey Weitzel's third year at the Military Academy that he solidified his place as one of the top students, ranking fourth in both philosophy and chemistry out of just forty-four who now remained in his class.[12] By June, Godfrey and his classmates were anxious for the graduation of the Class of 1854 so that the juniors could rightfully claim the title of "First Class" at the Academy. Godfrey's overall standing by the end of his junior year remained the same as his second year, third overall. Only two cadets stood between Cadet Weitzel and first place—Cyrus B. Comstock and Cornelius Van Camp. Though Godfrey had been cited for just six demerits since January, he and Cyrus tied with twenty-nine demerits each for the school year.[13]

Finally, Cadets of the "First Class"

The Corps of Cadets was organized like a battalion of infantry, consisting of four companies. The officers of the corps came from the senior class, appointed as the lieutenants and captains based on class rank and merit. The sergeants were appointed from the junior class, and the corporals from the sophomore class.

On June 16 the entire student body assembled for parade, the last one for the graduating Class of 1854. Anticipation was high to find out which cadets would be made officers in the Battalion of Cadets, especially who would be named first captains, the highest position in the Corps of Cadets. Only four seniors would receive this honor, one for each of the four companies. The first captain was responsible for maintaining discipline in his own company as well as within the entire corps. Only the top cadets in the senior class were chosen for this honor, those who showed "soldier-like performance of duties" and exemplary general conduct.[14]

The commandant of cadets, Major Robert Garnett, read the appointments to the anxious assembly. Godfrey Weitzel was named first captain of C Company! To the astonishment of his academic rival, Cyrus Comstock was passed over for an officer's appointment. "Weitzel 1st Captain!" he wrote with exclamation in his diary, showing his secret envy and bitterness. He attributed Weitzel's position to favoritism shown by Commandant Garnett.[15]

In celebration of graduation for the Class of '54, there was a nighttime ceremony, complete with fireworks. The Academy band played "Home, Sweet Home," as was tradition, bringing a lump to the throat of every cadet and a few tears to the eyes of some. The band played a special serenade to the Class of '55, which was now the "First Class" of the school. Everyone was feeling pretty proud of themselves, but none more than newly appointed First Captain Godfrey Weitzel, who, in just three short years, had gone from being the youngest cadet at the entire school to one of its top students, and now one of its top senior officers.

The next morning the graduates left campus. Among them were the superintendent's son Custis Lee and his classmates, including J. E. B. "Beauty" Stuart. "'Tis our turn next," wrote Cyrus Comstock in his diary.[16]

Jefferson Davis Visits Campus

Fall term began and the boys fell into a regular routine, interrupted only by occasional visits from dignitaries or celebrities, such as singer Jenny Lind. On Saturday night, October 28, a grand party was held at the residence of Superintendent Lee for a dozen top senior cadets, who had each received a special invitation. Godfrey Weitzel enjoyed visiting with Colonel Lee and a few ladies who were invited for the soiree, which included a dinner and socializing. The superintendent advised the cadets that a special guest was coming to campus the next week, Secretary of War Jefferson Davis, and he wanted the officers to make a good showing. Three days later, preparations began for the secretary's visit, with muster at 6:00 a.m., half an hour before sunrise. At 11:00 a.m., Secretary Davis arrived and was treated to a salute from the cadets and an excellent squadron drill. For First Captain Weitzel of C Company, it was his first up close and personal look at Jefferson Davis, an impressive man with deep-set eyes, chiseled cheekbones, and a firm jaw. In eleven short years Godfrey would occupy Davis's home, eat his abandoned breakfast, and sleep in his bed in Richmond as the Confederate president slipped out of town to avoid capture by troops commanded by Godfrey Weitzel.

The next day, November 1, was Godfrey's nineteenth birthday, but the celebration was for Secretary Davis, who was still on campus. At eleven o'clock that morning, the cadets pulled off a "splendid artillery drill" for the secretary and classes were suspended. A light rain fell and by afternoon it had turned into a torrent, so the cadet battalion was dismissed to quarters and Secretary Davis left the Academy, thoroughly impressed but also thoroughly wet.

The Christmas Day Caper, 1854

Holidays were few at West Point and therefore were special events for the students. Christmas and New Year's were each celebrated by a suspension of classes for the day. Christmas Eve dinner was a feast, starting with a traditional holiday meal of stewed and raw oysters, hot biscuits, and coffee. Then, at 2:00 p.m. on December 25, the boys were treated to turkey and all the trimmings in the dining hall. Those students who lived close to the Academy could obtain a pass to go home for a day or two if their grades were sufficient, but most of the cadets lived too far away and, therefore, spent the Christmas holiday on the campus.

The day's activities were sedate and, of course, refreshments were non-alcoholic. It being winter in New York, outdoor activities were limited by the weather. If the Hudson River was frozen over, cadets could go ice-skating. There were reports, however, of some boys sneaking off to obtain whiskey and hold their own private celebrations after hours. One such occasion resulted in a couple of inebriated cadets pelting a few officers with lumps of coal.[17]

As a cadet, Robert E. Lee went all four years at West Point without accumulating a single demerit, a seemingly impossible task. When he issued his usual order giving the cadets Christmas Day off, Lee warned them to obey the school's code of conduct nonetheless, so that "no irregularity or violation of the regulations may mar the enjoyment of the day."[18] As was tradition, the holiday order required that the cadets of all classes be in their rooms for inspection by 7:00 p.m. and that all violators would be arrested and strictly disciplined.

On Christmas Eve, after the holiday meal, Superintendent Lee invited about twenty of the top senior cadets to his residence for an open house, including two of his favorites—Cyrus Comstock and Godfrey Weitzel. Mrs. Lee also invited several single ladies to join them and mingle with the handsome young cadets. Colonel Lee and his wife were gracious hosts, but the superintendent never lost sight of his role as chief disciplinarian of the Academy, even on Christmas Day.

It seems that the Class of '55 was just too tempted to make "a run of it," despite Lee's hospitality and his stern order. Almost all of the seniors (other than teetotaler Cyrus B. Comstock) went to Benny Havens' Tavern that Christmas night, ignoring Lee's posted orders. It was this holiday excursion that put the only significant black mark on Cadet Captain Weitzel's relatively clean record.

While the official records are not completely clear on this escapade, it is known that after evening taps, on December 25, 1854, Godfrey Weitzel and six other cadets were reported absent from their quarters for a little over an hour. Superintendent Lee ordered Captains Church and Weitzel arrested on their return. Godfrey had apparently given in to temptation, along with classmates John R. Church, George H. Elliot, David McMurtrie Gregg, James H. Hill, and two of their chums, who broke Lee's rules by celebrating Christmas Day past curfew, most likely off campus at that infamous tavern in nearby Buttermilk Falls.

The superintendent's penalty was harsh but made Lee's point when he issued Special Orders No. 156 four days later, on December 29. The order was read at assembly for all to hear: Weitzel and Church were stripped of their officers' roles as first captains. Lee doled out similar demotions to Cadets Elliott, Gregg, and Hill, who were each deprived of their appointments as lieutenants.[19] Adding to the humiliation, the cadet officers had their chevrons removed from their uniforms.

After four days of imprisonment, Colonel Lee ordered that all seven of the cadets be released from arrest and returned to duty.[20] To make matters worse, however, and to drive home his point, as Godfrey was stripped of his rank, Cyrus Comstock—passed over as a class officer back in June—was appointed as lieutenant and quartermaster in the Battalion of Cadets.[21]

Of his new position as quartermaster, Comstock boasted privately: "'Tis the best office in the Corps. No roll calls to attend, no marching to meals, nothing military to do. I must not get too lazy. I half expected to get it last June, but it will do now." The self-righteous Comstock felt that the discipline against the officers was long overdue for his carousing classmates. He wrote in his diary the night the officers were demoted, "I begin to believe more and more strongly that justice, truth and honesty are quite as important possessions as gold, character, or anything else."[22]

It was a lesson that Godfrey Weitzel never forgot, though he never held it against his beloved superintendent, Robert E. Lee. In just ten years, Weitzel and Lee would confront each other on the battlefield. While he sat in confinement those four days in December, 1854, perhaps Godfrey hummed to himself that irresistible anthem:

> When you, and I, and Benny, and General Jackson too—
> Are brought before the final Board, our course of life t'review,
> May we never fess on any point—but then be told to go,
> To join the army of the blest—at Benny Havens' O.
>
> Come, fill your glasses fellows, and
> Stand up in a row
> So we'll sing our reminiscences of
> Benny Havens', O![23]

Final Semester: Politics at West Point

On March 31, 1855, just two and a half months before Godfrey's graduation, Superintendent Robert E. Lee was relieved of his post at the Academy. Lee was reassigned as lieutenant colonel in the Second Cavalry and left West Point to attend to his new duties. Lee had become a favorite among the cadets, and he regretted not overseeing the final June examinations and graduation for the Class of 1855. The Lee family returned to their beloved home at Arlington, Virginia, just across the Potomac River from the nation's capital. The new superintendent was Captain John G. Barnard, a West Point graduate four years behind Lee.

Three decades earlier, the Dialectic Society had been formed at West Point as a literary and debating society. The top senior cadets were members of the society, which in 1855 included Cyrus Comstock, Godfrey Weitzel, and David

Gregg. Cadet Gregg was president of the club until he resigned in October, frustrated over his inability to ignite their discussions. In the 1840s, the club was dissolved for a year because it was debating such controversial subjects as whether a state—under any circumstances—had the right to nullify an act of Congress. When Superintendent Richard Delafield allowed the society to reorganize, he limited it to "non-controversial" topics. His admonishment was soon derailed by the weighty issues of the day. Cadets in the club were from all sections of the country and, as political passions rose, their meetings became heated, sometimes resulting in fistfights.

During their last semester, Godfrey and his classmates began to tackle the topic of slavery. Godfrey's roommate was Francis Redding Tillou Nicholls, a native of Donaldsonville, Louisiana, a member of the "century club" with 106 demerits for the year, and one of only two cadets remaining in the senior class from Southern states.[24] The two surely discussed the most popular novel at the time, Harriet Beecher Stowe's antislavery tale *Uncle Tom's Cabin*, first published in March 1852. The *Boston Post* reported, "Everybody has read it, is reading, or is about to read it. And certainly it is one of the most remarkable literary productions of the time."[25] Not surprising, opinions on the book were divided between cadets from the Northern industrial and the Southern agricultural states. Rooming with a Southerner, especially Francis Nicholls, may have helped form Godfrey's views on slavery. Ironically, much of Godfrey's military career would be spent in and around his roommate's hometown of Donaldsonville, where the name Weitzel became hated by the locals.

An Impressive Finish

For the soon-to-be military engineers, senior year included courses on the design and construction of permanent and field fortifications. Classes during the fall term consisted of civil engineering, architecture, stonecutting, and engineering drawing. The spring term focused more on areas of military engineering, such as field fortifications. Perhaps the most important class of the senior year was Professor Dennis Hart Mahan's military and civil engineering class. This included a six-lesson, nine-hour course titled "The Science of War," which gave instruction on the composition and organization of armies, order of battle, reconnaissance, attack, and defense.[26] Such lessons on strategy would soon prove to be essential for the senior class of 1855, who just six years later would find themselves in command of thousands of troops.

Mahan was a demanding instructor with an annoying habit of clearing his throat as he spoke. He would bark at even the seniors, saying, "Stand at attention! First class officers should always observe rules and set an example to those in the Corps, *ehem, ehem,* but I have made the observation, *ehem, ehem,* that they are the first, *ehem, ehem,* to infringe them. Stand attention, Sir!"[27]

"Mr. Freedley," Mahan chided one senior, "if you are a snake, squirm; if you are a man, stand still!" Godfrey Weitzel was also once the victim of Professor Mahan's tirade. Cyrus Comstock wrote that Mahan "tore [Samuel] Breck and Weitzel to pieces, finely."[28] The boys nicknamed him "Denny" Mahan and grew to dislike the man. Cyrus Comstock noted in his diary, "Good Lord, deliver us," adding that a few professors had annoying ticks, "but Denny's *ehem, ehem* is far worse!"[29]

Godfrey learned from Mahan about surveying military positions, the layout of fieldworks, supervising work parties, constructing scale models of field fortifications, and building floating bridges. Perhaps refocused on his studies to make up for the Christmas Day embarrassment, Godfrey finished strong his last semester and in the final exams in June. He rose to second in his engineering class as well as in the infantry tactics course, and was ranked third in artillery. Despite this impressive performance, Godfrey still fell behind his academic rival, the older Cyrus B. Comstock, who locked in first place in every course except one, cavalry tactics, where Godfrey Weitzel held the top grade.[30] After falling from his horse just a few years prior, senior cadet Weitzel made a remarkable improvement in horsemanship, placing fifth among his graduating class.[31] For this, he was recommended for the mounted corps.[32]

Graduation for the Class of 1855

After a delightful Saturday evening party for the now just thirty-four members of the senior class, the cadets prepared for graduation. On Sunday morning, June 10, 1855, the cadets of the First Class walked across campus to their final church service, the last sermon to endure from Reverend Sprole. As he did for each graduating class, the campus chaplain gave the cadets words of encouragement, a message that touched them in an unexpected way. After four years, they had mixed emotions about leaving the Point and entering the world again. It was absolutely true what an older cadet had told Godfrey as a new plebe: "After a year at West Point, you could not be driven away from here."[33]

Final grades were posted the next week, and Godfrey was shocked when the rankings in infantry were posted, listing him second behind Cyrus Comstock— even though Godfrey's score was 0.6 point better than Comstock's! Comstock, it turns out, had done better on the final examination. Cyrus wrote in his diary that night about Godfrey's reaction: "It disappoints him more than it pleases me, for I should have been perfectly satisfied [with second place]."[34] It was good to see that despite their academic rivalry, feelings of friendship were growing between the two young men.

Comstock had his own disappointment, however, when the final conduct grades were posted. Despite the Christmas Day caper, Godfrey graduated with only eighteen demerits for the year, the fewest in his entire class. The always-proper Cyrus Comstock had nineteen, finishing second! Godfrey often referred to himself as a "lucky dog," and he certainly was in this instance. The few demerits earned by these two cadets was quite remarkable considering that two-thirds of the seniors were members of the "Century Club," with more than one hundred demerits each for the year. Two of their classmates, Francis Vinton and Marcus Reno, were suspended with more than two hundred demerits each, barring their graduation. At last, on Thursday, June 14, all classes were finished, examinations over. "We are through. Hurrah! Ah!" wrote a jubilant Comstock in his diary.[35] The next day, they would graduate as officers in the United States Army.

Graduations during the pre–Civil War period at West Point did not involve speeches by distinguished visitors or a formal procession for diplomas as do modern-day commencement exercises.[36] Instead, there was a parade of the graduating class and a spectacular fireworks display, followed by a reading of the final class rankings. An order was read by Superintendent Barnard relieving the young men from duties with the Battalion of Cadets and assigning them to their respective corps. For the Class of 1855, the rankings were not surprising:

First, Cyrus B. Comstock;
Second, Godfrey Weitzel.[37]

Due to his high standing, Godfrey was recommended for promotion in each category of military service including engineers, topographical engineers (or "topogs," as they were known), ordnance, artillery, infantry, dragoons, mounted, and cavalry.[38] Superintendent Barnard told the boys that after settling their accounts with the treasurer of the Academy, they were to proceed to their respective homes and await further orders.[39] This simple instruction formally ended the cadets' four-year experience at the Academy.

The four years of military and engineering training was received during peacetime. But in just six years, the nation would be at war—not from any foreign enemy, but from within. The classmates from West Point would take up arms against one another, some commanding troops from the South while others fought for the North. Who could have imagined the strange twist of fate that would pit student against teacher, roommates against one another? The nation was about to be put to its greatest test.

CHAPTER 4

Early Career in New Orleans

Home in Cincinnati—July 1855

The West Point Military Academy leaders knew from experience that their new graduates needed some time off, having had only one furlough in four grueling years at West Point. Godfrey Weitzel returned to Cincinnati and waited at his parents' home to receive orders for his first assignment. He was quite a celebrity in the Over-the-Rhine neighborhood, wearing his officer's uniform to church on Sunday. His German neighbors were so proud that one of their own had graduated from the United States Military Academy, ranked second in his entire class, at such a young age. His father, Lewis, was especially proud of "Gottfried." From being poor immigrants to having a son as an officer in the United States Army— it was quite an accomplishment for the family from Winzeln.

The Weitzels had additional cause to celebrate America's Independence Day of 1855 after they received an official letter that their nineteen-year-old son had been promoted to brevet second lieutenant, a position given to only the best students, and he was attached to the Corps of Engineers.[1] Godfrey was anxious to start his new career, but his orders gave him three months' leave, until October 1.[2]

In early October, the long-awaited orders arrived at the Weitzel home. Godfrey anxiously opened the envelope bearing the letterhead of the United States Army, Corps of Engineers, and read the contents of Special Order No. 183, dated October 1, 1855. He was assigned to duty in another river city—New Orleans, Louisiana—some seven hundred miles south, near the Gulf of Mexico. There, he was to report to a thirty-seven-year-old Army major named Beauregard, and to serve as his engineering assistant to design, build, and repair the defenses for the port city.

Little did Godfrey know at the time that this assignment would last for the next four years, until August 1859. The position would change his life and propel his career like a slingshot from obscurity to national headlines. Godfrey's career would advance largely on his being the right person at the right place at the right time. New Orleans was the right place to start his military career.

P. G. T. Beauregard, "The Little Napoleon"

Captain and Brevet-Major Major Pierre Gustave Toutant ("P.G.T.") Beauregard was seventeen years older than Second Lieutenant Weitzel, but at five feet seven inches tall, he was dwarfed by his six-foot-four assistant, who sometimes playfully called himself "a long-legged Dutchman."[3] The major had graduated from West Point in 1838 and, much like Weitzel, had excelled both as an artilleryman and a military engineer. Like Weitzel and Robert E. Lee, Beauregard had also graduated second in his class.

The Creole major was a widower, whose wife of nine years, Marie Laure Villere, died during childbirth in 1850. She was the daughter of a wealthy Louisiana planter. After the death of his beloved Marie, Beauregard used his engineering work as a diversion during his period of mourning. There was plenty of work to be done in New Orleans, especially on two fortifications miles below along the river—Forts St. Philip and Jackson.[4] Pierre needed a hardworking assistant, one with youth and brains, to keep up with his pace.

Forts Jackson and St. Philip

It was necessary to protect the strategic city of New Orleans, not only from naval forces entering the nearby lakes, but also from enemy vessels coming up the Mississippi River. Whoever controlled New Orleans controlled the Mississippi, and any ships trying to enter from the Gulf had to pass by its ports. Two forts were built to guard the city, both located on opposing banks of the river, some thirty-two nautical miles up from the Gulf of Mexico and sixty-five miles below New Orleans. Fort Jackson was located on the west bank and Fort St. Philip on the east bank. The two forts faced each other, and ships had to slow down at a bend in the river to pass them. Any enemy vessels would be torn apart by cannon fire from both sides. At least that was the plan.

Fort Jackson was a massive star-shaped masonry structure that could accommodate four to five hundred men within its towering twenty-five-foot gray-and-red granite walls. The fort was constructed after the War of 1812 on the advice of Andrew Jackson, its namesake. It was surrounded by a moat, with heavy guns mounted on its stone parapets, mostly to prevent an attack from the waterside. In the center was a bombproof barracks with a roof made of heavy timbers and covered with one foot of earth.[5] A drawbridge, lifted by huge weights and chains, provided the entrance over the moat.

On the opposite bank stood Fort St. Philip, located about eleven hundred yards away, on the site of an older eighteenth-century fort built by the Spanish during their control of Louisiana. The fort was taken over in 1808 as a part of the Louisiana Purchase and its name changed from the Spanish Fort San Felipe to St. Philip. Unlike the star-shaped Fort Jackson, this fort was an irregular-shaped brickwork that stretched along the left side of the river. It was inundated with more than eight feet of water during a hurricane in 1812, but it was the back-to-back hurricanes in 2005, Katrina and Rita, that virtually destroyed what was left of Fort St. Philip.

First Assignment: New Orleans

After celebrating his twentieth birthday in Ohio with his parents and brother, Godfrey bid his family good-bye once again from Public Landing and steamed south out of Cincinnati to where the Ohio River met the Mississippi, near Cairo, Illinois. From there, he floated with the current for another five hundred miles and arrived in the bustling city of New Orleans on November 7, 1855, fresh from his four-month furlough.[6]

Asking for directions at the steamship dock, the young engineer walked through the bustling streets looking for Canal Street and the partially finished Custom House. The sights and smells of the city were quite foreign to him. Beautiful women with parasols, sharply dressed men in top hats, and "Negroes," as the black population was called at that time. Growing up in Ohio and schooled in an all-white military academy in New York, Godfrey had not seen many black people in his life. In New Orleans, he saw not only colored men and boys engaged in manual labor loading bales of cotton onto cargo vessels, but "freemen" who dressed as finely as the whites.

After a thirty-minute walk from the port, he found the New Orleans Custom House and reported for duty to Major P. G. T. Beauregard. The major was hard at work designing reinforcements for Fort Jackson and Fort St. Philip, as well as constructing a breakwater on Lake Pontchartrain to protect the shore from the full impact of its waves. At the two forts, Beauregard insisted on more guns, all mounted in casements or on the parapets, and the powder magazine had to be enlarged. His objective was to protect New Orleans from an invasion by fast steamboats that might try to run past the fortified positions.[7] Beauregard would have been shocked to know that in less than six years, the final invasion to test the strength of these forts would be led by his new assistant, Godfrey Weitzel.

Godfrey gave the same effort to his engineering work in New Orleans that he had given to his four years of studies at West Point. He was a hard worker and fast learner, and his enthusiasm caught the attention of his supervisor, Major Beauregard, who recommended the tall young man for a promotion. In August 1856, at Beauregard's request, Secretary of War Jefferson Davis recommended that Godfrey Weitzel be elevated from brevet second lieutenant to the full rank of second lieutenant in the Army Corps of Engineers, effective July 27, 1856. The promotion was approved in September, and Godfrey became a full-fledged second lieutenant in the United States Army.[8]

About this same time, Godfrey's classmate Cyrus Comstock received his first orders to ship off to Baltimore, where he would join Captain Henry "Old Brew"

Brewerton, a former superintendent at West Point, as his assistant.[9] Though starting their careers at different cities, Comstock and Weitzel would meet again frequently during their military and engineering careers.

Godfrey Weitzel spent long days and late nights working on the Custom House and the two forts, as well as an entirely new fort located at Proctor's Landing, Louisiana. As a single man with no family nearby, Godfrey found that he had spare time alone, which allowed him to renew hobbies he had enjoyed in Ohio and West Point, fishing and hunting.

The team of Beauregard and Weitzel continued their labors through the winter of 1857–1858 and into the spring and hot summer of 1858 until July 1, when Godfrey was granted his first furlough since moving to New Orleans. It was a much-deserved leave of absence, and he had many stories to tell his family and friends back in Cincinnati.[10] The leave was later extended by special orders, and Godfrey did not return to his duties in New Orleans until mid-November, two weeks after his twenty-third birthday.

Furlough in Ohio, and a Special Young Lady

The summer of 1858 was a time of political upheaval and elections that gave a glimpse of things to come for the presidential elections of 1860. On June 16, 1858, a newcomer to national politics had given a rousing speech at the Republican State Convention in Springfield, Illinois. A forty-nine-year-old candidate for the U.S. Senate, Abraham Lincoln, stirred the delegates with his now-famous "House Divided" speech, using a biblical reference taken from the Gospel of Mark (3:23-26). Despite his powerful words, Lincoln lost that election to Stephen A. Douglas.

While on leave in Cincinnati, Godfrey was introduced to Louisa C. Moor, a seventeen-year-old beauty from his hometown. More than five years his junior, "Gottfried" never shared classes with her at Central High School. When he left for West Point, Louisa was only an eleven-year-old in pigtails whom he never noticed in the family grocery store. But what a darling she had grown into. Her father was Augustus Moor, a German immigrant who had opened a bakery on the corner of Main and Liberty Streets. Moor later expanded the business into a restaurant, coffeehouse, and beer garden, which grew quite popular with the town's German population. After a brief courtship, Godfrey proposed to Louisa, and the couple made plans for a wedding next autumn in Cincinnati.

Back in the Bayous

On his return to New Orleans, Godfrey wrote to Cyrus Comstock about his new love interest. "I am still a lucky dog," he wrote. "I am not married yet, although

I took advantage of my furlough to arrange the preliminaries to my marriage, which will probably take place some time next November."[11]

Rested and back from his extended visit home with fond memories of his new romantic interest, Godfrey pitched back into his work in New Orleans with renewed vigor. There, he assisted his mentor, Major P. G. T. Beauregard, for another nine months in preparing accurate measured drawings of the two major forts, as well as assisting with new construction.

His time at Fort Jackson became a rather dull routine, though, as reflected in a letter he wrote to Cyrus Comstock on New Year's Day of 1859: "At present, however, I take it easy," he wrote. "I sleep 12 hours, draw 3 and meditate 9 hours every day. I am leading the life of a regular hermit." Godfrey complained of boredom at the desolate fort, located so far from the city, where he was nearly alone, with only the ordnance seargent, the fort keeper, and a servant for company.[12]

As a cadet who never did well in Professor Weir's drawing class, Godfrey lamented the drudgery of "making a set of 5 new drawings (each in triplicate) of several portions of this work." When finished with those, Major Beauregard wanted Godfrey to move across the river to Fort St. Philip and make a new set of drawings there as well, "about 12 in number, each in triplicate," he complained. "Nothing but draw, draw, draw!" he wrote to Comstock. "Confound the infernal duty. I am completely out of patience. I have been drawing from the time I entered the corps until now, and will be from all appearance, until next year."[13] The irony in his protests was that this intimate knowledge of the two forts would be the single most important factor that would propel his military career in just a few short years.

Hunting and Fishing in the Bayous

To break the monotony of making triplicate drawings, Godfrey would spend some of his free time fishing and hunting in the waters among the many nearby islands that were inhabited by fishermen, oystermen, and duck hunters who supplied the city markets with the best seafood and wild ducks. It was a hunter's paradise, with bountiful marsh prairies that drew wild ducks by the thousands to feed on the grain of the grasses. "Dutch" Weitzel enjoyed catching fish and shooting ducks in the bayous and swamps near Forts Jackson and St. Philip. Over time he gained considerable knowledge of the ins and outs of the local waterways behind and around the two forts, always in search of the best spot to find ducks or red snapper. Godfrey studied the creeks and swamps and mapped them out in his head. This was useful information for a fisherman, but would come in handy for military purposes as well. Soon, he was catching rebels in those same swamps and bayous.

First Assignment to West Point

In late August 1859, Godfrey received new orders to wrap up his work in New Orleans and report to his alma mater of West Point. There, he was to begin a teaching position as acting assistant professor of engineering. Given the drudgery of his fieldwork, he jumped at the opportunity to return to that beautiful place on the banks of the Hudson, the "best school in the world."

Even in the years leading up to the war, cadets at West Point established "sectional lines" depending on their home states and their views toward slavery. George Custer recalled those days at the Academy, saying that the lines were "clearly defined and strongly drawn." Since cadets were recommended by the U.S. congressmen from their home districts, the boys tended to reflect the political sentiments of those districts. Although advocates on each side of the slavery debate were equally earnest and determined, the Ohio-born Custer observed that "those from the South were always the most talkative if not argumentative."[14]

Abraham Lincoln's June 1858 speech as a candidate for the U.S. Senate at his home state's Republican Convention in Springfield had fanned the Southern flames of secession. Lincoln's ominous remark that he did not believe the government could endure permanently half slave and half free sent a clear message to the South: If Lincoln was to be elected president, there would be a change in the nation—*either all slavery or none*. Since Lincoln was from the North, those words meant only one thing to men in Dixie—the end of slavery if Lincoln were in the White House. The Dialectic Society at West Point broiled with the discussion of "property rights" and "freedom." The match was lit.

The Student Becomes the Teacher

After four years in New Orleans, Godfrey had mixed emotions about leaving that beautiful city. The Custom House was not nearly finished, nor were the improvements to the two forts. More importantly, he would leave behind his superior officer, Major Beauregard, who had taught him many things and had given Godfrey responsibility to handle projects on his own, instilling in him the confidence that a young officer needed. And, of course, he would miss the sights and smells of New Orleans, including Mardi Gras and duck hunting and fishing in the Cajun backwaters.

Upon receiving his orders, Godfrey made his way to the Custom House in search of Major Beauregard, who wished him well. The diminutive major had already been advised of the transfer order as a courtesy, and he fully supported Weitzel's role as an assistant instructor. Beauregard himself had a secret desire to return to West Point, perhaps to teach, or even more if the opportunity presented itself. Godfrey packed up his belongings, bade a fond farewell to his coworkers and friends, and then headed down to the docks to catch a steamer going north. He was excited at the opportunity.

Twenty-three-year-old Godfrey Weitzel arrived at the Academy on August 23, 1859. Steaming upriver and rounding the bend in the Hudson, Godfrey arrived at the dock that brought back so many memories from his school days. The sight of the pitched white tents meant that the boys were still in encampment. Seeing the uniformed cadets engaged in drills made him smile. Wasn't it just eight years ago that he had been a naive plebe, marching on the Plain with his ragtag band of candidates? Now he had returned as an officer and an instructor.

Godfrey reported to Superintendent Richard Delafield and was informed that he had been assigned as an acting assistant professor of military and civil engineering under Professor Dennis (*"ehem"*) Mahan.[15]

No sooner had Godfrey found his quarters and unpacked than he learned that another classmate had been appointed an assistant professor as well. It was a name with whom he was quite familiar—Godfrey's old academic rival and friend, Cyrus Comstock. Cyrus arrived from his post in Baltimore under orders to become an assistant professor of natural and experimental philosophy, a post he would hold until July 1861.[16] What an irony that these two were inseparable.

Although Godfrey's mind was full of exciting plans for his upcoming marriage and his new teaching job, there was trouble brewing in other parts of the nation, big trouble that would soon rip apart the Academy and the nation. It was obvious when he reached West Point and spoke to some of the students and faculty: secession was in the air.

Godfrey and Louisa Are Married—November 1859

The autumn of 1859 was a foreshadowing of things to come. Presidential candidate Lincoln had just made a campaign speech at the Fifth Street Market in Cincinnati on September 17, 1859, the last of five speeches that Lincoln delivered in a two-day whistle-stop tour of Ohio. A month later, on Sunday, October 16, 1859, Kansas abolitionist John Brown led a group of twenty-one men across the Potomac River from Maryland into Virginia. "Talk! talk! talk!" Brown had complained at an abolitionist meeting in Boston. "That will never free the slaves. What is needed is action—action!" Brown's plan was to seize the cache of weapons stored at the Federal arsenal at Harper's Ferry, Virginia, and to free all Negro slaves in the state. Brown was captured two days later by U.S. Marines led by two of Godfrey's acquaintances, former West Point superintendent Colonel Robert E. Lee and former cadet Lieutenant J. E. B. Stuart. During the raid, in which the Federals stormed the building with sledgehammers, seven people were killed by guns and bayonets, including Brown's son Oliver. Ten more were injured. John Brown was arrested, convicted on charges of treason against Virginia, and hanged.

Lincoln's speech and John Brown's bold raid were in Cincinnati's German newspapers and secession was on everyone's lips when Godfrey arrived home on October 23 to marry his sweetheart, Louisa.[17] Superintendent Delafield extended Godfrey's leave to twenty-three days for a brief wedding and honeymoon.[18]

Godfrey and Louisa were married on Thursday, November 3, 1859, just two days after Godfrey's twenty-fourth birthday. His blushing bride looked beautiful in her white gown. Godfrey was equally impressive in his military dress uniform. It was a modest affair at St. Peter's German Lutheran Church, attended by Godfrey's parents and his brother, Lewis, by Judge Bellamy Storer and Heinrich Roedter, the Moor family, and a few close friends from the Over-the-Rhine neighborhood. Parts of the service were spoken in German by the minister.

After a brief honeymoon, Godfrey and Louisa headed east in mid-November for New York City and then to West Point. Godfrey had told Louisa so many stories about his days at the Academy and now he could show her the place. Once settled in their small campus house at West Point, Godfrey began his assistant professor role in the engineering department as Louisa settled into her role as a professor's wife. It was quite a change from Cincinnati. There weren't many women around—only boys and military men, and cannon fire!

Tragedy Hits Home—Thanksgiving Day, 1859

Assistant Professor and Mrs. Weitzel were just three weeks into their honeymoon when tragedy struck the young couple. It was common during this time period for homes to have a large open fireplace in the kitchen where all the cooking was done. A tin can of water was usually kept nearby in case the woman's large hoop-skirts caught a spark. It was Thanksgiving Day, November 24, 1859, and Louisa was cooking her first holiday meal for her husband. She labored for days to find all the right fresh ingredients, then spent the morning cooking up a delicious meal, with some of Godfrey's German favorites from home. As she walked past the fireplace, a spark popped and landed on Louisa's skirt, which suddenly caught fire. The cloth ignited rapidly and she was engulfed by the flames as Godfrey searched for enough water to put them out.

She screamed in pain as her husband tore pieces of burning fabric from her small body. Before the flames could be extinguished, Louisa suffered third-degree burns over large portions of her body and went into shock. Godfrey ran for help and campus doctors left their own holiday meals to rush to the Weitzel home. The physicians arrived too late to do anything for the badly burned woman. Fortunately, her suffering was not long and Louisa died within one hour, a death that cast a pall over the usually festive holiday campus atmosphere. She was only nineteen years old.

Through tears, her grief-stricken young husband composed a telegram to Louisa's parents and sent it that same night to the Moors in Cincinnati, informing them of the terrible death of their only child. The news broke the next day back home in a column titled "Sad Accident" in the German-language newspaper, *Cincinnati Volksfreund*:

> Yesterday we received the sad news that the daughter of General Moor, who a few weeks ago was married to Lieutenant Weitzel and since then was living in West Point was burned so severely that she died an hour later. The accident happened because her clothing made contact with

the open fire in the fire place and she was engulfed by the flames. All medical help was without success.[19]

Louisa's body was sent back to Cincinnati on a steamer a week later, where she was buried in Augustus Moor's family plot at Spring Grove Cemetery. Godfrey was granted an official leave of absence on November 26 for one week to accompany the coffin home, with permission to apply for an extension.[20] His friend and classmate Cyrus Comstock wrote of the tragedy: "Weitzel was married in November to a German lady of Cincinnati and after she had been here a week, she was so severely burned . . . Weitzel now has leave till next August and was going to Europe."[21] In Cincinnati, the *Daily Gazette* reported on Louisa's death, saying, "This most melancholy termination of a life that promised so much happiness, has filled the hearts of numerous friends in this city with sorrow."[22]

Given his grief, Godfrey could not return to his teaching post that semester, and Superintendent Delafield understood. Godfrey was granted an extended leave on December 14 for eight months, to August 28, 1860, with permission to travel abroad to his homeland of Germany.[23] Godfrey spent the next several months in mourning for the loss of his young wife of only three weeks.

The Presidential Campaign of 1860

Godfrey Weitzel caught a transatlantic steamer to Europe and spent several months traveling. He studied some of the engineering marvels there and kept notes on all that he saw. Everyone hoped that his trip abroad would help soothe the fresh wound he carried as a widower. As he traveled abroad, his father read newspaper accounts of the Democratic Party's presidential nominating convention being held in Charleston, South Carolina.

The convention was held from April 23 to May 3, 1860, for the purpose of choosing a candidate to run against the Republican nominee, the divisive Abraham Lincoln of Illinois. The Charleston convention was so hopelessly deadlocked, however, between proslavery, antislavery, and neutral factions that it broke up without nominating anyone as the Democrats' candidate for president. The different factions met separately later in the year and nominated three different candidates for president, thus virtually assuring that Lincoln would be elected in the fall.

When Godfrey Weitzel returned to Cincinnati in late spring 1860, he remained close to his in-laws, Augustus and Anna Moor, and he stayed for a period of time at the Moor home. Having lost their only child, the Moors adopted Godfrey as their son. He was at the Moor home on June 14 when the U.S. census taker came by to record the 1860 Census for Cincinnati, Hamilton County, Ohio. The residents at the Moor household list a twenty-four-year-old lieutenant, Godfrey Weitzel, who admitted in the presence of his German-immigrant father-in-law that he was in fact *a native of Bavaria.*

Although he had accomplished nothing of note since his wife's death in late November, Godfrey Weitzel learned in early July that he had been promoted to first lieutenant.[24] Someone was watching out for him, it seemed, and his career was continuing to advance. He needed to get back to West Point, however, back to teaching and a normal routine. He had traveled, he had cried, he had searched his soul for how he could have prevented Louisa's death. And, like Major Beauregard, he needed to get back to work to clear his mind and to move on with his life.

Seeds of War Begin to Grow

Godfrey's extended furlough expired late in August 1860 and he returned to his teaching position at West Point, arriving just in time for the ceremony marking the end of camp and the start of fall term classes. He had missed nearly an entire academic year at West Point, and the new plebe class was still camped on the Plain. It was a festive time with graduation ceremonies, parades, and fireworks, and Godfrey enjoyed the merriment as much as he could under the circumstances. But during these next few months the nation began to unravel at the seams over the controversial presidential election and the social issues it exposed. Republican candidate Lincoln faced three foes. North was pitted against South in these debates, and rumors of a *civil war* began to be heard in campus discussions.

As cadet George Custer wrote, "The election of Abraham Lincoln was not more hotly argued and contested by the regular stump speakers of either party than by the Northern and Southern cadets in their efforts to re-echo the political sentiments of their respective sections." The cadets from Dixie were so whipped up in their hatred of Lincoln that one night a group of them hanged a stuffed image of Honest Abe in effigy from the limb of the shade tree growing in front of the cadet barracks. Custer recalled that "the effigy was removed early in the morning—so early that few of the cadets or professors even knew of the occurrence." All the cadets and faculty knew what Lincoln's election would mean. "In the event of Lincoln's election," Custer wrote, "secession would be the only recourse left to the South."[25]

Beauregard Sets His Eye on a New Job

The position of superintendent of the Academy had been held by Richard Delafield since 1856, when he replaced Robert E. Lee's successor, Major John G. Barnard. But there was movement afoot to replace Delafield in 1860, and a

West Point graduate in New Orleans had his eye on that position. From his office in the Custom House, Major P. G. T. Beauregard wrote to Major Barnard on October 2, 1860, expressing his interest in the position of superintendent. Beauregard suggested quite arrogantly that with the exception of Barnard, "I know of none who would be better suited to the place." In return for Major Barnard's support, Beauregard suggested putting Barnard in charge of the New Custom House, on the condition that he would resign it in Beauregard's favor whenever he returned to Louisiana.[26]

Beauregard anticipated that his appointment might be opposed by the former secretary of war, now Mississippi senator Jefferson Davis, and urged Barnard to start a letter campaign on his behalf to Senator Davis and Louisiana senator, Judah P. Benjamin. With the former secretary of war and a U.S. senator supporting him, Beauregard felt that his chances of an appointment as superintendent would be strong. "They must be illuminated in writing on the subject," he wrote, "you must now go to work with Mahan and Weitzel, and prepare one in duplicate, giving them all the arguments they may require to oppose Davis & Co." He felt certain that he would have the cooperation of Professor Mahan and Assistant Professor Godfrey Weitzel, the protégé he had mentored for four years. Beauregard mentioned that he would personally talk to them both. Using a military phrase, Beauregard closed his letter, "We must trust in God but keep our powder dry." The presidential election of November 1860 was now just one month away. In an ironic understatement, Beauregard added a note to Barnard: "We have nothing new here—politics are running very high—but everybody seems to be bent on beating—Breck—Doug—or Bell—but never trouble themselves about Lincoln—who I think is our most dangerous enemy."[27]

Lincoln Is Elected President

Just as Beauregard feared, on November 6, Republican Abraham Lincoln defeated all three of his opponents. Though Lincoln had the most overall votes, he was not favored by most of the nation, winning less than 40 percent of the popular vote.

Within days, there was open debate in Georgia and Mississippi about seceding from the Union in protest. The controversy spread across the nation like a brushfire, landing on the campus of West Point, where boys from Northern and Southern states were already hotly arguing over states' rights and slavery. The cadets were being educated at the expense of the United States of America, and had pledged eight years of service to its Army. What would they do if their home states seceded? Would they maintain loyalty to the Federal government or align with their native states?

The common belief among the faculty was that two or three Southern states might try to secede, but no more. From his desk at West Point, Assistant Professor Cyrus Comstock wrote on November 7, "Lincoln was elected President yesterday. There is very little disunion talk here, though there are several officers from the South."[28] Some of the cadets from Dixie had been directed by their parents that if Lincoln were elected, they should resign and go home. Almost two weeks after Lincoln's election, Cadet Henry S. Farley from South Carolina tendered his resignation on November 19. Farley's name would go down in history, but not for quitting West Point.

Beauregard Appointed Superintendent of West Point

While the nation was focused on fallout from the election results, the secretary of war made a startling choice for the new superintendent of West Point. He appointed a Southerner, Pierre Gustave Toutant Beauregard, to replace Richard Delafield as the head of the nation's prestigious Military Academy on the Hudson. On November 21, 1860, Beauregard formally resigned his engineering position in New Orleans, effective January 1, 1861. True to his pledge to Barnard, Beauregard recommended the former West Point superintendent to replace him and to direct the work in New Orleans.[29] After wrapping up his affairs, Beauregard caught a steamship and headed for New York.

A Louisiana native was headed to West Point at a time when secession was being discussed in all the Southern states. The timing was bad for Beauregard. His tenure at the Academy would be short-lived.

The South Carolina legislature called a state convention that opened on December 17, 1860. With a vote of 160 to 0, South Carolina became the first state to secede. At West Point, a Christmas dance was held in the dining hall that same evening.[30] Despite the holiday music and food, there was a tension on campus quite different from years past. Secession was in the air, and one state had already seceded. Would more cadets flee? The question was answered on the day after Christmas, when two cadets from Alabama resigned their commissions.

John B. Floyd was the Secretary of War, and like Jefferson Davis before him, it was Floyd's job to oversee the Military Academy.[31] In December, Secretary Floyd—a Virginian—was accused of assisting the secessionist cause by sending military supplies to Southern arsenals in preparation for a possible war. President James Buchanan requested Floyd's resignation. Before leaving office on December 29, however, Floyd had appointed Louisiana native P. G. T. Beauregard to head the nation's Military Academy. It was his last official act of defiance against Buchanan's administration. All wondered what the president would do about Beauregard's appointment, especially in light of national affairs. They did not have to wait long for an answer.

The Prelude to War

Reports of a planned revolt in the Southern states reached West Point while Superintendent Delafield was still in charge. He had a young student body that was trained in field maneuvers and drills, perhaps as much as any foot soldier in the regular Army. He began to make plans, just in case the Academy was called on to supply troops to help suppress a rebellion.

Delafield felt that First Lieutenant Godfrey Weitzel's leadership skills were needed more in the protection of the Union against any uprising in the South than they were in the classroom in New York. On January 2, 1861, Weitzel was attached to Company A of the engineer soldiers from the Military Academy by order of the superintendent.[32] This company, like one that had been organized in 1858 to suppress an uprising by Mormons in Utah, would be led by Captain James C. Duane, then treasurer of the Academy. The special unit consisted entirely of cadets and officers from West Point.

Rumors proved to be accurate, and in early January 1861, Federal forts and armories found themselves under unprecedented attacks from within. Georgia residents seized Fort Pulaski on January 3; Alabamians seized the arsenal at Mount Vernon on January 4 and took Forts Morgan and Gaines the next day. Floridians seized the Apalachicola arsenal on January 6 and Fort Marion on the seventh. With such brazen movements against Federal positions, West Point's superintendent issued an order on January 6 for Captain Duane's engineering company to be ready to ship out at a moment's notice. Delafield also organized a field battery of four pieces and seventy young men.[33] Assistant Professor Godfrey Weitzel was relieved from his teaching duties and ordered to report to Captain Duane.[34]

Within the next two weeks, four more Southern states joined South Carolina by passing ordinances of secession: Mississippi, Florida, Alabama, and Georgia, in that order. The voting was not close in any of these states, and it became abundantly clear that the Union could not be held together. In Louisiana, a U.S. Marine hospital and a fort were seized just as Major P. G. T. Beauregard packed for his trip to New York. Beauregard was fully aware of the rebellious activities in his home state, but as long as Louisiana remained part of the Union, he vowed to fulfill his duties at West Point.

Beauregard Comes . . . and Goes!

Godfrey Weitzel was anxious when he learned that his former mentor and friend of four years' duty in New Orleans was appointed as the thirteenth superintendent of the West Point Military Academy. After all, Godfrey had helped Beauregard to get the job and now looked forward to being reunited with him. Cyrus Comstock wrote on January 20, 1861, that "Major Beauregard arrived yesterday or day before. [This] evening, Craighill and I called to see Major Beauregard."[35] The Louisiana native took formal command of the Academy on Monday, January 23. That very same day, a convention was opened at the statehouse in Baton Rouge to discuss Louisiana's secession.

Delegates at Baton Rouge voted overwhelmingly 113 to 7 for Louisiana to secede from the Union. The next day, on January 27, former secretary of war John Floyd was indicted by a District of Columbia grand jury for conspiracy and treason. It was this Virginian who had appointed Beauregard as superintendent. Surely, many suspected, this was part of Floyd's treasonous plot, to give control of the nation's military school to a Southerner.

It was no surprise, except perhaps to Major Beauregard, that on January 28, just one day after Floyd's indictment, the new secretary of war, Joseph Holt, revoked Beauregard's appointment. Holt ordered the reinstatement of former superintendent Richard Delafield. Holt was genuinely concerned about the Southern major's loyalty to the Union, especially after the secession ordinance was passed in Louisiana. Beauregard's tenure as superintendent continues to hold the record for the shortest in the institute's history, lasting only five days.

The explosive Beauregard was livid and protested his embarrassing removal, which he saw as an insult to his integrity. He argued that he had no intention of going with his home state unless Louisiana's secession finally resulted in war.[36] Despite his pleas, however, Secretary Holt had made his decision and was unwilling to run the risk. Holt moved promptly to replace Beauregard, reassigning him to duty back at the unfinished Custom House . . . in New Orleans. Assistant Professor Comstock summed up the week's extraordinary activities in his diary: "Major Beauregard had been in command one day when the order was countermanded and he was afterward ordered to resume his duties at New Orleans. . . . He was much hurt."[37]

Beauregard was apparently well liked during his brief administration, and Cyrus Comstock reflected the mood among the faculty: "We all regret his going." The faculty gave a dinner in Beauregard's honor the night before he left, followed by a serenade. General Totten tried to smooth things over, writing to Beauregard that the change, so far as he knew, was political and was no reflection on him.[38] Beauregard may have accepted the explanation on the outside, but inside he was steaming.

CHAPTER 5

Lincoln's Inauguration and War Begins

A Rebel Nation Is Born

Secession's wave continued to roll across the South, and on February 1, 1861, a state convention was convened in Austin. The Ordinance of Secession was overwhelmingly approved in a 166-to-8 vote, making Texas the seventh state to secede. President James Buchanan refused to surrender the Federal forts to the seceding states, prompting newly organized militias in the Southern states to seize all remaining forts inside their borders. They succeeded except for two, Fort Pickens—outside Pensacola, and Fort Sumter—in Charleston Harbor. The Union braced for conflicts at both locations and began plans to reinforce the two forts with more troops.

Three days after the Texas ordinance, delegates from the first six seceding states gathered in the state capitol building in Montgomery, Alabama, to form a new nation—a confederacy of Southern states. Texas, which had only days before voted to secede, was not represented. The Montgomery gathering included a distinguished group of Southern leaders who drafted a new constitution. It was patterned after the United States Constitution, but stressed the autonomy of each state. The new constitution was adopted on February 8, 1861, and the Confederate States of America were born.

Five hundred and fifty miles to the north, newly elected U.S. president Abraham Lincoln left his home in Springfield, Illinois, by rail to make his way to Washington for his inauguration. Along the way, Lincoln made stops in various states, during which he attempted to reaffirm his desire to avoid war. A plot to assassinate Lincoln in Baltimore was discovered and measures were put in place to protect him. It was rumored that some secessionist congressmen were planning to kidnap lame-duck President Buchanan so that Vice President John C. Breckinridge, a Southern Democrat, could seize power. It was also rumored that "minutemen" from Virginia and Maryland were ready to invade the city. Tension was high in anticipation of a terrorist act against Lincoln, Buchanan, or others.

Security was tightened all along Lincoln's route, and he was safely smuggled into Washington City in the wee hours of February 23. Lincoln regretted having to slip into the capital "like a thief in the night." Bodyguards were organized to protect the president-elect as plans were being finalized for the inauguration ceremony. Captain James C. Duane and his Company A of the engineer soldiers from West Point arrived in Washington, D.C., about this same time, with First Lieutenant Godfrey Weitzel as part of the contingent. Their orders had nothing to do with "engineering," but instead to serve as additional bodyguards for Abe Lincoln.

Jefferson Davis Inaugurated

Speaking at the rail depot in Montgomery, Alabama, on February 16, 1861, former U.S. secretary of war and Mississippi senator Jefferson Davis said, "The time for compromise has now passed. The South is determined to maintain her position, and make all who oppose her smell Southern powder and feel Southern steel."[1] With brash optimism like this, two days later, on February 18, Davis was elected and inaugurated as the president of the new Confederate States of America, beating Lincoln to the official oath. Davis delivered his inaugural address at the Alabama state capitol.

"For purposes of defense," Davis began, "the Confederate States may, under ordinary circumstances, rely mainly upon their militia, but it is deemed advisable, in the present condition of affairs, that there should be a well-instructed and disciplined army, more numerous than would usually be required on a peace establishment." Davis also called for the formation of a navy, "for the protection of our harbors and commerce on the high seas."[2] His message was clear: the Confederacy needed to be ready for whatever action Lincoln might take.

Lincoln's Inauguration

There was no cable television to watch the ceremony in 1861, and the nation waited anxiously for word on not only Lincoln's safety as he took the oath of office, but also on the message he would deliver in his address. From his desk at West Point, Cyrus Comstock wrote: "Today, I suppose Lincoln was inaugurated. We are waiting with interest for tomorrow's papers to see *First*, if there was any trouble, *Second*, what is the program of his administration."[3]

On Monday afternoon, March 4, at about one o'clock, President-elect Abraham Lincoln left the elegant Willard Hotel and stepped into an open carriage in the company of outgoing president James Buchanan. The pair rode southeast along Pennsylvania Avenue to the U.S. Capitol Building for the ceremony. Mounted Federal troops escorted the carriage the entire mile and a quarter ride from the Willard to the Capitol, while others guarded the parade route. All points along the inaugural route were protected by cavalry and infantry, with sharpshooters perched even in windows of the Capitol Building. "The sight was very brilliant," wrote one reporter, "and the crowd enormous."[4]

Security was an incredible challenge, as twenty-five thousand strangers had flooded into the city to view the historic ceremony, many sleeping on the streets or in the Capitol Building itself since all the hotels were full.[5] The nation's capital was not only threatened with invasion from the South, but was also endangered by the secessionist element from within the city. First Lieutenant Godfrey Weitzel and his fellow soldiers of Company A were stationed strategically with orders to watch the crowd for any unusual activity.[6] Every eye scanned the crowd for signs of a gun, sudden movement of a spectator, or a rifle barrel in an upper window or on a rooftop.

All soldiers stood at attention, bayonets fixed to the tips of their rifles. The excited crowd waved and cheered as the carriage passed by, some climbing fences or stone pedestals to get a better view. Despite all the security, the mob pressed close to the presidential carriage and forced it to stop frequently.

A tall, semicircular wooden platform had been built for the occasion on the west side of the unfinished Capitol, facing the Mall. The platform was about thirty feet tall, giving the crowd a good look at the ceremony. Tucked below the huge platform where Lincoln and the other dignitaries stood, more soldiers were placed with orders to watch for explosives.

Lincoln and Buchanan arrived at the Capitol Building after a twenty-minute carriage ride and rested inside for a few minutes before proceeding onto the newly erected platform on the portico. Scaffolding and huge steel trusses poked through the white Capitol Building, which was still under construction. The members of the U.S. Supreme Court (including Southerner Associate Justice A. Campbell), the members of the Senate and House, and other dignitaries were seated on the speaker's platform.

At about 1:30 p.m., the six-foot-four Abraham Lincoln stepped up to the wooden podium and gave his address to the nation. This was the first time that either Godfrey Weitzel or Justice John Campbell had laid eyes on Abraham Lincoln. The young lieutenant and older Supreme Court judge would get a more up close view of Mr. Lincoln in just four years in a different capital city, Richmond. The crowd quieted as Lincoln began to speak. He opened with a statement directed at calming the fears of the Southerners: "Apprehension seems to exist among the people of the Southern States," he said, "that by the accession of a Republican Administration their property and their peace and personal security are to be endangered." Lincoln continued, "There has never been any reasonable cause for such apprehension. Indeed, the most ample evidence to the contrary has all the while existed and been open to their inspection. It is found in nearly all the published speeches of him who now addresses you."[7]

While trying to calm the growing rebellion, Lincoln's inaugural address also made a firm statement of policy concerning the seizure of Federal forts and possessions. "We denounce the lawless invasion by armed force of the soil of any State or Territory," he said, "no matter what pretext, as among the gravest of crimes." Lincoln closed with a last attempt to calm the Southern passions, knowing that his words would be reprinted in newspapers throughout the South. "We are not enemies, *but friends,*" he assured. "We must *not* be enemies. Though passion may have strained, it must not break our bonds of affection. The mystic chords of memory, stretching from every battlefield and patriot grave—to every living heart and hearthstone all over this broad land—will yet swell the chorus of the Union, when again touched, as surely they will be, by the better angels of our nature."[8] After the speech, Abraham Lincoln raised his right hand, placed his left on the Bible, and was sworn in as the sixteenth president of the United States by Chief Justice Roger Taney.

A month after the inauguration, on Friday, April 5, Godfrey Weitzel returned to West Point from his brief guard duty in Washington, accompanied by some of the cadets from Company A. The remainder of Captain Duane's engineering company stayed behind in New York City, preparing to embark for some uncertain destination. Weitzel arrived aboard a steamer on that now familiar cruise up the Hudson River, disembarking and heading up the hill to his assistant professor's quarters. "He came up for some clothes," Cyrus Comstock recalled of his classmate. Comstock wanted details from his chum, a firsthand account of the inauguration.[9]

Weitzel shared the news with Comstock that a large force was being assembled, but he did not yet know where they were headed. One rumor was that the troops were to ship off to aid San Domingo (the Dominican Republic) in the Caribbean. Spain had recently announced in March that it was annexing the Caribbean island of San Domingo, a bold move prompted by a belief that the United States had its hands full with rumblings of a civil war and would not retaliate in the Caribbean. Others thought the Federals would sail to Texas or to Fort Pickens in Florida, with most believing the latter as the likely secret destination.[10] Fort Pickens was surely a target of the Confederates, being just one of two Southern forts remaining under Federal control, and reinforcements were needed.

Beauregard Gets His Revenge—April 12, 1861

In the Deep South, a similar military mission was forming, with the same destinations in mind. Having been unjustly ousted, in his mind, from his post at West Point, P. G. T. Beauregard was glad to be welcomed into the Confederate States Army by President Jefferson Davis as a full general. Beauregard was promptly placed in charge of the South Carolina troops in Charleston

Harbor across from Fort Sumter. On April 8, 1861, General Beauregard received a telegraph message from Confederate secretary of war L. P. Walker that read, "Under no circumstances are you to allow provisions to be sent to Fort Sumter." That was followed two days later with a directive: "You will at once demand its evacuation, and if this is refused, proceed in such manner as you may determine to reduce it." Beauregard responded that he would make the demand at noon the following day, April 11.

That next morning, Southern volunteers of the First Louisiana Regulars shipped out of New Orleans for duty in Pensacola, Florida. Their objective was the seizure of Fort Pickens. On the same day, up in Charleston, a brash and confident General Beauregard demanded that the Federal officer in charge of Fort Sumter surrender. When Major Robert Anderson rejected his demand, Beauregard sent an aide with another terse warning on April 12: "By virtue of Brigadier General Beauregard's command, we have the honor to notify you that he will open the line of his batteries on Fort Sumter in one hour from this time." Anderson offered to evacuate Fort Sumter three days later, at noon on April 15. This delay was unacceptable to Pierre Beauregard.[11]

The first cadet to formally resign from West Point following Lincoln's election in 1860, red-haired Henry S. Farley from South Carolina, was summoned by Beauregard for special duty. Perhaps to spite his humiliating removal as West Point's superintendent, General Beauregard personally chose Farley for the honor of firing the first signal gun that opened the bombardment on Fort Sumter. For that act, Farley has been forever locked into the history of the Civil War along with Beauregard as the one who fired the first shot to start a bloody four-year war.

The "Little Napoleon" ordered Farley and his other Confederate gunners to open fire on Fort Sumter in the early morning hours of April 12. Thirty-four hours of bombardment left Fort Sumter severely damaged, and Anderson was forced to surrender on the afternoon of April 13, 1861. Thus began the four-year war that pitted North against South.

Lincoln Responds: The War Is On

Beauregard's brazen assault on Fort Sumter prompted President Lincoln to issue a call of his own on April 15 for volunteers to assist in suppressing "the rebellion." That day Lincoln issued his famous call for 75,000 men to volunteer for service, a number that was about five times the number of soldiers then in the ranks of the United States Army—but still less than the 100,000 that Davis had called for a month prior. Lincoln asked the volunteers to serve for a period of only three months, thinking that the conflict would be short-lived.

On April 18, three days after Lincoln's call to arms, Colonel Robert E. Lee declined an offer to command the Union Army in suppressing the Southern rebellion. His home state of Virginia had voted to secede from the Union the day before, and Lee was—above all—a loyal Virginian. On April 20, Lee resigned from the United States Army, rode to Richmond, and accepted command of the military and naval forces of Virginia.

Violence in Baltimore

Although lacking in any significant military experience, politician and attorney Benjamin Franklin Butler was made a brigadier general in the Massachusetts State Militia at the age of thirty-eight, making him at that time the youngest general in the United States.[12] So it is not surprising that Butler promoted young officers who were loyal to him. He found his protégé in an unlikely candidate, a lanky German lieutenant from Cincinnati. The sharp-minded trial lawyer Ben Butler saw an opportunity in Lincoln's April 14 call for volunteers. Butler was a general in the Massachusetts militia and promptly fired off a message to his senator, Henry Wilson, recommending that a brigadier general accompany his state's troops to the nation's capital. Wilson agreed and pressured Governor John A. Andrew to sign orders giving Butler command of a portion of the state's militia. Armed with this appointment, General Butler boarded a train and accompanied the Eighth Massachusetts Militia on its ride to Baltimore en route to Washington.

Talk of secession was spreading in Maryland, and the Union troops would have to pass through hostile territory on their way to Washington. The first branch of the Massachusetts Volunteers to reach Baltimore was the Sixth Militia, which arrived in that city on April 19 to change trains. A violent mob greeted the troops, who opened fire on the stone-throwing secessionist crowd. Several of the Massachusetts militiamen were injured and four of the soldiers were killed, in addition to a dozen civilians. In the rebel capital of Richmond, Virginia, the news that Federal troops had been attacked in Baltimore was met with cheers and a torchlight procession that snaked through the city.[13]

Federal troops had to cross Maryland to defend Washington, which was surrounded by slave states. Ben Butler was not about to be deterred from getting his militiamen through Baltimore. His trainful of soldiers was already headed south for Baltimore when word spread that secessionists were cutting telegraph lines, burning bridges, and blocking rail passage to the South. With his determined style of leadership, the lawyer-turned-general decided to push on through to Baltimore despite the recent riot. The quick-thinking Butler stopped the train at the next depot and ordered a group of his officers to seize the railway's good-sized ferryboat. He then loaded coal and drinking water on board the transport, and embarked his seven hundred militiamen for nearby Annapolis, bypassing the contentious Baltimore. The Massachusetts troopers spread out and secured the town of Annapolis and the U.S. Naval Academy as a base of operations. In a brilliant stroke, Butler sent armed troops to the Maryland State House to take possession of the official seal of Maryland, so that legislators would be unable to affix the Great Seal and thus unable to make legal any ordinance of secession.[14] Butler's aggressive tactics were reported in the Northern press, who praised him for preventing Maryland's secession.

Butler's Fame Spreads in the North

On May 13, 1861, less than one month after Lincoln's call for volunteers, Ben Butler led two regiments of volunteers and a battery of artillery of Federal troops into the heart of Baltimore by train, where they secured the city. His Massachusetts militia took over the newspaper and the rail station, and seized fifteen wagonloads of stashed firearms. A few days later, Butler proceeded triumphantly into Washington, where he was received with cheers at the National Hotel. Basking in his newfound celebrity status, Butler made a speech to his admirers: "The Union must be preserved at all hazards of money," he said, "and if need be, of every life this side of the Arctic regions."[15] The crowd erupted in applause and President Lincoln knew that he had a decisive military man in Butler, one who might serve the North well in other hot spots. Two days later, Butler was promoted to the rank of major general of U.S. Volunteers.

Ben Butler was sent to Fort Monroe in Virginia, where the mouth of the James River meets Chesapeake Bay, to take command there. President Lincoln urged Butler to continue to use the same energy he had shown at Annapolis and Baltimore.

The "Negro Question" and Contraband Property

Virginia was, of course, a slave state, and a Union occupation of its key military fortress created a perceived safe haven for runaway slaves. While Butler occupied Fort Monroe, several slaves belonging to an officer of the Virginia militia escaped and came within Union lines for protection. North Carolina had just seceded from the Union on May 20, and the black field hands reported that their master had intended to send them to North Carolina to work on Confederate fortifications.[16] Hearing of the master's plans for his slave labor, the clever lawyer-general Ben Butler sent a receipt to the rebel officer, as was the custom when seizing any other private property. A puzzled agent of the slave master arrived at Fort Monroe under flag of truce and asked Butler's intentions as to the escaped slaves. After all, given the mandate of the Fugitive Slave Act, Butler was required to return runaway slaves to their masters.

Butler's response shocked the Virginian: "I intend to hold them." He explained that since Virginia had seceded from the Union, its citizens were now those of a foreign nation, no longer protected by the act. "I shall hold these Negroes as *contraband of war*," said Butler, "since they are engaged in the construction of your battery and are claimed as your property."[17] Just as he might seize a horse, wagon, rifle, or cannon being used by the enemy, Butler reasoned that since the Virginians saw the slaves as mere property, they were now subject to the same treatment as any other enemy property that fell into Union hands.

Butler's characterization of runaway slaves as "contraband" fueled his critics in the South, where he was already being vilified and denounced in the Dixie press. By contrast, Northern abolitionists were delighted at Ben Butler's legalistic approach to save slaves from reprisal at the hands of their cruel masters. The War Department also gave its approval to Butler's actions. Word spread among Virginia's black population that they could find protection within Federal forts. Within days the numbers of escaped slaves within many Federal camps increased. Black men, women, and children streamed into what they called Butler's "Fort Freedom" to seek protection. As many as forty slaves arrived each day, and by the end of May, Butler reported the influx of black slaves as a "disaster," not knowing whether to rejoice or weep.[18] He had indirectly liberated Virginia's slaves before Lincoln could emancipate them!

Lieutenant Weitzel Is Sent to Reinforce Fort Pickens

After the forced surrender of Fort Sumter in mid-April, all eyes were on the only remaining Federal fort in the South still in Union hands—Fort Pickens in the Florida panhandle. Pickens was the largest of a group of forts designed to fortify Pensacola Harbor. It was strategically located at the western tip of Santa Rosa Island and guarded the island and the entrance to the harbor. Confederate brigadier general Braxton Bragg had amassed approximately seven thousand Confederate troops in the Pensacola area with an eye on attacking Fort Pickens. Federal troops were rushed south to reinforce the position.

Captain James C. Duane and Company A of his engineer soldiers arrived from New York at Fort Pickens early morning on April 13, 1861, and disembarked from longboats. First Lieutenant Godfrey Weitzel was among the reinforcements stationed there for nearly five months, from mid-April until September 1861, where he oversaw the repair of the fort using skills he had picked up at West Point and in New Orleans. Five Union Navy vessels anchored off the coast of Pensacola to defend from any attack by sea, and Fort Pickens remained in Union hands throughout the War. Years later General Ben Butler credited Godfrey for his excellent work, saying that Weitzel had "fortified Fort Pickens so that it stood a bombardment without the loss of a man."[19]

After fresh reinforcements showed up in September, Captain James Duane and his engineer soldiers were sent back to West Point. Lieutenant Weitzel had barely settled into his assistant professor's quarters when he received new orders on October 14. He was being sent back to his hometown of Cincinnati, to report there to Brigadier General Ormsby Mitchel's headquarters. His job would be to help recruit troops for a new Company D of the engineer soldiers, the "Engineers Battalion."[20]

While Godfrey was at Fort Pickens, his father, Lewis Weitzel, died of a heart attack on August 29, 1861, and was buried at Spring Grove Cemetery alongside his recently departed daughter-in-law, Louisa C. Moor-Weitzel, in plots owned by Augustus Moor.[21] Godfrey was anxious to see his widowed mother and his brother, and to visit the graves of his father and wife, so the reassignment was a welcome one. Plus, he knew so many good young German men in Cincinnati, he was certain he could raise a regiment for the cause. He boarded a steamer back to the Queen City.

CHAPTER 6

From Cincinnati to New Orleans

A German Call to Arms!

By the mid-nineteenth century, the so-called Over-the-Rhine neighborhood of Cincinnati had become an important center of German immigrant culture. Germans had their own churches, beer gardens, social clubs, and even native-language newspapers. When the November 1860 election presented many with their first time to vote, the majority of German-Americans embraced Lincoln and his Republican Party platform. Lincoln had courted the German vote, even quietly purchasing a German-language newspaper in Illinois, the *Staatsanzeiger*, for $400 and leasing it back to its editors on the condition that it support the Republican Party platform.[1]

When Beauregard's artillery fired on Fort Sumter, a swell of patriotism rose in the hearts of Cincinnati's Germans, who responded without hesitation to Lincoln's call for volunteers. A community meeting was organized at the Turner Hall to recruit soldiers for an all-German company. The memory was still fresh in their minds of the awful results of disunion among the German states, and the new immigrants did not want to see the United States similarly divided. The recruitment was a success, resulting in the formation of an all-German regiment designated the "First German Regiment."

Godfrey Weitzel's father-in-law, the local beer garden owner Augustus Moor, helped to rally his fellow German immigrants to enlist. When still more Germans responded to Lincoln's call, another all-German regiment was formed, named the "Second German Regiment." The forty-six-year-old barrel-chested Moor gladly accepted a commission as its colonel.

Godfrey Returns Home, Again

Cincinnati's port on the Ohio River was bustling with activity not only from the normal civilian commerce, but now from the movement of troops and military supplies. The port served a key role in supplying goods and troops for the Union

Army, so fortification was essential to protect the supply line. Cincinnati served as the headquarters for much of the war for the Department of the Ohio, which was charged with the defense of the region.

Pursuant to his orders of October 14, 1861, Godfrey Weitzl returned home and reported to General Mitchel's headquarters there.[2] His newly widowed mother, Susanna Weitzel, was comforted to have her son back home and out of harm's way. While his father-in-law, Colonel Augustus Moor, fought battles in northern Virginia, Godfrey Weitzel was assigned the far less dangerous task of recruiting troops in the city he knew so well. By now, Godfrey was somewhat of a legend in the Over-the-Rhine neighborhood and looked the part in his first lieutenant's uniform. His job was twofold: first, to help engineer fortifications for General Ormsby M. Mitchel's District of Ohio; and second, as a recruiter to fill new Company D.

General Mitchel appointed the Cincinnati native as his chief engineer and put him to work designing the fortifications of the city when not assisting in recruitment. Godfrey's younger brother, Lewis Jr., eventually signed up, with his brother's coaxing, on December 15, 1861. Lewis Jr. was immediately made a lieutenant second class in Company C, Twenty-Eighth Infantry Regiment Ohio, where he served under the command of Godfrey's father-in-law, Colonel Augustus Moor.

Godfrey spoke German fluently and knew the city well, making him effective in rounding up more fellow immigrants to serve in his new company. "Guten morgen, Herr Schultz!" Godfrey would greet a new recruit. "Wie geht es dir?" He stressed that the men would receive their orders and instructions in their native language, from *German* officers. This persuaded those immigrants less proficient in English to enlist along with their fellow countrymen. Recruitment ads appealed to the German sense of ethnic duty and national pride, using terms like "holy war," "warriors," and "thieving hordes."[3] Godfrey Weitzel and other Union recruiters stressed ethnic pride and the advantages of serving in an all-German regiment. It was not long before Godfrey had all the men he needed for Company D to help with the fortifications in the city.

Back to Washington, D.C.

Godfrey celebrated his twenty-sixth birthday on November 1, 1861, with his mother, his brother, and other friends in Cincinnati. That same day, back in Washington, Winfield Scott stepped down and George McClellan replaced him as the new general-in-chief of the Union Army. Three weeks later, on November 22, a two-day battle broke out at Fort Pickens in Florida, which Godfrey had just left. During those two days, thousands of Union and Confederate shells were fired, with reverberations so strong that they shattered windows seven miles away in the town of Pensacola. But the assault was unsuccessful, and the fort remained in Northern control. The following day, Godfrey Weitzel received orders to leave

Cincinnati and report for duty in Washington City with General McClellan's Army of the Potomac.[4]

Weitzel arrived in Washington in early December and reported to General McClellan for duty. McClellan had purposely set up his winter quarters in the former home of Confederate general Robert E. Lee on his abandoned family plantation in Arlington, Virginia. McClellan occupied Lee's impressive Greek-inspired mansion on the hilltop, which gave a perfect view of the nation's capital just across the Potomac River. If General Lee wanted his house back, all he had to do was come home and claim it. He would have a grand reception, courtesy of the Union Army.

The irony must have been apparent to young Weitzel as he strode up the hillside leading to the imposing Lee mansion, past the slave quarters of the former Lee family servants and the temporary white tents of the Union soldiers. Godfrey entered the huge portico, held up by massive stone columns, passed security guards, removed his hat, and entered his former superintendent's house to meet General McClellan.

George McClellan had striking good looks, with a full head of neatly combed black hair, piercing eyes, and a broad mustache. Only the hint of a goatee grew below his lower lip. Like Weitzel, Lee, and Beauregard, George "Little Mac" McClellan ranked second in his class at West Point when he graduated in 1846. He made an intimidating presence as he strode about General Lee's home in his riding boots. McClellan received the young officer and assigned Godfrey Weitzel to work once again under Captain James Duane, but now to enhance the defenses of Washington sufficient to fend off any Confederate assault. Godfrey informed McClellan that he needed to organize a company of engineers just as he had done in Cincinnati. Once he had his team assembled, they would set to work on building some of the defenses and several pontoon bridges for the Army's use in Virginia. McClellan approved and Godfrey set off to find Captain Duane.

Duane had great news for Weitzel. His gallant service at Fort Pickens had not gone unnoticed. Though it took many months to make official, President Lincoln himself had submitted to the U.S. Senate a list of officers to be promoted "by brevet" in the Army of the United States. Included in that list was a request that First Lieutenant Godfrey Weitzel, Corps of Engineers, be promoted to brevet captain for "distinguished services at Fort Pickens, Florida."[5] This was the first of many promotions that would skyrocket the career of the young engineer up through the ranks of the regular and Volunteer armies. Captain Godfrey Weitzel was only twenty-six years old, but he would be a brigadier general within the year.

With his new promotion, Captain Weitzel was transferred on December 10 to the Engineer Battalion of the Army of the Potomac and placed in command of his first company of soldiers. He was also assigned to the special duty of putting together some of the pontoon trains for the Army. Perfect timing was a key to each success in Godfrey Weitzel's life, and his presence in Washington in early 1862 launched him into a major role that would change his entire future.

Plans to Attack New Orleans

"The most important event of the War of the Rebellion," said Commander David Dixon Porter, "with the exception of the fall of Richmond, was the capture of New Orleans and the forts Jackson and St. Philip, guarding the approach to that city."[6] Godfrey Weitzel was not only present at both events, but largely credited with the capture of both key Confederate cities. His participation in these two critical military events was triggered by meetings that had been going on in Washington since November to plan for a blockade of the Gulf Coast and the capture of its major ports. He was in the right place at the right time.

New Orleans and the Gulf inlet of the Mississippi River below that city was, and is today, a key commercial passage. From the inlet, ships could easily sail north some 75 miles to New Orleans, and from there another 360 miles upstream to the commercial port of Memphis. From Memphis, ships could steam north just over 200 miles to the bustling city of Cairo, Illinois, where the Ohio River joined the Mississippi and gave naval passage to the Northern port cities, such as Louisville, Cincinnati, and Pittsburgh. At St. Louis, the Missouri River joined the Mississippi and provided both military and commercial access to points west of Kansas City and north to Omaha. All this access to the river routes hinged upon control of New Orleans, and the Union was determined to have it.

At the War Department offices next to the White House, Secretary of the Navy Gideon Welles had formed an advisory board on naval strategy to conduct the Southern blockade. The board's recommendation was to focus on the Southern port cities of Mobile and New Orleans. In November 1861, naval officer Commander Porter had been summoned to Washington to meet with Welles. Porter had just returned from duty with the Gulf Blockading Squadron where his steam frigate *Powhatan* had been stationed near the mouth of the Mississippi. Therefore, Porter had a current assessment of the situation in the Gulf.[7]

Porter appropriately called the Mississippi River "the backbone of the Rebellion," for its strategic route through the rebel states.[8] The river would be essential to supplying the Confederate Army, thus making it one of the Union's first military objectives. It was clear to Welles and Porter that if you broke the supply line in the South, you would break the back of the enemy. The place to start that operation was at the port of entry into the Gulf of Mexico—the city of New Orleans. Secretary Welles planned to capture that city as soon as enough ships could be assembled to combat and defeat the two forts that guarded the southern approach to New Orleans—Forts Jackson and St. Philip.[9]

Unbeknownst to the secretary was that living in Washington, D.C., at that time was a young brevet captain and first lieutenant who was intimately familiar with both forts through his four years spent reinforcing them. He knew their strengths and weaknesses from his months of drawing them, in triplicate, to the point where he knew them from memory. The young captain was, of course, Godfrey Weitzel, the bright young German officer recently relocated from Cincinnati to the nation's capital.

Secretary Welles realized that an attack from the north would mean moving thousands of Union soldiers on transports down through Confederate-dominated points along the Mississippi River. This was not feasible, and it became apparent that an assault from the south, up the mouth of the river, was the only realistic way to take control of New Orleans. The recently fortified Forts Jackson and St. Philip presented major obstacles to such an assault, with their powerful guns positioned on opposite sides of a sharp bend in the river where ships had to slow their approach in order to make the turn. Making matters worse, it was believed that nobody in the Union Army or Navy had good knowledge on the current status of either fort. The engineer in charge, P. G. T. Beauregard, was now a Confederate general, and nobody else had current knowledge of the condition of the two forts—or so it was thought!

Porter enthusiastically supported the planned naval assault of New Orleans, adding that he felt it would be necessary to bombard the two forts with mortar boats to weaken their defenses. A mortar boat was essentially a converted sailing schooner on which was mounted a single, thirteen-inch stub of a cannon, looking more like a cauldron than a gun. These mortars were capable of throwing a 285-pound projectile a considerable distance, usually with a timed explosive device that would detonate on impact. Porter felt that the size and weight of the mortar shells could reduce Forts Jackson and St. Philip to rubble within forty-eight hours of constant bombardment. He discussed his plan with the secretary of the Navy and several U.S. senators.[10] The plan was so well received that the group took it to Secretary of War Edwin M. Stanton, who enthusiastically endorsed the idea; then next door to the Executive Mansion (as it was called), where they met with President Lincoln.

Lincoln understood the importance of the Mississippi River as a supply line to the Southern states. Whoever controlled New Orleans could cut off that line. However, the president wanted the endorsement of his new general-in-chief, George B. McClellan. The growing contingent of Federal officials was now joined by Secretary of State William H. Seward, and all proceeded by carriage to McClellan's headquarters at the Lee homestead across the Potomac. The meeting with McClellan solidified the plan. "We will leave this matter in the hands of you two gentlemen," Lincoln said to McClellan and Porter. "Make your plans, and let me have your report as soon as possible."[11] Lincoln then departed to allow his military leaders to strategize on the expedition.

To command the Army troops, McClellan selected General Benjamin F. Butler, whom Porter described as "a man supposed to be of high administrative ability, and at that time one of the most zealous of the Union commanders."[12] For the Navy's command, while Porter had conceived of the plan, another officer was selected, Captain David G. Farragut, whom Porter had known since childhood.

Ben Butler was called to Washington to meet with Secretary of War Stanton and President Lincoln. He was told that he was to work in concert with Farragut and Porter to attack New Orleans. As Butler left President Lincoln's office, Secretary Stanton pulled him aside. "You take New Orleans," Stanton said, "and you shall be Lieutenant-General."[13] These words stayed in Butler's mind for the next several months and became his life's goal.

Word soon made its way to Butler and Porter and their team of advisers that a newly promoted captain from Cincinnati had intimate knowledge of both forts from his four years spent living and working in New Orleans under Beauregard prior to the outbreak of war. Godfrey Weitzel knew the plans of each fort by heart and he was right there—in Washington! A call went out to "find Weitzel" and bring him to Butler's office at once. Soon Godfrey became a critical part of the planning team. His days of fishing and hunting ducks in the bayous behind the two forts, and of drawing each fort in triplicate, were about to pay off handsomely.

With Farragut to lead the Navy, Ben Butler began to assemble his Army officers for the joint expedition, handpicking the regimental commanders, several from his political contacts. He selected a successful lawyer and strong Democrat, George F. Shepley, to command a regiment of soldiers from Maine. Shepley was well known before the war, having been nominated by President Buchanan as attorney of the United States for the District of Maine.[14]

Preparations for the Assault

Butler's expedition was held up for more than two months by McClellan, who harbored reservations about the mission. General McClellan feared that the Navy could not safely sail up the Mississippi past the two fort strongholds of Jackson and St. Philip. Nonetheless, plans for the operation continued to take shape, and in December 1861 the first wave of troops arrived on a staging area in the Gulf at Ship Island.

In Washington, on February 19, 1862, Godfrey Weitzel was unexpectedly ordered to report in person to General McClellan for instructions.[15] Weitzel was not sure what to expect due to the secrecy of Butler's mission. He returned once again to Arlington, to the impressive two-story antebellum home of his former superintendent, Robert E. Lee, to discuss his new assignment with McClellan. With his reputation as an effective military engineer becoming widely known, and his four years of experience in New Orleans, the twenty-six-year-old Weitzel was promptly reassigned and ordered to report without delay to General Benjamin F. Butler at Hampton Roads, Virginia, where he would attach himself to the Department of the Gulf as Butler's chief engineer.[16]

There was no time to waste and Butler needed him at Hampton Roads. Godfrey, who understood the importance of his new orders, stood, saluted General McClellan, and turned and left for an adventure that would take him on a wild ride for the next two years.

Chief engineer! And New Orleans! The city in which he had spent nearly four years under P. G. T. Beauregard reinforcing the defenses! Godfrey must have paused as he left that meeting with McClellan, taking in the view from the front porch of the former Lee home. Peering out at the impressive city across the Potomac, with the unfinished dome of the white Capitol Building and the stub of the halted Washington Monument standing out, he must have wondered if Robert E. Lee would ever again take in the breathtaking view.

To Hampton Roads

Captain Godfrey Weitzel arrived at the bustling port in the Hampton Roads harbor, which was filled with tall-masted ships, and reported to General Butler's headquarters. Sitting behind a wooden desk was Ben Butler, whose square-shaped balding head was flanked by thin reddish locks that spilled over his ears and curled slightly in the back. His narrow nose separated two puffy eyes, and his wiry mustache drooped over his upper lip. Butler sized up the tall, bearded young engineer. After exchanging brief introductions, Ben Butler outlined to Godfrey his secret mission. Given Weitzel's knowledge of the Crescent City and his formal military training, Butler asked Weitzel what he thought would be the best method of assault on the two forts guarding the approach to New Orleans and what he would need for such a mission.

West Point had trained him for just such a situation, and Godfrey began to draw on his memory from Professor Dennis Mahan's classes on military tactics. The young lieutenant surprised Butler with the information that it was possible to land troops from the Gulf side and to attack Fort St. Philip virtually unopposed, since there were no guns on that side. Ben Butler squinted and suppressed a smile; he was intrigued at the idea. The words of Secretary Stanton came flooding back, just as clear as the day he'd sat in President Lincoln's office: "*You take New Orleans, and you shall be Lieutenant-General.*" Weitzel might be his ticket to that big promotion. With Butler's approval, Godfrey set to work planning the mission and securing all the supplies that would be required to capture the city he knew so well.

Butler later praised this bright young man for helping organize the expedition: "Through the energy of Lieutenant Weitzel, my chief engineer, those accessories of the expedition were fully got ready and put on board ship."[17] Among the supplies he would need, Godfrey procured scaling ladders to be used to get troops over the high stone walls of the two forts.[18]

As Godfrey explained the possibility of a land assault, the two men decided that the expedition should include mechanics to build boats with which to get through the bayous, lagoons, and morasses at the rear of Fort St. Philip. They would also need carpenters to build ladders for scaling the parapets, plus rafts and flatboats to transport field artillery and troops through the shallow swamps of Louisiana. Godfrey explained it all, and Butler approved it. They made a good team.

More Federal Troops Ship Out

Back at the Executive Mansion, an anxious Abraham Lincoln was growing weary of inaction by George McClellan. On January 27, 1862, Lincoln had ordered that all of his armies begin offensive operations by February 22, George Washington's birthday. Butler and Farragut knew that they would not be in position to assault New Orleans by that date, but now moved without delay to send thousands of men, plus necessary supplies and weapons, to the Gulf. On February 3, Captain David Farragut sailed out from Hampton Roads in his massive flagship the USS *Hartford* through Chesapeake Bay and into the Atlantic Ocean.[19] Commander David Porter's mortar flotilla set sail for the Gulf more than a week later. With their preparations made, Butler and Godfrey Weitzel set sail from Hampton Roads onboard the transport appropriately named *Mississippi* on February 21 with fifteen hundred of Butler's New England recruits and his wife, Sarah, as a civilian passenger.[20] The trip south was delayed by storms and rolling seas, which tested the fortitude of the Yankee farmers and merchants, now volunteer soldiers.

After a rough landing, which included Butler's ship getting tangled with another ship anchored in the harbor, Butler and his wife, Weitzel, and their troops arrived at their new island home.[21] Anchoring in the deep harbor of Ship Island, each regiment disembarked one by one and joined the tent city assembled on the sand island. As the men carried crates of supplies from the ship, Lieutenant Weitzel inspected their condition and checked them off the list of preparations he had made back in Hampton Roads.

Weitzel's Meeting with Farragut and Butler

General Butler paid a visit to Flag Officer David Farragut, accompanied by his chief engineer, Captain Weitzel. Butler explained that the young man had been stationed at Forts Jackson and St. Philip for four years and had valuable information. This captured Farragut's attention. After all, who better to give advice about the two forts than a man who had himself worked on them? The three men sat down on board Farragut's impressive flagship *Hartford*, and Godfrey Weitzel began to give a narrative about the layout, armament, and surroundings of each fort. At Godfrey's recommendation, Butler had brought with him more than one hundred Massachusetts carpenters and mechanics. They would build boats to move troops through the shallow swamps at the rear of Fort St. Philip. Godfrey had seen to it that the needed supplies and ammunition were all in order. When the time was right, Butler was ready to place six thousand of his men in the Mississippi River to take out the two enemy forts. Then it was up to the Navy to run past them, all the way to New Orleans. That promotion to lieutenant general was within Butler's reach.

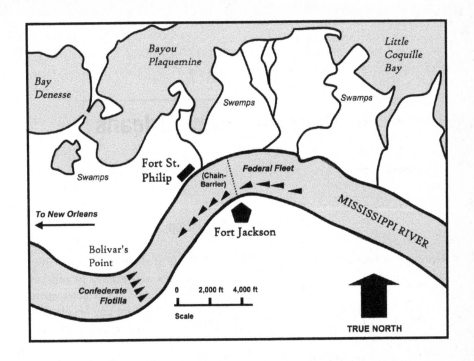

Bay Denesse

Bayou Plaquemine

Little Coquille Bay

Swamps

Swamps

Swamps

Fort St. Philip

(Chain-Barrier)

Federal Fleet

MISSISSIPPI RIVER

To New Orleans

Fort Jackson

Bolivar's Point

Confederate Flotilla

0   2,000 ft   4,000 ft

Scale

TRUE NORTH

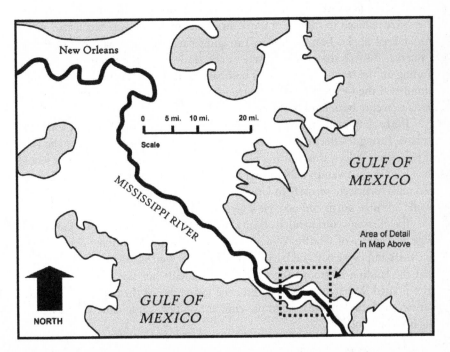

New Orleans

0   5 mi.   10 mi.   20 mi.

Scale

GULF OF MEXICO

MISSISSIPPI RIVER

Area of Detail in Map Above

GULF OF MEXICO

NORTH

FIGURE 6.1. Forts Jackson and St. Philip on the Mississippi River, April 24, 1862.

CHAPTER 7

The Capture of New Orleans

Running Up the Mississippi

Reports that Federal warships had started a blockade at the mouth of the river caused considerable concern in New Orleans. Residents were assured by officials that the two forts could protect the city from any invasion. Local newspapers reported, "The Mississippi is fortified so as to be impassable for any hostile fleet or flotilla."[1] Godfrey Weitzel must have smiled when he saw those reports. He knew how to do it.

Under the agreed plan of attack, Captain David Porter's fleet of twenty-one "bomb-schooners" were to anchor below the two forts and fire continuously until they were reduced to rubble, or until Porter's ammunition was exhausted. While Porter kept up his bombardment, Farragut's fleet was to remain out of fire, as a reserve. Butler's troops would stay at the ready, near the mouth of the river, waiting on the results of the Navy's bombardment. When Porter had sufficiently pummeled the two forts, the Army troops would advance up the river on transports to secure both land positions.

The backup plan, in case Porter's bombardment did not silence the forts, was to have Farragut's fleet of steamers attempt to run by them and clear the river of the enemy's fleet, thus cutting off supplies to the forts. Butler's troops would then land in the swamps behind Fort St. Philip and attempt an assault. When the two rebel forts were securely in Union hands, the rest of the land and naval force would advance north and take New Orleans by force.

The mission's commanders, Butler and Farragut, relied heavily on the knowledge and advice of Godfrey Weitzel, who knew the most intimate details of the two forts and every bay and bayou around them.[2] Weitzel assured General Butler that the landing of troops there would be difficult but not impossible. Butler later praised Weitzel, saying, "Both in the formation of the plan and in its execution, the local knowledge and pre-eminent skill of Lieutenant Weitzel were of the utmost value."[3]

The Assault Begins

The Navy's fleet now assembled in the Gulf consisted of forty-seven armed vessels, plus troop transports. On April 7, 1862, Farragut finally succeeded in getting his ships over the bar at the mouth of the Mississippi River. He notified General Butler that the Navy would be ready within four or five days, and invited Butler to come along.[4] Butler accepted the invitation. At daylight on April 13, the surveying steamer *Sachem* and the gunboats of the flotilla got under way, with the naval vessels following. The significance of the date was not lost on anyone, as it was one year to the day since Fort Sumter had surrendered in Charleston Harbor.

The survey team got within three miles of Fort St. Philip, close enough to see its flagstaff. The next day, the *Sachem* continued north to inspect the condition of sunken hulls that had been placed in the river to prevent passage.[5] A larger portion of the fleet crept to within two miles of Fort Jackson and drew fire from the enemy. With new intelligence on the condition of the forts and the blockages in the river, Porter and Farragut conferred with Butler and Weitzel and finalized their plans.

On April 16, the flotilla started up the river, with Porter's mortar boats in the lead. To disguise the ships along the tree-lined banks of the Mississippi, their hulls were smeared with mud and the riggings covered with branches of trees as camouflage. The odd-looking vessels made their way up the Mississippi and took positions below the two forts. The mortar vessels covered their mastheads and rigging with green branches and when tied up along the tree-lined riverbank, their masts looked like trees.[6]

The leading vessels moored about three thousand yards below the two forts, and the bombardment began. Each vessel fired at the rate of one shell every ten minutes, drawing return fire from Forts Jackson and St. Philip. About 5:00 p.m., fire was seen to break out inside Fort Jackson, and the guns were silenced as men worked to put out the flames.[7] Porter's fleet fired continuously, creating a noisy "*Boom! Boom! Boom!*" all day and all night. The work exhausted the sailors on the mortar boats, and by nightfall, the rate was reduced to one shell every half hour.

The orange-and-white arc of the mortar shells could be sixty miles away at Ship Island, where thousands of infantry soldiers awaited the outcome of the naval assault. Shells that fell outside the forts drove some twelve to fourteen feet into the soft ground, then exploded, making the whole fort tremble with the shock.[8] Those shells that fell inside the fort did even more damage, setting fire to the wooden barracks and officers' quarters of Fort St. Philip, which lit the sky as it burned all night. Porter ordered the firing to cease, presuming that the blaze would force the rebels to surrender. However, the fire cleared the fort of obstructions but did no serious damage to the stone fort itself. When the occupants failed to surrender, Porter resumed firing the next morning. Return fire from the defiant fort pierced the hull of a Union schooner, which sank in twenty minutes.[9]

"After we had kept up the bombardment for two or three days," Godfrey recalled, "a deserter came from the fort, and he was brought to Admiral (then Commander) Porter."[10] The deserter knew the position of every new gun that had been added to Fort Jackson and was able to mark them on a map with accuracy.

But after four days of bombardment and thousands of shells, no real damage had been inflicted upon the seemingly impenetrable forts that were so expertly designed and built by engineers Beauregard and Weitzel. While Godfrey wanted the Union mission to be a success, he must have taken some secret pleasure in seeing how well his designs had held up against such an overwhelming naval assault. General Butler directed his chief engineer to take a small reconnaissance party to the mouth of the Mississippi River and to bring back updated information about the construction of the forts that the Navy would encounter.

As a result of the failed bombardment, the backup plan was put into action for Farragut's fleet to make a run past the forts, with an Army assault to the rear of Fort St. Philip. However, the Confederates had anticipated an attempt to run past the forts and obstructed the river with a chain cable to prevent passage.[11]

Unlike the iron chain that George Washington had built at West Point, this chain connected several schooners anchored thirty yards apart in a line extending across the river. One end of this fortified chain was securely fastened to the shore on each side of the ships, with the chain woven through the schooners from one to another in between. This improved chain allowed the driftwood floating downriver to pass between the schooners without damaging the integrity of the barrier.

"The Forts Should Be Run"

On April 20, Farragut felt the time had come and issued a general order for his fleet to weigh anchor and start its journey upriver. "The forts should be run," he said.[12] Two days later, Chief Engineer Weitzel returned from his stealth mission up to the forts with fresh information. There were still no guns mounted on the swampy back side of Fort St. Philip and thus troops could be brought in from the Gulf on the east, rather than upriver, on small boats. They would need to take a narrow channel known as Maunels Canal, which Weitzel knew well from his duck hunting days. But first, Farragut would have to devise a way to break the chain-barrier if he was to run past the forts and into New Orleans.

The rear approach to Fort St. Philip was no easy task, however, and for several miles the approach was only a marsh covered with water and short shrubbery. But Godfrey Weitzel assured General Butler that "troops who were in earnest could get through it."[13] He was right. Butler sent one of the officers from his Massachusetts battery to scout out the rear of Fort St. Philip from a little bayou that ran from the Mississippi River into the Gulf. The scout reported to Butler that on the first night he found that he could get anywhere he wanted along the rear of Fort St. Philip without being noticed. The next night the brave scout took a slightly heavier boat and some men behind Fort St. Philip again. He reported back, just as Weitzel had advised, that there were no guns at all mounted on the rear that would prevent the transports from coming up the canal.

Time for Action!

By April 23, David Farragut had concluded that there was no more reason to wait. The condition of the river and the chain warranted an attempt to pass the forts. Days of bombing by Porter's fleet had not reduced the two forts, although Confederate deserters reported that considerable damage had been done inside the forts and that the men were "in a desperate and demoralized condition."[14] Farragut and his officers peered through telescopes from the *Hartford*. In the darkness they could make out a flotilla of at least twelve rebel steamers lurking around the bend and above the forts. A council of the commanding officers was held, and they decided to run past the forts early on the morning of April 24.

At Farragut's request, Lieutenant Godfrey Weitzel gave a briefing to all of the assembled naval commanders on the condition and formation of the forts. Weitzel explained that both were positioned very low to the water, especially Fort St. Philip. The young officer noted that the rebel gunners of all the batteries had been firing their guns at a high elevation in an attempt to reach the Union fleet five miles away. Weitzel predicted that the gunners would most likely keep the cannons at that same angle as the fleet approached.[15] He then made a very gutsy suggestion: If the Navy's vessels passed by the two forts within a close range of just fifty yards, the guns of the forts would probably fire *over* the ships, due to their angle. Weitzel added that the naval fleet could open fire with grape and canister at such close range, driving every rebel from his gun.

The naval commanders scowled, questioning the wisdom of running huge ships so close to an enemy fort. But Weitzel was an engineer, and he knew these forts better than anyone in the entire expedition. With Farragut's endorsement, the plan was agreed upon. They would move upriver after midnight and stay close to the forts. Farragut had outfitted his fleet with chain cables, fastened in "festoons" along both sides of the vessels, to protect the engines and boilers from cannon balls. He broke the fleet into five divisions, which were to be followed closely by General Butler in his headquarters boat, the *Saxon*.

On Thursday morning, April 24, 1862, the air was still, with a light breeze coming upriver and bringing with it a haze that clung to the water. At 1:30 a.m. an "all hands on deck" was called in anticipation of the signal from David Farragut. A red light was run up the *Hartford*'s masthead promptly at 2:00 a.m., signaling that the fleet was to weigh anchor and begin its perilous advance against the strong three-mile-per-hour current. From a distance of five miles—out of range of the guns—the Navy's five divisions proceeded to steam up the river.[16]

At 3:40 a.m., the first boats came within range of Fort St. Philip, and the enemy opened fire. The Stars and Stripes was hoisted on each ship and snapped in the breeze. "Full speed ahead!" orders were given to the engine rooms, and the fleet proceeded north. Farragut's gunships opened fire just before four o'clock, sending a plume of smoke and fire, followed by a nine-inch shell, into Fort Jackson. The big guns mounted on the broadside commenced firing, and the rebel forts responded with a volley of cannon fire. The battle was raging on the land and water, creating a deafening roar.[17]

General Butler called it an "appalling scene" defying description. One of Butler's staff officers wrote, "Imagine all the earthquakes in the world, and all the thunder and lightning storms together, in a space of two miles, all going off at once; that would be like it."[18] Just as Godfrey Weitzel had predicted, the enemy's cannon fire was hot, but most fortunately too high to stop the fleet.

"Such another scene was never witnessed by mortal man," wrote one journalist embedded on a Union ship. "Splinters flying in all directions, and shells bursting overhead!" It was equally terrifying to most of the sailors who had no battle experience, and even to the veterans. "Shot and shell whistling like locomotive demons around, above, before, and in the rear of you; flames from fire-rafts encircling you!" The noise was described as dreadful, as "shot, shell, grape, and canister filled the air with deadly missiles."[19]

Amid all this flash and fire, Butler's men borrowed the light-draft steamer *Miami* from Commander Porter and boarded the Twenty-Sixth Massachusetts and Fourth Wisconsin Regiments from their transport lying far below the forts.[20] Following Godfrey Weitzel's brilliant plan, the vessel steamed *south*, back into the Gulf and around the east side of the peninsula until it reached a position five miles above Fort St. Philip. There, the men were transferred into thirty rowboats and paddled upstream through the narrow and shallow bayous of Maunels Canal and into the swamps at the back of the fort.

The Federals had to abandon their rowboats and wade in the hip-deep water for the last mile. Thoughts of alligators and snakes must have crossed their minds, but Confederate rifle fire was a more realistic concern. The soaked men succeeded in landing on the back side of Fort St. Philip and took the enemy by surprise. The rebel garrison surrendered without resistance, many claiming that they had been conscripted into the service and did not want to fight anymore.

It was Farragut's opinion that "men trained to arms will never fail, if properly led."[21] His large flagship, the *Hartford*, bore the brunt of the battle with the gallant Farragut at the fore-rigging, standing confidently with his spyglass in hand. The courageous naval commander (who would later coin the phrase "Damn the torpedoes! Full speed ahead!") was under fire from both forts at the same time.

"The river and its banks were one sheet of flame," wrote one witness as Farragut's fleet poured it on with shell and grape from the onboard guns.[22] Rebel

FIGURE 7.1. *The Battle of New Orleans*, by Thomas S. Sinclair, April 24, 1862. (Library of Congress, Prints and Photographs Division, Reproduction No. LC-USZ62-15627.)

boats were on fire and others were sinking. Union sailors cheered loudly as each shell exploded onshore or when an enemy vessel sank. After a battle of just one hour and twenty minutes, Farragut's fleet was past the forts, though badly cut up. The Union ships were still afloat, but riddled from stem to stern.

With the resistance subdued and with sails dropped, Farragut's fleet successfully steamed past and up the swollen Mississippi River for New Orleans.

The Occupation of New Orleans Begins

Having participated in the surrender of the forts, General Benjamin Butler headed back up the river on the gunboat *Wissahickon* to join David Farragut and plan the next moves for securing the Crescent City. All rebel troops there had evacuated, as had many citizens who boarded steamers and went up the river to Alexandria, Louisiana, and beyond. Immense quantities of sugar, rosin, tobacco, and coal had been burned and destroyed rather than have the Federals seize it. The New Orleans riverfront was strewn with fifteen thousand bales of cotton that had also been set ablaze and dumped.

Black smoke billowed from the port as Butler arrived. He saw that Farragut's fleet was anchored in midstream, with one broadside of cannons facing the city of New Orleans to the east and the other facing the village of Algiers to the west. As Butler's gunboat passed, the Navy's sailors cheered him on, knowing that it was now up to the Army to complete the mission. Farragut was delighted to see Butler, whose troops were needed to suppress the rebellious citizens.

The Flag above the Mint

David Farragut sent a message to the city authorities demanding the surrender of New Orleans. While at first Confederate major general Mansfield Lovell refused, he was persuaded by the presence of impressive Union gunboats and tall ships arriving at the docks. He agreed to evacuate with his troops, estimated in number from eight to nine thousand, an act for which he was later criticized throughout the South. Farragut sent two officers ashore, who were confronted by a rowdy crowd who taunted the pair, even shaking cocked pistols in their faces. The stern-looking Yankees did not flinch, but marched through the gauntlet to City Hall to demand its surrender. A body of marines followed shortly behind the naval officers with fixed bayonets, followed by a battery of howitzers that rolled through the streets. One officer at last made his way to the rooftop of City Hall, where he pulled down the state flag of Louisiana.

One mile east of City Hall, Union troops raised the Stars and Stripes over the former U.S. Mint on Esplanade Avenue. Farragut warned Mayor John T. Monroe that as long as the Union flag waved high above the city, it would be understood that the city had surrendered. However, if the Stars and Stripes were ever taken down, that act would be a signal that the city had resumed hostilities, which would be followed by a naval bombardment.[23] No guard was placed at the top of the U.S. Mint, since any altercation or interference with the guard might give someone the excuse to haul down the flag. Instead, Farragut placed howitzers in the maintops of his flagship, the *Hartford*, with gun crews ordered to watch the flag. The gunners were instructed that if any persons were seen to interfere with the flag or take it down, they were to immediately open fire upon them with the howitzers. This would signal the *Hartford* to open fire upon the city, to be followed by firing along the line of the whole Union fleet stationed in the river.

On April 27, the Sunday morning following the Union occupation, fleet commander David Farragut called his officers and crew belowdecks on the *Hartford* for a religious service. He wanted to give thanks to God for keeping them safe during the great dangers and perils to which they had been exposed the past week. During the prayer service, a lookout in the maintop of the *Pensacola* suddenly shouted, "The flag is down, Sir!" A twelve-pound shell was instantly fired from the howitzer trained on the roof of the U.S. Mint, killing one of the four men on the roof but missing their ringleader, William B. Mumford.[24]

In the midst of the solemn service being held, the booming howitzers sent every man running to his battle post. Each gun was manned and the lanyards of the locks were pulled. The *Hartford*'s crew was ready to begin bombardment when a higher power intervened on that Sabbath Day. The sky suddenly clouded over and threatened to rain. As a result, Farragut's ordnance officer went around the battery and removed from the vents all the wafers by which the guns were fired, placing them in a receptacle where they would be kept dry.[25] Due to this divine intervention, none of the *Hartford's* guns were fired.

An angry David Farragut took out his spyglass and saw that the vandal who had removed the flag had run away. There was no movement indicating that an insurrection was afoot; therefore, Farragut ordered a cease-fire. In Butler's words, "And so the city was saved from bombardment." Farragut sent an officer ashore to find out why the flag had been removed. He soon learned that it was the rogue act of a small party headed by local resident William Mumford, who had torn down the flag, dragged it through the streets, spit on it, and then trampled on it until it was torn to pieces. The shreds were then distributed among the rabble, and each one thought it a high honor to get a piece of it and wear it.[26] Mumford was promptly arrested by Federal soldiers for his prank, which had nearly prompted an all-out naval assault.

Two days later, on April 29, 1862, Farragut wrote to Mayor Monroe warning that there should be no similar incidents of disrespect against the United States flag. The issue was far from settled, however, as Ben Butler was about to weigh in.

Godfrey Weitzel's intimate knowledge of the two forts, the swamps and bayous, and his military education on trajectory of cannons were key to the Union's success in taking New Orleans that day. In fact, Butler said, "Few men contributed more to the reduction of the city than he."[27] Butler bragged on his young protégé, saying, "The Country owes as much for our success at New Orleans as any other because of his intimate knowledge of the Forts and the State."[28] After the occupation of New Orleans, and in honor of his key role in the capture of that city, General Butler gave Godfrey Weitzel the title of assistant military commandant, Department of the Gulf.[29] The two officers set to work on securing and stabilizing the rebellious city, as well as establishing governance as an occupying force.

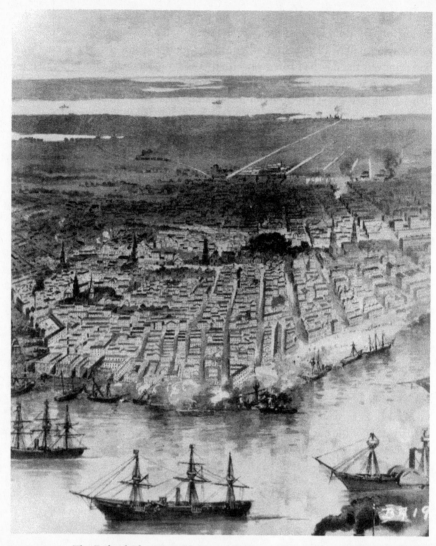

FIGURE 7.2. *The Federal Fleet at Anchor in the River, April 25th, 1862.* (From Rossiter Johnson, *Campfires and Battlefields*, New York [1894]. National Archives and Records Administration, Reference No. 111-BA-1921.)

CHAPTER 8

Occupation of the Crescent City

"Beast" Butler Arrives in the Crescent City

Together, the Army and the Navy had captured and occupied the jewel of the South—New Orleans, the Confederacy's most populous city and most important port. Now it was up to Butler to establish order and to secure the city as a Union stronghold in an otherwise Confederate state. It was a difficult task for any Union officer to lead the occupation of New Orleans, a city loyal to the rebellion. Butler needed to set up a command post for a myriad of civil and military operations and relied on his chief engineer, Godfrey Weitzel, for a recommendation.

Shortly after noon on May 1, General Butler issued his disembarkation order, and later that afternoon two Union regiments went ashore. They secured possession of the city at sundown. The river was very high, and the furious crowd of citizens could see the troop transports anchored along the levee, as well as Farragut's fleet, whose guns were trained menacingly upon their fair city.[1] A howling mob greeted the troops and the crowd grew steadily, as did their jeers and taunts, calling for Ben Butler to dare come ashore from his steamer.

The cautious Butler waited until dark to depart the safety of his steamer. He took the head of his troops and marched off to the Custom House on Canal Street, while the accompanying regimental band played "The Star-Spangled Banner."[2] The bluecoats marched without opposition to the Custom House, described by Butler as an "immense granite building covering some acres and making a complete citadel."[3] Although the massive structure had been under construction for more than a decade, its roof was not yet completed so that the spring rains seeped in and left a dank and musty smell.

General Butler housed the post office, the courts, and the military commissions all within the confines of the massive and partially finished Custom House—the strongest, most defensible position in the city. A fortress in itself, the Custom House served as the military center of operations for the Department of the Gulf. Butler's personal office was on the second floor, northeast corner.[4] His chief engineer and assistant, Godfrey Weitzel, officed nearby.[5]

The three-story building was impressive on the exterior, but not so inside. The building had not been completed or even roofed under Beauregard's supervision. Union troops found the building "filthy beyond expression." The walls were disfigured by disloyal and obscene inscriptions, and a mass of rubbish had been piled up in the numerous rooms. Butler's troops found scores of bronze and brass bells that had been donated by Southern churches in all parts of Louisianna and shipped to New Orleans to be melted down and reused as cannons. Union troops began to put the Custom House in order, using labor from the overwhelming influx of "contrabands" who came from every part of the South. The freed slaves gladly set to work cleaning the floors, ceilings, stairways, walls, drains, and casement. Godfrey Weitzel oversaw the construction of a handsome flight of stairs in the center of the front on Canal Street.[6]

As chief engineer, Godfrey had much work to do in assessing damage to the key buildings and forts and in allocating space and materials needed to secure the city from hostile forces. Butler had come to trust Weitzel because of his stellar performance in planning the assault on Forts Jackson and St. Philips, and Godfrey did not want to disappoint his new commanding officer.

Taming the Rebel City

New Orleans was a dangerous place, especially for the commander of the Union forces. Ben Butler had grabbed a rattlesnake by the neck, and he now had to figure out how to set it down without getting bit. A show of force was necessary, and so his Union soldiers set out each night to patrol the streets until morning. The New England regiments from Connecticut, Massachusetts, and Vermont, plus others from Indiana, Michigan, and Wisconsin, multiple batteries, and two companies of cavalry formed a significant occupation force to subdue the city. At nine o'clock each evening, an entire company of bluecoats escorted General Butler from the Custom House to his quarters at the opulent St. Charles Hotel.

The resistance was light, given that most of the local men of that city had volunteered or been conscripted into military service in Virginia and Tennessee, leaving a population of largely women, children, and free blacks. The white male population consisted of hooligans described by one Union officer as "the most villainous set of rascals to deal with." Deserters from both the Confederate and the Union armies, foreign rogues "from the four quarters of the world," gamblers, thieves, and cutthroats, a sort of devil's regiment of thugs. They needed a master and they found one in Ben Butler, who governed the city with an iron fist.[7]

Butler tolerated no disloyalty from the residents of New Orleans. Hearing "hurrahs" for Jefferson Davis and P. G. T. Beauregard, Ben Butler sentenced a group of local men to three months' hard labor at Fort Jackson. He sentenced another man to two years' hard labor on Ship Island for allegedly making a cross from the bones of a Union soldier, and a local bookstore owner to the same sentence for displaying a human skeleton in his bookstore window, claiming it was a dead Yankee. Butler ordered another local woman to solitary confinement at Ship Island for wearing a Confederate flag "in order to incite riot."[8] Such strict discipline eventually subdued the mob, but never their dissension. A loud, angry crowd once gathered outside the posh St. Charles Hotel and made so much noise that an irritated Butler ordered artillery brought in to disperse them.

The Woman's Order

General Butler busied himself in writing general as well as special military orders. One issued on November 9, 1862, directed Federal troops to confiscate property in the lush plantation land of Lafourche County, for which Butler thought he would get at least one million dollars' worth of goods for the government, namely, sugar.[9] Jefferson Davis responded with a proclamation on December 23 that condemned Butler's order. According to Davis, Butler's actions condemned "to punishment by starvation" at least a quarter of a million people, both male and female, of all ages and conditions.[10] But it was another of Butler's orders that brought about the greatest condemnation from Jefferson Davis—the infamous Woman's Order.

Ben Butler boasted that the city was so secured under his command that "from the second day after we landed, we had the men of New Orleans so completely under our control that our officers and soldiers could go anywhere in the city without being interfered with" (*BB*, 414). He bragged that he could walk or ride by day or by night through the streets of New Orleans unmolested *by the men* of the city, "anywhere I chose between Chalmette and Carrollton without any attendant or guard, or pretence of one, save a single orderly in attendance" (414). But not so with *the women* of New Orleans.

Union soldiers and officers found the female population of New Orleans a resistant and defiant lot who resented their Union occupiers and showed it in their actions. "A state of ugliness and vindictiveness hardly to be expressed," said one Vermont officer, "women seemed to be filled with the spirit of the Evil One."[11] One of the major problems was the verbal and even physical abuse Butler's soldiers endured from bitter and loyal Southern ladies who were resentful of the Union occupation. There were many reported incidents that whenever any man wearing a Union uniform was present, the women would contemptuously gather in their skirts, cross the street, or leave the room. Ladies would cast hateful glances or make rude comments. The more brazen among them *spit* on soldiers' uniforms and instructed their children to do the same, under the belief that women and children would not be arrested or punished (*BB*, 417). When one Union officer was asked why he didn't take more firm action, he responded, "What could I do, . . . to two women?" Another Union officer

FIGURE 8.1. *The Ladies of New Orleans before General Butler's Proclamation.* (From *Harper's Weekly*, 12 July 1862.)

responded coldly, "Well, you ought to have taken your revolver and shot the first *he* rebel you met" (418).

For Butler, the final straw came when a woman in the French Quarter emptied her chamber pot *onto Captain David G. Farragut* from her upper-level window. Farragut was understandably furious. Though the Federals showed remarkable restraint, Butler realized it was only a matter of time until one of his men would be pressed too far and would arrest a woman. If so, Butler feared that the local men would attempt a rescue and incite an armed conflict. He knew the situation was getting out of control and responded to Farragut, "I'll put a stop to this!" And he did (*BB*, 417–18).

After careful thought and deliberation over how to best quell these unpleasantries and what Butler characterized as a "dangerous entanglement," the lawyer-general came up with a clever legal solution. He recalled once reading an old English ordinance, which he thought, with a few changes, might accomplish the purpose. Butler drafted a local ordinance designed to execute itself and that would not require the local police to enforce it. On May 15, from his office in the Custom House, he took a pen and wrote out General Order No. 28, later known simply as the "Woman's Order." It read:

> As the officers and soldiers of the United States have been subject to repeated insults from the women (calling themselves ladies) of New Orleans, in return for the most scrupulous non-interference and courtesy on our part, it is ordered that hereafter when any female shall, by word, gesture, or movement, insult or show contempt for any officer or soldier of the United States, she shall be regarded and held liable to be treated as a woman of the town plying her avocation. (*BB*, 418)

When Butler handed the order to his chief of staff, General George Strong, the message was immediately understood. Disrespectful women would be deemed prostitutes, "common women," or "ladies of the evening," a reputation that the Southern belles did not desire. Strong cautioned Butler, saying, "This order may be misunderstood, General. It would be a great scandal if only one man should act upon it in the wrong way" (*BB*, 418). If by law, a local woman should be treated as one "plying her avocation," that is to be a prostitute—a local man or soldier might attempt to engage her services.

But Ben Butler's men were mostly New England soldiers, men whom he believed were well bred in every courtesy toward women. "Let us, then, have one case of aggression on our side," Butler replied. "I shall know how to deal with that case, so that it will never be repeated" (*BB*, 418–19). He would dole out the strictest and most public punishment to deter any similar conduct by a Union soldier, likely a public execution.

The order caused quite a stir among Southern men and was used by the Confederate officers to incite their troops—implying that "Beast Butler" was turning the local women of New Orleans into prostitutes! Rebel soldiers feared the worst for their wives and daughters back home, and Ben Butler became an evil villain in their minds and in the Southern press for turning the city into a brothel! The *Beast*!

The Hanging of Mumford

On June 5, after being found guilty of treason by a military commission for his removing of the United States flag above the U.S. Mint, General Butler signed Special Order No. 70 sentencing William B. Mumford to be executed on June 7.

Ben Butler felt that the public misunderstood the seriousness of Mumford's offense, one that Butler called "a most heinous one," from which dire results might have arisen had Farragut's warships opened fire on the city. Butler always felt his order was misunderstood and that the punishment fit the crime.

Despite a plea from Mumford's wife and children, who wept bitterly and fell about his knees, Benjamin Butler was unmoved. He wanted to make a public show of the execution so as to deter any further acts of treason. He ordered that Mumford be put to death near the Mint, with the flag of the United States flying overhead (*BB*, 441–42). Mumford was unrepentant and met his death as coolly as did John Brown on the Virginia scaffold.[12] While a crowd of onlookers watched in horror, Mumford swung by the neck. Butler recalled the scene: "There was a universal hush. . . . The crowd separated as quietly as if it were from the funeral of the most distinguished citizen. And no scene approaching general disorder was ever afterwards witnessed during my time" (*BB*, 443).

The French Threat and Godfrey's Reprimand

After the Union forces settled into their occupation of New Orleans, a small French vessel, the *Catinet*, came upriver and anchored at the head of the Union fleet. Butler had reopened the river to commerce and disbanded the blockade, so there was nothing unusual about a foreign ship anchoring in the river. However, General Butler learned soon afterward that the captain of the *Catinet* was a French spy on a reconnaissance mission for Emperor Napoleon III. Secretary of State Seward had learned through confidential channels from Paris that the French emperor was plotting an invasion of New Orleans to oust the Union occupiers in a land swap with the Confederates. Napoleon also made a proposal to the British government that their two nations unite in recognizing the independence of the Confederacy. Once recognized, the French would enter into a treaty, with Jefferson Davis's government seeking aid from the rebels if he should make an attack upon Mexico for the purpose of establishing an empire there under his puppet leader, Emperor Maximilian (*BB*, 464).

In support of the Mexican attack, Napoleon wanted to occupy New Orleans as a base of his operations. Once his fleet was in place, the French would declare war upon the United States and, without any further notice, attack and take Forts St. Philip and Jackson, and then move on to New Orleans. The Confederate Army would then launch an attack by land to free Louisiana from Yankee control. In return for helping the Confederacy regain Louisiana, Napoleon would have Texas reannexed to Mexico.

With a French spy in port and plans abroad for a French assault on New Orleans, General Butler was ordered to be on full alert to meet the attack. He was to put Forts Jackson and St. Philip in full repair and full armament. His instructions from Washington were to defend New Orleans "at all hazards," and if the French fleet tried to pass the forts, he was to open fire upon it. General Butler issued instructions to his trusted chief engineer, Godfrey Weitzel, to proceed with repairs from the April bombardment "with the utmost energy" (*BB*, 465).

Though badly battered by Farragut's hail of shells, Godfrey examined Fort Jackson and pronounced it "as strong as before the bombardment."[13] Surprisingly, Fort St. Philip was entirely unharmed. Ben Butler reviewed Weitzel's recommendations and soon came to the conclusion that the construction of a few new batteries could, "without doubt, hold the forts against the French fleet" (*BB*, 466). Butler was especially confident in the plan, knowing that if the French succeeded in passing the two forts, Farragut's fleet would crush them from the north. The plan seemed perfect, but young Weitzel was a by-the-book West Pointer. He knew from his prewar days in New Orleans that any improvement to a Federal fort required the approval of the Army's chief engineer, Joseph Gilbert Totten.

To Butler's utter astonishment, Godfrey challenged the order. "But, General," Godfrey said, "we cannot repair those forts without an order from Washington. I will write General Totten, the chief of engineers, about it." This was not peacetime, and Ben Butler saw no point in involving Totten. He asked Weitzel impatiently, "What has he got to do with it?" The naive lieutenant responded, "No fort can be repaired, General, by the Army regulations, without permission of the chief of engineers." "Well," Butler said, "I can get along without that permission, for I have money and men enough with which to do it, and I will send at once for the ordnance, if we are short." Weitzel was puzzled. "Oh, but, General, I do not see how I can do it" (*BB*, 466).

Thinking back on the conversation years later, Butler wrote, "I loved Weitzel then as I have ever since," but not knowing whether they actually had enough time to get the forts ready, the lawyer-general played a cruel mind game. Butler glared at Weitzel through his puffy eyelids, showing his disappointment. He drew a disgusted sigh and snapped back, "Well, if you cannot do as you are ordered I will get somebody else to do what I want done." To drive his point home, Butler dismissed Weitzel with a parting shot: "I should be to blame in this, not you, and my orders would justify you. You may go" (*BB*, 466).

Godfrey saluted his commander and left the office, feeling as though he had been punched in the stomach. He had let General Butler down, his mentor and commanding officer. Godfrey had never been spoken to by Ben Butler like this before. The twenty-six-year-old officer returned to his quarters, closed his door, and fell onto his bed and began to sob uncontrollably—so much so that he could not even speak.

Within the hour, as Butler sat at his desk pondering the challenges of a possible French invasion, his chief of staff, Major George Strong, knocked on Butler's door. "Come in," said Butler. After exchanging salutes, Strong's voice showed concern. "General, what have you been doing to poor Weitzel?" "Nothing," Butler answered wryly, "but telling him what I want him to do and what he can do." Strong came closer, his voice softer now. "But, General, you have broken his heart. A braver and stronger man doesn't live; but I found him in his quarters sobbing like a child and so broken down that he could not tell me what you had done." Weitzel was only able to tell Strong that Butler had "ordered him to do what he could not do." Strong added, in Weitzel's defense, "He says that he doesn't fear it on his own account, because the order of the commanding general will justify him in doing anything." Godfrey was more concerned that Ben Butler would be chastised and demoted for not following protocol. Of course, Weitzel told Strong, he would obey Butler's orders, but he feared for the backlash against his mentor. Strong added awkwardly, "He loves you, General, and he says it would be your ruin and the loss of your command to do what you want done" (*BB*, 466–67).

General Butler was both touched and slightly amused at young Weitzel's tender concern. He asked Strong to go get Weitzel from his quarters and bring him back to Butler's office. Within thirty minutes a red-eyed Godfrey Weitzel knocked and the general said to come in and to close the door.

"Strong has been telling me what your feelings are," Butler said. "I know what they are towards me, and I feel very grateful for them." He told Godfrey that he appreciated the concern for the political fate of his commander, which showed great loyalty. But the seasoned Massachusetts lawyer and legislator was taken aback by the young engineer's comment that Butler "did not know the risk" he was incurring. "I was both glad and sorry to hear that," Butler said. Then, in a fatherly tone he added, "I thought, Weitzel, you had been long enough with me to believe that I know more about military law and my responsibility than all the regular officers in the service put together" (*BB*, 467).

The conversation then turned more serious. "As a lawyer," Butler said, "I ought to know my duty, and as a man I am willing to do it without any regard to consequences" (*BB*, 467). Godfrey got the message, loud and clear—Benjamin Franklin Butler could look out for himself. He had sentenced Mumford to death, had spared others from a similar fate, had ordered the women of New Orleans tried as prostitutes, and was the head of the Army's operations in the largest Southern port city. He could look out for himself and would take the heat for his actions—right or wrong.

Butler dismissed Lieutenant Weitzel from the general's office with a simple instruction: "Now, you and Strong go together and draw any order that you two believe will justify you in obeying my commands in this matter," he said. In his characteristic manner, always protecting his junior officer, he added, "And I must and will take the responsibility." Butler added, "Upon reflection, I will not take no for an answer. Now go and make your order" (*BB*, 467).

Weitzel and Strong returned to Butler's office shortly to present the written order directing Weitzel in broad terms on what to do, the details to be arranged in writing afterward. Butler read the order, signed it, and handed it to Major Strong to be countersigned as Butler's chief of staff. He then gave his verbal instructions to the two junior officers: "Now, Strong," he said, "put that on the order book, and Weitzel, you go and get from the quartermaster anything you want, including any number of men you can use." There would be considerable cost, of course, to implement this plan. Butler added, "They may be hired if necessary,—and I will pay the bills." The process of implementing Butler's simple orders was taking too long and the general was getting impatient. He concluded the meeting abruptly. "We have lost three hours here," he said, "and I shall expect you by diligence to make it up. Good morning" (*BB*, 467). At that, Strong and Weitzel saluted, turned on their heels, and left Butler's office. They had work to do, and now they had an order to do it.

Under Godfrey Weitzel's direction, Forts Jackson and St. Philip "were put in apple-pie order" (*BB*, 468). Weitzel's redesign allowed the Union guns in both forts to point down upon the river so as to prevent a naval assault by anyone who might attempt to repeat Farragut's daring run past them. Godfrey Weitzel did not remain long as a mere engineering officer and soon found himself on the battlefield as a brigade commander.

The Two-Term Mayor

New Orleans mayor John T. Monroe angered General Butler when he objected to the Woman's Order and again when Monroe opened the city to French ships, a move that Butler viewed as opening the city *to foreign spies*. When evidence later surfaced that the mayor was possibly financing a Confederate company of troops known as the "Monroe Guards," Butler promptly had the mayor arrested and jailed in Fort Jackson. He also imprisoned several other members of the City Council who refused to swear oaths of allegiance to the Union. In Monroe's place, Butler needed to appoint someone to hold the office of military mayor of the city.[14]

Mayor George F. Shepley

With the town's elected mayor locked up in jail, on May 20, 1862, Ben Butler appointed forty-three-year-old lawyer Colonel George Foster Shepley as the first military mayor of New Orleans. Shepley was a safe choice, a New Englander born in Maine and son of the chief justice of the Maine Supreme Court. Shepley had studied law at Harvard and left a law practice in Bangor, Maine, to accept an appointment from President Polk as the U.S. attorney for the District of Maine, a post he held until the outbreak of civil war.

Shepley's term as mayor was short at just under two months, until July 14, one day after he was promoted to brigadier general. The new mayor set to work on the sanitation problem by putting unemployed men to work cleaning the gutters and streets, which the City Council seemed unable to maintain. The Union's action averted the spread of disease in the Crescent City during the hot summer of 1862, particularly the spread of the fatal yellow fever. For this reason, Butler's efforts during the period of occupation have generally been regarded as unusually good, particularly for avoiding an outbreak of disease.

Godfrey Weitzel's First Term as Mayor

Even though Louisiana had seceded from the Union, a small pocket of the state was now under Union control. Therefore, in July 1862, Secretary of War Edwin Stanton felt it appropriate to appoint a military governor for the state of Louisiana. After considering several candidates, Stanton chose newly promoted Brigadier General George Shepley for the post.[15] Pursuant to Stanton's direction, on July 14, Butler named Shepley as the governor of Louisiana, creating a vacancy in the municipal office of mayor. Unable to hold multiple offices, Shepley resigned as mayor, with his resignation "to take effect on the appointment of my successor."[16]

Ben Butler had another candidate in mind and immediately replaced Shepley with his chief of engineers and assistant military commander, the bright twenty-six-year-old Godfrey Weitzel. Mayor Weitzel took office that same day, in addition to the multiple other duties he held at the time.

Godfrey Weitzel was a natural choice for mayor due to his familiarity with the city and its people, despite his poor attempts at speaking French. After all, he had spent four years there prior to the war, living and working in New Orleans, a unique experience among the largely New England officers of Butler's occupation force. As assistant military commander, Lieutenant Weitzel had taken the lead in recruiting Louisiana Unionists for service in the United States Army and was familiar with many of the local families. Weitzel was, therefore, uniquely qualified to succeed Shepley as acting mayor. His first term, however, was a short one.

Attack on Baton Rouge—August 5, 1862

Seventy miles north of New Orleans lies the state capital of Baton Rouge. On April 25, one day before New Orleans fell to Farragut and Butler, the rebel government in Louisiana decided to abandon Baton Rouge, moving first about 60 miles west to Opelousas, and later about 190 miles northwest to Shreveport. In the typical style of the retreating rebels, all cotton in the area was torched in order to prevent its falling into Union hands. With the Confederates gone, the Yankees took possession of the abandoned town of Baton Rouge. Having lost New Orleans, however, the Confederates were determined to retake the Louisiana capital at least, and sent one of their brightest and best military generals to accomplish the task.

Confederate general John Cabell Breckinridge was a Kentucky lawyer, a politician, and a veteran of the Mexican-American War. He had been twice elected a member of the United States Congress and served at age thirty-five as vice president under President Buchanan, the youngest VP elected in U.S. history. He had run for president against Republican Abraham Lincoln in 1860 and carried all of the Deep South with his proslavery platform.

Breckinridge was not finished with politics, however, and was elected to the United States Senate. He took office on March 4, 1861, but when Kentucky formally sided with the Union, he fled south and joined the Confederate Army as a brigadier general. Upon resigning from the Senate, he said, "I exchange, with proud satisfaction, a term of six years in the United States Senate for the musket of a soldier."[17] On December 4, 1861, his colleagues in the Senate unanimously passed a resolution to expel him as a traitor.[18]

The deposed senator and declared traitor was anxious to take Baton Rouge back from the Yankee invaders, and on July 29, 1862, Breckinridge ordered a massive movement of two divisions toward the Union-held city, with the attack planned for early morning on August 5.

Brigadier General Thomas Williams was in command of the Union's occupation forces at Baton Rouge. He had received advance warning of the planned attack, and on August 4 he called together his commanding officers, who selected defensive positions to meet the rebels. In advance of the Confederate assault, General Butler ordered all public property that could be of any use to the enemy to be removed from Baton Rouge, including books from the state library and a statue of George Washington.

On the morning of August 5, Breckinridge attacked Baton Rouge as anticipated. When word reached Ben Butler in New Orleans, he dispatched Godfrey Weitzel to report on the condition of affairs there and to assess what reinforcements might be needed to repulse a renewed attack.[19] Weitzel headed out immediately, not knowing that the battle would last only about four hours. Due to his new assignment in Baton Rouge, Godfrey had to leave his post as mayor after just two weeks in office. Since New Orleans needed an active mayor, Godfrey was replaced on August 5 by Lieutenant Colonel Jonas H. French as acting military mayor. French, a Boston Democrat and lawyer, was another favorite aide to Ben Butler, one on whom Butler felt he could depend and control.

Upon reaching Baton Rouge and assessing the situation, Lieutenant Weitzel reported back to General Butler that Federal troops had been in an admirable position to await the coming attack (*BB*, 481). Breckinridge's assault was made under the cover of an almost impenetrable fog. The Confederate ram *Arkansas* came in support of the troops to engage the Northern gunboats *Essex*, *Sumter*, and *Kenio*. The *Arkansas* opened fire on Captain David Porter's gunboat *Essex* near the river's bend, four miles above Baton Rouge, but ran aground (483).

Union troops in Baton Rouge were sick and weakened by the summer heat of Louisiana. But upon learning of the Confederate attack, soldiers came out of their hospital beds to defend the position. Breckinridge's fighters drove back the Union troops a quarter of a mile from their original position, overtaking the camps of three Union regiments and destroying much of their equipment.[20] The outnumbered Union forces suffered many casualties, including General Thomas Williams, who was killed by a rifle-ball wound in the chest. Nonetheless, the Yankees eventually drove Breckinridge's men back several miles. Although the Confederates achieved some modest success, the day was marked as a Union victory.

With General Williams dead, Ben Butler looked to Godfrey Weitzel to take command at Baton Rouge. On August 6, 1862, Butler sent a message to Godfrey through an aide that he felt the main attack had been made on Baton Rouge and that Weitzel could hold the city with the troops he had.[21] Butler felt he could not send reinforcements, however, fearing this would weaken his defense of New Orleans, which he thought was the ultimate object of the Confederates.

The next day Butler directed Lieutenant Weitzel to "examine and determine the best positions for holding the town."[22] He urged Weitzel to check the position of Breckinridge's troops and his equipment and report back to headquarters as soon as possible. Godfrey Weitzel's August 7 report boasted of a "glorious victory" at Baton Rouge by Brigadier General Williams over the Confederate forces under Breckinridge's command. Weitzel reported the enemy's attack as "a complete failure," adding, "The ram is blown up. Their troops were repulsed."[23]

Since Weitzel's report confirmed that Baton Rouge was now firmly in Union hands, General Butler ordered Godfrey to return to New Orleans on August 9 for a full debriefing on the situation.[24] Butler also instructed that before leaving Baton Rouge, Weitzel should see to it that all "contrabands" that could be seized be employed, and any white secessionists, as necessary, be "impressed into service." This mixed-race work crew was to build earthworks and dig trenches to secure the Union position. As ordered, Godfrey returned to New Orleans several days later after overseeing the improvements to Baton Rouge's defenses.

Weitzel's Second Term as Mayor

On his return from Baton Rouge, Godfrey Weitzel resumed his role as military mayor, starting his second term on August 21, 1862. This term lasted just a little over a month, until September 30. Technically, Godfrey Weitzel served as the twenty-first mayor and the twenty-third mayor of New Orleans, with the city's interim mayor, Jonas H. French, being the twenty-second. In addition to being named mayor, on August 25 Godfrey Weitzel was given the added responsibility and title of superintendent of exchange of prisoners.[25] This added to his other titles of brevet captain, first lieutenant, chief of engineers, and assistant military commander, and showed the type of trust that Ben Butler placed in the young man.

With his new mayor in place, Butler continued to direct his attention to the defenses of New Orleans. Forts Jackson and St. Philip had been repaired and reinforced to Butler's satisfaction by Godfrey Weitzel—without General Totten's approval. In Butler's words, Godfrey Weitzel "had put the forts in perfect equipment for defence" (*BB*, 490).

Slaves in the Federal Camps

The question of escaped slaves entering Union Army camps had been a recurring logistical problem ever since Ben Butler coined the term "contraband" back at Fort Monroe. The issue reemerged during the summer of 1862 when large numbers of runaway slaves sought protection in Union Army camps outside New Orleans. They believed that the Yankee soldiers were like a God-sent Moses and were to deliver their race from bondage. Protection behind the Union lines was the first step on the road to freedom.

General Butler and his officers were perplexed at what to do with these colored masses that had thrown themselves upon the soldiers for protection. Some felt that since slavery was "an unmitigated evil," the Army had a duty to protect the poor slaves from being forced back to their masters under the Fugitive Slave Act. Others believed that it was not for the military to arbitrate the claims of local citizens to their "private property." The abolitionists within Butler's New England Division, in particular, felt a compassion for the slaves and could not find it in their hearts to return the helpless fugitives to their masters.[26]

The crowd of refugees tripled the number of mouths to feed, from 1,000 to 3,000, such that the Army's quartermaster was not able to cater to the mob and care for the Union troops as well. When the situation was brought to Mayor Weitzel, he gave permission to feed the black men, care for their sick, and employ them for any service in which they could be made available.

In July 1862, the military governor of Louisiana, General George Shepley, was called to Washington to meet with President Lincoln and his secretaries of state and of war to give them a current report on the situation in Louisiana. Shepley presented a request for another fifteen thousand troops to be sent to New Orleans to help fend off threats of an attack. His request was denied, however, since every department of the Army was seeking more troops at the time. Stanton promised that more troops would be sent when available.[27] The discussion then turned to employing freed blacks in the military service, but the president and his cabinet members rejected the idea, urging instead that Butler and Shepley continue the current policies in relation to treatment of the black population of Louisiana.

CHAPTER 9

The Lafourche Campaign

The Youngest General of the Civil War

It is often suggested that George Custer was the youngest Union general, appointed at age twenty-three. However, Generals Charles Cleveland Dodge and Edmund Kirby were both younger than Custer when they were promoted at ages twenty-one and twenty-three, respectively. Civil War buffs know that the youngest Yankee general of the great conflict was not Custer, Dodge, or Kirby—but Galusha Pennypacker, who was nominated at the age of twenty years and eight months, not then old enough to vote. Dodge was promoted in November 1862, Kirby in May 1863, and Custer in June 1863, while Pennypacker became a brigadier in February 1865. But before any of these twenty-somethings, it was Godfrey Weitzel who was the youngest Federal officer promoted to brigadier general at age twenty-six on August 29, 1862. He held that obscure record for three months until eclipsed by Charles Dodge.

In recognition of Godfrey's leadership and valued service during the operations leading up to the capture and occupation of New Orleans, Ben Butler recommended his protégé, First Lieutenant and Brevet Captain Godfrey Weitzel, for promotion to the rank of brigadier general of Volunteers. In Butler's words, Weitzel deserved the promotion, "for his capacity, conduct, and skill."[1] Ben Butler began his campaign on Weitzel's behalf in early July 1862, urging Secretary of War Stanton to recommend Godfrey's advancement to the president. Butler wrote:

> Godfrey Weitzel of Ohio, 1st Lieut. of Engineers, one of the first scholars of West Point, afterwards instructor there; who commanded the first Company which came to Washington to watch over the life of the President at the inauguration; who fortified Fort Pickens so that it stood a bombardment without the loss of a man; one whom the Country owes as much for our success at New Orleans as any other because of his intimate knowledge of the Forts and the State: for him I beg to press that he may be appointed a Brigadier General.[2]

Ben Butler explained that he needed another general to lead a brigade in Louisiana and, "there is no abler man for it in the Country" (*POC*, 43). If granted by Stanton, Godfrey would leapfrog over the ranks of major, lieutenant colonel, and colonel—straight to brigadier general. When Stanton did not immediately reply, Butler renewed his request one week later "for an experienced Brig. Gen., such as Lieut. Weitzel would be if he held that Commission" (54).

Later that same month, while meeting in Washington to brief President Lincoln and Secretary Stanton on the situation in New Orleans, General George Shepley reiterated Butler's request for Weitzel's promotion, which Stanton received very favorably. On his return to Louisiana, Shepley urged Butler to make one final push, guaranteeing that Godfrey would receive the promotion (*POC*, 147).

General Butler took Shepley's advice and wrote to the secretary of war one last time, on August 14, urging the promotion. Butler argued that his ranks were being depleted by disease and he was forced to recruit locals to fill up to one thousand needed positions. "I have determined to use the services of the free colored men," Butler wrote, "who were organized by the rebels into the 'Colored Brigade,' of which we have heard so much." Foreshadowing his ultimate plans, Butler continued, "I would like an experienced Brigadier General . . . and would again press the appointment of Lt. Weitzel of the Engineers" (*POC*, 192).

The recent death of General Williams at Baton Rouge and the resignation of another brigadier made the promotion all the more necessary. Not only did Butler believe that Weitzel deserved the promotion, but he also knew that with a higher rank there would be an increase in pay, which Godfrey needed to help support his widowed mother back home in Cincinnati. Butler even wrote to his wife, Sarah, seeking her opinion (*POC*, 352–53). Mrs. Butler was a fan of Godfrey Weitzel's, whom she had previously described as "wise and experienced," someone who could complete every detail "to the last degree" (201).

Butler's persistence paid off, and on August 29, 1862, Godfrey Weitzel was promoted to brigadier general of the U.S. Volunteers.[3] Ben Butler shared his excitement over the promotion in a short note to naval officer David Farragut, who had been promoted to rear admiral in July (*POC*, 273). Farragut admired the bright young engineer for his keen insight into the fortifications around New Orleans. Godfrey made his commanding officer and mentor proud in the years to come. Butler wrote in his 1892 autobiography about the wisdom of the promotion, saying, "[Weitzel's] great success in that [role], and his career afterwards during the whole war, fully justified the appointment."[4]

Weitzel's Reserve Brigade

After his appointment as brigadier general, Godfrey Weitzel was never again stationed in New Orleans itself, the city in which he had thus far spent the majority of his military career.[5] Now, his role was changed to that of a field general. With his trusted aide now officially able to command troops, General Butler put him to work in that capacity, giving Godfrey his own brigade in the Department of the Gulf.

Just a month after the promotion, on September 28, General Butler organized a "reserve brigade," which comprised five regiments, two batteries, and several companies of cavalry. Godfrey Weitzel was chosen to lead this new brigade. Four regiments from New England received orders to depart from the Custom House in New Orleans and other urban quarters in the city and to make camp at Carrollton, several miles above New Orleans. There, at a place christened "Camp Kearney," the regiments were assembled into Weitzel's Reserve Brigade.[6]

The brigade consisted of the Twelfth and Thirteenth Connecticut, the First Louisiana, the Seventy-Fifth New York, and the Eighth New Hampshire Regiments. Supporting the new brigade were the mounted troops from Perkins's Massachusetts Cavalry; Barret, Godfrey, and Williams's Louisiana Calvary; and the firepower of Carruth's Sixth Massachusetts Battery and Thompson's First Maine Battery. General Weitzel selected his staff officers from among the top men of these New England regiments. These officers were all much older than Godfrey, but would have to look to the tall twenty-six-year-old to lead them into battle. Some had their questions, and many had their doubts.

Arriving at Camp Kearney in Carrollton was like the old days back at West Point for Godfrey, encamped with his men and drilling them in formation. As a captain of the cadets and an assistant instructor, Godfrey had drilled his peers in formation and cavalry. It had been seven years since he had led such exercises, but he was sure he remembered how to do it.

One member of the Reserve Brigade recalled that "General Weitzel personally gave the officers instruction and practice in skirmishing, and showed himself an accomplished drill-master."[7] This was old hat for Godfrey, and he was delighted to get away from the administrative duties he had been assigned since his arrival in New Orleans. He drilled the New Englanders hard for nearly a month to prepare for upcoming expeditions in the field. This being his first opportunity to lead men into battle, Weitzel needed assurance that his men were up to the task.

Godfrey was initially concerned, however, when he learned that the Twelfth Connecticut was to be part of his brigade. There had been rumors that this regiment was "sickly, discouraged and undisciplined."[8] General Weitzel decided to check their condition for himself by putting them through a series of basic drills. As the men of the Twelfth Regiment were engaged in a battalion drill, Weitzel rode up confidently on horseback and introduced himself as their new commanding officer. At six feet four inches tall, he made quite an impression, towering over his officers and troops, who averaged only five feet seven. He had the looks of a general, if not the age. One of his Yankee soldiers described General Weitzel as "a man of attractive and imposing presence."[9]

From his mount, he personally took command of the drills, hurrying the men through a long series of double-quick movements. First he sent the New Englanders into a doubled column, then into a square, then into a column again, then into a line, and kept up the routine for a full thirty minutes as fast "as the men could trot." The exhausted soldiers felt that the West Pointer's intent was to confuse them so he could find grounds to report them as unfit for field service. To Godfrey's surprise, the Twelfth Connecticut obeyed every command with precision, responding "like a machine."[10]

Satisfied with the performance, General Weitzel rode off. The sweaty soldiers stood at ease. One of the Connecticut men commented that they were proud of their performance, but, "we were equally pleased with our lively young brigadier."[11] Godfrey quickly gained the respect of the entire Reserve Brigade, who called Weitzel "a competent and gentlemanly officer."[12]

Camp Life in Louisiana

Drilling his men was easy compared to the new problems General Weitzel had to address. Runaway slaves continued to stream into the Union camps as they had over the summer. Adding these to the captured and deserting Confederates held in prisons nearby created potential for a flash-fire uprising. There had always been concern that freed slaves would attempt some retribution against their former masters, and now those masters were confined in prison. The situation turned ugly on September 13, when an armed mob of twenty-eight blacks tried to storm a Union prison where Confederate soldiers were being held. The mob was stopped by guards posted by General Weitzel. Some of the blacks were wounded and all were arrested. One terrified rebel prisoner sent a note to Weitzel, pleading to have him paroled for fear of his life. Godfrey sent the note to General Butler with a cover letter asking, "What shall I do in this case? By your permission and authority this armed police was organized. What shall be done with the Negroes?" (*POC*, 297).

This was only the beginning of a long-term logistics problem for Godfrey Weitzel, who soon found that freed slaves followed his brigade wherever it went, by the hundreds. He sought Ben Butler's advice often on what was known as "the Negro Question."

Former Supreme Court justice John A. Campbell ran a small law office in New Orleans and had not been bothered by Ben Butler since the Union occupation. Campbell read about his new mayor, Godfrey Weitzel, and had no doubt seen the tall officer busy around town. The Confederacy needed smart leaders like Judge Campbell, and President Jefferson Davis eventually sneaked a message into New Orleans, asking the judge to become part of Davis's team of advisers in Richmond. Campbell quickly accepted the offer, quietly closed up his law office, and moved to the Confederate capital. There, he accepted a rather unlikely position for a man known as a "peacemaker." On October 21, 1862, Judge John A. Campbell was appointed assistant secretary of war for the Confederate States of America.

On to the Lafourche!

On October 4, 1862, Godfrey Weitzel ordered his Reserve Brigade into formation for inspection. The new brigadier general was impressed with what he saw and complimented the men. Within two weeks, Weitzel was so comfortable with his well-drilled brigade that on October 18 he marched them out of their camp and down Canal Street in New Orleans for a grand review and inspection by his proud mentor, Major General Benjamin Butler. Delighted with the performance, General Weitzel treated the men that night back at Camp Kearney to rations of water slightly tinged with whiskey.[13] It was a gesture that made his men love him even more. The brigade was bonding but getting anxious to take on the enemy.

With his successes in Baton Rouge and New Orleans, Ben Butler had thoughts of taking Galveston or Mobile, yet he was still short of troops for such bold campaigns and could not obtain enough reinforcements from Stanton. As a result, he focused on routing out the resistance in the bayou country of west-central Louisiana.[14]

Stanton made it clear to Butler from the start that controlling the Mississippi River meant capturing New Orleans and "clearing the rebels from the Mississippi, so as to open trade and commerce through that channel with the Gulf," which Stanton said "always appeared to be among the chief points of this war." Stanton told Butler, "You have successfully accomplished one, and I hope the other will not be long in its accomplishment."[15]

Butler's purpose for the venture into the bayou country was threefold: drive out the rebel resistance; take control of the railroads there; and seize the sugar from secessionist landowners. The plan was for Weitzel's Reserve Brigade to drive the enemy down Bayou Lafourche toward the town of Thibodeaux. There, the Eighth Vermont Regiment and the all-black First Louisiana Native Guards would intercept the enemy in the neighborhood of the Lafourche railroad crossing, about three miles south. Naval gunboats cooperating with the Twenty-First Indiana Regiment were to pass around the coast, ascend the Atchafalaya River as far as Brashear City, and cut off the enemy from its only available line of retreat across Berwick Bay.[16]

For the plan to work, it was essential that the arrival of troops by rail at the crossing below Thibodeaux and the arrival of the gunboats at Brashear City be nearly simultaneous with the successful advance of Weitzel on Thibodeaux. Timing was key to trap the "butternuts" and reduce the risk of an attack on New Orleans.

Bayou Lafourche

Lafourche is from the French for "the fork," and the name alludes to the bayou's large outflow into the Gulf. In the 1860s, Bayou Lafourche (pronounced "la-foosh" by locals) was a free-flowing river that ran from the Mississippi River at Donaldsonville some sixty-five miles southeast into the salt water of the Gulf of Mexico. Sugarcane production along its lush banks brought economic prosperity to the area, making the Lafourche region one of the richest parts of Louisiana during the nineteenth century. The riverbanks of the bayou were dotted with large plantations, slave quarters, and impressive antebellum mansions, all supporting the sweet sugar crops.

However, forty years after the great war, the river outlet was dammed up at Donaldsonville, cutting off much of the nourishment of a huge wetland in this part of the state. The dam changed the flowing bayou into a stagnant ditch. Left as a testimony to the once prosperous commerce are the huge plantation homes, turned into quaint bed-and-breakfasts and tourist museums to Louisiana's past. The mansions are well-preserved postcards of an era gone by, when sugar was king in the Lafourche.

The land either side of Bayou Lafourche is some of the most picturesque in the state, with fertile, flat sugarcane fields stretched out north and south of the waterway, interrupted by occasional cypress swamps. Today, the bayou is flanked by two roads, Louisiana's Highway 308 on the north and Highway 1 on the south, sometimes called "the longest main street." Across these same two roads slaves hauled sugarcane, and Union and Confederate troops hauled cannons behind thousands of foot soldiers and cavalry, stopping periodically to engage in bloody skirmishes.

It is easy to imagine their dusty marches and occasional battles along the bayou, in the cane fields, and in the front yards of the mansions that stand as mute witnesses to the past conflicts. Two-hundred-year-old massive oak trees recall a time when Union and Confederate troops fought under their shade, breaking off branches with their bullets and shells. At majestic plantation homes like Nottoway (in White Castle), St. Emma (south of Donaldsonville), and Madewood (in Napoleonville), the ghosts of young soldiers are said to still walk the hallways, porches, and fields.

Donaldsonville, Louisiana

The twisting Mississippi River takes a brief turn at Donaldsonville, where Bayou Lafourche once branched off. At that confluence, the town was founded, serving as the Louisiana capital for the period from 1830 to 1831, after New Orleans was deemed "too noisy" to conduct government business. The town's proximity to the major shipping lanes of the Mississippi River and Bayou Lafourche made Donaldsonville an important strategic location for both sides of the war.

In 1929, however, after massive flooding of the Mississippi River, the Army Corps of Engineers constructed a massive levee system designed to keep the river from ever breaching its banks again. Bayou Lafourche was closed off at Donaldsonville, eliminating it as an outlet to the Gulf and ending an era of the bayou as a free-flowing river. But in 1862, the water ran freely here, and the town's wharfs became a site for guerrilla warfare against passing Union ships, effective enough to outrage Rear Admiral David G. Farragut.

Farragut's Bombardment of the Town

Admiral Farragut had heard that rebel soldiers, and possibly even civilians, had taken frequent shots at Union steamers near Donaldsonville as they navigated the river above New Orleans. Farragut made a decision to put an end to the harassment of his vessels. He sent a ominous warning to the town's inhabitants: "If they did not discontinue this practice, I would destroy their town." When the attacks continued, Farragut sent an advance notice that he was launching a retaliatory attack and suggested that the citizens send the women and children away from town. "I certainly intended to destroy it on my way down the river," he told Secretary of the Navy Gideon Welles, "and I fulfilled my promise to a certain extent."[17]

On August 9, 1862, Rear Admiral Farragut anchored his massive flagship, the USS *Hartford,* in front of the town. It must have been an awesome sight, with his battle-worn three-masted ship anchored there, cannons aimed in the town's direction, sailors peering from the rail and rigging, and the well-dressed Farragut on deck ready to give the command. When he gave the signal "Fire!" a barrage of cannons and mortars pelted the town, causing great destruction.

When the blasts ceased, Admiral Farragut sent a detachment of marines to row ashore and set fire to the hotels, wharf buildings, and the home and other buildings owned by Phillippe Landry, a Donaldsonville resident reported to be a captain of guerrillas. Though Farragut had no taste for devastating private property, he felt justified in doing so if private citizens endangered the lives of his men. The bombardment was temporarily effective, and Union vessels sailed safely past the town for a short while thereafter. But rebel resistance to a Yankee presence soon made itself known.

Dick Taylor and Alfred Mouton

General Richard "Dick" Taylor was the son of United States President Zachary Taylor—"Old Rough and Ready." A native of Kentucky but educated at Yale, the younger Taylor persuaded his father to purchase a seven-hundred-acre sugarcane plantation in St. Charles Parish, Louisiana, known as "Fashion." Dick Taylor inherited the plantation after his father's untimely death in July 1850, just sixteen months into his presidency. Vice President Millard Fillmore succeeded Zachary

Taylor into office, signing Godfrey Weitzel's admittance letter to West Point in September 1850. When civil war broke out, the younger Taylor remained loyal to his adopted state of Louisiana. He was promoted to the rank of major general on July 28, 1862, at age thirty-six, making him the youngest major general in the Confederacy at the time.

Less famous than the Little Napoleon was another Confederate general from Louisiana, Jean Jacques Alfred Alexandre Mouton, more commonly known as just "Alfred Mouton." A West Pointer, born in Opelousas, Louisiana, and the son of a former Louisiana governor, Alfred Mouton was one of those impressive seniors in the class of 1850, graduating a year before Godfrey Weitzel arrived on campus. Prior to the war, he had taken up farming sugarcane in Lafayette Parish, so he was quite familiar with the cane fields and the backwoods of his home state.

The Donaldsonville Expedition Begins

In addition to Weitzel's Reserve Brigade of mostly New Englanders, two regiments of the newly formed Native Guard were also placed under Weitzel's command (POC, 400). The Native Guard was a former regiment of free blacks that had been recruited by local authorities in New Orleans before the Yankee invasion. A group of the men had called upon Ben Butler after the occupation to volunteer for Union service. When questioned if they would fight, one of the men responded, "General, we come of a fighting race. Our fathers were brought here slaves because they were captured in war, and in hand to hand fights, too. We are willing to fight." The response delighted Butler. "Pardon me, General," the black man continued, "but the only cowardly blood we have got in our veins is the white blood."[18] In late August, Ben Butler issued General Order No. 63 organizing a volunteer force from the Native Guard veterans and other freed blacks willing to serve.

To carry out the mission, General Butler ordered some light-draft steamers to accompany the brigade, with iron plating added to protect their boilers and engines. The plating had originally been designed for rebel gunboats but was confiscated by Butler in New Orleans and put to Union use. He also added light guns to each boat and ordered them to act in conjunction with Weitzel's brigade to penetrate the waters of Berwick Bay and attack enemy batteries there. Butler commented that he had high hopes for Weitzel's expedition, not only for operations in Louisiana, but "I should be glad if General Weitzel should be able to move upon Texas" as well (POC, 401). Once Taylor and Mouton were flushed out of the bayous and sugarcane fields, Butler planned for Weitzel to set up a base of operations in Galveston, the largest city and major seaport in Texas, which the Federals had recently seized.

As a follow-up to Farragut's assault on Donaldsonville in August, Brigadier General Godfrey Weitzel was ordered there to stifle renewed rebel activity. Confederate cavalry and artillery under General Mouton were believed to be stationed along the Mississippi River in and around Donaldsonville, ambushing Union gunboats once again with cannon fire and sharpshooters hidden along the riverbanks. A Union gunboat flotilla patrolled the river, but troops were needed on land to stop the harassment. Godfrey Weitzel was instructed to lead an expedition to Donaldsonville, defeat the enemy forces there, and take control of that stretch of the river once and for all. General Butler ordered that the expedition begin by October 24, 1862.

The evening of Tuesday, October 14, a group of distinguished local civilians held a dinner in New Orleans to honor General Weitzel, as it was understood that he would soon be departing with his new brigade upriver on "active service." Among the invited guests were many Federal officers from both the Army and the Navy. The acting military mayor, Colonel Henry C. Deming, a lawyer from Connecticut, gave an eloquent speech and toasted the Navy and its bravery in passing the two forts in April. The toast was returned by a naval officer, each noting the "harmony that had always existed in the Department of the Gulf between the military and naval forces of the Government."[19] It is not clear if the Navy's Captain David Porter was in attendance, since he would not have toasted to Ben Butler.

A Formal Review of Weitzel's Brigade

Four days later, on October 18, a clear Saturday afternoon, General Weitzel conducted a final review of his brigade, which marched four miles from Camp Kearney down into New Orleans. A reporter for the *New York Times* called the display "one of the finest ever witnessed in the military city of New-Orleans."[20] The large turnout from local citizens was attributed to the "warm personal interest" that Godfrey had taken in the city before and during the war. Weitzel's squadron of cavalry led his five regiments and two batteries of brass and iron artillery up Commerce Street in a column, then left at Lafayette and continuing right onto Magazine Street for five blocks, then turned west at the Custom House on Canal Street. Colorful flags marked each of the New England regiments as the brigade came to a halt and assembled in formation precisely at 3:00 p.m. at the intersection of Canal and St. Charles Streets.

"The men looked superb, and as they came tramping along," a Northern reporter noted, "it made the hearts of Union men beat with joy at the appearance of so much valor and strength, bearing the Union flag along highways that were but a few months ago desecrated by rebel rags, or made hideous by treasonable shouts." Major-General Ben Butler and his staff rode along the lines to conduct the inspection of troops. General Weitzel took a prominent position in front of the brigade, his first formal review as a brigadier. The young general "attracted universal attention, and commanded . . . intense interest" in the crowded streets, a reporter noted. Godfrey saluted General Butler as he rode past, beaming with satisfaction.[21]

Later that evening, a torchlight procession paraded through the streets of New Orleans, made up of three hundred local men who had labored all summer improving the city's canals. The men carried a large United States flag and were accompanied by a fine band as they headed toward General Butler's headquarters for a serenade of "Hail to the Chief." The leader of the group read a statement thanking General Butler "for the kind interest he has taken in the laboring classes of New Orleans, by giving them employment," rather than making them dependent on charity. But for his timely arrival, the men feared they would have been compelled to join the Confederate Army or face starvation in prison.[22]

Ben Butler appeared on his balcony and was moved at the affection shown by the locals, a contrast to his initial greeting back in late April. He thanked the torchbearers and pointed with pride to the flag they carried, assuring them that the day would soon draw near when the citizens of New Orleans would prove themselves "loyal enough" to take the affairs of the city government into their own hands. His remarks drew three hearty cheers and the band struck up "Hail Columbia." The crowd then moved on to the residence of military governor George Shepley for more music and speeches.

Leaving New Orleans

When it first began its expedition, the Weitzel Brigade numbered more than four thousand, with troops from Connecticut, Maine, Massachusetts, New York, and New Hampshire.[23] They were cleverly supplemented by whites recruited in Louisiana, called the First Louisiana Regiment, whose local knowledge of the bayou country was important to have along, as the Northerners did not know the territory or the terrain.

On the beautiful Indian summer afternoon of Friday, October 24, General Godfrey Weitzel's Reserve Brigade boarded transports at Carrollton, above New Orleans, and carefully steamed their way up the Mississippi River about one hundred miles, accompanied by the armored gunboat fleet from the U.S. Navy. Weitzel left only the Eighth Vermont Regiment behind at Camp Kearney to help protect New Orleans. The troop movement was no military secret, and the headline of an October 27, 1862, article in the *New York Times* announced: "Gen. Weitzel's Expedition at Donaldsonville, Its Probable Further Destination," followed nine days later with another headline, "Gen. Weitzel's Expedition after the Guerrillas." The flotilla consisted of Captain George M. Ransom's gunboat, the *Kineo*, plus three other gunboats, the *Sciota*, the *Katahdin*, and the *Itasca*. The temperature was dropping as autumn set in, and the cool breezes invigorated the Northern troops who had suffered in the sweltering heat of the Louisiana summer.

One onlooker wrote that "the fleet got well under way, followed by the grim-looking transports, and the grimmer-looking gunboats."[24] General Weitzel and his staff boarded the steamship *General Williams*, so named for the Union officer killed at Baton Rouge in August. They were accompanied by the Thirteenth Connecticut and assumed a position in the center of the fleet. The flotilla proceeded slowly up the wide river against the strong current, but soon increased its speed.

Another Union vessel, the USS *Calhoun,* left Lake Pontchartrain and proceeded to the Southwest Pass, where it was met by the steamers *Estrella* and *St. Mary's* under orders to support Brigadier General Weitzel in his efforts to control the Lafourche region.[25] The *Calhoun* was commanded by a brave young lieutenant commander named Thomas McKean Buchanan, who would soon play a major role in one of Godfrey's early successes.

Just as Ben Butler had done, Rear Admiral Farragut ordered that sheets of boiler iron be wrapped around the small gunboats to protect them against musketry so that they could safely run the length of the Atchafalaya River and catch rebel gunboats such as the formidable *J. A. Cotton*, a menacing ironclad ram patrolling Bayou Teche and the Atchafalaya.

The transports and gunboats made good time, and Weitzel's expedition landed without incident at 4:30 a.m. on Saturday, October 25, at Miner's Point, about six miles below the port town of Donaldsonville. Weitzel gave credit to his naval protectors, saying, "My transports were not fired upon at all, so well were they covered by the gunboats."[26] The disembarking process began in the early dawn hours as sleepy soldiers hauled gear and weaponry up a steep bank. By the time the Cajun sun rose, the bluecoats were off-loaded and formed in line on the riverbank at Miner's Point.[27] As the New Englanders left the transport *General Williams*, an escaped slave was brought on board Weitzel's steamer with information for the brigadier general. He revealed that as the Union fleet came upriver, his master mounted a horse and rode into Donaldsonville to join the rebel guerrillas there. General Weitzel thanked the man for the information and promptly ordered officers to seize the master's plantation, together with its mules and carts, and to appropriate them for troop transportation. More spoils of war.

Godfrey had heard about Donaldsonville from his West Point roommate Francis Nicholls, a native of the town and the first graduate of the U.S. Military Academy from Ascension Parish, Louisiana. He would not have time to pay any visit to the Nicholls family on this trip, however. General Weitzel sent out reconnaissance troops to determine where the enemy was located, and at what strength. The skirmishers encountered Confederate pickets, whom they easily drove back. A reporter for the *New York Times* wrote that Weitzel's cavalry made a brave dash against the enemy pickets, killing one and taking two others as prisoners, suffering only one man wounded in the assault.[28] The Yankee scouts returned to Weitzel with a report of three thousand rebel troops encamped on both sides of Bayou

Lafourche. General Weitzel determined that the Confederates planned to meet him thirty miles southeast along the bayou, at Thibodeaux.

Raiding Donaldsonville

The line of Union soldiers was formed and orders given to cautiously march along the riverbank toward Donaldsonville. About a mile outside of that town, they encountered the remains of a Confederate battery whose guns had been removed to a fortified position farther to the south, along Bayou Lafourche. Weitzel pushed his men on toward Donaldsonville, which they found deserted and in shambles. Farragut's shelling of August 9 had torn the place to pieces with his barrage of cannon fire and arson. In retaliation for firing upon Union gunboats, the once flourishing town had been reduced to a desert of smoke-blackened ruins. Escaped slaves came out to joyously greet the liberating Army. Some impersonated rebel soldiers, and "showed by their antics how the rebels skedaddled at our approach," wrote a traveling journalist.[29]

The fall day turned suddenly cooler, and the skies darkened. A strong wind began to blow, which announced the coming rain. General Weitzel ordered his men to take cover and to find shelter wherever they could. He set up a brigade headquarters and made plans for his mission into the Lafourche region in search of Mouton and Taylor. The troops began occupying the town that had been abandoned by enemy soldiers just one night before. The Twelfth Connecticut Regiment took up shelter in a Catholic church. Weitzel's quartermaster rounded up what horses and mules could be found, while the troops gathered up the poultry and pigs "that came their way."[30]

Foraging on the land of the enemy has been a tradition of great armies since at least the fifth century BC, when Chinese warrior Sun-tzu wrote, "A wise general makes a point of foraging on the enemy. One carload of the enemy's provisions is equivalent to twenty of one's own."[31] However, in order to maintain order, General Weitzel issued strict orders against "foraging" in the town itself.[32] Fires soon were lit in the hearths of abandoned houses as the troops sought to warm themselves and make a small meal before nightfall. Despite the commanding general's orders, foraging on their first major mission into enemy territory got out of hand and many excesses were committed by the soldiers of the Reserve Brigade.

General Weitzel took the blame personally, saying, "I have violated one of the first principles of campaigning, never to encamp in a village, when one can just as well remain outside."[33] He would never do so again. Weitzel's men added to the damage inflicted by Farragut's bombardment by pillaging livestock and goods in the deserted town. One foot soldier bragged about the bounty his regiment found waiting in Donaldsonville. "We lived high, you can bet! Pigs, geese, hens and honey!"[34]

The cavalry kept on the move that night, against the elements, and rounded up more than a hundred horses in fine condition. Slaves reported that the Confederates had abandoned Donaldsonville but had fortified themselves in positions to the southeast, along Bayou Lafourche. "We hear that the enemy is in large force in the fortification down the bayou," wrote a newspaper correspondent. "We shall in the morning march against the enemy."[35]

Mouton's Retreat

Alfred Mouton received a report late on October 25 that General Weitzel's gunboats and transports were moving slowly up the Mississippi, most likely bound for Donaldsonville. The Confederate brigadier mounted his horse and rode immediately to that town, where he found that his Confederate troops had fallen back about twelve miles to the south. Mouton's scouts reported that Weitzel's Union force numbered from 2,500 to 3,000 infantry, plus 250 cavalry, and two batteries of field artillery. Mouton knew that he could not match these impressive numbers since he had at his disposal only 600 infantry and about 250 cavalry, with one field battery. "The disparity was so great," he later wrote, "that I deemed it my duty still to recede until the re-enforcements I had ordered up arrived, and accordingly fell back to the [plantation] of Mr. Winn, 2 miles above Labadieville." There, his reinforcements from the Eighteenth Louisiana and Crescent Regiments reached him with another battery about 2:00 p.m., coming in from Berwick Bay and Bayou Boeuf.[36]

Moving Out!

At 6:00 a.m. on Sunday, October 26, the Union's First Louisiana Regiment, under Colonel Richard E. Holcomb, was left behind to hold Donaldsonville with the aid of three gunboats. The remainder of the Weitzel Reserve Brigade proceeded southeast along the bayou, throwing out skirmishers and flankers, including about five hundred cavalry, in pursuit of the enemy. The plan was to avoid any major battle until encountering the rebels at Thibodeaux, thought to be about two thousand in number, where they would concentrate at some strong position.[37]

With full bellies from that first night's forage and feast, General Weitzel ordered his men to proceed cautiously south along the bayou. As their tall, young brigadier general rode on horseback, the stub of a cigar clenched in his teeth, his troops followed the bayou south with one regiment of infantry and one troop of cavalry on the eastern bank, and the rest of Weitzel's brigade on the western bank.

Two enormous Mississippi flatboats were towed downstream from Donaldsonville along the bayou, pulled along by mules and escaped slaves who tugged ropes along the banks, keeping pace with the rear guard.[38] As Weitzel later wrote, "Believing that the enemy would, by means of the numerous flat-boat ferries

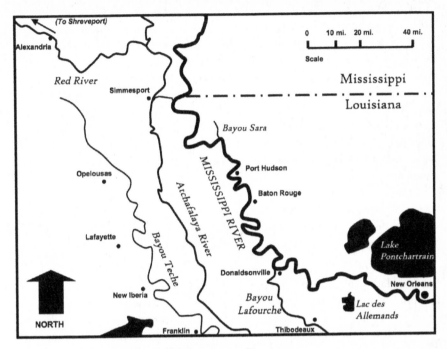

FIGURE 9.1. The Lafourche and Tech regions of Louisiana.

which I knew were in the bayou, probably cross from one side of the bayou to the other, I took in tow a flat-boat bridge and carried it with me all the way."[39] If troops needed to move across the waterway, the barges could be easily converted into a pontoon bridge. Weitzel's floating bridge would end up being the strategic turning point of the upcoming battle.

General Weitzel ordered one company of the Eighth New Hampshire, with an advance guard of cavalry, to begin their march down the right bank of Bayou Lafourche to clear the area of Confederate resistance. The enemy could be heard just a mile or two ahead as the Yankees marched along the banks of the free-flowing bayou. The Twelfth and Thirteenth Connecticut Regiments and the Seventy-Fifth New York followed behind the Eighth New Hampshire. Godfrey instructed his officers to destroy every boat they passed "as a prudential military measure" to prevent the rebels from crossing.[40]

Weitzel's Reserve Brigade made it some fifteen miles to Napoleonville without encountering the enemy, other than a few Confederate scouts. As the Union Army passed by local plantations, a contingent of soldiers and officers were sent to search for hiding rebels. Any landowners found at home were questioned regarding their loyalties to the North or the South. Those who answered correctly were spared, while others found their property at the mercy of "foraging" expeditions by Union soldiers and the escaped slaves who tagged along.

As the day wore on, enemy scouts were continually in sight of Weitzel's advance guard. Just before going into camp that evening, the Union advance guard killed one rebel captain and took three prisoners in for interrogation. Immediately afterward, one of the Eighth New Hampshire privates on the right bank was taken prisoner by the enemy. At that point, General Weitzel ordered his men to bivouac for the night and prepare for a firefight the next day.[41]

The troops camped in the open air, without the aid of tents or other shelter. Some made pillows out of cornstalks. It was a chilly late October night and some of the soldiers had difficulty sleeping with their exposure to the cold air. Others, however, snored soundly, exhausted from the day's march on rough terrain and their sore feet.

Godfrey Weitzel was among those who had difficulty sleeping, but not due to the night air. Since becoming a brigadier general in late August, he had not seen battle. Tomorrow would bring his first armed conflict in the field, and he knew it was also the first battle for every one of his regiments. He racked his brain for all of his West Point training in Professor Mahan's classes on military tactics. Had he made all needed preparations for battle?[42] At around 4:00 a.m., it hit him! Why hadn't he thought of it before? Godfrey had no corps of engineers to cut down the levee in case he needed to move troops and artillery across the bayou. How could the former chief of engineers for the Department of the Gulf have overlooked this? He promptly ordered a detail of soldiers and slaves for this task and furnished them with spades, picks, and axes to be in readiness for that work.[43] *Was that all?* he wondered. He retraced all of his preparations and was finally comfortable that all was in order. Godfrey lay down in his heavy light-blue cavalry overcoat and slept until an aide woke him to let him know the troops were ready to renew the march.[44] All was in order.

CHAPTER 10

Fighting in the Bayous

First Victory: The Battle of Georgia Landing

As General Weitzel advanced his Reserve Brigade down Bayou Lafourche, he met the enemy at Labadieville, a town twenty miles southeast of Donaldsonville, named after a local plantation owner. The area was then and is now in the heart of sugarcane country, where plantations have raised the coveted crop for more than two hundred years. Bayou Lafourche runs through the town, which today has less than two thousand residents. It is hardly a blip on the map, covering less than four square miles of land on the border of Assumption and Lafourche Parishes. Labadieville was the scene of Godfrey Weitzel's first battle on October 27, 1862. The engagement has been called the Battle of Georgia Landing, the Battle of Kock's Plantation, and the Battle of Labadieville. Godfrey Weitzel simply called it—a victory.

Prelude to Battle

Sleep was interrupted for Weitzel's men at dawn and they were ordered to renew the hunt downstream to find Mouton and his supporting band of rebs. Still unsure about the abilities of the untested Twelfth Connecticut he had drilled so hard back in Camp Kearney, Weitzel placed them at the rear of the brigade. Godfrey needed to push the brigade southeast toward Thibodeaux if he was to complete his mission of clearing the area of enemy resistance. At 6:00 a.m. on Monday, the twenty-seventh, after the troops had eaten a light breakfast, General Weitzel ordered his men to renew the march along both banks of the bayou toward Labadieville. His floating barge was towed not far behind.

"Boots and saddles" was sounded, and the troops of the Eighth New Hampshire set out on the left bank, with Perkins's Massachusetts Cavalry accompanying them on the right. It was General Weitzel's plan to move cautiously down the bayou, slowly getting a feel for the enemy's position and strength, and then to concentrate rapidly by means of his floating bridge on whichever side was needed. If successful, Weitzel would drive Mouton into the trap that had been laid at Berwick Bay, where his gunboats should have already arrived.

Mouton's plan, by contrast, was to concentrate his entire force upon a portion of the Federals by means of the Labadieville bridge. The Confederate general was unaware of Weitzel's floating pontoon bridge, which gave the Federals the ability to quickly retreat or to move troops to another side as needed.[1] This would prove an essential strategic advantage for the Yankees.

Weitzel set the bulk of his brigade along the west bank since it would provide the easiest line of retreat should that be necessary. As he rode alongside the men, Godfrey was disappointed in the lack of precision he saw from the New Englanders, who "marched like greenhorns, straggling about the road, the levee and the fields, and taking advantage of every discoverable cut-off."[2] Unaware of the enemy's true position and strength, nor which side of the bayou to expect resistance, the New England regiments marched on gaily for an hour or two that morning, with banners flying and music from their regimental bands.[3] This was no sneak attack, and Confederate scouts had already alerted Mouton to the oncoming Union brigade.

In the heart of Louisiana's sugarcane country, the line of marching bluecoats and mounted cavalry passed by more impressive plantations, with names such as Belle Alliance and the nearby Palo Alto, flourishing green farms covered in endless flats of waving cane. At several of the properties, gorgeous groves of oak trees lined the "alley" between the mansion and the bayou, forming a tunnel of green branches. Confederate troops had been quartered recently in the sugarhouses of several of the plantations, including the St. Emma plantation, located about four miles south of Donaldsonville and just west of Bayou Lafourche.

St. Emma was owned by Charles A. Kock, one of the leading sugar planters and largest slaveholders in Louisiana, with more than three hundred slaves. Perhaps since Mr. Kock was an emigrant from Breman, Germany, his fifteen-year-old Greek Revival–style home was not molested as General Weitzel passed by. The original five-bay-wide plantation house, with its tall columns, still stands today just east of Donaldsonville.

Most plantation owners had abandoned their property in advance of the Union occupation, and the area resembled a ghost town. "Not a vehicle, nor even an equestrian, appeared on the highways," said one Yankee foot soldier. It was eerily quiet when, suddenly, an old man appeared from one of the houses like a ghoul. Described as a "tall, cadaverous man" with the voice of a camp-meeting preacher, he shouted warnings to the passing troops: "Ah boys! Boys! You don't know what awaits you. You are going to your defeat and rout and slaughter!" he taunted. "Better turn back while you can! Better turn back!"[4] Some of the younger troopers yelled back at the old man, who promptly retreated into his house.

Although the white residents had fled, their slaves came out from various hiding places when they saw their noble liberators approaching. "The Negroes swarmed about us with acclamations of joy," said one Yankee. "God bless you, massas!" they cried. "Oh, de Lawd's name be praised! We knowed you'd come. Ise a gwine 'long with you!"[5] And they did, by the hundreds. Liberated slaves fell into the ranks, ready to do anything for their deliverers. One of the black men warned of a large force of rebel soldiers farther down the bayou, a report that had been confirmed by Weitzel's scouts.[6] The snaking line of white-faced, blue-coated soldiers was now mixed with ragtag and black-faced slaves as it continued the way along the banks of the waterway, marching band and all.

For hours the brigade plodded along without incident, the drums beating a rhythm to keep the pace. Colorful banners distinguished one New England regiment from the other as they tramped along the green banks of the bayou. As the line of Union bluecoats plodded along, they passed two rebel camps, only recently vacated, with campfires still blazing near cane-roofed huts.[7] Hoofprints and manure showed that a sizable force had bivouacked there the night before. The Federals quickly torched the huts as they continued the march. Local slaves reported that the camp had numbered about five hundred, mostly armed as mounted infantry. At several points the brigade also encountered hastily constructed breastworks and rifle pits, which the enemy had abandoned in its retreat. The fight was near now, and all the soldiers braced themselves for battle, as did their young general.

Miles ahead of the main body of foot soldiers, at about 9:00 a.m., the Eighth New Hampshire encountered Mouton's rear guard and skirmished with them for nearly one hour on the left bank. The engagement escalated when, at almost the same time, scouts from Perkins's cavalry encountered more skirmishers on the opposite bank.

The Enemy Is Encountered

The squad from Perkins's cavalry, consisting of a sergeant and five men on horseback, was scouting in advance of the Union column. It passed an open field about five hundred yards long and halted there, at a point between the levee and thick woods. One of the Yankees spotted some movement in the underbrush and whispered, "Sergeant, there they are—to the right, lying down." The sergeant scanned the thicket without turning his head and saw a rebel ambush lying in wait under tall grass. Trying to act nonchalant, the officer stood up in his stirrups and coolly surveyed the road in front of him, and then a country crossroad that fell in from the right. "Nothing here," he said loudly. "We'll ride back and report."[8]

The six mounted men rode off at a slow walk at first, and then with a "Hee-Yah!" kicked their spurs into their horses and made a run toward the advancing Eighth New Hampshire Regiment to warn them of the ambush. The cool actions of the sergeant saved his life and those of his five companions. A rebel captured three hours later told his captors, "If that sergeant hadn't been so cool, he would have caught his death. I had a bead drawn on him, but the officers wouldn't let us fire. They thought the coons didn't see us, and they allowed they was going to bag the whole column."[9]

Mouton had chosen a good position on a bend in Bayou Lafourche, about one mile above Labadieville, at a point known as Georgia Landing. Here they had dug extensive rifle pits and constructed embrasures in the levee, which served the purpose of a parapet.[10] Perkins now wheeled his cavalrymen about and the engagement began, first with a barrage aimed at the underbrush where the rebs were hiding. The ambushers responded in kind with rapid fire from sharpshooters.

Two companies of the Eighth New Hampshire Regiment moved into a skirmish line and relieved Perkins, while the other eight companies formed a square, just as they had been drilled to do back at Carrollton. The *bam! bam! bam!* of rifle fire cracked the air, with the occasional *boom!* of a Confederate piece of artillery. Shells splashed in the bayou and balls zinged past soldiers on both sides. Men in blue uniforms grabbed their chests or arms as blood began to pour; others fell dead where they stood. Several men were wounded, the first blood seen in battle by the fresh Federals.

Mouton's forces were much smaller than had been reported. The main rifle pit of the rebels concealed two full veteran regiments, who lay behind and almost directly under a stout cypress fence that ran nearly a quarter of a mile perpendicular to the bayou on its right bank. To the rear of this pit was a thick woods that concealed the remainder of Mouton's forces. Open ground in between the fence and the woods would expose the Federals to fire from the enemy sharpshooters hidden in a dense cluster of trees. The Yankees tossed off their knapsacks and overcoats, guarded by a few half-sick men, and the Thirteenth Connecticut and the Seventy-Fifth New York Regiments formed into line of battle. The untested Twelfth Connecticut acted as rear guard.[11] Adrenaline was rushing as guns were rapidly loaded and fired.

Crossing the Sugarcane Field

The adjacent field was covered with green, full-grown sugarcane, standing eight to ten feet high. The tall cane likely concealed enemy gunmen, making entry into it near suicide. Cautiously, the blue-coated soldiers pushed away stalks of cane with their rifles, stepping gently on stalks that broke beneath their feet. It was "a nearly impenetrable growth," one soldier recalled.[12] Deep drainage ditches that crossed these fields at right angles created temporary obstacles. Keeping a straight line of formation was impossible. Only the regimental colors could be seen above the green crop to guide the men forward irregularly. At any moment, the soldiers anticipated the flash of gunfire at point-blank range from between the tall green cane rods.

Fortunately for the Federals, no enemy resistance was encountered in the cane field until they emerged breathless and terrified at the opposite end of the green stalks. It was about 11:00 a.m. when Colonel Henry Birge emerged from the sugarcane, unable to locate his men. "Well, Captain," he said as another officer appeared, "where's the Thirteenth?" "There's one of them," the captain said, seeing one private pop out of the green stalks. "The rest of them will be here as soon as they can squeeze through."[13] Some officers had abandoned their horses, unable to get them through the tall cane.

As the Yankees waded through the field, Mouton's men had crossed a bridge in the rear, and were pouring down to their strong position on the right bank, hoping to catch a portion of the Union brigade by surprise and overpower them. As General Weitzel emerged from the cane field, he received a report from his advance guard that the enemy was in force about one mile ahead, on the left bank, with six pieces of artillery.[14] Weitzel quickly figured out their plans.

He sensed that the main body of Mouton's Army was elsewhere. "We are on the wrong track," Godfrey said. "This is a false scent. The fighting will be on the other bank."[15] He immediately ordered the men back to the pontoon bridge, to cross it and support the Eighth New Hampshire. He also ordered four pieces of Carruth's battery up and directed that the Seventy-Fifth New York and the Thirteenth Connecticut form into battalion columns to prepare for what he believed would be the main battle.

A portion of Mouton's men had cleverly circled around behind the Union line while they were crossing the sugarcane field, and Weitzel soon learned that the enemy's cavalry was approaching from behind his rear guard, cutting off any retreat. Reentering the cane field, Weitzel's brigade found itself being shelled by the enemy, who was using the Union regimental flags for targets. Wounded were sent to the rear as the skirmish continued for an hour in the green sugarcane fields, which became riddled with bullets and cannonballs.

The Pontoon Bridge

Just as quickly as they had appeared, the rebel infantry suddenly fled. "Fearing some ruse," Weitzel recalled, "I immediately ordered the Thirteenth Connecticut across the bayou to support the Eighth New Hampshire and the Twelfth Connecticut."[16] He had an aide instruct the Twelfth Connecticut to break off two companies to guard the rear baggage train and move the rest up to the battlefield. Weitzel immediately swung his floating bridge across Bayou Lafourche so that the eight companies of the Twelfth Connecticut could cross to lend support.

Using his engineer's training, he also immediately ordered that a road be cut up the steep bank on both sides of the bayou for the passage of artillery and his supply train. The axes that Godfrey had remembered early that morning were used to chop up the levee, making a level road across the pontoon bridge. The engineer squad and some slaves hurried to dig a road through the levee as the barge that served as a pontoon bridge was swung into position to extend the road to the other bank.

Two twelve-pound howitzers were put into position to protect the crossing. Weitzel now ordered the men to cross the bayou over his floating bridge to the western bank where he felt that Mouton was waiting. The bluecoats crowded onto the pontoon bridge, some stooping carelessly to fill their canteens. "To the astonished eyes of the Rebels, it must have appeared the work of magic," one Union officer said as the bluecoats traversed the bayou in midstream. At that moment, General Mouton made his presence known with a barrage of cannon fire sent from his batteries half a mile west of the bayou on the right bank. The first shell screamed overhead and splashed into the muddy water. A second shell came closer and spattered some of the men, but without damaging the bridge. As General Weitzel phrased it, the enemy was "firing splendidly upon our forces and my bridge." One Union cavalryman was killed, another wounded, and two horses dropped dead, spilling their riders.[17]

A thick wood separated Weitzel from Mouton as the opposing batteries pounded away, though neither could see the other's position. On the opposite side now, shot and shells whistled over the heads of the Union soldiers. "We had great confidence in General Weitzel," one soldier recalled, "but not yet in ourselves. Would our men stand fire? Would they resist a cavalry charge? Would our men march straight against a bristling fence of bayonets?"[18] There was no time to speculate, as trees were split by enemy shells and the screaming sound of projectiles filled the air.

Crossing the bayou, the men were ordered quickly up the steep bank of the opposite side. The troops now hurried across and regrouped on the west bank. They then marched about five hundred yards from the bayou and formed a battle line. There was some initial confusion as orders were being barked out by various officers amid the din of battle: "Battalion, halt! Front! On the center, dress! Battalion! Forward! Guide Center! March!"

Nearby, Lieutenant Colonel Colburn, who commanded the Twelfth Connecticut Regiment, shouted for his men to straighten their line to the center person. "Center dress! Close up those gaps! Center dress!" His company officers repeated the same orders. The three regiments from Connecticut were now all together, marching through thick thornbushes and over stumps and ditches, pressing forward and struggling to maintain a straight line. They came to a rail fence that blocked their progress. "Break it down!" came the order, and the front rank rushed against it, striking it with their chests and flattening it in seconds.[19]

General Weitzel rode a short distance behind his men, dressed in a sky-blue overcoat, still smoking a cigar and surveying the scene. At six feet four and mounted on horseback, he was a tempting target for enemy riflemen. Nonetheless, Godfrey maintained his composure, although his junior officers and soldiers were busy dodging and ducking at every sound of a projectile.[20]

The gap between the opposing armies closed to just a quarter mile now. A Union scout rode up to report that the enemy's position was just on the other side of the woods, across the open field, behind a fence, and protected by a ditch in which they were lying. It was a good strategic position for the rebels and would force the Yankees into the open if Weitzel were to order an attack. The untested New Englanders entered the woods, knowing that their first battle lay now just five hundred yards ahead. The open field would expose them to rifle and cannon fire, and they braced for the next order to "Charge!"

Mouton's batteries caught sight of the bluecoats as they approached the edge of the woods and sent a shell screaming overhead, which passed through the lower branches of the trees and sent down a shower of leaves.[21] The shot was so low that most of the men ducked their heads for fear of losing them. The Southerners sent another flurry of shells aimed at the regimental banners, whose colors contrasted with the green foliage. Guns boomed rapidly from across the battlefield. The two Union howitzers back at the pontoon bridge did not respond for fear of killing their own troops.

With each shot, the rebel gunners lowered their aims, targeting the heads and torsos of the New Englanders hiding in the woods. Not wanting to show any fear that might discourage his men, a captain from the Twelfth Connecticut recalled thinking, "They will hurt somebody soon, but the missile will hit me about the time that I should hear it."[22] He knew his men were watching him and would follow his lead. No twitching or trembling could be seen from an officer, even in the face of such enemy fire.

Eventually, the First Maine battery of Weitzel's brigade commenced shelling the woods across the field. They missed their mark, however, with shells going a mile past the enemy.[23] At this point, only a quarter of a mile from the enemy line, the Yankee soldiers had not yet opened fire. Suddenly, Mouton's infantry unleashed a barrage, "with a rattle like the discharge of an endless string of fire-crackers."[24] The rifles found their marks, as blue jackets spurted red and men shrieked in pain. Some terrified foot soldiers and members of the drum corps lay low, refusing to advance. Others rushed for cover behind trees.

"We Must Charge Them!"

General Weitzel rode up confidently in his light-blue topcoat to inspire his men. "It's getting pretty warm," he said. "You'd better lie down." In obedience, an officer barked out the order to "Lie down!" which was quickly obeyed by soldiers who knew their chances of survival increased the lower to the ground they were. The order was odd to some troops who had been drilled to stand straight up without flinching in the face of enemy fire. General Weitzel sat upright on his horse, cigar clenched in his teeth, watching the enemy fire and evaluating the situation. Peering through the woods, he thought he caught a glimpse of movement approaching across the field. "Rise up!" he suddenly said. "Their cavalry are coming!"[25]

Yankee soldiers quickly fixed bayonets and awaited the next order. "You may lie down," Weitzel then shouted to the confused soldiers. "They're not coming." A rookie mistake as Godfrey misread movement in the distance. He watched and waited to be sure there was no enemy cavalry attack. Now certain that Mouton would stay in his wooded hideout, it was an opportunity to take the offensive. Giving a counterorder that must have confused his men once again, General Weitzel suddenly barked confidently, "We must charge them!"[26]

At this command, every soldier braced for the rush across the field, knowing it would be instant death for some and agonizing wounds for others, but this was how wars were fought. Following his orders, Colonel Henry Birge of the Thirteenth Connecticut shouted, "Rise up! Battalion, forward! Guide center!" It was the command for the final grand charge of the day. The time had come for the Yankees to advance into the open field and the orders were given to "March!" The bluecoats formed in the line of battle and marched through the brush and into the large open field. The boys in butternut then opened fire with their muskets as the Union troops came into range. They drew a bead on the approaching line and squeezed, raising puffs of smoke and fire. "The fun commenced," one private wrote, "and the first thing I know, a cannon ball came within six feet of my head. They kept firing, shot and shell, at us." Rebel sharpshooters fired continuously, sounding like a stick run along a picket fence, "only vastly louder," one soldier said.[27]

Bullets whizzed by and whiffs of dust jumped up where some of them hit the ground. Peering across the field and into the woods, a long roll of blue smoke curled upward from the unseen sharpshooters. All this time, Mouton's batteries kept up the roar to the right, emitting a thin cloud of gray smoke from their position.[28] A frightened color guard bearing the United States flag turned to the rear and began to retreat from the enemy fire. An officer who saw this and feared the entire regiment might follow the flag pounced upon him with his saber drawn. "Forward, or I'll split your head open!" he shouted. The solider was dazed and startled as the officer pushed him back into position to the front of the color guard, ordering "Forward!" Men began to fall now from bloody head and chest wounds. A lieutenant was hit in the chest by a shell fragment and killed; a private flung up both hands with a scream and dropped dead with a ball through his heart.[29]

General Weitzel was riding close behind and could see the disaster unfolding at the edge of the woods. He sent the Eighth New Hampshire to the rear to meet a reported rebel cavalry force trying to trap the Yankees in the woods. He also ordered the Thirteenth Connecticut forward to replace the Eighth New Hampshire. The boys of the Twelfth Connecticut continued ahead into the battlefield five hundred yards long and prepared for a severe hand-to-hand struggle, envisioning the worst carnage that close-range fire and bayonets could inflict.

The enemy continued the rain of gunfire from their cover in the woods and down in their rifle pits behind a stout fence. Puffs of white smoke were all the Yankee soldiers could see of the rebs in the distance. From the woods and rifle pits, however, the Southern boys had an altogether different view: four hundred men of the Twelfth Connecticut and a long line of six hundred bayonets of the Thirteenth Regiment, one thousand bluecoats in all, coming steadily forward in unbroken ranks. Holding their fire, the Federals continued to march ahead, some dropping here and there as enemy shots found their mark, the rest forging ahead. Two officers were killed, and it was all the other officers could do to restrain their men from returning fire out of anger.

To Godfrey's delight, his brave New England foot soldiers continued the advance without firing. They were more than halfway across the field before they could see any of the Confederates masked by shrubbery. More puffs of smoke gave away their positions. "How we longed to return the fire!" one soldier recalled. "But our leader seemed determined to rely on the bayonet alone." That was not Godfrey Weitzel's plan at all. By not stopping to fire their rifles and to reload, the thousand-man force made quick time across the field, a few men being sacrificed for the good of the others. "Forward, still forward we pressed, shoulder to shoulder, and still we were the targets of their two batteries and three infantry regiments," a Connecticut officer recalled. "Our impatience to be shooting grew extreme."[30]

The aggressive rush of bluecoats so surprised the Confederate sharpshooters that many began to retreat for fear of being overrun. The Yankees held their fire and continued their approach until the Southern troops "became frightened and ran up out of the ditch to skedaddle." Suddenly, the order was given and four hundred rifles of the Twelfth Connecticut opened fire. "Heavens! What a volley!" one soldier remembered. Other Union regiments followed suit, and there was "a tremendous roll of musketry." As continuous gunfire now rained into the woods, aimed at the places where white puffs had revealed the enemy's position, the Yankees advanced.[31]

The excitement grew intense as each man wondered if the rebs would stand to face a bayonet charge. Now close enough to see the enemy, Confederate officers frantically brandished their swords, trying to hold their men in place.

The Rebels Retreat—The Battle Is Won!
One of Weitzel's men bragged later, "We gave them a volley, some of them [left] on such a hurry that they forgot to take their muskets." With the rebs on the run, Colonel Henry Birge of the Thirteenth Connecticut Infantry ordered an attack on the double-quick. The bluecoats started with a yell that startled the retreating Confederates. With a rush, the excited, howling Federals shot into the air and in an instant rushed up and over the enemy rifle pit. As the oncoming Union troops got within one hundred yards of the enemy, some rebels retreated in a panic while others raised white handkerchiefs in surrender. Swarms of men in gray and butternut uniforms sprang out of the ditch that had sheltered them and fled at full speed.[32] "Such skeddadling you never saw," recalled one New Englander.[33]

Seeing their retreat, the Yankees let out an excited scream and increased their fire. The bluecoats spoiled the enemy's aim now by blasting away as they charged across the open field. The whistling of Union bullets and the flying of cypress splinters made the ditch "a most disagreeable hole to be in," according to one Confederate taken prisoner. There was, however, some risk in charging across the field while firing, in that the front rank might be shot from the rifles of the rear rank. Captain J. W. De Forest of the Eighth New Hampshire Regiment was hit in the neck by just such a shot, but he survived to write a detailed account of the battle.[34]

The rebel officer in charge, Colonel George P. McPheeters of the Crescent Regiment, had been watching the intense fighting with the advancing Eighth New Hampshire. When two Connecticut regiments joined the New Hampshire boys, he feared being overrun and trapped between the field and the swamp to the rear. He ordered the Confederates to retreat but stood in place himself as his men fled past, trying to remain calm in the face of a rapidly approaching enemy force.

Before McPheeters could join the retreat, he took a bullet through the head and was later found by the Yankees flat on his back with one eye lying on his cheek. General Weitzel delivered the body to some of his brother officers who were prisoners, and McPheeters was given a decent burial near the battlefield, with the chaplain of the Eighth New Hampshire officiating.[35]

"The sight of the escaping enemy was an irresistible temptation," the wounded Captain De Forest recalled, and the New Englanders ran more rapidly then, "yelling with delight and blazing away at the woods, although the enemy had vanished like a dream." The excited soldiers could hardly be restrained by their officers, all of whom were shocked at the early retreat of the Southerners. To save ammunition, a lieutenant colonel rode down the line shouting, "Cease firing!"[36]

The battle was over in just eighty minutes, leaving the field strewn with wounded and dead soldiers and more in the woods beyond. General Weitzel rode up fast from the rear in his light blue top coat and dark kepi hat, complimenting the men, who answered with enthusiastic cheers.[37] Two Union companies were ordered into the woods in search of any rebel stragglers. They captured more than two hundred of the enemy who were either wounded or too slow in their retreat. The remaining companies of Weitzel's brigade formed ranks, counted off, and had roll call to determine any casualties. It was for this reason that the plebes at West Point had been trained to stand in line for roll call several times a day. In battle, it was essential to take a head count frequently to assess the manpower of a regiment. Officers took down the numbers, tallying up the missing as each name was called.

The supremely proud General Weitzel rode up to each of the assembled regiments and congratulated them. As he made a speech to the Thirteenth Connecticut Regiment, the boys cheered their young commander who had won his first battle in such quick order. Weitzel then rode over to the next regiment, which stood at attention in the open field. "Twelfth Connecticut, you have done well. That is the way to do it. Never stop, and the enemy won't stay," he said. "That is the best speech I ever heard," whispered one of the boys in blue to another private. The regiment responded enthusiastically, shouting, "Hurrah! Hurrah!" for the brigadier general . . . and for itself. One soldier wrote, "The general is justly proud of his brigade, and he enjoys the entire confidence of every man in the expedition. It is impossible for a general to have more fully the moral support of an army, than that possessed by General Weitzel."[38] One Vermont officer noted candidly that "General Weitzel was a young man to hold so responsible a position."[39] But his age became irrelevant in the face of his clever victory.

In all the backslapping and congratulating, the soldiers had almost forgotten about Mouton's cavalry approaching from the rear. Just like that, shots were heard from the enemy's Second Louisiana Cavalry as they began skirmishing with the baggage guard that had been left behind. The Eighth New Hampshire Regiment promptly responded and drove them off. Realizing that Mouton's force had retreated, the enemy cavalry turned and rode off to Thibodeaux at a gallop. Scattered fighting continued for another thirty minutes between Union cavalry and remnants of Mouton's Louisiana boys, guns booming farther and farther southward as the rebels retreated down Bayou Lafourche into the heart of sugarcane country.

It was a good day for General Weitzel's Reserve Brigade. It had won its first battle and captured a fieldpiece as well as more than two hundred prisoners by day's end. Although the battle was a Union victory, it was not without its casualties. The Weitzel brigade lost eighty-six men in this short fight, eighteen killed and sixty-eight wounded.[40] The Confederates suffered fewer casualties, with only sixty killed and wounded, including the brave Colonel McPheeters. Two hundred and sixty-eight rebels were taken as prisoners, all later released on parole.[41] Weitzel's men buried all of the enemy's dead and took another seventeen wounded into a local house that was turned into a field hospital. The Union dead were buried and the wounded cared for before General Weitzel ordered his brigade to camp for the night.

On to Thibodeaux

For the untested regiments in Weitzel's brigade, that first day's battle was invaluable. A first victory gave the troops encouragement and a thirst for a second battle. Godfrey Weitzel believed that Mouton's original plan was to march his rebel column up Bayou Lafourche and establish fortifications on the Mississippi at Donaldsonville to harass the Union fleet and prevent passage north. After the first encounter, however, Weitzel felt certain that he could defeat Mouton by chasing him back to Brashear City. With support from a gunboat fleet, he could prevent Mouton from escaping across Bayou Teche.

Locals at Carrollton and New Orleans had spread false information that Mouton had fifteen thousand men at Thibodeaux, drilled and heavily armed, that would smash Weitzel's brigade. This proved to be a gross exaggeration, called by one Yankee a "bugaboo invention" created by Mouton himself. In truth, the rebels under Mouton numbered only about twenty-five hundred soldiers including militia, outnumbered by Weitzel's brigade two to one.

Having brushed away the small rebel army at Labadieville, the way was now cleared to Thibodeaux, the capital of the Lafourche Parish. General Weitzel marched his brigade nine miles from Labadieville to Thibodeaux, where Union scouts reported that the enemy was going to make a stand. Whenever enemy movement was reported, a Union artillery group fired a few rounds that were so loud on a quiet Tuesday morning, "it made the woods ring." The townspeople of Thibodeaux rolled out of bed and poured into the streets in their nightclothes. "I don't blame them for being frightened," observed one Union soldier. The towns-folk were not the only ones afraid, as that same Yankee soldier wrote home, "I am so nervous that I can't write so that I can read it myself. If you can, you will do well!"[42]

The Weitzel Reserve Brigade cautiously entered Thibodeaux without en-countering any further opposition. The town was nearly abandoned, other than women and some slaves who had not yet escaped. Mouton's force was nowhere to be found. The troops marched through the empty streets waving their regimental banners as well as the hated Stars and Stripes. They kept step to the music from the accompanying band, which celebrated with a mocking rendition of "Dixie," followed by "Yankee Doodle."[43] Southern women closed their doors and shut-tered their windows, sometimes sneaking a peak at the blue-coated foot soldiers and cavalrymen passing through the town.

From the smoke of burning bridges in the distance, General Weitzel knew that Mouton's forces were retreating west toward Berwick Bay. He immediately ordered his cavalry in pursuit, who followed as closely as possible to prevent the total destruction of additional bridges, including two important railroad bridges across Bayou Lafourche and Bayou Terre Bonne.[44] The cavalry were successful in harassing Mouton's forces as they fled. However, the retreating enemy burned bridges across Bayou Boeuf and Bayou Terre Bonne to prevent Weitzel's cavalry from continuing the pursuit.

The Pied Piper of Thibodeaux

As it became clear that Thibodeaux was safely in Union hands, black men and women from all over the region swarmed into town to greet their liberators with elation. They brought along horses, wagons, furniture, bundles of clothing and bedding, and children. The snaking columns of Federal soldiers were swelled with their tagalongs. "Every soldier had a Negro, and every Negro a mule," said one of the troops. Another observer wrote, "The Negroes everywhere flocked to the army, as to their deliverers, and many of the plantations were entirely deserted."[45]

As the mobs of newly freed blacks joined in the parade, General Weitzel had a logistics problem far greater than had been encountered back in Carrollton. This was an army on the move, not a camp. Adding to the growing problem, Mouton's troops left more than four hundred wagonloads of slaves behind at Brashear City as they fled the Union gunboats.

Godfrey Weitzel wrote to Major George Strong, Ben Butler's chief of staff, asking candidly, "Now what shall I do with them?" The ranks of escaped slaves were

FIGURE 10.1. "The Man Who Won the Elephant at the Raffle." (1863; Civil War Cartoon Collection, American Antiquarian Society.) (GEN. WEITZEL: "But the question is, What am I to do with the Creature?")

swelling to a point that Godfrey felt he had twice as many escaped slaves and their children in and around camp as he had soldiers within. "I cannot feed them," he wrote to Major Strong. "As a consequence they must feed themselves."[46]

When his report was published, a political cartoon (see fig. 10.1) soon showed up in Northern newspapers showing a giant black man in the morphed form of an elephant, with a tiny Union officer leading him along. The caption reads, "The Man Who Won the Elephant at the Raffle." The cartoon shows an exasperated Weitzel saying, "But the question is—What am I to do with the creature?"

Godfrey Weitzel wrote to his mentor, Ben Butler, about the growing black population now trailing his brigade. Butler sidestepped the issue, writing back: "I sympathize with you in the matter of the Negroes. By the Act of Congress they are clearly free, still you must not encumber yourself with them." Butler advised Weitzel to hold the freed slaves at Thibodeaux until the railroad was running again, then the Army would move them to the camp at Algiers, outside New Orleans. "If they pillage, of course, we cannot help it," Butler wrote. "It is one of the necessary evils following this system of labor, and the rebellion, as far as I can see."[47]

Camp Stevens

With their mission nearly accomplished after only one battle, Weitzel's Reserve Brigade went into camp on a plantation about one mile below Thibodeaux. From his camp, Godfrey Weitzel sent field reports to General Butler on October 28 and 29 listing those killed and wounded in skirmishes with Mouton's small force. Weitzel's men also collected a large number of Confederate cavalry and artillery horses, as well as pack mules. However, the engagement had used up quite a bit of ammunition, and Weitzel pleaded with the department headquarters to quickly send more.

Ben Butler was proud of his protégé's success and wrote back, "I cannot speak too highly of the admirable conduct of your troops, and your own brilliant success in the expedition."[48] A portion of Weitzel's brigade marched to the town of Raceland, Louisiana—some fourteen miles farther down the bayou from Thibodeaux—where it had been reported that a small hostile force was hiding out. General Weitzel selected Thibodeaux as the place to set up a central command and ordered the men into camp on the abandoned Acadia plantation that was about a mile south of town. The encampment was named "Camp Stevens," which today is a residential development just south of Nicholls State University at Thibodeaux.

The "Negro Question" Returns

There were entirely too many escaped slaves falling in with the Union brigade for General Weitzel to house and feed. Godfrey decided to order some of the slaves who were the property of local sugar plantation farmers back to their homes to help them get their crops planted. However, his contact with the local farmers and citizens in the Lafourche District showed him that trouble was in the air with black Union troops and escaped slaves roaming the region. Although many of the local community had sworn their allegiance to the Union, General Weitzel wrote that the community "is in great terror, fearing trouble with the Negroes. They beg me to allow them to retain their arms."[49] This created a dilemma, in that arming the local whites might calm their fears of a slave insurrection or retribution, but it would put Union troops at risk. His pickets had already been fired on by unknown persons with shotguns.

Godfrey knew that he could not allow the Southern citizens to keep weapons without authority from his commanding officer. He proposed to Ben Butler that only those residents who had taken the oath, as well as paroled rebel soldiers, could retain their arms. In a November 2, 1862, letter, General Butler rephrased the issue: "By the Act of Congress, independent of the President's proclamation, having come from rebel masters into our lines, in occupation of rebel territory since the passage of that act, they are free. But the question recurs. What shall we do with them?" He could not return them to their former masters as "property," but that meant he had to take care of them in addition to carrying out his military duties. Butler explained that it was now the Union Army's duty to care for these slaves, who could not now be returned to their disloyal masters. "Put them as far as possible upon plantations, use every energy to have the sugar crop made and preserved for the owners that are loyal, and for the United States when the owners are disloyal."[50]

Weitzel's expedition into the Lafourche District was a success, and on Godfrey's twenty-seventh birthday, November 1, 1862, he wrote, "I have undisputed possession of this country now, and this part of the campaign is a perfect success."[51] He had earned the respect of his troops and officers alike. More than one hundred officers from the various regiments called at his quarters at Camp Stevens to congratulate him on his birthday. "He requested his staff officers, all of whom were older than himself, to aid in entertaining his guests," one officer recalled. The outpouring of affection nearly brought Godfrey to tears. "Never had they seen him come so near showing the 'white feather,' and having his wonted gravity of manner disturbed," a witness observed. To toast their young leader, an officer said, "To the gallant young brigadier general, Godfrey Weitzel." Embarrassed at the attention, Godfrey modestly said, "This is not an official occasion, gentlemen. Please call me G. Weitzel, lieutenant of engineers. This brigadier-general commission I have yet to earn."[52]

By defeating Mouton, Weitzel began the opening of the Opelousas Railroad to Brashear City, Louisiana, a feat that was ultimately accomplished on December 8. Weitzel's engineering training came into play during this exercise as his troops had to put in order eighty miles of road, build two bridges covering 1,150 feet, rebuild four miles of track, and open up complete railroad and telegraph communication between Algiers and Berwick Bay.[53] He assigned troops from the colored Louisiana Native Guards to picket the roads with orders to hold Boutte Station, Bayou des Allemands Bridge, Tigerville, Bayou Lafourche Bridge, and Terre Bonne Bridge, among others. In short, Godfrey Weitzel seemed in complete control of the Lafourche region. The goal of the entire expedition was to open the whole region of the Bayou Lafourche to Union occupation, and he had done it.

Weitzel Declines Command of New Districts

Weitzel's success so impressed General Butler that he recommended the barely twenty-seven-year-old West Point graduate be placed in charge of the entire district, including the District of Bayou Teche. Ben Butler informed Godfrey Weitzel on November 2 that his duties were to be expanded. The portion of Louisiana to the west of the Mississippi River was to be called the "Military District of Lafourche" and would be placed under Weitzel's command. In a bold and surprising move, General Weitzel wrote to Butler to decline command of the Lafourche District, a letter that shocked Ben Butler.

After much thought, Weitzel wrote to Butler on November 5 stating simply, "I desire, most respectfully, to decline the command of the district which has just been created." His reason? Not that he was unfit for the task, but that accepting the command would place him in command of *all the troops* in the district. Weitzel shocked his commanding officer by adding, "I cannot command those Negro regiments."[54] Godfrey also had concerns about overseeing both the Teche and the Lafourche regions, as the Teche was not yet under Union control.

Butler told Weitzel that the command was "in compliment to your skill and gallantry." Putting so large a force under the young general's command was Butler's way "to show a mark of confidence in your discrimination and judgment," he said. In a blatantly racist comment, Weitzel confessed to Butler that he had no confidence in the two all-black regiments of Native Guards under his command, and he did not think they would fight.[55]

Ben Butler Visits Camp Stevens

On November 8, Ben Butler showed up at Camp Stevens, a rare field visit. He was not there to inspect the troops but had important news to share with his protégé, and he wanted to personally talk to Godfrey about his decision regarding the command of colored troops. It would not do to simply write letters back and forth for the former trial lawyer. Ben Butler needed a face-to-face discussion with Weitzel. Butler had learned that movement was afoot in Washington to replace him as department commander. Godfrey could not understand why anyone would replace his beloved general. Yes, his methods were rough, but his motives were pure, and the results showed the wisdom of his actions. But the decision had been made at the very top of the Federal government—by Abraham Lincoln.

History is muddled as to why Ben Butler was removed from his post in New Orleans. There were charges of rampant corruption by Union officials under Butler's watch, including his own brother, but no proof of wrongdoing was ever found against General Butler himself. Nonetheless, the rumors of his graft earned him the nickname "Spoons," for allegedly stealing silverware from the mansions of the wealthy. Edwin Stanton later claimed the reassignment was due to a misunderstanding about Butler's views on the Emancipation Proclamation. Whatever the reason, in Washington, the complaints about Butler

FIGURE 10.2. Major General Benjamin Franklin Butler, the "Beast" of New Orleans (1818–1893). (Library of Congress, Manuscript Division, Reference No. LC-MSS-44297-33-155.)

were too loud and too frequent to ignore. Both Lincoln and Stanton decided it was time for a change.

On the day after Butler's visit to Camp Stevens, War Department secretary Stanton issued the order placing command of the Department of the Gulf into the hands of General Nathaniel P. Banks, the former congressman and governor from Massachusetts. Stanton's order had the approval of the president himself.[56] The "Beast" of New Orleans was no longer in command, and Godfrey Weitzel would have a new boss. This was the first time since the invasion of New Orleans that Godfrey was separated from his mentor's supervision and protection. Their separation would only be temporary.

CHAPTER 11

Commanding Black Troops

Unlikely Prejudice

Ben Butler characterized Weitzel's rejection of the offer to command black regiments as pure racial prejudice. In Butler's autobiography, written eight years after Weitzel died, he admitted: "I can now give a curious instance of the exhibition of this prejudice by one of the ablest men and best loved members of my staff, a life-long friend of whom I have heretofore spoken and shall hereafter speak in terms of affection, friendship, and admiring regard, Gen. Godfrey Weitzel."[1] Butler then recalled the story of his appointment of Godfrey to command the all-black Louisiana Native Guard, and the initial rejection of that command on purely racial grounds.

No junior officer refused an offer of promotion, and none said "no" to Ben Butler. Godfrey's letter rejecting the offer to command two black regiments of the Native Guard shocked Butler. With freed slaves outnumbering whites in the region, Godfrey feared an insurrection precipitated by the presence of armed black men. Stealing, plundering, and other crimes would be a distraction from his military duties. It was only at the urging of Butler, Weitzel's mentor and a strong abolitionist, that Godfrey was convinced to reconsider.

In New Orleans, Godfrey had discussed the topic of black soldiers directly with General Butler, stating, "The commanding general knows well my private opinions on this subject. What I stated to him privately, while on his staff, I see now before my eyes." In Weitzel's view, the arrival of uniformed black soldiers, armed and part of the Union force commanding Lafourche, had fueled symptoms of an insurrection among the black community there. Godfrey pleaded with his friend not to assign him to this task, saying, "I beg you therefore to keep the Negro brigade directly under your own command or place someone over both mine and it."[2]

From a practical standpoint, Godfrey worried how he could suppress a local uprising of freed slaves without breaking up his Reserve Brigade into small forces here and there. With smaller companies of all-black troops roaming the region, Weitzel feared what havoc they might cause, and how they might be treated by the locals. He also felt that the presence of armed black men would terrorize a region where most white men were away from their homes. "I cannot assume the command of such a force," Godfrey wrote, "and thus be responsible for its conduct. I have no confidence in the organization [of the Native Guard]. Its moral effect in this community, which is stripped of nearly all its able-bodied men and will be stripped of a great many of its arms, is terrible."[3]

For the loyal protégé of Ben Butler to refuse this command came as a tremendous disappointment. Butler said, "My surprise may not be imagined when I received these reports from Weitzel, especially that one in which he declared he would not obey my orders to command colored troops."[4] The junior officer's refusal prompted Butler to challenge him in a November 6 letter, which strongly rebuked Weitzel's racist explanation. "That you should have declined the command is the occasion of regret, arising *most of all* from the reasons given for doing so."[5]

Godfrey Weitzel felt that the colored local regiments should be assigned only to guard duties in locations such as along the railroad. Why, asked Butler, did Weitzel permit the colored troops to guard his lines of communications by railroad if he felt the Native Guard somehow weakened his defense? The trial lawyer challenged Weitzel's logic, asking him pointedly, "You do not complain in your report that they either failed to do their duty in that respect or that they have acted otherwise than correctly and obediently to the commands of their officers."[6] Butler pushed Weitzel to explain himself, pointing out that the colored troops were not accused of committing any outrage or pillage upon the inhabitants of the area to date.

Was Weitzel's objection simply racism or a legitimate military or social concern? Butler was aware of Weitzel's opinion "that colored men will not fight," but he challenged that premise by asking for proof. "You have failed to show, by the conduct of these freemen so far, anything to sustain that opinion," said Butler. He pressed Weitzel to explain his refusal to command the Native Guard, saying, "especially as you express a willingness to go forward to meet the only organized enemy with your own brigade alone without further support."[7]

Godfrey Weitzel's objections were not entirely based on his perceptions of the fighting ability of the black soldier. He had been stationed in New Orleans for years, where he observed firsthand the interaction of Louisiana residents and freemen, as well as black slaves. His concern was as much about the civilian reaction to the sight of colored troops with weapons as it was his naive belief that the colored soldier would not fight. Godfrey worried that the women and children, living without a white male adult in the home, would be terrified of armed black men in their communities.

Slavery was a cruel and evil institution. "No pen, no book, no time can do justice to the wrongs it honors," wrote Elizabeth Van Lew of Virginia.[8] Would the armed former slaves seek retribution against their persecutors? Locals had voiced their fear of rape, murder, plunder, and revenge by armed ex-slaves, a terror that Weitzel thought would demoralize the Lafourche and Teche regions.

His bleeding heart went out to them. "Women and children, and even men, are in terror. It is heart-rending, and I cannot make myself responsible for it. I will gladly go anywhere with my own brigade that you see fit to order me."[9] He just did not want to bring the black soldiers into the Lafourche.

Godfrey wrote to Butler that abandoned slaves rounded up by Mouton's forces had been returned to local sugarcane plantation owners such as David Pugh. However, the slaves refused to work and assaulted both the overseer and Mr. Pugh, injuring them severely, as well as a man who came to their defense. Weitzel also reported a similar "outbreak" at another plantation on the Terre Bonne Road. He told Ben Butler that "the entire community thereabout are in hourly expectation and terror of a general [up]rising."[10]

Ben Butler did not share Weitzel's concern for protecting the disloyal Southern residents, nor their property, and he felt that the young general should be less concerned about protecting the wives and children of the enemy "from the consequences of their own rebellious wickedness."[11] Ben Butler considered the Southern population to have severed its ties with the Federal government and, therefore, could not rely on the government for protection. In Butler's opinion, the Southern population deserved their fate and could choose to either surrender or face an insurrection they'd brought on themselves by the evil institution of slavery.

"Perhaps, the more terror-stricken the inhabitants are that are left in your rear, the more safe will be your lines of communication," he concluded. As to the terrified women and children, Butler asked Weitzel rhetorically, "Is not the remedy to be found in the surrender of the neighbors, fathers, brothers, and sons of the terror-stricken women and children, who are now in arms against the government within twenty miles of you?" Like a trial lawyer appealing to a jury, Butler made his closing argument: "And, when that is done, and you have no longer to fear from these organized forces, and they have returned peaceably to their homes, you will be able to use the full power of your troops to insure your safety from the so-much-feared (by them, not by you) servile insurrection."[12]

Godfrey also expressed his concern about the treatment that black soldiers might receive if captured. His fear was born out in May 1863, when there was a small uprising in St. Mary Parish against local slave owners incited by a white "jayhawker." Frightened citizens formed a vigilante committee and with the help of thirty-five Confederate soldiers broke up the rebellion. They hanged fifty of the black men along with their white ringleader.[13] Then there were the more notorious atrocities at Fort Pillow, north of Memphis, where Confederate cavalrymen were accused in April 1864 of murdering black soldiers who had surrendered. A congressional investigation later concluded that the black troops had been mercilessly butchered by Southern soldiers.[14]

Enough was said on the topic. As Ben Butler recalled it years later, "With a bleeding heart lest Weitzel might still be so far misled as to disobey my orders, after reasoning with him upon his conduct, I wrote an order leaving him no option but to obey it—which he did."[15]

Godfrey was not convinced by General Butler's arguments, but as a loyal officer he reluctantly accepted the command. Black soldiers served him well for the duration of the war. With some irony, Butler wrote in his memoirs that "eventually, a major general, Weitzel would command the only all-black army corps in American military history."[16] He would march them into the streets of Richmond!

The Black Flag Raised by Jeff Davis

Godfrey Weitzel's concern over Southern reaction to the use of armed black soldiers was soon validated, in part, in an official proclamation by the Confederate president. All Negro slaves captured in arms were to be handed over to the state law officials, "to be dealt with according to the laws of said States." As for the white officers under command of Benjamin F. Butler, who had armed the colored troops, they would be deemed criminals, "whenever captured, reserved for execution."[17]

New General in Town

The time had finally come, and on December 16, 1862, General Nathaniel P. Banks assumed command of the Department of the Gulf, which placed General Weitzel's brigade under his supervision. As the new head of the department, Banks was charged with opening the Mississippi River. This would require him to capture or level key rebel fortifications along the river at Vicksburg and at Port Hudson. Lincoln regarded the opening of the Mississippi River as "the first and most important of all our military and naval operations," and informed Banks flatly, "It is hoped that you will not lose a moment in accomplishing it."[18] Capturing the two forts would give the Union domination over the river, splitting the Confederacy in two.

On December 17, news reached Camp Stevens of the arrival in New Orleans of General Nathaniel Banks, the new department commander, under orders to relieve General Butler. That same day a portion of Banks's force arrived at Baton Rouge. Ten days later, a portion of the Weitzel brigade received orders to break camp and meet up with Banks's troops in Baton Rouge. On Monday morning, December 29, Godfrey Weitzel's troops left Thibodeaux for a slow march through rain and deep mud for twenty miles, retracing their tracks back up Bayou Lafourche. After camping for the night, the march resumed to Donaldsonville, where troop transports ferried the men sixty miles up the Mississippi River to Baton Rouge.

Weitzel's brigade arrived at Baton Rouge on New Year's Eve and promptly made camp on the same battleground where John Breckenridge had been defeated in August. Camp was later moved to just inside a strong breastworks that was still under construction. There, the brigade resumed drills and awaited deployment under the new department commander, General Banks.

Butler's Farewell to New Orleans and Friends

The privately humiliated but publicly emboldened Ben Butler wrote a farewell address to the citizens of New Orleans, which was published on Christmas Eve, 1862. Despite all the friction generated by his strong-arm administration, he wrote, "I shall speak in no bitterness, because I am not conscious of a single animosity." He boasted that when he entered the city, he found its inhabitants conquered and disorderly, "incapable of taking care of yourselves. . . . I restored order, punished crime, opened commerce, brought provisions to your starving people, reformed your currency, and gave you quiet protection, such as you had not enjoyed for many years." How did the citizens of New Orleans respond to his magnanimous efforts? "My soldiers were subjected to obloquy, reproach, and insult," he said.[19]

Butler took the opportunity at his exit podium to give his views on slavery, realizing they would be published in the morning papers. Speaking to the citizens of Louisiana, he extolled: "There is but one thing that stands in the way . . . one thing that at this hour stands between you and your government—and that is slavery." Butler called it an institution "cursed of God," which had taken root in Louisiana. But with God's providence, it would be uprooted and quashed.[20]

Before leaving town, General Butler surprised some of his officers with a Christmas gift: their own likeness hand-painted on porcelain cups and saucers by a local New Orleans artist. The portraits included both Generals Shepley and Weitzel, a few other officers, and even Ben Butler's own wife, Sarah.[21] The gift was ironic, in that Butler was so hated in the South, porcelain chamber pots with Ben Butler's frowning image painted in the bottom were found in many Southern homes long after the war. Today, they are a collector's item and replicas are sold in New Orleans at the Confederate Museum.

Butler and Weitzel to Be Hanged If Captured

Jefferson Davis also had a Christmas gift for both Butler and Weitzel: *the black flag*—the death sentence, issued in a proclamation on December 23, 1862, from Richmond.

The Southern and European press had denounced Butler's Woman's Order as an affront to womanhood. British prime minister Palmerston condemned the order as "infamous," adding that "an Englishman must blush to think that such an act has been committed by one belonging to the Anglo-Saxon race."[22] In the Deep South, one Southern newspaper put a $10,000 price on Butler's head.[23]

The day before Ben Butler's Christmas Eve speech, Jefferson Davis issued General Order No. III expressing outrage over the hanging of a man who merely tore down the Union flag, the confiscation of sugar and other "property," and the infamous Woman's Order. Davis declared that General Benjamin F. Butler, his officers, and any other white officers commanding black troops be executed upon capture. The Confederate president branded Butler and his band of thugs as nothing more than outlaws who should be hanged. Davis grossly exaggerated the situation in New Orleans, writing from Richmond:

> The soldiers of the United States have been invited and encouraged by general orders to insult and outrage the wives, the mothers, and the sisters of our citizens. Helpless women have been torn from their homes and subjected to solitary confinement, some in fortresses and prisons and one especially on an island of barren sand under a tropical sun, have been fed with loathsome rations that had been condemned as unfit for soldiers, and have been exposed to the vilest insults.[24]

Davis declared Butler to be "a felon, deserving of capital punishment." His proclamation continued:

> I do order that he be no longer considered or treated simply as a public enemy of the Confederate States of America, but as an outlaw and common enemy of mankind, and that in the event of his capture the officer in command of the capturing force do cause him to be immediately executed by hanging.[25]

The mandate condemned Ben Butler's officers to death as well:

> That all commissioned officers in the command of said Benjamin F. Butler be declared not entitled to be considered as soldiers engaged in honorable warfare, but as robbers and criminals, deserving death; and that they and each of them be, whenever captured, reserved for execution.[26]

General Order No. III fanned the fears of armed ex-slaves roaming the South, as Godfrey Weitzel had warned. Davis wrote, "The African slaves have not only been excited to insurrection by every license and encouragement but numbers of them have actually been armed for a servile war—a war in its nature far exceeding in horrors the most merciless atrocities of the savages."[27]

The order was endorsed in May 1863 by a resolution passed by the Confederate Congress. While the proclamation named Ben Butler specifically, it clearly covered Butler's chief protégé, the twenty-seven-year-old brigadier general from Cincinnati. Godfrey had been reluctant to take command of colored troops in November, but agreed after being pressured by Butler. Now, as the commissioned officer in charge of two regiments of colored troops, Godfrey Weitzel would be hanged if captured.

Lincoln Promises to Reinstate Butler

On his return to Washington, Ben Butler learned that the order to remove him from New Orleans was based on a misunderstanding by Secretary Edwin Stanton about Butler's views on the Emancipation Proclamation, which had been issued by Lincoln on September 22, 1862, and was set to go into effect on January 1. Stanton met with Massachusetts senator Charles Sumner on the evening of January 7, 1863, to discuss Butler's situation. Sumner, a fellow abolitionist and friend of Butler's, demanded an explanation.

After hearing about Butler's abolitionist stance and his efforts to raise black troops, Stanton reportedly told Sumner that if he had known Butler's "real position" with regard to the proclamation, "he would have cut off his right hand" before he would have allowed anyone to take Butler's place in New Orleans.[28] Edwin Stanton wanted a commander in New Orleans to whom the president's proclamation that all slaves would be permanently freed in all areas of the Confederacy "would be a living letter." Stanton figured that a Republican would be more apt to embrace Lincoln's views, "rather than an old Democrat," such as the forty-four-year-old Butler. Ben Butler had initially been a Lincoln supporter but, ironically, backed Jefferson Davis of Mississippi as a candidate at the 1860 Democratic Convention.

After seeing Butler's passionate Christmas Eve farewell address and learning of his strong antislavery stance, President Lincoln promised to return Butler to New Orleans very soon. Lincoln added that he wished to keep Butler in the public service for all that he had done for the nation thus far in the war.

The media played up Butler's removal from the Department of the Gulf as a demotion, with humiliating cartoons and articles. To clear his name, during their private meeting at the Executive Mansion, Butler asked the president quite candidly why he had been replaced. "The country does not know why I was recalled from New Orleans," he told Lincoln. "That leaves me open to the suspicion that it had been done because of the truth of some infamous charges that the Rebels and Copperheads have made against me." Abraham Lincoln reassured Butler that he had not been demoted. "I have seen no reason to change my opinion of you, which, from the beginning, has been of the highest character, as you know," Lincoln replied. The president did not intend to ask for Butler's resignation. Instead, he told the stocky balding general, "I want to give you a command quite

FIGURE II.I. "Uncle Abe Welcomes Ben Butler." (From *Harper's Weekly*, January 17, 1863.)
UNCLE ABE: "Hello! Ben, is that you? Glad to see you!"
BUTLER: "Yes, Uncle Abe. Got through with that New Orleans job. Cleaned them out and scrubbed them up! Any more scrubbing to give out?"

equal in extent and importance to the one which you won for yourself at New Orleans. In it you can do great good to the country."[29] Ben Butler was relieved.

Lincoln rolled out some maps that showed the slave population by territories and districts. Pointing to the region along the Mississippi River, someone had shaded various areas where slavery was most prevalent. Looking up from the maps, the president said, "The question of abolition of slavery is now settled. I want you to go down on the Mississippi River, take command there, and enlist, arm, and organize as many negro troops as can be had."[30] Butler had been successful in recruiting and organizing colored troops in New Orleans. Lincoln wanted him to do more of it!

The president played to Butler's famous ego and flattered him, saying, "I know of no one who can do this as well as yourself. From our correspondence, I see that you thoroughly believe in negro troops." Lincoln told Butler that he could name any officers he wanted to accompany him and assured him, "I will endorse them by appointments."[31] Butler already had one young general in mind.

CHAPTER 12

Destroying the *J. A. Cotton*

The young brigadier was no longer under the command of "Beast" Butler. Would this relieve him of the death sentence imposed by Jeff Davis? Godfrey Weitzel did not have time to ponder such things since he had a new nemesis to battle—a dreaded rebel gunboat, the *J. A. Cotton.*

Weitzel's Brigade Reassigned to Bayou Teche

Due to Union losses in December, General Banks decided that he needed to re-inforce the defenses below New Orleans and on Ship Island.[1] He ordered that the Second Regiment of Native Guards be redeployed to the defenses of Mississippi Sound. As a result, on January 9, General Weitzel relieved that regiment from his command and ordered it to New Orleans, with the balance of his brigade sent back to Thibodeaux. After just two days of rest there, Godfrey received orders for a new expedition. He was to clear the area of harassment by the Confederate gun-boat *J. A. Cotton*, which was located in Bayou Teche. Before embarking on this new expedition, however, Godfrey Weitzel was relieved of the command of his colored troops. The action had nothing at all to do with Jefferson Davis's death sentence. In truth, Nathaniel Banks disapproved of the use of black soldiers, and when he took over for Ben Butler, he quickly weeded out the colored regiments, including any black officers, under the claim of incompetence.[2]

Weitzel Joins the Nineteenth Army Corps

Major General Nathaniel P. Banks was now fully in control of the Department of the Gulf, and he began to pick his leaders for the various divisions. On January 12, 1863, Banks selected the successful Brigadier General Godfrey Weitzel to com-mand the Second Brigade, First Division of the Nineteenth Army Corps, a position Weitzel would hold until mid-May. Before Banks could send troops northward to help Grant seal off the upper portions of the Mississippi, he first had to capture or scatter the Confederate units in the lower regions of the Teche country.

Impressed with how Godfrey Weitzel had driven Alfred Mouton out of the Lafourche region the previous October, General Banks chose Godfrey once again to flush out Louisiana rebels. The plan was for Weitzel's brigade to make a drive to the west and rid the region of not only Mouton, but the impressive armored gunboat *J. A. Cotton* as well. At once, the young engineer-general began to plan his expedition into the Teche District. Godfrey recommended that available funds be used to build a few light-draft gunboats that could support his troops in Berwick Bay.

For his new mission, Godfrey Weitzel brought up about forty-five hundred men, including seven infantry regiments, four artillery batteries, and two cavalry companies who settled back in at the familiar Camp Stevens outside Thibodeaux.³ Some twenty-two miles to the west was Brashear City, a strategic spot that controlled the mouth of the Atchafalaya River and, therefore, the entrance to Bayou Teche to the west and all points south. Godfrey knew that Berwick Bay was a key logistical and strategic waterway, of highest importance to the rebels. If the Confederates gained possession of the bay and its waterways, they could make frequent raids by bayous and streams that the land forces could not prevent. Weitzel felt that only by holding the waterways in and around Berwick Bay could the Federals effectively disrupt rebel lines of communication from Port Hudson westward. In Godfrey's mind, a naval force in Berwick Bay, in cooperation with a suitable land force, was the only and the proper way to maintain control of this area.⁴

General Weitzel received reliable intelligence reports that the enemy was planning an attack on his forces at Berwick Bay. He also learned that the rebels were increasing the firepower of the already impenetrable gunboat *J. A. Cotton*, both in caliber and in the number of guns. The *Cotton* was a giant Mississippi steamer partially clad in iron, 185 feet in length and nearly 35 feet wide, with seven big guns mounted on her deck.⁵ The *Cotton* had become the nemesis of Union forces operating in the Bayou Teche region, and it had to be destroyed. Godfrey Weitzel decided to launch a decisive and preemptive attack instead of waiting for the Confederates to advance.

General Weitzel called for naval commander Lieutenant Thomas Buchanan to join him immediately. Together they would make a run up the Bayou Teche to capture or destroy the *Cotton*.⁶ Their first attempt was delayed, however, when the weather turned violent and a "strong northwester" prevented the light boats from making progress. The rebels sneaked across the bay and into Bayou Teche under protection of the *Cotton*, which then anchored in the bayou.⁷ Weitzel's brigade was not large enough to secure lines of communication with General Banks in New Orleans. Therefore, he could not get permission to cross Berwick Bay. As a result, the by-the-book officer had his four gunboats patrolling the bay, keeping it and adjacent waters clear of any more rebel crafts.

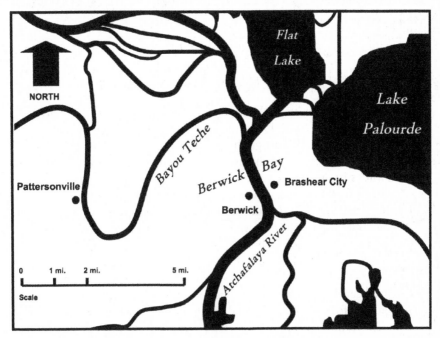

FIGURE 12.1. Map of Berwick Bay Area and Bayou Teche.

When proper orders arrived, in the wee hours of Tuesday morning, January 13, General Weitzel moved his artillery and cavalry west, across Berwick Bay and upriver to Bayou Teche, using Buchanan's gunboats as transports. The process began at 3:00 a.m. and ended seven and one-half hours later. Weitzel boarded a gunboat at 11:00 a.m. and made the crossing from Brashear City. Once across, an orderly had a fresh horse waiting for the general, which took Godfrey west along the bayou with his cavalry, the artillery and troops marching on the west bank. General Weitzel had two objectives: first, remove the obstructions in the waterway that protected the *Cotton*; and second, destroy the rebel gunboat.

Battling the *J. A. Cotton*

Weitzel's brigade formed in line of battle about 3:00 p.m. at Pattersonville (today, Patterson) and then marched two more miles north up the bayou, protected by the gunboats *Diana*, *Kinsman*, *Estrella*, and *Calhoun*. General Weitzel directed the Navy's Lieutenant Buchanan to make a reconnaissance up Bayou Teche to scout the rebel position and report back on the enemy's strength. Upon Buchanan's return, Weitzel moved his whole force to an area called Lynch's Point, about twelve miles below the parish seat city of Franklin. There, his entire brigade set up camp for the night on a plantation within sight of the *Cotton*.[8] The four Union gunboats dropped anchor in the bayou between the encampment and the *Cotton*, separated by a formidable obstruction that the Confederates had placed in the water. Both sides prepared for the battle that would surely take place the next day.

The following morning of Wednesday, January 14, was cold and rainy, with a strong wind blowing from the southeast. The march was resumed about 8:00 a.m., with Yankee troops and gunboats advancing on the enemy's position. The Union boats reached the obstruction that protected the *Cotton* at a place called Corney's Bridge, named after the local plantation owner. The rebels had destroyed Mr. Corney's bridge, leaving nothing but some remnants of the old bridge that stuck up three to four feet above the water. Against the rubble the rebels had sunk an old steamer, which they had first filled with bricks and then topped with even more rubbish.[9] The blockage made it impossible for the *Cotton* to come downriver or for the Union to advance upriver beyond the old bridge.

Weitzel sent the Eighth Vermont Regiment up the east bank of Bayou Teche to clear out Confederate rifle pits and their supporting cavalry. The Vermont boys proved their worth, successfully taking forty-one prisoners, including one officer. As the rest of the Union forces, including the Seventy-Fifth New York Regiment and cavalry, advanced on the west bank to attack the *Cotton*, the bayou came alive with activity. General Weitzel selected sixty men from the Eighth Vermont to pick the gunners off the deck of the *Cotton*, which they did effectively, in addition to driving back a small Confederate field battery.[10]

Battle lines were formed and the four Union gunboats began firing on the *Cotton* as Weitzel's land forces ran up both banks of Bayou Teche. Godfrey Weitzel was determined to rid the region not only of the *Cotton*, but of as many of Mouton's troops as possible.[11]

Lieutenant James E. Whiteside of the Seventy-Fifth New York led his sixty Volunteers up the west bank opposite the *Cotton* and boldly ordered the rebels to surrender and to "haul down her flag." The Confederates responded defiantly by immediately shooting Whiteside, who ordered his men to "keep on and take the ship" before he died there on the bank. The sharpshooters from New York were inspired at the bravery of their lieutenant and unleashed a torrent of lead upon the *Cotton* with deadly accuracy, taking out everyone in sight and completely silencing the armored gunboat.[12]

Even the pilot of the *Cotton* had to abandon his post under the hot fire of the Yankee sharpshooters.[13] Captain Fuller, the commander of the *Cotton*, remained at his post. He later complimented the brave bluecoats in his report of the engagement: "The Yankees fought like tigers," he said, "and exhibited feats of great daring and bravery."[14]

Firing began in earnest at 9:00 a.m., with gunboats *Kinsman* and *Estrella* engaging the *Cotton* and Union artillery attacking at the same time. As the convoy neared the obstructions in the river, rebel sharpshooters fired from rifle pits on the northern bank and the *Cotton* finally opened fire as well. Suddenly there was a tremendous explosion under the gunboat *Kinsman*, and the stern of the boat rose violently into the air. An enemy torpedo had exploded under the vessel, damaging her rudder.

One of General Weitzel's aides galloped up quickly to tell the *Kinsman*'s crew of another torpedo that was planted immediately ahead, the tip coming from a "contraband" who had escaped from the *Cotton*.[15] The *Kinsman* cautiously pulled back down the bayou, after warning both the *Estrella* and the *Calhoun* of the mines.

Death of Commander Buchanan

Godfrey Weitzel was characterized by "an almost brutal honesty."[16] Writing of the day's events, he claimed that the Navy's Lieutenant Commander Buchanan made a fatal mistake by advancing too soon, "the only fault of a very brave and honorable man."[17] Buchanan tried to force his way over the rebel obstructions to attack the *Cotton*. It was a bold move to try to run over the sunken hulls, but a fatal mistake for Buchanan. When the *Calhoun*'s captain disobeyed Buchanan's orders to proceed to the obstructions, Buchanan barked out, "Then move out of the way and I will go!" as he took the helm.[18]

The Confederates now concentrated most of their fire on Buchanan's advancing gunboat, and as one Union man fell under fire, another promptly took his place at the *Calhoun*'s guns.[19] A shot rang out and struck Buchanan in the right side of his head, immediately below the temple, passing out the opposite side.[20] "*Oh, God!*" he exclaimed as his spyglass went over his shoulder, and he collapsed. During the confusion, the *Calhoun* ran aground with its bow on the same shore as the rifle pits. It was now about 10:00 a.m., and the Confederate sharpshooters poured forth "a most murderous volley" from behind their concealed rifle pits on the helpless Calhoun. Two more sailors on board were killed and six wounded in the ensuing slaughter. The gunboat *Cotton* then opened up its guns to attack the Union batteries, and the river fight became severe and hot.[21]

With Buchanan dead and his gunboat run aground, the crew and vessel were in imminent danger of capture. Weitzel ordered the Eighth Vermont Regiment forward, and the men promptly rushed up the bank on the double-quick to the rescue of the *Calhoun*'s trapped crew. The New Englanders attacked the rebels in the rear of their rifle pits. Skirmishers were thrown out on the right flank and sixty more men advanced on the left.

The coordinated charge was handled with such speed that the entire regiment swept into and over the enemy rifle pits, killing seven Confederates, wounding twenty-seven others, and capturing fifty-seven prisoners. The *Calhoun* was saved from destruction, and its crew members were able to free her from the shore by using the current to sweep the bullet-riddled boat around until it floated free.[22]

The other Union gunboats and various regiments continued to pour their fire onto the *Cotton*. At this point, General Weitzel ordered his artillery to open up on the broadside of the *Cotton*. "For hours the roar of artillery was almost incessant, and the high wind which had been prevailing seemed frightened into silence," wrote one participant.[23] Firing was kept up until dark and did extensive damage to the *Cotton*.

Confederate captain Fuller of the *Cotton* was shot through both arms, yet is reported to have "stood like granite at his post," bleeding from his wounds.[24] The Union assault was too much, however, and with the loss of their wounded captain the Confederates determined to destroy their massive gunboat to prevent her from falling into Union hands. At about 11:00 p.m., fire was set to the *Cotton*, which then drifted down the Teche, "a pillar of fire," and sank.[25]

Although General Weitzel had something to celebrate in watching the *Cotton* burn and sink, he later learned that the Confederates had saved the vessel's cannons, which became part of the artillery guarding Fort Bisland. The mission was largely a Union success, other than the new river obstruction. Weitzel's men captured more than fifty Confederate prisoners and several horses, with only the loss of five Union troops and two brave officers—the Navy's Lieutenant Commander Thomas Buchanan, and the Army's Lieutenant James Whiteside—with another twenty-seven wounded. The Confederates suffered the loss of three of their officers and another thirteen privates killed on land and on water, with an unknown number wounded (including the *Cotton*'s Captain Fuller), plus the sinking of the *J. A. Cotton*.[26]

Back to Berwick Bay

With the *Cotton* silenced and her supporting rebel force largely defeated or taken prisoner, General Weitzel's column retreated slowly down the river the next morning under cover of Union gunboats. The troops reached Franklin, Louisiana, by land and then boarded transports back to Berwick Bay.[27] According to a Southern newspaper report, the Union troops destroyed three houses in their retreat to Berwick Bay, leaving "the smoldering ruins which mark their backward march . . . cruel remembrances of their fanatical hate behind them."[28]

The gunboat flotilla arrived at Berwick Bay at 5:00 p.m. that day, having succeeded in their mission. Weitzel reported that his men "behaved magnificently," clearing Bayou Teche and opening up the river. The regiments floated back into Berwick Bay, which they safely crossed before midnight. Weary soldiers then marched more than twenty miles east to Camp Stevens at Thibodeaux.[29] Lieutenant Buchanan's funeral was held on January 16 on the ferry wharf at the foot of Canal Street in New Orleans. General Weitzel was there to honor the gallant Buchanan.

Weitzel Promoted for Success on the Teche

General Nathaniel Banks was so impressed with Weitzel's swift success on the Teche that on January 16 he wrote to Major General Henry W. Halleck, general-in-chief, urging Weitzel's promotion. Banks bragged, "That gallant and energetic officer is again entitled to the thanks of the general commanding this department for the skillful manner in which he has performed the task confided to him."[30] Banks's recommendation was accepted in Washington, and Godfrey Weitzel was promoted to a full captain and brigadier general of Volunteers on March 3, 1863.[31]

Back at Camp Stevens, Weitzel's Second Brigade, First Division of the Nineteenth Corps, went to work constructing two major fortifications, one called Fort Brashear and the other Fort Buchanan, named after the recently fallen naval officer. The brigade remained there until January 26, when orders were received to pack up and move into camp a mile outside Baton Rouge, near the Port Hudson road.[32]

Ben Butler Returns to New Orleans

Although Nathaniel Banks was in command in Louisiana, movement was afoot in Washington to reinstate Ben Butler. The egotistical Butler let it be known that he did not want to return to New Orleans in a *junior* role to General Banks. He was not willing to return unless he was restored to the command of the Department of the Gulf. Lincoln wrote to Secretary Stanton on January 23 directing that General Butler be sent to New Orleans at once. "He should start by the 1st of February, and should take some force with him," the president wrote.[33]

Lincoln was concerned about wounding General Banks's feelings, since he had been given command only in November, and it would surely be an embarrassment to be relieved of command so soon. Banks had originally wanted to go to Texas, not Louisiana, and so Lincoln cleverly ordered Stanton to make arrangements to send Banks there with a substantial force before Butler arrived in New Orleans. On January 28, President Lincoln sent a telegram to Butler with a short message: "Please come here immediately. Telegraph me about what time you will arrive."[34] Lincoln wanted to personally deliver the good news to Butler about his reassignment to the Gulf. He urged Stanton to move rapidly upon Butler's appointment, saying, "I think we cannot longer dispense with General Butler's services."[35]

Fighting in the Atchafalaya River Basin

From its intersection with the Lower Atchafalaya River at Berwick Bay, near what is today called Morgan City, Bayou Teche extends almost seventy winding miles north and west to the town of Port Barre in St. Landry Parish, where it intersects Bayou Courtableau. The twisting bayou got its name "Teche" from a Chitimacha Indian word meaning "snake." The region from Brashear City to Opelousas is in the Atchafalaya River Basin, an area bordered on both sides by wide expanses of swamp.

The Yankee boys from New England were not accustomed to the sweltering Louisiana weather, nor to the wildlife. The murky waters of the swamps and bayous were lurking not only with Mouton's two-legged dangers, but others with four and eight legs. Huge golden silk spiders, called "banana" spiders due to their large yellow bodies, spun invisible webs between the cypress trees in the forests and swamps, making a sticky trap for the unwary Union soldier. Though the spider's bite was not fatal, it was painful. The more prevalent and hazardous predators lurking on the banks and in the muddy waters of the swamps and bayous were alligators, whose bellowing kept the troops awake and jittery all night long.[36]

On March 9, 1863, General Nathaniel Banks gave orders for his men to break camp and begin their march for an enemy fort at Port Hudson.[37] There, a major Navy-Army assault was being planned under Admiral Farragut, who wanted to repeat his success at New Orleans by running past impressive rebel batteries at a bend in the Mississippi River while Banks attacked the fort from the landside. Farragut's run was only a partial success on the night of March 14. General Banks was unable to assault the rebel fort due to insufficient manpower. Therefore, Banks waited for a second opportunity while more troops gathered at Baton Rouge.

From mid- to late March, General Weitzel's brigade marched and camped in the most miserable of conditions, wading through mud mile after mile, their boots filled with water and caked earth, or marching on dusty backroads to chase down rebels still embedded in the lower Teche. The brigade marched from Brashear to Baton Rouge, then steamed back to the familiar port of Donaldsonville on troop transports.

On Tuesday, March 31, General Weitzel moved his men south in the early morning mist along the right bank of Bayou Lafourche, the same path they had taken just five months ago, passing familiar plantations and cane fields.

Encountering little resistance, Weitzel's brigade was sent back to Bayou Teche to attack Fort Bisland, a rebel earthworks about three-fourths of a mile long with an impassable swamp on its right and armored gunboats in the bayou on its left.[38] Familiar foes, Confederate generals Alfred Mouton and Dick Taylor, were there and ready for the invasion.

Battle of Fort Bisland

On April 13, Godfrey Weitzel faced off against Mouton at the confluence of the Teche and the Atchafalaya. (See Fig. 12.1). Weitzel's brigade was ordered to push forward in order to draw the enemy's fire and "amuse him." In a single long line, stretching from the woods on the left well toward the river on the right, Weitzel's bluecoats moved slowly toward Fort Bisland. It was dangerous and rigorous work advancing through the eight- to nine-foot-high rows of sugarcane that had been left unharvested as a result of the war. As soldiers emerged from the cane stalks in broken ranks, stragglers began to come up from the rear and re-form the lines. General Weitzel straightened up in his stirrups and peered through his spyglass across a field. One-third of a mile straight ahead he could see the enemy's long embankment, Fort Bisland. Between Weitzel's position and the fort lay a long, narrow cane field, bounded by forests rising out of swamps. To the right, Godfrey saw two half-demolished brick sugarhouses on a local plantation. Approaching the fortified position was made difficult by a battery of cannons in the swampy wood to the right, which would annihilate an attacking column. On the left, the rebels were protected by armored gunboats in Bayou Teche, including a captured Union gunboat, the *Diana*. "The scene was one of perfect quietness and silence and desertion," recalled one eyewitness.[39] All that was about to change.

"*Bang! Bang! Bang!*" roared an unseen enemy battery. "*Jiz! Jiz! Jiz!*" screeched the stream of lead balls over the heads of General Weitzel and his men. Instinctively, the Union soldiers returned fire with rifles and muskets. For twenty minutes or more the initial volley continued, like a rowdy Fourth of July. The *Diana*, now under command of Confederate captain Raphael Semmes, concentrated its Parrott guns toward the center of Weitzel's advancing troops for most effect.[40]

Taking in the scene from his position in the rear, General Weitzel gave the order to fall back and regroup as a frontal assault did not seem wise. Hearing the command, the regiment turned about-face and started rushing to the rear in confusion and panic away from Fort Bisland's guns. Officers tried to restore order, one rushing through the ranks with his sword drawn, ordering and threatening until he brought his own company from a double-quick pace down to an ordinary marching step. Seeing his lead, every other officer did the same and regained control of the controversial Twelfth Connecticut as they marched to the rear. Once assembled, Weitzel gave the order to bivouac for the night as he and his officers planned the next day's assault.[41]

Tuesday, April 14, began with a barrage from the heavy guns of Captain Semmes's boats in Bayou Teche. Union batteries of the Twenty-First Indiana returned fire, sending their deadly shells into the rebels' positions on land and into the twisting bayou. By 10:00 a.m., the sun had burned off the morning haze, but puffs of smoke from the exchanges of cannon fire gave a hazy filter to the open space between the two armies. Weitzel formed his brigade once again into one long line, three men deep, and began a second march slowly through the sugar-cane fields toward Mouton's fort. The flagbearers showed their regimental colors, again giving the rebels something to aim at.

As the Union blue emerged from the light green of the cane forest, Confederate batteries opened up lively. The first cannon shot arched through the sky and struck the ground some sixty to eighty feet in front of a regimental color guard. It threw up the plowed soil of the field in a small cloud of brown dirt, bounced up, and whizzed over the heads of the New England boys, landing one hundred feet behind them, where it went bounding off to the rear. A Union officer remarked to his men with an encouraging smile, "That's bad for the fellows behind us." The rebel artillerymen adjusted their aim and their next shot struck within thirty feet of the Union line, bounced up, and whistled to the rear. Every man on the front line had the same thought, *You'll hit us next time!* But the Yankees were about to catch a break.[42]

Right on cue, one of Weitzel's batteries entered the game with a roar of explosions and screeching shells that must have startled the Confederates, as their next shot sailed well over the regimental colors, hitting the ground far behind the regiment. The rebel gunners never recovered their dangerously accurate range.[43] The hot artillery exchange went on all day until dusk, with cannons dueling across the open field. Weitzel's troops suffered very few losses in the day's battle.

After a full day of battle, an order was given about 5:00 p.m. for the infantry to pull back out of the range of fire. The New Englanders slowly retreated into the cane field, having gained no advantage all day. Night brought the stinging bites of large mosquitoes, plus intermittent rain, which prevented the soldiers from getting much sleep on the wet ground.

Realizing he was badly outnumbered, General Dick Taylor ordered General Mouton to abandon Fort Bisland, withdraw toward New Iberia, and join the main body of the rebel army north of Franklin. Though the Confederates had fought fiercely, Taylor knew they could not stop the overwhelming Union forces General Banks had assembled. He also knew that General Cuvier Grover's division had landed in his rear, cutting off his retreat. Therefore, after dark, Mouton quietly began evacuating supplies, men, and weapons from the fort, completely giving Weitzel the slip.[44]

About 2:00 a.m., Union pickets detected the rumbling of Confederate cannons being hitched up and moved. Several hours later, a young colonel in charge of the pickets came to General Weitzel and reported the news: "I heard their artillery [rolling] off about two o'clock," the colonel reported. Weitzel looked at his pocket watch in shock. "Good God, sir! Why didn't you inform me of it immediately?" The colonel replied, "Why, General, I thought you wanted them to clear out . . . and I didn't like to disturb you after such a hard day's work."[45]

By now Mouton had five to six hours head start. Weitzel dismissed the messenger and the young general turned his attention to the change in plans. Weitzel had intended a frontal assault while Grover blocked the rear, eventually squeezing Mouton in the middle. Now, with Mouton and Taylor on the move, it was essential to break camp and not allow any more distance between the two armies.

General Weitzel called his officers together and orders were rushed among the various regiments to pack up and be ready to march. There would be no time for breakfast. Texans on horseback could travel faster than Yankees on foot, so each minute of delay increased the distance. With Fort Bisland evacuated, Union forces quickly moved over its walls and occupied it.[46]

Another Month of Chasing Mouton

"Sling blankets and shoulder arms was the order now, and we set off on our long chase to Alexandria," recalled one officer.[47] Weitzel's men marched furiously that hot April day and made an impressive twenty-four miles before nightfall.

The humid air of the Louisiana bayous was unbearable to many of the Yankees wearing thick wool uniforms. Worse yet were swarms of mosquitoes that continued to feast on sweaty skin. Daily marching on dusty roads with blistered feet became torture for the fatigued men, who grimaced at each step. "Louisiana mud, snakes, mosquitoes, lice—they soon ceased to have any terrors for us," one officer said, as the men became hardened to life in the swampy marshlands of the Deep South.[48]

Forced marching continued until April 17, when Godfrey Weitzel finally caught up with the elusive Mouton. The two armies were so close that a "great distant dust" could be seen in the sky ahead, a sure sign of a retreating army of cavalry, foot soldiers, wagons, cannons, and horses on dirt roads, "kicking up a storm" in their retreat. Faces became caked, and even eyelashes and hair were discolored.

Although the Federal infantrymen were dirty, thirsty, and exhausted, the rebels were equally worn out. Confederate stragglers waved their caps and handkerchiefs as a sign of surrender. "We were marching the Louisiana infantry to tatters," an officer said. The prisoners reported that if they had not been under the threat of death at the hands of their own officers, Mouton's whole force would have gone to pieces under the exhaustion of the retreat. This was encouraging news to General Weitzel. If Mouton's men were at their physical and moral low, perhaps they could be captured, if not defeated. The Union bluecoats picked up the pace "with renewed energy."[49]

CHAPTER 13

Battle of Port Hudson

Aware of Ben Butler's prior efforts to seize sugar and cotton, Alfred Mouton was determined that none of the valuable Louisiana crops should fall into enemy hands. As Mouton passed through cotton plantations in retreat, his men ignited the fluffy white plant, and the smoke of burning cotton created a haze in the sky. At night, the path of destruction was even more visible as the glow of burning cotton lit the horizon.

On April 20, the Nineteenth Corps reached the town of Opelousas, the third-oldest city in Louisiana and Mouton's hometown. The marching ceased for just a few days and General Banks allowed his Nineteenth Corps to get some much-needed rest. A new mission awaited Weitzel's brigade, one that did not involve extensive marching. To the contrary, Port Hudson would be a waiting game and the longest siege of the entire Civil War.

Grant Orders the Nineteenth Corps to Port Hudson

On April 23, General Grant wrote to General Nathaniel Banks advising that he could spare twenty thousand men for the assault on Port Hudson. Assuming that Port Hudson would fall before Vicksburg, Grant ordered that Banks send all the troops he could spare to Vicksburg after the reduction of Port Hudson.[1] The slippery Alfred Mouton would have to wait for another day.

Port Hudson was about forty-five miles east of Opelousas, as the crow flies, and would take several days' marching to reach. General Banks disbanded his headquarters at Opelousas on May 5 and ordered his Nineteenth Army Corps to march toward Alexandria, a three-day march that covered an impressive distance of nearly one hundred miles. The blistered feet had barely hardened to calluses when General Weitzel told his men to break camp. Banks instructed Weitzel to push as rapidly as possible to Alexandria.[2] On May 8, the weary men strapped on heavy loads and at 5:00 p.m. began once again to march some sixteen miles in the dark until they finally bivouacked at 3:00 a.m. Pickets guarded the camp while exhausted regiments caught some sleep.

At sunrise on Saturday, May 9, drums beat the signal to fall in, and General Weitzel's sleepy brigade set off on another twenty-seven-mile march until nightfall. The following morning, having bivouacked by the side of a flowing stream, the men bathed and rested until orders came to resume the march, this time making another twenty-four miles by 3:00 p.m.[3] General Banks soon joined the column and was heard to say, "We must reach Alexandria tonight!" As the order, "Fall in!" was barked, the soldiers' brief rest was over, and for the next ten miles they struggled to keep pace. Unlike the way most generals were greeted, no soldier cheered when Nathaniel Banks rode by. Staggering drummers beat out a rhythm for the exhausted regiments while officers tried to keep spirits up. One lieutenant colonel from New York ran footraces against a private in his big boots just to get his soldiers to laugh at the unusual skit.

At last the weary Weitzel brigade "reeled, crawled, and almost rolled into Alexandria."[4] The men had marched a grueling thirty-four miles in one day, and eighty-seven miles in the past seventy-six hours. The soldiers bivouacked quickly, many going to sleep without a meal, others going on nighttime foraging missions to find local chickens, which were devoured with gusto back at camp.

Once at Alexandria, on the south bank of the Red River, General Banks allowed the troops to rest again for several days as leg muscles regained strength and feet healed. Later that week, General Banks moved a portion of his troops out of Alexandria and toward Port Hudson, as Grant had ordered. The lucky ones rode on river transports, while the rest made a difficult march that crisscrossed the Atchafalaya and Mississippi Rivers. Generals Weitzel and William Dwight were directed to hold their respective brigades in Alexandria until May 17 and then follow to Port Hudson.

The Plan Was Obvious to Both Sides

To take command of the lower portion of the Mississippi River, the Federals had to capture the strategic positions of Vicksburg, Mississippi, and Port Hudson, Louisiana. Jefferson Davis fully understood this. In a speech given at Jackson, Mississippi, on the day after Christmas 1862, two days after delivering his "death sentence" to Ben Butler and his officers, Davis exposed the Union's strategy. "Vicksburg and Port Hudson are the real points of attack," he predicted. "Every effort will be made to capture those places with the object of forcing the navigation of the Mississippi, of cutting off our communications with the Trans-Mississippi Department, and of severing the western from the eastern portion of the Confederacy." He implored the loyal men of the South to "assist in preserving the Mississippi River, that great artery of the country!" Only by controlling this key waterway could he perpetuate the Confederacy, he told the crowd, "and the success of the cause."[5]

Davis was absolutely right about the Union's intentions. The Federals had finalized their plans to attack the fort at Port Hudson in mid-November of 1862.

It would be no easy task, however, and would end up the longest siege ever for the United States military, a forty-eight-day ordeal. Godfrey Weitzel was, once again, at the right place at the right time to mark his place in history.

Port Hudson and Its Surroundings

About 115 miles south of Vicksburg, the Mississippi River used to take an acute 90-degree turn as it snaked its way south to Baton Rouge another fifteen miles below. The swift current at this bend cut a deep channel in the earth—nearly a mile long around the sharp bend, with bluffs seventy feet high. On the plateau above that, the Confederates commanded a key strategic position and built a semicircular fort some two miles in diameter at Port Hudson. The fort was a long earthwork formed in a zigzag, interwoven with woods and ravines. Rough terrain consisting of long stretches of broken ground, with hills, woods, natural gullies, and ravines, made access difficult from the landside. The likely approaches to the fort were blocked by natural obstacles that deterred assaulting Union columns. In between these creeks and trenches, a continuous line of parapets with an abatis of felled trees encircled the fort.

Today, the area around Port Hudson is populated with oil refineries and paper mills. The air is tainted with a pungent smell of petroleum from the large BP Amoco plant, the smell of money to locals. Trucks hauling loads of freshly cut trees populate Highway 61 and the roadways around the former Confederate fortress on their way to the Georgia-Pacific pulp and paper mill nearby. Just behind the Port Hudson National Cemetery, huge stacks of logs looking like oversized breastworks are sprayed with water to keep them moist in the hot sun. Although the river has since changed course, in 1863 Port Hudson sat on the summit of a seven-story cliff on the east bank of the mighty river. From its high place commanding the bend below, the Confederate Army positioned almost twenty huge Columbiads and many more smaller cannons in a continuous line. With this impressive mass of iron weaponry, the rebel artillery could rain shot and shell onto the decks of any Union vessel foolish enough to attempt to pass upstream.

The Mississippi River was very swift and narrow here, shallow on the side opposite the fort, but very deep on the east side, where the village and fortifications stood.[6] Due to the bend in the Mississippi here, any ship would necessarily have to reduce its speed, making it an easy target for cannons perched high above. This made Port Hudson the perfect location for either side to control river traffic.

Off to Port Hudson

From mid-March to mid-May, it was rumored that the enemy strength inside the fort was reduced to no more than 4,000 troops. Deserters picked up by the

Union Navy reported that Port Hudson's garrison was perhaps as small as even 2,500 to 3,000. With this information, Banks immediately recalled all of his generals and their divisions to Port Hudson to make another attempt to seize the fort or to engage in a siege that would starve out the small garrison inside.

At 2:00 a.m. on May 25, the Weitzel brigade commenced a brisk five-mile march south along the riverbank. The troop movement was not begun a moment too soon, for while en route, Weitzel received word to "hurry forward with all speed," as it was rumored that the Confederate garrison at Port Hudson might attempt to evacuate the place and escape. Godfrey had experienced this at Fort Bisland when Mouton slipped away, and he did not want to see a repeat. General Weitzel ordered his exhausted men to march on the double-quick, and they soon went into position in line of battle on the right wing, near Foster's Creek.[7]

Always the engineer, General Weitzel mounted up about 6:00 a.m. and rode with one of his aides to the front to do some reconnaissance.[8] On his return that morning, the Nineteenth Army Corps' artillery began shelling Port Hudson as preparations were made for an assault amid speculation that the rebels had significantly reduced their numbers. The reports proved to be woefully inaccurate, however, as the Confederate forces within the fortifications numbered from 7,000 to 8,000, with another 2,500 cavalry, plus a small force on the west side of the river commanding the enemy batteries, for a total force of between 10,000 and 11,000. General Banks had less than 13,000 men total at this point in time, and twenty of his regiments were "nine-months" men, whose terms began to expire in May. Banks did not have a sufficient force to capture Port Hudson, which he felt would require a force of three Yankees to every one rebel.

At 4:15 p.m. on May 25, Banks sent a message to General Weitzel directing him to assume command of the right wing at Port Hudson. This included the Third Division under Colonel Halbert Paine, as well as General William Dwight's brigade, Prince's cavalry, and Weitzel's own brigade. With Weitzel occupying the right, Generals Christopher Augur and Cuvier Grover set up positions in the center, and General Thomas W. Sherman took the left to balance out the landside attack.[9]

On the waterside, Admiral Farragut's flagship the *Hartford*, which had bravely run the gauntlet and passed Port Hudson on March 14, was now positioned above the rebel fort. A fleet of Union steamships and gunboats were stationed below and were prepared to engage the rebel batteries perched on the high cliffs. General Banks ordered the gunboats to begin firing at will, starting at midnight, to ensure that the enemy garrison would get no sleep.

On Tuesday, May 26, the rebels made an attack on Weitzel's exhausted brigade. The Yankees responded with an exchange of rifle and musket fire until the Confederates were driven back behind their defenses. The Nineteenth Corps then placed its artillery in position for the assault to come.

General Banks wrote confidently to Admiral David Farragut that day, "At daylight to-morrow (27th), unless something unexpected occurs, I shall order the works to be carried by assault. Please let the mortars destroy the enemy's rest at night." Farragut was delighted to oblige Banks's request, responding, "I shall continue to harass the enemy occasionally day and night. . . . It seems to me that you have only to make the assault and they must fall." That night, the battle plan was fully outlined to the commanders of brigades, regiments, and batteries. General Nathaniel Banks ordered the attack to open simultaneously all along the lines. "Port Hudson must be taken to-morrow," the generals were told. But this would not be.[10]

First Bloody Assault—May 27, 1863

General Banks hoped that a massive infantry attack on May 27 would break the enemy's line, despite the anticipated loss of lives. A victory was well worth it, in his mind.[11] Storming parties have suffered considerable loss throughout history, and this one would be remembered for the bloody slaughter of nearly two thousand Union men. There was no gain whatsoever, unfortunately, only death and casualties. It was a day that General Godfrey Weitzel would never forget.

The advance of Weitzel's brigade on the far right was to be supported by Colonel Edward Chapin's brigade on the left and General Thomas Sherman's division on the extreme left. Both Chapin and Sherman would be wounded as they led their troops, Sherman losing his leg and Chapin his life. The five regiments of General Cuvier Grover's division plus General Christopher Augur's men were to hold the center, separated from the others by thick woods. Colonel Nathan Dudley's brigade was on the right near Weitzel to provide a balanced attack. The plan was for all of the Union commanders to advance their skirmishers in a co-ordinated assault.[12]

After Farragut harassed the Confederates all night, the land attack began at dawn. At first light, the Union artillery opened up with more light shelling of the rebel fort, followed by heavier artillery.[13] By 6:00 a.m., there was furious cannon fire all along the entire front and the Confederates responded with return volleys. The earth trembled and everyone felt confident, especially General Banks, who signaled to the naval fleet at 6:15 a.m., "Port Hudson will be ours to-day."[14] However, even with the best-laid plans, timing is everything.

On cue, Farragut's fleet opened with its guns and rained shot and shell upon the enemy garrison from the river. In return, the Confederate land batteries pounded away, launching missiles down onto the approaching vessels. The barrage was so intense that "the ground fairly shook, while the air echoed with the noise of battle."[15]

The initial wave of the land assault had only a slim chance of success from the start. As Captain John De Forest of the Twelfth Connecticut said, "It is no easy job to march half a mile under a telling fire, and then climb ramparts defended by cool-headed [enemy] sharpshooters."[16] Weitzel's brigade lined up that morning in a long, narrow clearing, hemmed in between a forest to its rear and a thickly wooded incline in front.[17] The forest would provide Weitzel's men with limited cover to only about 250 yards from the fort. The field between the woods and the earthworks was in part the cleared land of a plantation, but it was obstructed by fences and hedges, recently felled timbers, and other natural obstructions.[18] This presented a challenge to the brigades, who had to traverse the field under continuous fire.

Each division commander had his own plan to cross a ditch that separated the Union position from the enemy fort. These plans ranged from cotton bags to wood planks.[19] Godfrey Weitzel's brigade moved into action in three lines from the right. As orders were given for men to fall into formation, Godfrey Weitzel studied the faces of his troops. Many were mere boys, and nearly all were relatively inexperienced in matters of war. No West Pointers here, they were all volunteers from New England who had left their jobs as farmers, grocers, carpenters, teachers, tailors, and even lawyers to heed Lincoln's call for help. They left behind their mothers, wives, and children, as well as their homes and opportunities. But the troops were anxious and ready.

The order of advance was first Dwight's brigade and then Weitzel's brigade, which was led by Vermont's Colonel Stephen Thomas. Dwight's brigade was led by the Ninety-First New York Infantry Regiment, which moved into the forest.[20] When General Weitzel felt that the planned movements to his left were advanced far enough, he ordered his columns of bluecoats forward.[21] They trampled their way through the dense woods, anticipating the obstructed field in their front. The sound of birds chirping was deceivingly peaceful amid the noise of the trampling of a thousand feet.

Footing was uncertain on uneven ground, and regiments struggled to maintain formation. After twenty minutes of marching through the woods, the first cannon shots were heard, signaling that the battle had begun. "The shells howled and burst over our heads incessantly and deafeningly," said one Yankee soldier.[22] As cannons shattered the woods, tree trunks split and tall trees fell with a crash to the forest floor. While some waited for their turn at battle, the wounded from Dwight's first wave came streaming toward the rear. Men in agony with gaping wounds, missing limbs, bloody flesh and bone protruding, passed by. Horrified hearts pounded fast now, stomachs churned, and the New Englanders of Weitzel's brigade waited nervously for the young general's order: "Forward! March!"

Three days prior to the assault, the enemy lines in front of Weitzel's position were not fortified. The rebels had relied upon the natural obstructions and uneven ground as sufficient to deter an infantry attack. However, Confederate general Franklin Gardner detected indications that warned of the Yankees' plans, so he had light breastworks quickly erected.[23] As a result, the first order of business for Weitzel's attack was to clear big logs and felled trees that choked ravines and blocked the way. This created a deadly situation where troops could not even see the enemy, nor could they move quickly due to the obstructions. At great peril, men with axes would have to work to open a path for the infantry.

Shells continued to rip into the woods more rapidly now, startling the waiting men and sending splinters of wood and clods of dirt and shrapnel flying. Bodies began to drop as the rebels hit their mark; others slumped with flesh wounds. Waiting for orders, the roar of cannon fire and the sight of the wounded raised the tension as anxious faces stared back at one another.

Finally orders came to deploy and take positions under what cover could be found outside the woods. Some men advanced into a natural valley, while others huddled along the brow of the crest, and the remainder took up position on a nearby bluff.[24] Then came a directive to relieve the advance troops in the field, an order that amounted to almost certain death for those obeying. Officers turned to their loyal troops, all eyes fixed upon the regimental commander. "Fall in!" Within minutes the men were advancing into the gauntlet of gunfire and cannon shot raining down from the earthworks at Port Hudson. Officers shouted with enthusiasm and urged their men forward. Bullets whistled past heads, sometimes finding their targets.[25]

Though the attack was supposed to be simultaneous, there were unexplained delays for several hours by divisions in the center and the left. The result was that Weitzel's men on the right suffered the full attention of the rebel guns, sustaining numerous casualties. It was a beating the likes of which Godfrey had never before experienced.

As the morning's battle blazed on, Godfrey Weitzel listened for the sound of gunfire on his left, which would tell him that either Augur or Sherman had joined the fight. However, there was nothing but artillery fire, which did not seem right. Nonetheless, Godfrey thought that if the various regiments advanced according to the battle plan, he might gain a foothold on the high ground held by the rebels.[26] As it turned out, all of the brigades and divisions had dutifully carried out their orders except for General Thomas Sherman on the left, who delayed without excuse. An outraged General Banks sent word to Weitzel at 1:45 p.m., saying, "General Sherman has failed utterly and criminally to bring his men into the field." At noon, Banks caught General Sherman dining with his staff officers, "all with their horses unsaddled, and none knowing where to find their command."[27] Banks was livid. General Weitzel's men were dying in the field while Sherman ate lunch!

Godfrey was confused and understandably bitter about the lack of support from Auger, Grover, and Sherman. The West Pointer from Cincinnati sent word to General Banks that he had "yet to learn that any other general had co-operated in the assault, which was ordered to be simultaneous."[28] Godfrey did not know the actual topography of the ground before him, which caused him concern about ordering his men forward. Would they be forced to retreat or would they find a break that would result in the capture of the fort?

Due to obstacles in the thick forest and being completely exposed to raking Confederate sharpshooters, progress was very slow. Men in the first two advancing lines fell rapidly, riddled with bullets. Their lines were so badly broken that General Weitzel ordered Colonel Stephen Thomas's third line of the Eighth Vermont Regiment to charge ahead in support of the first two. Within a few moments, the Eighth Vermont passed the broken lines of the first two regiments and engaged the rebels with such surprise that they captured many and scared the rest back into their fortifications.[29]

In the frantic assault, however, Colonel Thomas soon realized that he had ordered his men to halt only fifty yards from the main earthworks, where the Yankees were dangerously exposed to rebel fire. The Confederates instantly seized the opportunity and fired upon the Green Mountain boys, picking them off with ease as blue uniforms became splattered with red blood. The failure of Sherman and Auger to promptly join in the attack left the enemy free to concentrate all their fire upon Weitzel's men. Thomas knew that he could not remain at this spot, nor attempt to scale the works—for either option "was wholesale butchery."[30] "Fall back!" he finally shouted over the din of gunfire as his men sought the cover of a ravine.

With no choice but to remain under cover, Colonel Thomas sent a message back to General Weitzel advising what he had done. Assessing the situation from his command position to the rear, Godfrey Weitzel sent word forward that Thomas should hold his position if possible. Weitzel's brigade was, at this point, the first line of battle, which they continued to hold despite a loss of a dozen killed and another sixty-seven wounded, including Vermont's brave Colonel Thomas.[31]

By 2:15 p.m. Sherman had finished his lunch and joined with Augur's columns to assist Weitzel in assaulting the enemy. However, the morning's disastrous confusion doomed their late efforts to salvage the day. At 3:00 p.m., General Augur's men at last advanced from the woods across an open area of about a mile in length obstructed by abatis and underbrush. Immediately they encountered heavy grape, shell, and canister fire from the Confederate artillery. General Banks issued an order at 4:00 p.m. that General Sherman "carry the works at all hazards." Generals Thomas Sherman and Neal Dow were both wounded and carried off the field that afternoon, and Dow's brigade had to fall back in defeat. Sherman's late charge was repulsed, losing even more men than Generals Weitzel and Grover. A wound to Sherman's right leg later required amputation to save his life.

Weitzel reported to Banks that he thought he could make another attempt during the night or the following morning. However, none of the generals were able to fulfill their mission during the day. By nightfall, Port Hudson remained in Confederate hands and the fierce combat settled into silence. The assault was a total disaster. Godfrey Weitzel's brigade retreated to tend to its wounded and count its dead.

Overall, Union troops suffered the loss of 293 killed, another 1,549 wounded, and 157 missing (likely dead) in the day's assault, with no ground gained—a complete rebel victory. By contrast, Confederate casualties totaled only 250–275 killed, wounded, and missing. Men slept in the woods under huge magnolias scarred by bullets and splintered by cannon shell. Stretchers carried the wounded to field hospitals at the rear, which were soon filled to overflowing with more than 1,800 Union soldiers and officers killed or wounded in the day's battle.

With the disaster of the May 27 attack, Nathaniel Banks abandoned for a time any further attempt to attack and, instead, made preparations for a protracted siege. An agreement was reached for the morbid exercise of retrieving the dead bodies the following morning. One curious Yankee soldier climbed a high point to peer across at the enemy's position during the cease-fire. "Sallow, darkly sunburnt men, in dirty reddish homespun and broad-brimmed wool hats, stared back at me in grim silence," he reported.[32] They were merely waiting for the signal to resume the battle.

The "Negro Charge"

The battle of May 27 is perhaps best known for the ferocity shown by the troops of the Second Louisiana Volunteers, an all-black regiment under the command of Colonel Charles Paine. Whatever doubts Godfrey Weitzel still held about the ability of black soldiers to fight were wiped away by what he witnessed that day. In between the attacks of Generals Weitzel and Augur, an assault was ordered by the two black regiments of the Native Guard as a diversion. Their ground was very difficult, and when the Confederates saw the charge by blacks in uniform, "the garrison received them with special temper and exasperation."[33] The black soldiers fought without panic but suffered severely. All who witnessed the battle were impressed with their bravery.

Two of the Union regiments came out of a willow swamp close to the river and entered a clearing of six or seven hundred feet. In the clearing was a line of Confederate rifle pits backed up by two small howitzers. The black soldiers charged at a double-quick as soon as they reached clear ground, but concealed skirmishers in rifle pits fired indiscriminately on the black troops, followed by a simultaneous discharge of the rebel howitzers. When they got within 150 yards of the front of the bluff, every cannon, heavy and light, double-shot, and every rifle turned loose on them. More than 250 of the black troops were either killed in the barrage or were too badly wounded to crawl out of sight. A rebel officer described it as a "horrid scene of war," as the dead and wounded lay "among the willows."[34]

The Longest Siege

The Confederate garrison inside Port Hudson was under command of forty-year-old Major General Franklin Gardner, who knew his men were trapped.

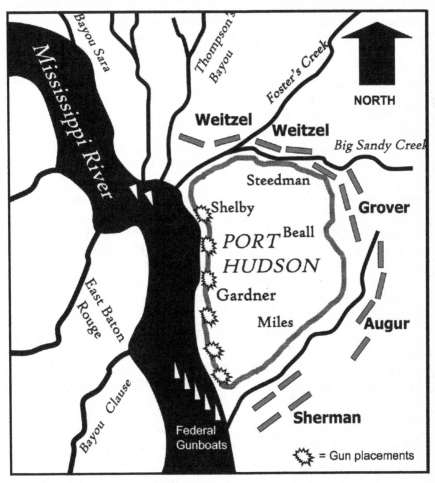

FIGURE 13.1. Map of Port Hudson, Louisiana, ca. May to July 1863.

Gardner was a West Point grad, an 1843 classmate of Ulysses S. Grant and a respected engineer. Though born in New York, Gardner had married the daughter of Louisiana governor Alexander Mouton, the sister of General Alfred Mouton, and decided to fight for the South. With Gardner's men entrenched behind his impressive earthworks, and multiple Union brigades surrounding the place, officers on both sides began to anticipate a prolonged siege—a waiting game. It would be only a matter of time until the fortress was out of food, water, and the will to fight. Admiral Farragut sized up the situation aptly and wrote to General Banks: "You must overcome them," he encouraged, "by a little perseverance."[35]

"A Little Perseverance"

The siege was now in place, and all the Union brigadiers set to work strengthening their lines, mounting guns, and selecting sharpshooters. The Federal line snaked for several miles around the north and east of Port Hudson in a "C" shape to cut off any supplies or escape routes. All available men were needed to guard the perimeter, even those who suffered minor wounds in the bloody first assault of May 27.

On May 30, a signal officer was finally able to open communications between the Army and the Navy by climbing to the top of a tree on the extreme right of Weitzel's line.[36] From that treetop, General Weitzel gave coordinates to the U.S. sloop of war *Richmond*, which flung shells into the enemy's fort and rifle pits.[37] In return, the rebels kept Weitzel's troops awake all night long with a barrage from a huge ten-inch cannon that the Union boys nick-named Old Demoralizer. Chinese warrior Sun-tzu wrote in the fifth century BC that if your enemy is "taking his ease, give him no rest."[38] The Confederates took this to heart, and the next morning, a groggy General Weitzel signaled to Admiral Farragut, "Let the mortars fire on that gun which shot at us last night." Farragut gave orders for the mortars to concentrate fire "on the 10-inch Columbiad . . . which generally annoys Weitzel."[39] With its position signaled from a treetop to the USS *Hartford* in the river below, the Navy obliged.

As troops on both sides sweated out the June heat along the banks of the Mississippi, there were daily exchanges of musketry and artillery fire along the lines. "Every morning I was awakened by the popping of rifles and the whistling of Minie balls," one Yankee wrote. "Hardly a day passed that I did not hear the loud exclamations of the wounded, or see corpses borne to the rear."[40] Confederate artillery sent thunderous blasts screaming overhead and crashing through the trees near Union positions. Farragut's mortar fleet returned the fire and lit up the night. Occasionally a Union shell hit its mark, setting fire to some building within the Southern stronghold, and an orange glow could be seen over the parapets.

Two weeks after the first assault, General Banks became impatient for another assault. On June 10, he ordered Weitzel's brigade to conduct a night reconnaissance, hoping to draw out the enemy's fire and thereby confirm the location of their artillery. It was muggy and cloudy when at about midnight the order was given to fall into line. Seventeen companies were sent over the Union breastworks and waited for the signal to move forward. After three hours of preparations, the advance was begun at 3:00 a.m. as the Federals marched cautiously forward.

Suddenly, the movement caught the attention of the enemy, who opened up with a crack of heavy musketry fire. Weitzel's men endured a hail of lead that pierced their blue uniforms. Pinned down by enemy fire, and their pathway blocked by obstructions, General Weitzel ordered the troops to remain as they were until daylight. The skirmishers suffered heavy losses during the reconnaissance and with no gain. Godfrey called his men back in just before daybreak, when another temporary truce was agreed to collect the dead and wounded from the field.[41]

It was apparent to all the officers and skirmishers alike that the only way to drive the Confederates out from Port Hudson's protection was with another all-out advance, which would result in severe Union losses. Eventually, word came down along the lines to prepare for the second assault. General Banks gave orders to his officers to be ready in just two days to make a grand attack on the main works. Still mindful of the disastrous assault of May 27, Godfrey Weitzel made plans and consulted his officers on the best strategy for the upcoming offensive.

The Second Major Assault—June 14, 1863

In the first two weeks of June, details of Federal troops dug nightly inside a winding ravine to create protected approaches for the upcoming assault. It was hoped that the trenches would prevent a slaughter of advancing on open ground. Like gophers, the bluecoats labored to excavate a deep pathway that eventually led up to a bluff from the woods, just south of Weitzel's position. It was no secret to the Confederates, who could observe the night's progress at sunrise. While they made no all-out assault on the workers, rebel gunners did occasionally harass the work crews "with casual sharpshooting, which did little harm in the darkness."[42]

After two weeks of nocturnal digging, a half-mile of trench was carved out, averaging six feet deep and ten feet wide, covered with a lid of trees for protection. Despite its depth, the pathway offered only limited protection from the enemy sharpshooters firing from a higher position inside the fort. Worse yet, the trench ended eighty yards short of the fort's walls, leaving the infantry totally exposed to enemy fire during their final dash to the parapet.[43] Even today's Olympic sprinters would have failed to make the distance safely, let alone the undernourished Union troops carrying knapsacks and rifles. Despite the risk, it was decided by Generals Banks and Grant to attempt another assault through the ravine on Sunday morning, June 14.

Banks made his opening salvo Saturday afternoon, when Union artillery unleashed a furious bombardment to which the enemy vigorously responded. Several Confederate guns were dismounted from the explosions, as hoped. Presumptuously, General Banks sent a flag of truce to Confederate general Franklin Gardner demanding his surrender, which Gardner refused. The firing was not resumed as both sides prepared for the anticipated assault.

Although the next day was a Sunday, it was no day of rest. Banks had issued orders that the Army should make a major offensive in the early morning hours. General Weitzel cleverly designed his assault column to consist first of two New York regiments of skirmishers, followed closely by one regiment with hand grenades, then another with cotton bags that would be used to fill the ditch in front of the breastworks. Three more armed regiments were then to bring up the rear as an assaulting party.[44] It seemed like a good plan, perhaps something right out of Professor Dennis Mahan's military and civil engineering class at West Point. If all proceeded as planned, the Yankees would scale the walls and the enemy fort would fall.

Officers were given their instructions, and the men made their final preparations by checking ammunition, filling cotton bags, reading from Bibles, and writing notes for loved ones. Instructions were quietly explained to each company. Particularly anxious were the men of the Twelfth and Seventy-Fifth New York Regiments, who had been chosen to lead the column through the ravine, then exit and spread along the base of the enemy ramparts. Their job was to annoy the defenders while other Federals made their advance with the grenades and cotton bags. The Eighth Vermont was given the dangerous assignment of leading the third wave as the assaulting column.

At 1:00 a.m. on June 14, the Yankee troops were given a light breakfast. Each man knew that the day would end in bloodshed and death, perhaps his own. Godfrey Weitzel followed his orders as a dutiful West Pointer would, hoping his men could carry the day and the enemy works. He gave a nod to Colonel Elisha B. Smith to start the assault. It was about 3:00 a.m., and Smith quietly spread the word for each regiment to take up their positions. The anxious New Englanders formed into a column for the perilous march through the newly completed trench. As recalled by one captain, "Not an order was uttered aloud" to carry out the sneak attack.[45]

Dense fog blanketed the morning, casting a strange veil over the battlefield. An owl hooted "Tu who, tu who!" In the dim night and thick mist, the Union regiments and batteries were assembled silently. An "army of ghosts," as one man described it.[46] The men waited in a long, dark, and solemn suspense. Soon came the whispered order "Stand to arms," and the men rose and marched down into the trench.

The New Yorkers were the first ones in, stumbling in the darkness into the deep ravine, followed by the Eighth Vermont and the other regiments. Once inside, the bluecoats moved very slowly, halting occasionally as they bunched up along the half-mile trench. Their approach was detected, and rebel bullets began to hit the logs covering the trench, forcing men to crouch a little lower. Troops behind piled into the muddy gulch, and taller men ducked their heads so as not to knock off the covering in the subterranean path. Despite the width and depth of the enhanced ravine, it was still too narrow and too shallow. Nervous troops were jammed up inside. By 5:00 a.m., the lines were formed and Weitzel's seven regiments were in place, waiting for the signal.

The sun had just begun to rise and the fog lifted when, after almost two hours of waiting, orders were given for the first wave of skirmishers to advance up and out of the tunnel. The Seventy-Fifth New York jumped out first with "a sudden and furious roar of musketry . . . followed by the charging yell" to serve as skirmishers for the rest of the column.[47] The brave men hoped to make the eighty-yard dash across the open space in front of the parapets before getting picked off. Confederate sentinels were on the alert, and the New York skirmishers were barely out of their trenches when the Southerners let loose with musket fire from behind their works. The barrage of gunfire was so intense that the cotton bag and hand grenade regiments could not make their way forward the eighty yards to execute their commands. The onrush of Federals lacked direction, as no generals, nor any regular officers, went near the ramparts during the entire day's assault.[48] Leadership was left to volunteer colonels and lieutenant colonels, untrained in the methods to attack enemy fortifications.

As the doomed assault proceeded, Colonel Halbert E. Paine's brigade held the center and the colonel went to the extreme front to encourage his men. He was hit in the leg by a Confederate sharpshooter and fell at the foot of the ramparts, severely wounded. Part of his brigade actually entered the earthworks but, without their leader and lacking support, failed to capture the fort. Colonel Paine remained lying in the open field all day in the hot sun, unable to move without drawing enemy fire.[49] Brave soldiers who tried to reach him were likewise gunned down and fell near their commander. Paine was later rescued, but his leg had to be amputated.

Just as it seemed that the Yankees would be driven back, the Eighth Vermont marched forward with its cotton bags and entered the fray. As one officer yelled, "Forward, Eighth Vermont!" he fell dead from a Confederate bullet. The men obeyed nonetheless and marched into the hail of gunfire under the command of a lieutenant colonel. "Hurry up, boys! They want you ahead!" shouted one New Yorker whose face was covered with blood.[50] It was as brutal a scene as anyone had witnessed. Within five minutes, sixty of the Vermonters dropped to the ground, many with fatal wounds. By daybreak, about eighteen hundred lay dead or were wounded or missing, with twenty to thirty more taken prisoner inside the fort. Another disaster was unfolding.

Though a portion of Weitzel's forces eventually reached the ditch in front of the breastworks and a few even touched the wall, the cotton bags that were supposed to fill the ditch and the hand grenades that were to be thrown over the parapet never made it that far. Only one soldier, a brave young man in his twenties, reached the base and tossed his grenade inside. He was promptly cut down by a rebel sentinel with a shot through the abdomen.[51] Those who were able took refuge in the fort's trenches only to find that they were trapped, unable to get back. They had to protect themselves by hugging tightly to the walls or crouching behind cotton bags and stumps of trees in plain daylight.

With little protection, the brave Federals hunkered down as the morning dragged on, realizing they might be stuck in their positions until nightfall. The Confederate gunners picked off anything that moved. Many who lay wounded before the works were killed during the day, and those brave men who tried to rescue their fallen mates were ruthlessly shot.[52] The Confederates celebrated the repulse of the Union's second grand assault with drums and trumpets, singing their anthem, the "Bonny Blue Flag," and other "secesh" songs as the sun began to set a little after 7:00 p.m.

The June 14 assault on Port Hudson was another Confederate victory. Just like the first attempt, nothing was accomplished. The Eighth Vermont alone saw twenty-one of its men killed and another seventy-five wounded, seven of whom died later.[53] Admiral Farragut sent in two surgeons to assist the Army with their wounded.

Victory at Last!

After another extended siege, 135 miles to the north, Ulysses S. Grant began negotiations for the surrender of the rebel position at Vicksburg on July 3, 1863. Grant's siege was likewise taking its toll on the thirty thousand hungry Confederates there. Surrender was finalized on July 4—Independence Day. Word of Grant's success did not reach General Banks, however, until early on Tuesday, July 7.[54] When Banks received the news, it spread along the Union lines like wildfire.

As news broke of Vicksburg's surrender, there was "a mighty hurrah" from the Yankee side of Port Hudson. Cheers erupted in the trenches and from behind Federal breastworks as each soldier learned the news. General Banks signaled to Admiral Farragut to begin a celebration. "Bands will play," he said, "and we shall fire salute of one hundred guns from right and left at noon. I shall be glad if you will participate with us."[55] Farragut joined in the festivities by issuing a similar order to the upper and lower fleets stationed on the river. The surrender of Vicksburg on July 4 was an early birthday present for Admiral David Farragut, who turned sixty-two the next day.[56]

When Gardner's men heard the salute at noon on July 7 and the Yankees' hardy cheers, the Confederates knew that something important had occurred. Curious, they called out to the Union troops. "What are you yelling about?" an Alabamian asked from the fort. "What's the news, Yanks?" yelled another. "Vicksburg has gone up!" a score of Federals shouted. "Hell!" came the rebel response.[57] General Gardner knew that with the fall of Vicksburg, Grant was now free to turn his full attention to Port Hudson.

At half past midnight, a cease-fire was agreed to, and a Confederate officer under a truce flag delivered a message to a Union colonel, who forwarded it to Banks's headquarters. After the forty-eight-day standoff, two failed assaults, the illness, tension, heat, and filth were over. Early on the morning of July 8, Godfrey Weitzel and the other Federals saw a wonderful sight. A white flag of truce was formally mounted above the enemy's earthworks. General Gardner had surrendered!

General Banks personally selected the young brigadier general Godfrey Weitzel to receive the surrender of Port Hudson, saying that Weitzel was "more closely identified with the whole campaign than any other officer." Banks wrote to Weitzel, saying: "I shall designate you as the officer to receive the surrender of General Gardner." To Banks's surprise, the humble Weitzel declined to accept the surrender. Banks was shocked and wrote to Weitzel, "I am sorry that you do not accept the surrender."[58] Nonetheless, for his meritorious service in the siege and two assaults against the rebel fort, Godfrey received another honorary brevet of lieutenant colonel.

With Port Hudson now in Union hands, the last Confederate defense on the Mississippi was removed. A free waterway was opened from Cairo, Illinois, all the way to the Gulf of Mexico. The backbone of the Confederacy was broken at last and, despite great loss of life, there was celebrating in Washington.

CHAPTER 14

Thibodeaux and the Sabine Pass

With the long siege finally broken at Port Hudson, General Nathaniel Banks ordered that immediately after the July 9, 1863, formal surrender ceremony and review of the troops, General Weitzel's brigade should be prepared to move out. Despite all of Godfrey's efforts, the Confederates were back in possession of Brashear City and the surrounding area, as well as Donaldsonville. Rebel batteries on the banks of the Mississippi River were harassing Union gunboats and transports night and day, crippling several vessels and interrupting communications with New Orleans. Weitzel was needed back in the Lafourche—again!

Third Tour of Duty in the Lafourche

Now that he could spare the manpower, General Banks wanted to send two divisions of the Nineteenth Corps to Donaldsonville. With no time to waste, Banks informed Weitzel that his transports would be ready for his brigade after the surrender ceremony. Godfrey was to lead *an entire division* back along Bayou Lafourche to hunt down the Confederate occupiers, finishing what he had attempted twice before. All the territory that had been secured by Weitzel's troops had fallen back into enemy hands while Union forces were tied up at Port Hudson.

Following the formalities of Gardner's surrender, General Weitzel and his Second Brigade made their way from the tall precipice of Port Hudson down to the riverbank below. As their comrades from other brigades prepared to bed down for the evening, Weitzel's men packed two days' rations in their haversacks and boarded the transports. The steamers were stocked with three days' additional rations plus a full supply of ammunition, mounted cannons, and cavalry horses. After the bulk of his men had filed onto the boats, Godfrey Weitzel boarded the crowded steamer *Laurel Hill* and slipped down the Mississippi, past Baton Rouge, in the relative darkness of a waning crescent moon.

Colonel Joseph S. Morgan followed Weitzel about midnight of July 10 with General Grover's First Brigade and Nims's Battery. Grover followed with two more brigades on July 11.[1] At 4:00 a.m. on the morning of July 11, Godfrey Weitzel and his brigade arrived at Point Pleasant Landing, just above Donaldsonville.[2] As his soldiers disembarked, one of Grover's men asked, "What troops are those?" Upon learning the identity, he remarked, "Weitzel's brigade, hey! Oh, they'll give it to 'em!" a compliment to the successful young brigadier.[3]

To be certain all were accounted for, General Weitzel ordered his men into formation in an open field opposite a tall forest of thick trees. An aide from Grover's brigade rode up in a hurry with a warning not to be startled by the tactics of the rebels, who had attacked them with both cavalry and infantry, "uttering deafening yells." This brought a grin to the worn faces of Weitzel's men at the mere suggestion that they would be scared off by a hollering band of Southerners. "We were anxious for a field fight," said one of the officers, expressing the frustration of the entire brigade at the forty-eight-day siege just ended. "We could win an easy vengeance on open ground," the Yank concluded, though he would have to wait for his chance.[4] Orders were finally given to bivouac for the night.

Confederate brigadier general Tom Green had seen Weitzel's transports coming down the Mississippi River crowded with troops, but he did not know that Port Hudson had fallen. He simply thought the troops were coming to attack *him*.[5] The Texan had concentrated four regiments and four guns on the east bank of Bayou Lafourche, and on the west bank he posted three more regiments and two guns. However, the body of bluecoats arriving above Donaldsonville was such an intimidating presence that Green immediately withdrew all guns from the riverbank and called all detachments back. He and Dick Taylor understood the threat of Weitzel's and Grover's arrivals.

Morning broke on July 12 and Weitzel's troops were ordered to "fall in" for a brisk march south on the double-quick. Repeating their now-familiar trek, Godfrey spread his men out along the bayou with a regiment on each bank. Farther to the south, the enemy waited for the Federals. Green was prepared for the Union invaders and had learned from Mouton's prior failure. General Weitzel sent an advance guard of cavalry and four companies of infantry to flush out the enemy, just as a hunter would send out a bird dog after pheasants.

Soon, the advancing skirmishers encountered Tom Green's Texans. Artillery was rolled forward and fired four or five cannon shots to drive the Confederates back. The crack of rifle fire kept up from both sides of the bayou as the Yankees pushed south. Skirmishing continued all day on July 12 with occasional exchanges of artillery. The tables were soon turned, however, as the outnumbered Confederates bravely attacked the next day.

Second Battle at Kock's Plantation

About four miles south of Donaldsonville, as he passed an elegant two-story mansion, Godfrey recognized the St. Emma plantation. It was the same plantation where Weitzel's Reserve Brigade had first encountered Mouton in late October 1862. It was near here that the old ghoul had warned, "Better turn back while you can!"[6] This time Godfrey would have been wise to heed that warning, for a bloodbath awaited his division.

On July 13, Weitzel's division joined up with General Cuvier Grover's division. In the morning twilight, a foraging detachment and advance guard were sent out along both banks.[7] With Charles Paine's brigade on one descending bank of the bayou and Nathan Dudley's on the other, the Federals headed slowly south until they reached Kock's Plantation, south of Donaldsonville. Green's skirmishers were waiting there and opened fire, forcing the Federals back.

Green took the offensive and attacked the heads of both Yankee columns, taking the Union commanders by surprise. The Texans drove the bluecoats back almost one mile in a panic. Behind Paine's and Dudley's brigades was the bulk of Weitzel's division, which now advanced down the bayou in large numbers on the double-quick at the sound of enemy fire. A fierce battle soon raged along the creek's banks and in the adjacent cane fields and ditches. The Federals had been caught by surprise, resulting in little time to rally and gather their broken forces.

The battle was a succession of charges as the rebels pummeled and pushed the Yankees. General Grover rode out to see the situation firsthand and immediately ordered a withdrawal of his entire force.[8] The brief battle was an embarrassing defeat for Godfrey Weitzel, who had squashed Alfred Mouton's small force with ease just nine months earlier along this same bayou. It was made all the worse by the number of casualties suffered. Although Green had the smaller force, his men inflicted the far greater damage. The North suffered the loss of 2 officers and 54 men killed, plus another 7 officers and 210 men wounded, with many more missing or captured.[9] By contrast, the Confederates reported only 3 killed and 30 wounded. General Tom Green boasted that he had also captured about 250 Yankee prisoners. To make the victory even sweeter, the Texans had captured numerous small arms, Enfield rifles, and three pieces of Union artillery, as well as wagons, teams, and equipment, plus a flag from a New York regiment.[10] It was a complete rout, and not at all what General Banks had ordered.

Dick Taylor wrote of the day's victory: "I have the honor to announce a brilliant success gained by a portion of my forces, under the command of Brigadier-General Green, over Weitzel and Dwight." Taylor bragged appropriately that although the enemy was over four thousand men strong, Green—with only twelve hundred men—drove the Union troops from the field and all the way back to Donaldsonville.[11] The scapegoat for the loss was Union colonel Joseph S. Morgan, who had commanded Grover's troops that day. He was later arrested and arraigned before a general court-martial on charges of misbehavior before the enemy and drunkenness on duty, and ultimately found guilty of both charges.[12]

When General Banks received the news of the defeat on July 14 at Port Hudson, he went immediately to Donaldsonville to meet with Generals Weitzel and Grover for a debriefing and strategy session. It was agreed that the only appropriate response was to press Dick Taylor's troops hard and slow them down enough to permit Union gunboats to reenter Berwick Bay and cut off Taylor's line of retreat. Nathaniel Banks left and continued south to New Orleans to petition the Navy for more gunboats. His orders were for the Nineteenth Army to go into "summer quarters."[13]

Godfrey Becomes a Division Commander

Word quickly went out along Union wires to other brigades advancing on Lafourche that read: "Be very cautious how you advance. There is a report Weitzel has been repulsed on the Lafourche. Hold your force in readiness to fall back." The July 1863 expedition into the Lafourche completely failed in its objective and left much of the interior of the Acadian region in control of Dick Taylor's rebel forces, with the exception of the Union's Fort Butler at Donaldsonville. Berwick Bay, long controlled by the Union, was back in Confederate hands, controlling a key port on the Lower Atchafalaya River.

General Christopher Augur had been sick ever since Port Hudson, and eventually acknowledged he was unfit for the summer's duties. On July 15, Augur formally turned over command of his First Division to Godfrey Weitzel and took leave for treatment in the North.[14] Weitzel was now officially a division commander at the age of twenty-seven, as he continued his meteoric rise up the Volunteer Army ladder.

Back to Thibodeaux and New Orleans

Godfrey Weitzel's newly enhanced division stayed in temporary quarters near Donaldsonville until he received orders in late July that his division was to pull back some thirty miles to the southeast at Thibodeaux. Dick Taylor's forces had abandoned that area as more Federals arrived, leaving Weitzel free to move in and take control. Following orders, Godfrey Weitzel packed up his men and their animals and equipment and marched farther down the familiar bayou to take up summer quarters near Thibodeaux, where he set up a command headquarters.[15] Weitzel named the place "Camp Hubbard" in memory of one of his officers who fell at Port Hudson during the first May 27 attack.[16] Days were spent foraging there in the bountiful orchards of the lush Lafourche region. Always one to keep his men drilled and ready, General Weitzel held regular evening dress parades.

Camp Hubbard was full of rumors that something was about to happen. Troops sensed something in the air as they saw unusual activity at General Weitzel's headquarters, with the coming and going of orderlies and messengers. Their suspicion was confirmed when an order came through for the cooks to prepare three days' rations for the men. That could only mean that a "grand movement" would soon follow to some unknown destination.

Reshuffling of the Nineteenth Army Corps

In late July and August, nearly thirty of the nine-months Volunteer Regiments of the Nineteenth Army Corps went home to be mustered out. This added to the severe loss of men in the two Port Hudson assaults and the more recent defeat at Kock's Plantation. The corps was stretched even thinner when one regiment was ordered to Key West and the Tortugas and yet another sent to Pensacola, Florida. A third regiment was shipped down to Forts Jackson and St. Philip to protect New Orleans against a rumored invasion. As a result, the Nineteenth Corps was reorganized, with the First and Third Brigades of the First Division combined into one. The Second Division was broken up and ceased to exist. Weitzel's original brigade was reassigned to Augur's First Division, which Godfrey now commanded.[17]

As part of the restructuring, General William B. Franklin assumed command of the Nineteenth Army Corps on August 15, and Godfrey Weitzel was confirmed to head its First Division, which promptly took a post at Baton Rouge.[18]

On to the Sabine Pass

French emperor Napoleon III had sent more than thirty-five thousand troops into Mexico and ousted President Benito Juárez in June 1863. It was reported in Washington that Confederate diplomats sought to negotiate an agreement with France to recognize the rebel nation. In return, the South would lend its support to Napoleon's regime in Mexico. With the Mississippi River now in Union hands, Lincoln wanted to send an expedition to Texas to discourage any French thoughts of crossing the Rio Grande in support of Jefferson Davis's government.[19] General Banks ordered an expedition under General Franklin to occupy the mouth of the Sabine River. Within days, Godfrey Weitzel received orders to join Franklin and to lead an assault upon a rebel fort there.

The Sabine River separates Texas and Louisiana. It runs from the prairie country of northeast Texas some 550 miles to the south, where it empties into the warm salt water of the Gulf of Mexico. A small island known as Oyster Reef splits the river channel into two streams, east and west. Like the Mississippi River below New Orleans, the Sabine provided a port of entry from the Gulf to points north and a supply line for the blockade-runners to aid the rebellion. To protect the port, a rebel fort, known as Fort Sabine, was built on the west bank. In order to complete the monopoly on Southern ports, Lincoln wanted the Sabine River under Union control.

Much has been written about the rebel victory on September 8, 1863, at the Sabine Pass against an overwhelming Union naval and Army force. The battle made the name of Confederate Lieutenant Dick Dowling a household word in south Texas. The exploits of his small band of forty-four men are legendary. Years later, Jefferson Davis would refer to the success of Dowling and his small band as "more remarkable than the battle of Thermopylae," where a small Greek force held off Xerxes' massive Persian army against all odds in 480 BC.[20]

This would be a continuation of Godfrey Weitzel's string of losses since his arrival at Port Hudson in May 1863. He has been criticized soundly by at least one author as a fabricator and spineless officer, lacking nerve during battle on the Sabine.[21] Hardly the same man described by Major George C. Strong as the strongest and bravest man alive.[22] However, the events of the Sabine expedition need to be explained in sequence to fully appreciate the factors that led to the Confederacy's unlikely victory. It was no lack of nerve on Godfrey's part, but rather a combination of mechanical breakdowns, navigational errors, shallow water, and dead-on accurate cannon fire by Dowling's artillery that doomed the mission.

Setting the Stage

Although the Texas port at Galveston had been under blockade since early July 1861, the Sabine Pass was underestimated in its importance. It was not until late September 1862 that any Union blockade was ordered of the Sabine. Ben Butler had ruled out an invasion there due to its shallow entrance and a sandbar that prohibited deep-draft vessels from entering.[23] Nonetheless, on September 23, 1862, a small Navy expedition led by Union captain Frederick Crocker crossed the bar and entered the pass. He encountered no opposition but fired three shells into the enemy fort guarding the pass just to be sure.[24] Crocker was surprised to find that the Confederates had abandoned their position and spiked their guns.

The Union Navy seized Fort Sabine without any resistance and the town of Sabine City soon surrendered, making it the first major Texas city of the war captured by Union forces.[25] The fort remained under Federal control until late January 1863, when a fleet of cotton-clad rebel steamers crept down the Sabine River from the north and boldly attacked a small blockade force at the mouth of the pass. The Confederates captured two Union vessels, twelve heavy guns, more than one hundred prisoners, and a cache of medical and military supplies.[26]

With the Sabine back under Confederate control, a new fort was recommended. Confederate general John B. Magruder sent thirty engineers and an estimated five hundred slaves to the Sabine Pass to build a stronger fort there. The new fort was triangular in shape and overlooked the Sabine River. It housed six gun emplacements and had bombproofs built into its saw-toothed front. The earthworks were reinforced by large timbers and railroad iron. The fort was named Fort Griffin and placed under command of Lieutenant Dick Dowling and a forty-four-man crew of the "Davis Guard."

Weitzel had been so successful in his earlier campaigns in Louisiana that residents of Texas feared that an attack at the Sabine was inevitable. Brigadier General Godfrey Weitzel's reputation was spreading not only among the Union Army and Navy, but in the Southern states as well. Families actually began to move out of Houston in late 1862 in fear of an attack by General Weitzel.[27]

The Sabine Assault Is Planned

The attack upon Fort Griffin would be another joint Army-Navy project, with troop transports and gunboats needed to ferry Union soldiers over the sandbar. General Banks organized a force of four thousand men under General Franklin's Nineteenth Corps to make a landing at Sabine Pass. Banks requested the co-operation of the Navy, which supplied the light-draft steamers *Clifton, Sachem, Arizona,* and *Granite City* for the mission. Two of these vessels, the *Sachem* and the *Clifton,* had a history of mechanical problems. The *Clifton* was an old Staten Island ferryboat that had no protection for its boilers, machinery, or men. Admiral Farragut wrote that "her crew are so completely demoralized that I find it impossible to send her back to you as an efficient vessel."[28] Godfrey Weitzel agreed with the admiral's assessment of the gunboats, writing, "These gunboats are now in a very bad condition."[29] In fighting at Galveston Bay, the *Clifton* and the *Sachem* were disabled by the sea, and the *Sachem* lost its propeller, rendering them both useless in that conflict.[30] Even General Banks complained about the worn-out and often-repaired *Clifton* and *Sachem,* saying, "These were all old boats of decayed frames and weak machinery, constantly out of repair, even when engaged in the ordinary service of the river."[31] Those two gunboats would prove to be the downfall of Weitzel's expedition into Sabine Pass.

On September 1, 1863, Godfrey Weitzel arrived at Baton Rouge with orders to prepare his men for an assault upon the rebel works at the Sabine Pass. The next day, the first of Weitzel's brigades assembled on the docks and shipped out of Baton Rouge on board three transport steamers bound for New Orleans. Two other brigades followed afterward with artillery that headed out into the Mississippi Delta to the Gulf of Mexico.[32] In order to conceal their true destination, General Banks staffed a few of the vessels with pilots who were known for their work in Mobile Bay.[33]

With his troops having safely shipped out, General Weitzel left the port at New Orleans at 5:00 p.m. on Friday, September 4, on the steamer *Belvidere.* He was accompanied by about one thousand infantry, one battery of thirty-pounder Parrott guns, and one twenty-pounder of the First Indiana Artillery, as well as the ships *General Banks*, *I. C. Landis*, and *Saint Charles*. Generals Emory and Franklin were aboard the steamers *Crescent* and *Suffolk*, respectively.

That night, the transports steamed south past Forts Jackson and St. Philip and splashed out into open waters. Turning right, they sailed another 108 nautical miles past Terrabone Bay and Atchafalaya Bay, arriving at the Southwest Pass by 6:00 a.m. on Saturday, September 5. The flotilla paused there for several hours, accompanied by the gunboat *Arizona*, while General Weitzel waited to be joined by Captain Frederick Crocker and his naval gunboats, the worn-out *Clifton* and *Sachem*. It was the same Crocker whose small expedition had captured the abandoned rebel fort at Sabine Pass in September 1862 without opposition. All seemed in order for a successful mission.

Weitzel's transports arrived at the Southwest Pass at 11:00 a.m., where they joined the remainder of the First Division's convoy under protection of the Union gunboat *Arizona*. The following morning, the *Clifton* and the *Sachem* showed up. General Weitzel placed two officers and seventy-five sharpshooters of the Seventy-Fifth New York Volunteers onto the *Clifton*, with an additional officer and twenty-five riflemen from the 161st New York Volunteers on board the *Sachem*.[34] The convoy weighed anchor and sailed westward another eighty miles to the Sabine Pass, hoping for an early morning surprise attack.

There were no Union blockaders off the Sabine Pass on Sunday night, causing Captain Crocker's gunboat *Clifton* to run *past* the mouth of the Pass to the west. His pilot, who was very familiar with the channel of the Sabine Pass, was on board the gunboat *Granite City*, which did not arrive at the pass until Monday afternoon. Due to the absence of the Union naval blockade and the missing pilot, Crocker's entire convoy sailed right past the mouth of the Sabine.

After hours at sea, General Weitzel was shocked to receive a message from Captain Crocker that the convoy had missed its mark and was now somewhere *to the west* of the Sabine Pass! Crocker ordered all the boats to reverse direction, and the entire convoy turned around mid-sea and headed back east.[35] This was not the end of the navigational nightmare, however.

At seven o'clock on Monday morning, September 7, the embarrassed Captain Crocker pulled alongside Weitzel's ship, the *Belvidere*, and went aboard. He confessed to the puzzled young general that he had blundered *a second time* in his navigation, and that the convoy was not west of the pass at all as he had thought—but actually about twenty-five miles *east* of the Sabine Pass, off the Calcasieu River. It is not certain how long the convoy had sailed in the wrong direction each way, crisscrossing the coast line, but Godfrey Weitzel was surely losing confidence in Captain Crocker's judgment. The navigational errors had cost the convoy precious time, confusing the mission and adding to the eventual failure of the entire expedition.

Crocker's warning came too late to catch the entire convoy, and General Franklin's fleet from New Orleans had already sailed unseen past the *Belvidere* and the *Clifton* at Calcasieu Pass. Adding to the mounting delays, Weitzel found that two of his military transports, the *General Banks* and the *Saint Charles*, were now disabled with mechanical problems. Frustrated, Godfrey Weitzel rolled out maps on board the *Belvidere* and discussed the situation with Crocker. The Navy captain advised that an attempt should be made right away to run up the Sabine and launch an attack before word spread of the expedition's arrival.[36] After all, Crocker had taken Fort Sabine once before, and he felt he could do it again, given the chance.

Weitzel rejected Crocker's idea and decided that under the circumstances, it would be best to attempt to stop the entire convoy at the point where they were, near Lake Calcasieu, repair the two transports, and regroup. He felt that he had no choice now but to postpone the attack. With more than twenty Union steamers seen by locals off the Southern coast, the element of surprise was now surely lost. "We will attempt to dash on the enemy's works on the next morning," Godfrey told Crocker.[37] The squadron dropped anchor at 10:00 a.m., after more than six hours of wasted maneuvers, and was soon joined by Brigadier General William H. Emory's fleet.[38] General Franklin's fleet arrived alone at Sabine Pass about an hour later, wondering what had happened to Weitzel and Emory.

The group off the Calcasieu River could not communicate with General Franklin. Anxiously, Godfrey Weitzel had to wait until the repairs were completed, nearly 5:00 p.m., before he could start his fleet once again for the Sabine Pass.[39] The entire day had been lost, as it was not until nine o'clock that evening that the squadron arrived outside the pass. With the element of surprise clearly gone, the fleet of twenty-three steam transports and three gunboats did not attempt to hide their lights. Perhaps the Confederate guard would abandon Fort Griffin in fright as they had done the last time Crocker attacked. The assembly of lighted ships was so impressive that one soldier wrote in his diary that it "was probably the gayest night Sabine Pass ever saw. In appearance it was more like New York. Every vessel showed all the lights they could and others kept coming in."[40] Soldiers crowded the decks of their ships to take in the sight, laughing and chatting in speculation of the coming events. They could not have imagined the debacle about to occur.

The Day of the Invasion—September 8, 1863

At six o'clock the next morning, the impressive fleet weighed anchor and steamed to the mouth of the Sabine Pass. As the *Clifton* approached the bar, the Federals announced their presence by firing on Fort Griffin, which did not respond. Three hours later, the *Sachem*, the *Arizona*, and the *Granite City*, followed by the two troop transports, made their way over the sandbar in the shallow river water. The six vessels headed upstream and anchored two miles south of the fort at 11:00 a.m. Under protection of the four gunboats, around 1:00 p.m. Godfrey Weitzel made

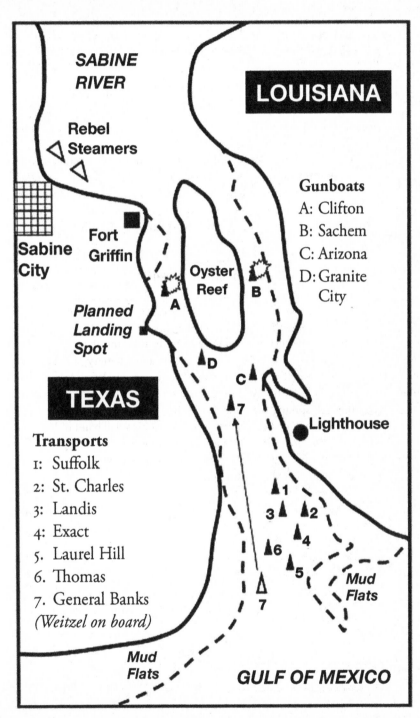

FIGURE 14.1. Map of the Sabine River assault, September 8, 1863.

a personal reconnaissance of the proposed landing spot and the Confederates' position. He was accompanied by General Franklin and Captain Crocker. It was decided that the best place to land the troops was at a location called "Old Battery Point," located just above the site of the former Confederate Fort Sabine.[41] After conferring with Crocker and Franklin, General Weitzel ordered five hundred men from the Seventy-Fifth New York to transfer from the *Belvidere* onto the river steamer *Thomas*. The captain of the *Thomas* followed the *Clifton* and the gunboat fleet over the bar at the mouth of the pass.[42]

General Weitzel accompanied a landing party of another five hundred men from the Seventy-Fifth New York who boarded the transport boat *General Banks* with instructions to follow behind the rear gunboat, *Granite City*, as soon as the attack was commenced. This battalion would attempt a landing at the chosen spot. An hour later, the transports steamed for the bar, geared for battle.

Things Go Terribly Wrong

The Davis Guard at Fort Griffin under Dick Dowling could see the assembly of half a dozen vessels entering the channel and waited patiently for their arrival. The Union intelligence on the fort was seriously in error, thinking that the defenses ashore and afloat had only two thirty-two-pounders and a battery of fieldpieces. In fact, the fort had more than three times that many guns in place. Dowling had orders permitting him to withdraw if that were the only viable option. One of his officers recommended spiking the guns and fleeing, just as had been done a year prior at old Fort Sabine. Dowling put the question to his small band of less than fifty men: "What do we do?" The response was a resounding, "Fight! Fight!" from his brave Texans. "We will stay by the fort until she goes down," the men said. "And if she goes down, we will go with her!"[43]

Weitzel and Crocker's plan was for the gunboat *Sachem* to lead the parade into the pass, followed by sister gunboats *Arizona* and *Clifton*, in that order. The gunboat *Granite City* would start in just behind the *Clifton* in order to screen the landing of one thousand New Yorkers aboard the transports *Thomas* and *General Banks*. The gunboat *Clifton* had another seventy-seven troops from the Seventy-Fifth New York on board, with twenty-six more men from the 161st New York on the *Sachem*. Of the 103 men on these last two vessels, only six would escape the upcoming disaster.

Most of the morning and early afternoon was spent trying to get the gunboats and transports over the bar and into the pass itself. Everything was proceeding according to plan. At 3:45 p.m. the *Sachem*, followed by the *Arizona*, steamed up the eastern channel of the pass, the "Louisiana Channel," to draw the fire of the fort. The *Clifton* advanced up the western "Texas Channel," followed by the

Granite City. Close behind was General Weitzel and his five hundred New Yorkers on the transport *General Banks*.

The first Union gunboats opened fire on the rebel battery, but Dowling's guns made no reply until the Federals were nearly abreast of the fort. When the *Sachem* was about twelve hundred yards away, Dowling gave the command "Load and fire at will!"[44] At that, the Confederates unleashed eight guns, surprising the Yankees, who anticipated only two guns at most. A hot battle ensued between the *Sachem* and the rebel fort.

Disaster struck before the gunboat *Granite City* ever got to its assigned position, which was designed to cover Weitzel's landing. As the *Sachem* reached midpoint of Oyster Reef, which separated the two channels, it ran aground there, stuck in the mud. Dowling's guns pummeled the steamer as it sat helpless in the stream. "We were riddled from stem to stern," recalled one Yankee. With a whistling noise that sailed across the reef, a rebel shell found its mark as it entered the *Sachem*'s steam engine, bursting its steam dome. Clouds of scalding steam erupted from the boiler, killing crewmen below and above deck as the ship became engulfed in hot steam. It was horrible as men were cooked alive. "God grant that I may never witness another such scene," said one observer.[45]

Captain Crocker took his gunboat, the *Clifton*, up the western channel at full speed when it, too, ran aground on the shallow river bottom, "unfortunately," as Weitzel explained, "in exact range of my proposed point of landing."[46] The *Clifton* made a gallant fight, despite its poor physical condition, turning its three guns on the broadside against Fort Griffin. With Dowling's Irish luck, two well-aimed shells struck the *Clifton*, one hitting the smokestack and another penetrating her boiler, causing an explosion that disabled the ship. Many were killed by the explosion, which enveloped the vessel in intense steam, forcing the New Yorkers to jump into the river. The Confederate sharpshooters were merciless in picking off any man left on the deck of the *Clifton*. Crocker made the decision to hoist the white flag of surrender.

Through his binoculars, General Weitzel saw the disaster unfolding before him. He had to make a quick decision, taking into account the unraveling naval efforts and lack of protection for his landing. He decided to attempt the landing and gave that order when, suddenly, he saw the colors of the *Clifton* lowered and the white flag of surrender raised on the *Sachem*. The white flag then appeared on the fore of the *Clifton* as well. To add to the mayhem, Godfrey saw that a third gunboat, the *Arizona*, had run aground. Grounded by the stern, the ebb tide of the river caught her bow and swung the steamer across the channel. From that position, the *Arizona* had great difficulty extracting herself as the steam engine became overheated from mud in the boilers.

With three of the Union protectors disabled or surrendered, it was now impossible to safely land troops.[47] A few moments later, orders were sent by signalmen to General Weitzel to retreat.[48] The entire battle had lasted only about

FIGURE 14.2. Map of Weitzel's battles and encampments in Texas and Louisiana.

one hour. Light-draft rebel steamers took the *Clifton* and *Sachem* in tow within twenty minutes of their surrender, capturing their New York crews.

Godfrey Weitzel still wanted to make another attempt to capture Fort Griffin, but his request was denied. By 6:00 p.m. the troops had returned to their original transports in the Gulf.[49] Later that night a frustrated Godfrey Weitzel received orders to return with his transports and troops back to the Southwest Pass. Even this movement was delayed, however, since one of the ships, the *Laurel Hill*, was disabled and had to be towed. The promising mission had turned into a complete disaster.

On September 11, 1863, orders were signaled to Generals Weitzel and Emory to disembark their troops at Algiers outside New Orleans, where they arrived at eleven o'clock that night. While steaming home on board the steamer *Suffolk*, somewhere near the Southwest Pass, Godfrey Weitzel sat down to write his official account of the failed Sabine expedition. He wrote that of the seventy-seven men and officers of the Seventy-Fifth New York Regiment on the *Clifton*, only six of them had escaped. He added that of the one officer and twenty-five men from the 161st New York on board the *Sachem*, he did not know how many had been killed or wounded, but counted the day's total loss as three officers and ninety-four men. Nearly all who survived were taken prisoners, including Captain Crocker.[50]

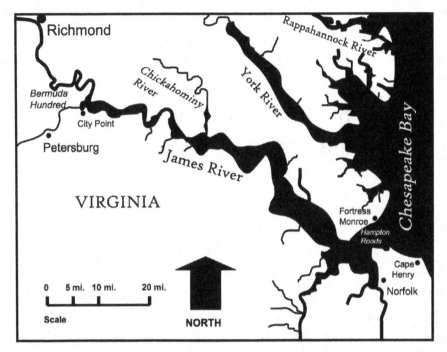

FIGURE 14.3. The James River, from Chesapeake Bay to Richmond, Virginia.

The controversial failure at Sabine Pass was blamed on the ineptness of the Navy or the Army, depending on which branch was writing the report. Had the mission been a success, it was believed that control of the pass would have led to the control of Texas. Instead, Dick Dowling would go down in history as the hero of the Sabine Pass. Even today, there are Dowling elementary and middle schools in the Texas towns of Houston, Odessa, and Port Arthur. These schools pay tribute to Dowling's courage and to the Irish luck of one well-aimed shot and of sandbars that hung up the Union gunboats.

CHAPTER 15

Reunited: Drewry's Bluff and the Spring Campaign of 1864

Back to the Bayou

It had been a slow and nightmarish trip of more than three days on the troop transports back to New Orleans. The vessels were tossed by heavy winds and giant waves that so frightened the troops, some threatened a mutiny.[1] Godfrey replayed the events of Sabine Pass in his mind over and over as the seasick men slipped around the windswept decks. He kept seeing that fatal shot fired into Captain Crocker's vessel, the *Clifton*, as the mission unfolded into disaster. It was an embarrassment to him, his men, and to the Union Army.

Finally, between six and seven on the morning of September 11, the ordeal was ended and Weitzel's demoralized and dizzied First Division of the Nineteenth Corps arrived at the mouth of the Mississippi River, with the damaged *Laurel Hill* still in tow.[2] The squadron anchored there for most of the day, sailing upriver for New Orleans about 3:00 p.m. Godfrey stood on the deck as he passed the familiar Fort Jackson on the left, then St. Philips on the right, making a sharp turn in the river where he had spent so many years. It was not the triumphal return he had hoped for. The transports anchored in the river, where Godfrey and his troops spent one last night aboard ship before landing in New Orleans the next morning. Weitzel's men made camp at Algiers, a spot that one officer called "a dirty, rascally suburb of New Orleans."[3]

Godfrey reported to General Banks, who was still in command at New Orleans, on the failed mission in Texas. His officers and men rested at Algiers for three days, anxious to leave the filthy place. On September 15, they got their wish, as General Banks changed strategy on how to get a toehold in Texas. He directed Emory's and Weitzel's divisions of the Nineteenth Army Corps, under command of General Franklin, to move back to Berwick Bay. Following orders, the First and Third Brigades of Weitzel's division packed up and proceeded to Brashear City, accompanied by a battery of artillery. At Brashear City, the troops crossed the bay and set up camp at Bisland on the lower Teche. Once all regiments were concentrated, orders were given to march through New Iberia and Opelousas to Carrion Crow Bayou. At this spot, which is today called *Carencro*, a Cajun word for the local buzzards that nested in cypress trees, a new camp was set up. On September 20, Weitzel's division broke camp and moved to Washington Smith's plantation, where they were joined by the First Maine Battery, and set up camp again. Six days later, Weitzel's First Division moved from the Smith plantation, marching ten miles to set up a new camp at Tarleton's plantation, where the troops remained for the remainder of the month. It was an uneventful few weeks of marching, camping, and drilling until early October.

Reunited with the "Beast"

In November, President Lincoln reassigned General Benjamin F. Butler, giving him command of the Department of Virginia and North Carolina.[4] This put the Eighteenth Army Corps under Butler's command. Godfrey would soon be reunited with his mentor. Back in Louisiana, an urgent message was delivered to Major General Franklin on December 9: "General, as soon as General Weitzel can be spared, please send him to New Orleans, to report at these headquarters for special temporary duty in the north."[5] Franklin issued the order that same day, and General William Emory was given temporary command of Weitzel's division.

When Godfrey arrived in New Orleans, he reported to General Banks and received his new orders. He was to head for an area called "the Bermuda Hundred," in the Department of Virginia and North Carolina, now commanded by General Benjamin Butler. This would be his first assignment outside Louisiana since the assault on New Orleans. When he returned to camp, the young general broke the news of his reassignment to his officers, some of whom had been with him for the duration of his service in Louisiana. Weitzel formed the men in line, and as he rode his horse in front of them for one final inspection, the men gave him "hearty, though sad, parting cheers." Godfrey was loved by his men, and both the officers and the troops were said to have "learned to esteem him highly for his personal qualities and military knowledge. His kindliness of heart won their love; his ability and skillful management gained their confidence; his careful provision for their wants and comfort inspired their trust in his sagacity and prudence" (*BB*, 897).

The Bermuda Hundred and Drewry's Bluff

The area in Virginia known as the "Bermuda Hundred" was established in 1613. It was the home of tobacco farmer John Rolfe, the English colonist who married Pocahontas, daughter of Powhatan. New plantations made by the colonists were called "hundreds," an old Norman term used to divide England into districts that could each supply one hundred soldiers. The name Bermuda Hundred came from the traumatic wreck in 1609 of a ship en route from England to Virginia. All 150 passengers and crew on board survived the incident, and most remained in Bermuda for ten months. The castaways took the wrecked ship apart and built two smaller ships to finally get to Virginia. Shakespeare incorporated the tale into his play *The Tempest*. Several of the voyagers died while shipwrecked and were buried in Bermuda, including John Rolfe's first wife and child.

West of the Bermuda Hundred was Drewry's Bluff, a fortified position ninety feet above the James River, about eight miles below the Confederate capital of Richmond. Here, as was the case with so many strategic sites, the river took a sharp S-curve, slowing any Union vessel attempting to make the bend. An impressive fortification perched there, called Fort Darling, was in an ideal setting to sink Yankee transports and gunboats bold enough to approach Richmond. Drewry's Bluff served as the biggest obstacle to the success of any such attempt, and capturing that location became an objective of the Federals. It was here that Godfrey Weitzel confronted his former mentor—"Little Napoleon"—General P. G. T. Beauregard, in May 1864.

On April 1, 1864, General Grant met with General Butler at Fort Monroe to discuss the status of the upcoming spring campaign against Richmond. It was the first time the two famous generals had ever met. Grant looked over maps of the area as Butler explained the lay of the land around Richmond. Grant thought the campaign could be best conducted by having the Army of the Potomac attack Lee's army and drive it back to Richmond. An army under Butler's command could then be put around Richmond on the south side of the James River. The two armies would then join above Richmond and "scoop it out of the Confederacy," cutting off all the sources of supply for Lee's army (*BB*, 627, 628).

On April 2, Godfrey Weitzel was relieved of his duties under General Banks in the Department of the Gulf and ordered to report "without delay" to Ben Butler in the Department of Virginia and North Carolina for further assignment to duty.[6] As Godfrey Weitzel headed north, a battle took place on April 8 in De Soto Parish, Louisiana, between Union troops and Confederates under Dick Taylor, Alfred Mouton, and Tom Green, Godfrey Weitzel's nemesis from the Lafourche Campaign. The Confederates had won the day's battle and Mouton pursued the fleeing Federals. As he passed a group of thirty-five Union soldiers, they threw down their arms to signal their surrender. Mouton turned and lifted his hand to stop the firing on his prisoners. It was reported that five Federals then stooped down, picked up their guns, and shot Alfred Mouton, who dropped from his saddle. Confederates who witnessed this cold-blooded murder gave a rebel yell and before their officers could stop them, all thirty-five Yankees lay dead.[7] It was a tragedy for each side, and an unworthy end for the Cajun general who had tormented Weitzel's brigade in the cane fields of Louisiana.

The Spring Campaign Begins

Back at Fort Monroe, on April 28, Grant gave General Butler his final instructions on a campaign against Richmond. "Start your forces the night of the 4th," Grant said, "so as to be as far up James River as you can get by daylight of the morning of the 5th, and push from that time with all your might for the accomplishment of the object before you."[8] Butler's plan was to seize the land between the Appomattox and James Rivers, establish a base there, and then move up north, following the south bank of the James River all the way into Richmond.

The Eighteenth Army Corps had been encamped at Yorktown, Virginia, at the mouth of Chesapeake Bay in preparation for the springtime campaign. With Godfrey Weitzel back under his command, Ben Butler tapped his friend to lead the Second Division of the Eighteenth Army Corps, a position he would hold until October 1864.[9] As restructured, the Eighteenth Corps now contained three divisions, commanded by Generals William T. H. Brooks, Godfrey Weitzel, and Edward Winslow Hincks, the division of the latter being composed of nearly all black troops led by white officers. During the next five months, the Eighteenth Army Corps would have six different commanders, with four changes of command in the month of September alone.[10] Its last commander would be Godfrey Weitzel, who was, once again, at the right place at the right time.

Following Grant's orders, on May 3, Ben Butler departed from Yorktown and made a feint up the York River, landing a group of men from transports, pretending that he would advance on Richmond from that point. "This deceived the enemy," *Harper's Weekly* reported, "who at once hurried their forces from Fort Powhatan and other defenses on the James River to meet the threatening column."[11] On the evening of May 5, General Butler received a letter from Elizabeth Van Lew, a Union spy in Richmond, advising that nearly all the troops had departed Richmond to join Lee's army, and that the capital was temporarily unguarded. She wrote that if Butler would send up his troops at once, Richmond could be taken before troops returned (*BB*, 640–41). Excited by this news, Ben Butler planned to march his troops the short fourteen miles north toward Richmond and, at a minimum, seize Drewry's Bluff, the key outpost high above the James River that commanded the river passage.

To his surprise, Butler's plan was opposed by two of his generals, William "Baldy" Smith and Quincy Gillmore, who felt it was a poor idea, based on unverified information from a spy. Even Godfrey Weitzel was reluctant to attack the rebel capital, which he called exceedingly hazardous. "General," Godfrey said, "I shall go if you order me to, as you know, and do the very best I can" (*BB*, 642). But Weitzel was worried about his mentor's fate if the assault failed. A loss in Richmond would bolster the Confederate resolve and be a humiliation to the Union. "General, . . . if it should fail after your two corps commanders, Smith and Gillmore, have so strenuously advised that it should not be undertaken, it would entirely ruin you." Godfrey would sacrifice his own reputation to fulfill

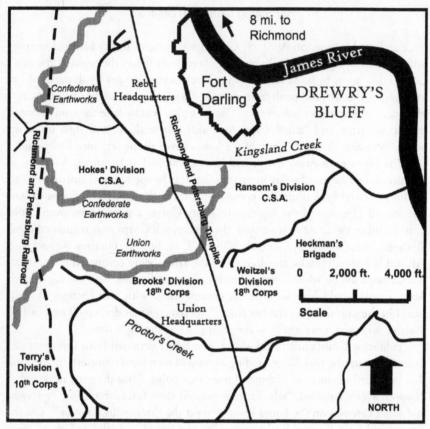

FIGURE 15.1. Map of Drewry's Bluff, May 16, 1864.

Butler's plans, stating that "to take charge of it under your orders would not harm me." Ben Butler was not prepared for Weitzel's next sentence. "As your strongest friend, I myself must advise against it" (642). Butler paused to consider Godfrey's advice. To fail against the opposition of three generals would give Butler's opponents fresh fodder against him. It could end his military career. Outnumbered three to one, Butler agreed to abandon the idea.

As more troops landed in early May, Butler set up camp on the Bermuda Hundred, fortifying his base of operations there. In addition to constructing a five-mile channel across the isthmus from the James River to the Appomattox River, he had observation towers built on a high plateau overlooking a great bend in the Appomattox River known as the Point of Rocks. From this tall vantage point, Yankees could see the church spires in Petersburg across the valley below. Days were spent in reconnaissance and skirmishing, as well as destroying a portion of the railroad between Richmond and Petersburg so as to cut off communication between those points and interrupt the flow of troops and supplies from the South to Lee's army (*BB*, 643).

Battle of Drewry's Bluff

On May 8, Godfrey wrote a letter from his headquarters on Cobb's Hill saying, "We can see Petersburg easy. My division arrived here on Friday morning last. . . . Beauregard is in command of the rebels out here."[12] Those "rebels" were defending Richmond and consisted of a meager force of about 6,000 troops—no match for Butler's 30,000 bluecoats in the Army of the James. However, rebel reinforcements were constantly arriving to bolster the defenses. Rather than make a surge against P. G. T. Beauregard's smaller forces, Butler sent General August Kautz's cavalry on a raid against the Weldon Railroad. This delay gave Beauregard time to amass 30,000 rebel troops at his position near Drewry's Bluff, equaling the Union forces.

Shortly after daybreak on May 12, General Kautz's cavalry made a second raid on the railroads, which were protected by the Eighteenth Corps as well as a division of the Tenth Corps. Godfrey Weitzel's Second Division of the Eighteenth Corps soon began skirmishing with the enemy and gradually pressed them back to a creek. There, the Confederates under Godfrey's former friend and mentor P. G. T. Beauregard opened fire with two pieces of artillery. Rebel guns were quickly dislodged by Union shells, allowing Weitzel to form his men into a line of battle on the north side of the creek.

While several regiments of New Englanders forced their way through a marsh and a dense thicket, Generals Godfrey Weitzel and John Turner forged ahead into more open country, driving Beauregard back across Proctor's Creek. Later that day, General Quincy Gillmore came up to reinforce Weitzel and Turner with part of the Tenth Corps and a battery. The Little Napoleon was being pushed into a corner and needed reinforcements. After three days of skirmishing with no significant results, Beauregard learned that Confederate general Robert Ransom Jr.'s brigade of about eighteen hundred men and officers would arrive in the evening to reinforce him. Ransom's men had been involved in the fortification of Drewry's Bluff and knew the area well. With this information, Beauregard decided to play offense rather than defense. He instructed his men to make an assault at daybreak, hoping to cut off the Union Army from its base of operations and either capture or destroy it.

Beauregard would test the cunning of his former protégé Godfrey Weitzel with a frontal attack on his position. If the Union line showed any sign of giving way, Beauregard would push his entire force to the front and overwhelm the bluecoats.

On May 15, General Weitzel had his men of the Eighteenth Corps build a crude breastwork of logs along his entire front. The Tenth Corps was defended by the outer line of the enemy's entrenchments, which the Union had seized and used in reverse—hunkering down on the outside of the berms that the Confederates had built. The Union's breast-high entrenchments were in a field, just out of range of the enemy's cannons. These earthworks left only a small open space of a quarter-mile between the winding James River and the right of the Union line. That space was patrolled and held by Yankee cavalry acting as pickets (*BB*, 657).

Seeing the early morning mist rise from the river, Godfrey began to devise a plan to prevent a surprise attack, which he anticipated any day. The engineer-soldier came up with a clever idea that had not been tried before by Union or Confederate armies.

The Fog of War

Although credit for the concept remains in dispute, Union troops had procured nine miles of telegraph wire taken down from poles along the railroad so as to disrupt communications with Richmond. With all this wire, Weitzel suggested to Butler that he be allowed to wrap the wire calf-high around the stumps of trees about fifty yards in front of the Union positions and around posts driven into the ground. If the enemy were to make a nighttime charge, or one in the early morning fog, men would stumble over the wires within muzzle-shot of the Yankee position. Butler, who always liked unique approaches to battle, promptly approved of the idea (*BB*, 658). Wires were strung in front of the left and center divisions of the Eighteenth Corps, in front of Brooks's and Weitzel's men, and wound tightly around tree stumps. The idea worked as planned.

In the moonlight of May 15, Weitzel's sentinels could see that something was going on along the Confederate line. While the pickets exchanged a few shots, no news was reported to General Weitzel of any activity on his front. As anticipated, about five o'clock on the morning of May 16, Beauregard made a surprise advance shielded by a dense fog. The enemy opposing Weitzel consisted of six brigades and one regiment, outnumbering General Weitzel's two brigades and three regiments by about two to one.[13] The telegraph wire evened the odds.

As the rebels sneaked closer to Weitzel's position, hundreds of Confederate foot soldiers stumbled over the wires in confusion. When their voices and groans were heard, Union pickets opened with a barrage of rifle shots. The Federal position was so well protected that General Weitzel reported, "The enemy, in falling over the telegraph wire, were slaughtered like partridges." Godfrey added that the regiments making up his line did not move until they had twice repulsed the enemy "with terrible slaughter, they being piled in heaps over the telegraph wire." A Confederate colonel called it "a Yankee trick."[14] Writing to a friend about the battle, Godfrey said,

At daybreak, in a dense fog the enemy who had been heavily reinforced during the night from Richmond . . . got on the right flank and rear of my line which was nearest to the front and in a very short time overwhelmed one of my brigades and broke it. I never have been under such fire nor ever seen such men slaughtered so. The rebels came on to my line in dense masses determined to drive me, and they were just piled up in heaps. During the night before I had made my men make log breastworks in front of their line, and there I made them take some telegraph wire and stretch it along my whole front near the ground, winding it firmly around stump &c. The rebels came on to charge my breastworks. Every time they came to the wire, as it was foggy, they stumbled and fell over it and then I peppered it to them.[15]

General Charles Heckman's brigade was not as fortunate, lacking the advantage of the trip wire. According to members of the Eighteenth Corps, there was not wire enough to go around the entire Union line and Generals Brooks and Weitzel were extremely close to the enemy, while Heckman was not in such danger of a sudden rush. Therefore, the wire was used only for those troops in the most peril, the divisions of Brooks and Weitzel.[16]

The mist was so thick that morning, an object ten feet away could not be seen. "A dense fog enveloped us," Heckman wrote, "completely concealing the enemy from view" (*BB*, 663). Heckman claimed that the fog was so thick, he could not see the enemy's advance until they were five paces in front, their metal bayonets coming into clear sight. A red-hot volley of musket fire was unleashed by Union troops, driving the rebel column back in confusion. Confederate officers were not deterred and encouraged the attackers to try and try again, five times.

Despite the thick fog, Ransom's brigade overpowered Heckman's troops in just an hour of fighting and Heckman was forced to retreat. "I never at any other time experienced such a musketry fire as on that day," Heckman recalled, adding that he lost nearly all of his field and line officers (*BB*, 663). The rebels captured several hundred Union troops, and even General Heckman himself, who was sent to a prison at Charleston.

Weitzel to the Rescue

The fog and smoke from rifle fire on May 16 was so dense that soldiers could not see even a horseman fifteen yards away.[17] In the "fog of war," General Weitzel's orderly got lost and strayed into enemy territory, where he was captured by one of Beauregard's pickets. The frightened orderly called out to General Weitzel, who had boldly moved to the front with his skirmishers. "General, a Johnny has got me prisoner!" the prisoner yelled. "Come out here and save me!"[18] The lanky young general sprang out with his pistol in hand and rescued the orderly, capturing the rebel picket as well. He must have seemed like a ghoul at six feet four, coming out of the fog and surprising the Confederate picket. As he placed his long silver revolver to the head of the captor, forcing him to give his rifle to the orderly, the terrified young Southerner begged Weitzel not to shoot. The rebel picket was astonished to learn that he had just been taken prisoner by a division commander and brigadier general!

The orderly, once prisoner—now victor, marched the terrified enemy picket to the Union rear.[19] Soon the story spread among the ranks of the Eighteenth Corps, endearing General Weitzel to his troops for his bravery in action without regard to his rank. Coupled with his clever trip wire, this had been a good day for Godfrey, though a Confederate victory overall.

Around noon, as Confederate reinforcements came in from Petersburg, Ben Butler ordered his entire force to retreat to the Union entrenchments and secure their positions in the fortified safety of the Bermuda Hundred. All divisions fell back, leaving Drewry's Bluff to P. G. T. Beauregard for another day.

The Little Napoleon Attacks

On May 18, Confederates attacked on the right of the Union line but were repulsed. Beauregard had now amassed an impressive force of 25,000 men, not counting those guarding the towns of Petersburg and Richmond. Outnumbering Butler's forces of 20,000 bluecoats, the Louisiana-born general ordered a second assault against the Union position on May 19, which was more to test the Yankee lines in preparation for the major attack the next day.

Beauregard's main attack came on the morning of May 20, when he charged against the weakest point in Butler's lines. The Confederates started a brush fire between 9:00 and 10:00 a.m., igniting the chevaux-de-frise of dry wood that had been placed in front of the Union position as an obstacle. The smoke created a man-made fog between the two opposing armies. Through the hazy smoke, the enemy came rushing forward with its famous rebel yell. The Yankees fought them off, holding the Union position and repulsing each attempt to dislodge them (BB, 665).

On May 21, 1864, Godfrey wrote to a friend, "Last night General Butler sent for me and told me that he must have me near him. The truth is that he did not know how to manage so large an army and wants me to help him."[20]

That morning, P. G. T. Beauregard ordered yet another attack, but with Weitzel's help, Butler's men repulsed the attack (BB, 666). Beauregard regrouped to evaluate the two-day effort and decided to make no further advances against the strong Union lines. He ordered about nine thousand of his men sent to General Robert E. Lee by the way of Richmond.

Comstock Arrives; The Siege of Petersburg Begins

On June 9, 1864, Godfrey Weitzel was reunited again with his college chum Cyrus Comstock, who was now General Grant's chief engineer. The two classmates rode together along the very strong Union line at Bermuda Hundred, stopping at General Butler's headquarters. The pair of chief engineers entered Ben Butler's office and saluted the forty-five-year-old general from Massachusetts. Also in the room was the German-born cavalry officer from Cincinnati, August V. Kautz.

Having failed to take Richmond, Butler yearned to now capture Petersburg, a desire that he said, "lay near my heart" (*BB*, 672). Butler told Comstock that with "Baldy" Smith's Eighteenth Corps, he could hold the line against Lee's army.[21] August Kautz joined the conversation, adding that he did not think the rebels had more than fifteen hundred men in Petersburg. This fueled Butler's desire to take Petersburg by storm. Cyrus Comstock was invited by his classmate Godfrey Weitzel to spend the night before returning to General Grant with his report. It was good to see an old friend in times like these.

Cyrus Comstock returned again to Butler's camp at Bermuda Hundred on June 28 to discuss strategy with Generals Weitzel and Butler. Godfrey now believed that it would be feasible to make a run at Richmond, a view shared by other generals. Comstock reported Weitzel's assessment to General Grant, adding that while the plan was certainly practicable, it would not have the needed effect. "Even if we put our whole force there," Comstock told Grant, "I do not think it would make Lee leave Petersburg."[22] If the effort did not move General Robert E. Lee's army, then Comstock doubted the viability of an attack. Such a deployment would only weaken the Federal line on the James River and make it subject to being broken by the Confederates.

Grant took in the advice of both Weitzel and Comstock and replied, "We must do it or move farther 'round Petersburg so as to cut the Weldon-Lynchburg railroad." Grant stroked his beard and said, "I have not decided which option to take," adding that General George G. Meade did not think he could pull it off. Comstock advised that if the Army could not cut Lee's line now, then it could never do it.[23] These were words Grant did not want to hear, since that meant a siege would be necessary to weaken Lee to the point of submission.

To get a better assessment of the rebel strength, Comstock went the next day to one of General Butler's observation towers. Climbing to the top and peering through field glasses, Cyrus could distinctly make out an entrenched line running from Port Walthall Junction to Swift Creek, with one strong earthwork blocking the ground over which the Federals would have to move. He concluded that neither Butler nor Weitzel knew of the long earthwork since they did not mention it in their meeting. "This would make a surprise [attack] difficult," Cyrus wrote, "and make a repulse disastrous."[24] When Comstock gave his report to General Grant that evening, the lieutenant general abandoned the idea of a surge into Richmond. It would be a siege after all.

Weitzel Promotoed and Chosen for a Special Mission

In the July heat General Weitzel suffered a sunstroke that rendered him unable to leave his quarters for several weeks.[25] His illness continued into August, causing Godfrey to take an extended sick leave.[26] Despite his illness, for his gallantry in the battle of Drewry's Bluff and in the Bermuda Hundred in general, on August 26 Godfrey Weitzel was rewarded with the brevet of major general of Volunteers. This was only a temporary promotion, however, and within just a few months Godfrey would be made a full major general at age twenty-nine.

A few weeks after his promotion, Godfrey Weitzel was summoned by General Grant for a meeting at City Point. The young general entered Grant's office, unaware of the agenda. "He there told me that an expedition was being prepared to close the mouth of Cape Fear River, near Wilmington," Godfrey recalled. "It was to be composed of a large naval force, and of a land force consisting of from 6,000 to 10,000 men."[27] His mission would be to silence and capture an impressive enemy fort guarding Wilmington, North Carolina, known as Fort Fisher. Although the War Department had originally selected another officer to command the land forces of the expedition, Grant rejected that officer, "as he had once shown timidity." Instead, Ulysses S. Grant chose Major General Godfrey Weitzel to command the land forces of the important Wilmington expedition, a considerable vote of confidence.

"Weitzel," Grant said, "this is to be another Mobile affair. The navy will run some of their vessels into Cape Fear River, and I would advise you to land your troops and take a position across the peninsula, and then Fort Fisher and these works will fall exactly as Fort Morgan did."[28] Grant gave Godfrey no orders about entrenching if the fort did not fall. The plan was for the Navy to run past the fort, just as Farragut had done below New Orleans and at Port Hudson. Weitzel would then land his men.

Grant advised that David Porter, who was now an admiral, would command the Navy's fleet, with whom Godfrey was well acquainted since New Orleans. Grant told Godfrey to go meet with Porter in Washington, where the two were to confer and work out the logistics. General Grant provided Weitzel with all the charts and papers he had relating to the expedition and told Godfrey to read them over carefully and make any suggestions.

Godfrey pored over the documents, examining them late into the evening at City Point. The following day, he called on General Grant again before departing. "As I am to command the expedition, I think I should go down off Wilmington, reconnoiter the ground, and get all the information I can of the character and strength of the enemy's works at the mouth of Cape Fear River," Weitzel said.[29] Grant agreed and assigned Godfrey the Army gunboat USS *Chamberlain* for the task.

Weitzel steamed down the coast abord the *Chamberlain* on September 27, coming near the mouth of New Inlet, not far from the rebel-held Fort Fisher.

He met with naval officers from the Wilmington blockade, some of whom had been positioned there for more than two years. He also interviewed several of the naval pilots who were from North Carolina and "knew every green pine tree between Wilmington and the mouth of Cape Fear River."[30] After three days of gathering information, Godfrey pulled into the harbor near Fort Monroe. There was no time to meet with Admiral Porter in Washington, however, since an awaiting telegraph message ordered Weitzel to return to the battlefield, on the north side of James River, as quickly as he could ride there. A fight was raging between Union and Confederate forces south of Richmond at a place called Fort Harrison. Many generals had been wounded, and Ben Butler wanted Weitzel there to assume command!

The Capture of Fort Harrison

The Battle of Chaffin's Farm is noted not only for the capture of Fort Harrison, but also for the great heroism and tragic loss of black troops in the engagement. The Fourth and Sixth U.S. Colored Infantry each lost more than 50 percent of their men, killed and wounded. In a joint assault by the Tenth Army Corps under General David Birney and the Eighteenth Corps under General Edward Ord, the Federals were massed on the north side of the James River, near Deep Bottom. At daybreak on September 29, the entire force was thrown at Fort Harrison. Brigades formed in battle lines with orders to strike and drive the enemy as rapidly as possible. General Ord's assault was led by Brigadier General George Stannard, a veteran of Gettysburg. All three of Stannard's brigade commanders were wounded or killed in the fighting, including General Hiram Burnham, in whose honor the captured fort was renamed. General Ord was also critically wounded in the battle. He was replaced temporarily by General Charles Heckman, who had only recently been released from a rebel prison after his capture in the fog at Drewry's Bluff.

When fighting ceased, Federal troops had occupied the U-shaped earthworks. They worked through the night to close up the open north end of the fort, which faced Richmond and the enemy. General Butler arrived at Fort Harrison to inspect the new Union prize and was surprised to find General Grant already there. Butler knew that it would take up to twelve hours for Lee to get any sufficient reinforcements from Petersburg to attempt to dislodge the Yankees from the fort. His confidence amused Grant, who responded laughingly, "Well, General, if you say so, and as this is your expedition, I do not think I ought to interfere" (*BB*, 736). Grant returned to Petersburg after giving Butler's officers a hardy congratulations on their effort.

General Grant had left before newly brevetted Major General Godfrey Weitzel arrived that evening, fresh from his reconnaissance trip to Wilmington. "I rode over there and found the Army of the James engaged in battle with

the enemy," Godfrey recalled. After reporting in, Ben Butler promptly transferred command of the Eighteenth Army Corps to Weitzel, replacing Heckman,
who was standing in for the injured Ord. Godfrey was initially concerned that
this command might interfere with his expedition to Wilmington, but General
Grant told Godfrey to continue the preparations.[31]

With command of the Eighteenth Corps came responsibility for the captured Fort Harrison. Godfrey immediately began preparations to defend an anticipated counterattack by Robert E. Lee.

Weitzel Faces Off with Robert E. Lee

Realizing the strategic loss of Fort Harrison, Robert E. Lee planned overnight
to personally accompany ten thousand reinforcements from Petersburg under
General Charles Field to recapture the fort guarding Richmond. He would face
his former student and top cadet, Godfrey Weitzel, who now commanded the
captured fort.

It was perhaps inevitable that former Cadet Weitzel and his respected superintendent, Robert E. Lee, would meet inVirginia before the war's end. That day
came on Friday, September 30, 1864, when Weitzel's Eighteenth Corps of barely
five thousand men successfully held Fort Harrison against counterattacks by two
divisions personally commanded by General Lee. Godfrey wrote that "the rebels
in much superior force tried to retake what they had lost, and I repulsed their two
desperate assaults."[32] Grant wrote, "All their efforts failed, their attacks being all
repulsed with very heavy loss."[33]

Friday was rainy, and Lee's attempt was ineffective, as different brigades
attacked throughout the day, mostly from the north. Three times, the Union
line was charged by Lee's troops, but Weitzel's men held firm. The rebuilt fort
proved an impenetrable position and remained in Union hands. Lee kept up the
attack until nearly nightfall, when he finally withdrew in defeat. Against Lee's
much larger force, Weitzel's Eighteenth Corps captured more than eight hundred
Confederate prisoners and eight battle flags. Lee's loss was sizable, as Godfrey reported that his Federals "buried 264 rebels on that day and only lost 15 killed and
79 wounded." As a new corps commander, it was his first victory, within hours
of taking charge of the Eighteenth Corps. Benjamin Butler wrote that Weitzel's
men "most bravely and inflexibly" held the position, adding that "every man was
a hero on that day" (BB, 737).

A few weeks later, in mid-October, General Grant showed up at Weitzel's
headquarters on the James to find out how his reconnaissance trip went at
Wilmington. Godfrey reported that based on the plan Grant had outlined
during their first meeting at City Point, "I thought that 6,000 men would be
sufficient" to capture Fort Fisher. Grant wanted to delay the expedition a bit,
since information had leaked to rebel newspapers "and it was known all over

the South."[34] He wanted Weitzel to continue his preparations, but wait for further orders on the date to move out.

The Second Battle of Fair Oaks

General David B. Birney became severely ill and was ordered home to Philadelphia, where he later died on October 18, 1864. As a result, the command of the Tenth Army Corps was transferred to General Alfred Terry. With Godfrey Weitzel now in command of the Eighteenth Corps and General Terry commanding troops from the Tenth Corps, orders were given for a joint operation to stretch out Lee's line. Grant ordered Butler's Army of the James to create "a diversion" north of the James River so that Lee could not reinforce his Petersburg lines with troops from Richmond. Rather than a mere diversion, however, Ben Butler sensed the time was right to do more than test Lee's lines. Butler still wanted to storm into Richmond.

He presented his case to Grant and to Grant's chief engineer, Cyrus Comstock, on October 2. If he could borrow another corps from General Meade, Butler felt certain he could capture the rebel capital. Comstock was not warm to the idea. He felt that at best, the Federals might carry the outside line, but not the interior line. Comstock told Butler that he would lose much more than the enemy, and his troops would eventually have to fall back.[35] Contrary to Comstock's intuition, Grant was at first inclined to let Butler try his plan, but after hearing Comstock's pessimism, refused the request. Grant allowed a diversion to be attempted, but no assault on Richmond. The so-called diversion took place on October 27–28 around the town of Fair Oaks Station and has, therefore, been called the Second Battle of Fair Oaks.

The first Battle of Fair Oaks occurred on May 31–June 1, 1862, when Union troops under General George McClellan first reached the outskirts of Richmond. It was the second-largest loss of life in the early stages of the war, with more than eleven thousand casualties over two days of intense fighting at close range. Also known as the Battle of Seven Pines, since that was where the heaviest fighting occurred, the 1862 conflict there was a stalemate with nearly equal losses on both sides. The second battle on this same ground proved, however, to be one of Godfrey Weitzel's most devastating losses.

Although Weitzel's Eighteenth Army Corps now firmly held Fort Harrison, it was nearly surrounded by Confederate troops under the leadership of Confederate lieutenant general James Longstreet, who commanded the Richmond defenses. At daylight on October 27, Ben Butler ordered a joint test of the Confederate lines by both Terry's Tenth and Weitzel's Eighteenth Army Corps. Terry was to advance up the Darbytown and Charles City Roads and create a diversion to the north of Fort Gilmer, blocking those routes into the city. Meanwhile, Weitzel was to pass behind Terry and surprise the graycoats by flanking them at the intersection of the

Williamsburg Road and the York River Railroad. Butler hoped that if successful on the Williamsburg Road, Weitzel could push toward Richmond if the enemy was undermanned.[36]

"Butler thought he could take Richmond," Comstock later wrote, "and gave instructions accordingly." Ben Butler seemed perfectly willing to run the risk of losing 2,000 to 3,000 men in an unsuccessful assault, Comstock felt, even though there "was not one chance in ten of doing it."[37] Despite Grant's orders and under pressure from General Butler, at 1:00 p.m. on October 27, Weitzel's Eighteenth Corps reached the Williamsburg Road after an eight-hour march and turned west. Longstreet realized that the Union skirmishers from Terry's Tenth Corps were merely trying to distract attention. Suspecting an attempt to surprise the left, Longstreet promptly ordered Confederate general Charles Field's division to extend itself in that direction.

At 3:30 p.m. Weitzel sent two of his seven brigades to attack across open ground. Field's division and a few pieces of artillery arrived just in time to meet Weitzel's surprise attack. The Union assault was so undermanned that both Confederate brigades charged out from behind their breastworks after stopping the initial Federal thrust and captured several hundred prisoners. It was an embarrassing defeat, resulting in 516 killed and wounded Federals, with another 587 missing, for a total loss of 1,103 casualties. By contrast, Longstreet reported only 64 killed, wounded, and missing, since his troops were protected behind entrenchments. While the figure may be too low, the disparity reflects the ease with which Longstreet stopped Butler's attempt to storm Richmond. Grant ordered the troops back to their camps.

Weitzel Makes Full Major General and Is Given Command of the Only All-Black Corps

Godfrey Weitzel celebrated his twenty-ninth birthday five days after the Second Battle of Fair Oaks, on a chilly November 1, 1864. A week later, Abraham Lincoln was reelected president, defeating the Democratic candidate George McClellan, the "peace candidate." Lincoln carried 22 states to just 3 for General McClellan, although the popular vote was closer at 55 percent to 45 percent. A bitter McClellan remarked, "For my country's sake, I deplore the result."[38]

Despite his loss at Fair Oaks, Godfrey received the highest military promotion of his career, appointed as a major general of Volunteers on December 12, 1864. This was no mere "brevet," as was his promotion in August, but a full two-star major general, nominated by the reelected president Abraham Lincoln. The promotion was made retroactive to November 17 and was accelerated, in part, by the death of General David Birney on October 18, which resulted in the need for another major general in the Army of the James. With his new title, the Army had yet another new assignment for the twenty-nine-year-old officer,

FIGURE 15.2. Field photo of Major General Benjamin F. Butler (seated in chair) and his loyal protégé, Brigadier General Godfrey Weitzel (center, sitting), Bermuda Hundred, Virginia (spring 1864). (Photograph by Mathew Brady; National Archives, Reference No. NWDNS-111-B-194.)

one that was unique among all officers in the war—command of an all-black Army corps.

The War Department issued General Order No. 297 on December 3, 1864, making substantial changes in the composition of the Army of the James. Godfrey Weitzel's Eighteenth Army Corps was disbanded. The white troops of Terry's Tenth and Weitzel's Eighteenth Corps were organized into a new combined corps, designated the Twenty-Fourth Army Corps, and commanded by the now-recovered Major General Edward Ord. The black troops belonging to the Tenth and Eighteenth Corps were then organized into an all-black unit, designated the Twenty-Fifth Army Corps. All of the black troops of the Department of Virginia and North Carolina, no matter what corps or regiment, were then assigned to this new corps. The only white troops, other than officers attached to the Twenty-Fifth, were the artillery brigade of the Tenth Corps with its existing staff.

The Twenty-Fifth Corps was the very last Union Corps formed during the Civil War, and the only all-black corps. Ben Butler knew exactly who he wanted to lead it—Godfrey Weitzel! It was a fitting irony for Weitzel, who two years earlier in Louisiana had told Ben Butler, "I cannot command these Negro regiments." Now it was not just two regiments of Native Guards, but an entire Army corps, consisting of nine black regiments in three divisions. The Twenty-Fifth Corps was assigned to the Army of the James.

For whatever doubts Weitzel initially harbored about all-black units, he was a changed man by the end of the war. On January 31, 1866, he said of his black troops, "Its organization was an experiment which has proven a perfect success. The conduct of its soldiers has been such to draw praise from persons most prejudiced against color, and there is no record which should give the colored race more pride than that left by the 25th Army Corps." This would be Godfrey's last command of the war, but the most eventful and, ultimately, the most historic. He would seize Richmond and march these black troops into the heart of the Confederate capital.

CHAPTER 16

Fort Fisher and Ben Butler's Powder Boat

History has been kind to Godfrey Weitzel and his role in the aborted Christmas Day assault on Fort Fisher. Ben Butler took full responsibility for the mission's failure. Butler was used to criticism by this point in the war and never made any effort to deflect the blame onto his protégé, even after a congressional inquiry. The failed attempt to seize Fort Fisher would go down in history as another Ben Butler folly, rather than being attributed to the Navy's delays, bad weather, and high seas, which doomed the land assault. Fortunately for the mission's official commander, Godfrey Weitzel, no blame was laid at his feet.

The Fort Fisher Expedition

At the southern tip of the triangular peninsula that separates the Atlantic Ocean from the Cape Fear River lies the sandy ruins of the once great Confederate stronghold named Fort Fisher. Ben Butler called it "the strongest earthwork built by the Confederacy."[1] Only about a fourth of the fort remains today, the rest lost to the sea. Carolina hurricanes and erosion of the seacoast have stolen most of the gunports that guarded the north approach and swept away all of the east-facing earthworks. The grass-covered slopes are silent reminders of the two grandest naval assaults of the four-year war.

To continue its strangulation of the South, the Union had to put a noose around the Cape Fear River and shut off its supply line into the port of Wilmington, North Carolina. "This port was of immense importance to the Confederates," General Grant wrote, "because it formed their principal inlet for blockade runners by means of which they brought in from abroad such supplies and munitions of war as they could not produce at home."[2] Grant determined, with the concurrence of the Navy Department, that he would send a joint Navy-Army expedition against the fort, thus cutting off a major supply artery feeding the Southern cause.

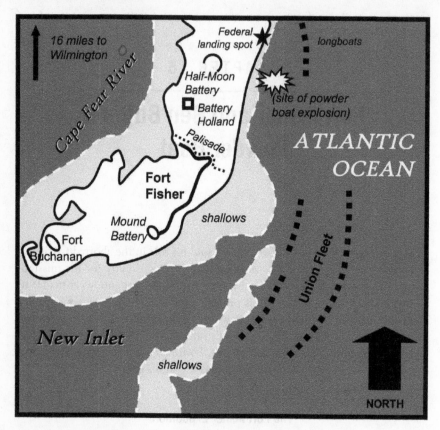

FIGURE 16.1. Map of Fort Fisher and surroundings.

Fort Fisher was named after Colonel Charles F. Fisher, a North Carolina native who fell at the First Battle of Manassas. Sometimes referred to as the "Gibraltar of the South," the dune-fort was the last major coastal stronghold of the Confederacy. Its tall walls were built of sand and earth that created more than twenty separate mounds, between which there were heavy guns mounted on wooden platforms. An armament of twenty-one guns and three mortars guarded the landside to the north, plus another twenty-four guns faced east, toward the Atlantic. These guns could be wheeled in a 360-degree arc to fire on any approaching enemy. Underground passageways were built with heavy timbers, and bombproof rooms were tucked deep below the giant mounds. From behind the dunes and inside protective bomb shelters, the rebels who occupied the fort felt they were safe from even the most aggressive of land or sea assaults. That presumption would soon be tested by the Union Army and Navy.

Blockade-runners leaving Wilmington via the Cape Fear River set sail for friendly outposts in the Bahamas, Bermuda, or even Nova Scotia, where they could trade Southern cotton and tobacco for British war supplies. Coastal geography favored the runners at the wide mouth of the river, which split between Smith's Island and the Frying Pan Shoals.[3] A sandbar prevented any sizable Union vessel from approaching the fort but allowed the low-hulled smuggling vessels to glide in and out at will. A man-made channel called "New Inlet" cut across the peninsula just south of Fort Fisher, allowing the sleek runners to slip in under protection of rebel artillery.

The rebel fort was under the command of William Lamb, a colonel of the Second North Carolina Artillery, who had anticipated a Union assault for many months.[4] He stockpiled about thirty-six hundred shot and shell and strengthened the earthworks.

Ben Butler commanded the Department of Virginia and North Carolina and, therefore, was Godfrey Weitzel's senior officer. Butler weighed in on the planning for the Fort Fisher assault, confirming that the expedition would consist of about 6,500 infantry, plus two batteries of artillery and fifty mounted cavalry. General Adelbert Ames's division of the Twenty-Fourth Army Corps and General Charles Paine's division of Weitzel's Twenty-Fifth Corps would supply the necessary troops. Godfrey was to meet with both Ames and Paine and instruct them "to select their best men."[5] The troops were to be supplied with ample ammunition and five days' rations. Weitzel and his men were scheduled to depart from Deep Bottom on December 7 for the North Carolina coast. And there was one last detail that Ben Butler had in mind, one that he felt certain would ease the capture of Fort Fisher: the "powder boat."

The "Powder Boat" Idea

A newspaper article caught Ben Butler's attention about great destruction for many miles created by an explosion of gunpowder at Erith, England. He also knew of the devastation caused by rebel sabotage when a barge loaded with ammunition exploded at City Point in August 1864. After further study, Butler became convinced that by igniting a large mass of explosives on a boat floated to within four or five hundred yards of Fort Fisher, the sand-dune garrison would be leveled, or "at least be so far paralyzed as to enable, by a prompt landing of men, a seizure of the fort" (*BB*, 775).

While in Washington, D.C., in November 1864, Butler had the opportunity to suggest the "powder experiment" to President Lincoln, to the secretary of the Navy, and to General Halleck. "It was readily embraced by the Secretary of the Navy," said Butler, "and with more caution by the President. Further investigation was suggested, and I left the matter in the hands of the navy" (*BB*, 775). Ben Butler shared the idea with his trusted engineer, Godfrey Weitzel, saying that "the Rebels had frequently used torpedoes against us . . . we are going to use one against them—larger than any they had ever used!"[6] Assuring Weitzel that this was Butler's idea and its success or failure would be on his shoulders, he said, "I am going to take you with two divisions down there, and see that this powder boat is exploded properly."[7]

Butler wanted to level the fort with a bomb, then send in the infantry under his protégé's command to seize the place. Godfrey would handle the details while Butler grabbed the glory. Butler presented his novel plan to General Grant and Admiral Porter in November, predicting that such a huge explosion would flatten the fort's earthen walls and kill most inside. With Grant's and Lincoln's endorsement, Admiral Porter agreed to provide the explosives and a barge to transport the bomb. He selected the USS *Louisiana*, a flat-bottomed, shallow-draft vessel assigned to blockade duty. It was disarmed, cut down, and camouflaged to look like a blockade-runner. Butler's men then loaded the boat with 150 to 200 tons of gunpowder and attached an elaborate ignition system.

The idea was novel in its day, but in modern times the use of car bombs and even "powder boats" by terrorists have had incredible effect, such as the Oklahoma City bombing in 1995 and the attack on the USS *Cole* in 2000. Eerily, Butler foretold that if his powder boat was effective, "the whole system of offensive warfare by naval procedure would be changed," for no forts near harbors would be safe if a small vessel loaded with gunpowder was run ashore and exploded, destroying all the people in the fort. It was an early weapon of mass destruction, and Butler predicted that the enemy would abandon their forts whenever a powder boat approached (*BB*, 775). Tight security today around naval ports and ships shows that his prediction was accurate.

Moving Ahead with the Expedition

Grant was anxious for the expedition to get started due to fine weather.[8] Upon receipt of Grant's direction, Butler wrote to Admiral Porter in Norfolk on December 4. "When can you be ready with our little experiment?" Butler asked. "Time is valuable from the news we get." Porter replied, "We are ready for the 150 tons of powder."[9] Each day was critical to success.

Two days later, Grant sent orders to Butler explaining the mission's objectives: "The first object of the expedition under General Weitzel," Grant wrote, "is to close to the enemy the port of Wilmington. If successful in this, the second will be the capture of Wilmington itself" (*BB*, 782). Grant continued in words that would later be omitted by Ben Butler when communicating with Godfrey Weitzel on the night of battle. "The object of the expedition will be gained on effecting a landing on the mainland between Cape Fear River and the Atlantic, north of the north entrance to the river." Should Weitzel be able to pull off such a landing, Grant added, "whether the enemy hold Fort Fisher or the batteries guarding the entrance to the river there, the troops *should intrench* [sic] *themselves*, and by co-operation with the navy effect the reduction and capture of those places." With the fort and the batteries in Union hands, "the navy could enter the harbor, and the port of Wilmington would be sealed" (782).

Godfrey Weitzel was not told that Butler was under orders to "entrench" if the fort did not fall—a key omission that ultimately led to Butler's dismissal from the Army—he never showed Grant's orders to Weitzel. In fact, it was not until January 1865 that Godfrey first saw Grant's orders, when published in the Cincinnati newspaper.

The Mission Goes Forward

On December 7, Ben Butler received a dispatch from General Grant instructing him to let Weitzel get off to North Carolina as soon as possible. The time to strike Fort Fisher was at hand (*BB*, 784). From his headquarters at the Bermuda Hundred, General Weitzel ordered Ames's division of the Twenty-Fourth Corps and Paine's division of the Twenty-Fifth Corps to prepare to cross the James River that night. Under cover of darkness, the troops boarded transports with directions to rendezvous at Fort Monroe at Hampton Roads—just across the bay from Norfolk (784). From there, the Army flotilla was ordered to meet Admiral Porter's fleet far off the coast of Wilmington, over the horizon and out of sight of Colonel Lamb and his rebel sand fort. Butler left that same day, stopping only at City Point to shake hands with General Grant and let him know the expedition had begun.

Grant was surprised to see Butler aboard, having directed that General Weitzel lead the expedition. "[General Butler] knew that it was not intended that he should go," Grant recalled, "but my orders and instructions were sent through him as commander of the department."[10] Therefore, Grant did not question Butler's presence as a supervisor. Out of caution, Grant assigned his trusted chief engineer, Colonel Cyrus B. Comstock, to accompany the expedition and to keep an eye on the unpredictable Butler. Godfrey was delighted to see Cyrus and welcomed his assistance in planning the complicated land and sea assault. "He is an engineer officer, and was a class-mate of mine," Godfrey said. "We are quite intimate friends."[11]

On December 9 the Army transports began arriving at Hampton Roads, where the men, rations, and horses were transferred to large ocean steamers. Generals Butler and Weitzel took the opportunity to pay a visit with Colonel Comstock to Admiral David Porter, whose flagship the USS *Malvern* was docked close by, at Norfolk. On Saturday afternoon, December 10, Butler and the two West Pointers steamed across the bay where Butler informed Porter that the Army was all packed and ready for action. To Butler's surprise, the admiral informed him that the powder boat was not quite ready. He also cautioned Butler that he should not put his troops at sea, given the condition of the weather (*BB*, 785).

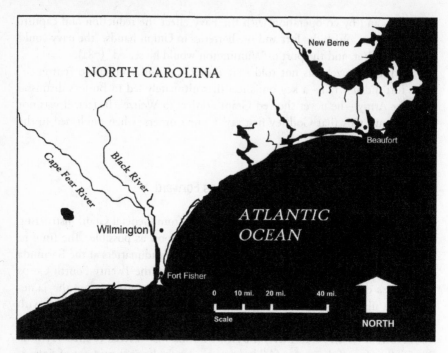

FIGURE 16.2. Map of the Atlantic Coast, from Wilmington to Beaufort, North Carolina.

Admiral Porter took the opportunity to take a shot at his rival Butler, writing to the assistant secretary of the Navy, Gustavus Fox, on December 10 that "Butler has just put his troops on board the transports in all the rain and storm, and is now in a great hurry to get off." In a mocking tone, Porter continued, "I believe the troops are all Negroes, and I believe Butler is going himself to look on or direct—he had better leave it to Weitzel" (*BB*, 283). In fact, the Army's ocean transports stayed in port to ride out inclement weather. The fleet took on board twenty days' additional rations and lay at anchor waiting for a terrific storm to break.

Waiting at Sea

"We lay here until the 13th instant," a frustrated Godfrey Weitzel wrote, "awaiting for the navy to get ready and the weather to improve."[12] As the storm let up, Porter advised Butler that they could set sail on December 13, but that the admiral wanted a thirty-six-hour head start on the troop transports so that he could move his slower and heavier monitors, as well as the powder boat, into position. In the wee hours of Tuesday morning, the transport fleet sneaked out of Hampton Roads, with the confident Ben Butler and a less-confident Godfrey Weitzel on deck. In the feint move, the transports steamed north up the Chesapeake Bay and then ran up the Potomac River to Mathias Point.[13] Butler ordered the Army transports to put out to sea the following morning. Without lights, on December 14, the ocean steamers carrying two divisions of sixty-five hundred white and black soldiers moved south along the coast before proceeding out into the Atlantic.

Admiral Porter had assembled an impressive armada of fifty-seven ironclads, frigates, and gunboats. Together with Butler's two divisions, this was an awesome military force, one for which capturing Fort Fisher would seem to be child's play. Butler made arrangements to meet up with the fleet twenty-five miles off New Inlet, the man-made channel just below Fort Fisher. Weitzel and Butler made good time and reached the blockading squadron off the rendezvous point at Masonborough Inlet on the evening of December 15 between 6:00 and 7:00 p.m.[14] Grant's engineer, Cyrus Comstock, had no prior experience at sea, and he became quite sick after two days on the ocean transports. Although Comstock's diary reported the water as smooth, his entry for December 15 said simply, "Sick all day."[15]

Due to a miscommunication, Admiral Porter claimed he did not know about Butler's feint to the north and presumed that with a thirty-six-hour advance departure, Butler and Weitzel must have passed his fleet and were now miles ahead of him to the south, not behind. As a result, when Porter rounded the Pamlico Sound and arrived at his advance base at Beaufort, North Carolina, some ninety miles north of Wilmington, he was surprised not to see Butler's transports.

On Friday, December 16, Butler kept his vessels with the blockading fleet off the coast until noon. The Army transports then steamed east twenty-five miles in search of the planned rendezvous with Admiral Porter. Cyrus Comstock's diary entry said it all: "No Admiral. Smooth water."[16] Butler waited impatiently at sea while Porter proceeded to load ammunition and finish the packing of the powder boat back at Beaufort. The process of loading Porter's fleet took three days in port while the Army bobbed at sea waiting. With Porter nowhere to be found and perfect sailing conditions, General Butler sent the two West Point engineers, Weitzel and Comstock, on the gunboat *Chamberlain* to make a reconnaissance of Fort Fisher. The pair ran in close to the shore so as to draw fire from the fort's batteries and test their range (*BB*, 788).

Weitzel reported that the fort appeared to be "a square bastioned work," with a high relief, protected by a wide and deep ditch on all sides except for the sea front. The fort had bombproofs sufficiently large to hold its entire garrison.[17] His assessment of a square-shaped fort was an error, not discovered until much later.

Saturday, December 17, was yet another fine day lost due to the absence of Porter's fleet. Godfrey Weitzel took the opportunity to run in again with his

FIGURE 16.3. Captain Cyrus Ballou Comstock (1831–1910), Godfrey Weitzel's academic rival and friend. (Library of Congress, Prints and Photographs Division, Reference No. LC-USZ62-110551.)

chum Cyrus Comstock and another West Point grad, General Adelbert Ames, aboard a smaller craft as close as possible to Fort Fisher for more reconnaissance. There was a thick fog, which Weitzel hoped would prevent the trio of officers from being seen, but it also hampered their ability to see much of the fort. When they were spotted by Confederate sentries and fired on several times, Weitzel ordered the captain to turn the vessel back out to sea and return to the fleet.[18]

The Navy Finally Arrives!

After three picture-perfect days of waiting, Porter showed up with his armada at the rendezvous spot on the evening of Sunday, December 18. "The weather during sixty hours of this period had been perfectly calm, and the sea smooth," Godfrey wrote, "but on the evening of the 18th there was quite a rough sea, making it impossible for troops to be landed on the beach." Porter arrived about nightfall, just as the sea turned choppy and Colonel Comstock became seasick again. Due to rough seas, Admiral Porter was requested to delay his attack, "until the sea became smooth," Weitzel wrote, "so that we could co-operate with him."[19]

From his flagship the *Malvern*, Porter advised Butler that the powder boat was "as complete as human ingenuity could make her," packed with 235 tons of powder (*BB*, 788). However, the perfect weather of the last few days was turning suddenly threatening, and Ben Butler could see a storm was approaching. As a result, Generals Butler and Weitzel agreed that the explosion of the powder boat should be delayed due to the challenge of landing men and supplies in rough surf.

Butler sent the two engineers, Weitzel and Comstock, on a small craft to see Admiral Porter on board the *Malvern* and to explain the Army's concerns.[20] He wanted the officers to convey to Porter that there would be no use in exploding the powder boat if the troops could not land. The seas were so rough that night, Weitzel and Comstock had difficulty boarding Porter's flagship. When the pair returned they reported to Butler that the admiral had agreed, and would hold off on the detonation as Butler wanted. Porter suggested instead that the fleet of troop transports move back to the advance base at Beaufort, where they could ride out the impending storm and take on more coal and fresh water. The assault would need to be delayed until the weather cooperated.

Butler and Weitzel lamented the loss of three days of perfect weather as they idled their time off the coast waiting on Porter's fleet. Butler called those three days of waiting "the finest possible weather and the smoothest sea."[21] The loss of these three days would prove crucial to the success of the expedition.

Monday morning, December 19, Admiral Porter signaled to Ben Butler that it was still too rough to land troops, so he proposed "to exercise his fleet" (*BB*, 789). Porter proceeded to assemble the armada in a line of battle by divisions. By that night, a gale-force wind whipped up to the northeast, and it became evident to all there could be no landing of troop transports in the rough seas. Supplies of coal and water were running low among Butler's transports and gunships. The best-laid plans were unraveling. Seeing the inclement weather, and that nothing could be accomplished to fulfill the mission for three or four more days, Butler sent a message to the transport fleet to head back into Beaufort harbor and renew supplies of coal and water (789). Ben Butler steamed to Beaufort to supervise the operations there himself.

Porter's fleet, including the powder boat, remained anchored for the next four days while the storm whipped up the waves and pounded the shore. Ben

Butler was still furious after losing three days of beautiful weather due to Porter's incompetent delays. Now, he would have to wait out four more days of severe storms before the mission could commence. The enemy was clearly aware now of the enormous Union fleet hunkering off the coast and could be sending reinforcements to Fort Fisher at any time. The game plan had gone awry and, in Butler's mind, the Navy was to blame.

The rebels were now on full alert of an impending attack. The expected fleet was seen off Fort Fisher, with its wooden hulls down just below the horizon (DFF, 358). The Federal fleet sailed in toward land from its position just over the horizon and anchored several miles offshore, beyond the range of the Confederate guns. Dropping sails, the line of wooden masts looked like a winter forest of trees oddly lining the Atlantic coastline. The large hulls on the Union vessels prevented an attack until high tide. This gave the Confederates time to make final preparations. Meanwhile, the Army was still ninety miles away at Beaufort, taking on coal and water.

Although an assault had long been anticipated, Fort Fisher was far from full strength in manpower. Colonel Lamb had only half of his garrison, consisting of five companies of the Thirty-Sixth North Carolina. The other half had been sent south to Georgia to rebuff Sherman's famous advance to the sea (DFF, 358). Lamb had not more than 500 men within the sand fortress, contrasted to Weitzel and Butler's 6,500 troops.

During the afternoon of December 20, a strong gale kicked up from the northeast and continued to blow all night long. Rough seas delayed messages between Porter and Butler over the next forty-eight crucial hours. Porter sent a message to Butler that he planned to explode the powder boat at 1:00 a.m., on Thursday, December 22. Wednesday passed in great anticipation as the Confederates braced for the attack (DFF, 358).

On Thursday, the twenty-second, the heavy winds whipped the sea into a white foam and rocked the Army transports to the point that several horses were lost overboard (DFF, 358). Most of the vessels of the transport fleet had to seek shelter in Beaufort Harbor.[22]

Finally, on Friday, December 23, General Butler sent word to Admiral Porter that he would finish getting supplies in Beaufort and be ready to commence the attack two days later on Christmas morning, Sunday, December 25, when he hoped the seas would have calmed from the four-day storm. Porter, however, felt that the landing conditions would be fine on Saturday, Christmas Eve, and replied to Butler that he would explode the powder boat at 1:00 a.m. that morning. Butler was outraged at Porter's lack of patience. The brash admiral would surely claim the glory for leveling the great fortress and taking control of the Cape Fear River and Wilmington, leaving Butler only to do the cleanup necessary to take prisoners and secure the fort. Thinking that Porter might have already exploded the powder boat, Butler started immediately for Fort Fisher, ordering Weitzel and his transports to follow him. No matter that Grant had chosen Godfrey to head the mission, Ben Butler was taking charge!

With the naval armada having shown itself off the coastline, Colonel Lamb was delighted at the arrival of Major James Reilly with 225 North Carolinians, plus 140 "junior reserves," boys between the ages of sixteen and eighteen. The addition of these troops increased the total strength of Fort Fisher to nearly 900 men and boys. There was not a cloud in the sky as the sun set behind the Cape Fear River, the last rays shining through the sand mounds of Fort Fisher, lighting the tops of the Federal masts with an orange glow. "With its parting rays, the gale subsided," wrote Colonel Lamb. The battle would come now (DFF, 359).

The Powder Boat Explosion, Christmas Eve, 1864

Around midnight on Friday, December 23, the disguised powder boat *Louisiana* was towed near Fort Fisher and the barge's engines were started to bring the fake runner even closer. Fuses were lit, and the crew abandoned the floating bomb. About 1:00 a.m., Confederate sentinels saw what looked like a vessel on fire up the beach, about a mile from the fort (DFF, 360). They had no idea it was an explosive-laden Union barge that had been ignited to annihilate Fort Fisher.

The officer of the day reported the unidentified burning object to Colonel Lamb, thinking it was another blockade-runner. Lamb climbed to the top of the ramparts to see for himself. "I watched the burning vessel for half an hour," said Lamb, noting that the burning object was a mile away (DFF, 360). Though anxious at what the dawn would bring, the puzzled colonel returned to his quarters at about 1:40 a.m. in hopes of getting some brief sleep. His slumber was suddenly disturbed as the gunpowder ignited and the powder boat exploded in the darkness.

"I had hardly lain down before I felt a gentle rocking of the small brick house," Lamb recalled. The odd shaking of the earth caused the colonel to think it was a dream, or perhaps vertigo, but it was followed instantly by an explosion. Rebel sentinels were confused at the quake, which sounded like a ten-inch Columbiad. Men and boys came running from all directions to report that the burning vessel off the coast had just blown up—having absolutely no effect on the fort! Lamb sent a telegram to General William Whiting in Wilmington, where the shock was also felt. Lamb was convinced that a blockade-runner had run aground, her crew setting the fire that destroyed the hull (DFF, 361). What other explanation could there be, after all? He lay back down to rest, knowing that the morning would test him, his men, and his fort.

For all of the planning in Washington, and the efforts to load, transport, and ignite the vessel, the powder boat was a dud. It is suspected that much of the gunpowder on board blew into the ocean before the barge was ignited, resulting

FIGURE 16.4. Admiral David Dixon Porter (1818–1891). (Photograph by Mathew Brady; Library of Congress, Prints and Photographs Division, Reference No. LC-DIG-cwpb-04806.)

in the smaller-than-expected blast. Ben Butler blamed the failure squarely on the Navy, "who, through some of its officers, failed utterly to carry it out properly" (*BB*, 807). The episode has been called one of the most ludicrous fiascoes of the war. Butler wrote in his postwar autobiography, "I was blamed and ridiculed for the powder boat all over the country, and those who ridiculed me knew no more of the subject than they knew of the events of an unknown world. Thus it will be seen that this experiment was another of Butler's failures through the inefficiency of some of the officers of the navy" (807).

CHAPTER 17

Christmas Day, 1864:
Attack on Fort Fisher

The gale-force winds that had whipped the sea for four days finally subsided. The ocean waters were dead calm, and the rising sun warmed the balmy salt air. From inside his fort, Colonel William Lamb observed that "Saturday, December 24, was one of those perfect winter days that are occasionally experienced in the latitude of the Cape Fear. . . . The deep blue sea was as calm as a lake, and broke lazily on the bar and beach."[1] As the sun rose over the Atlantic, the North Carolina boys and men talked about last night's odd explosion, each one speculating on the cause. Deep sleepers had not even noticed the slight vibration inside the fort, while those on the beach felt its impact more fully. A thick fog began to roll across the ocean as the grand Union armada moved into battle position off Federal Point.

The Navy Shelling Commences

The attention of all within the rebel fort was soon drawn to the horizon as the impressive Federal fleet came into view. "A grander sight than the approach of Porter's formidable armada towards the fort was never witnessed on our coast," Lamb wrote (DFF, 361). The tall masts could be seen by the Wilmington lighthouse as the Navy's five largest frigates—*Susquehannah*, *Wabash*, *Colorado*, *Powhatan*, and *Minnesota*—crept forward. One by one, the Union vessels appeared, floating three-masted fortresses as long as a football field, each one mounting more guns on board than all of Fort Fisher's batteries. They were followed by ironclads, more than fifty men-of-war in all, looking even darker as they were backlit by the rising sun. The various vessels stretched in a semicircle around Fort Fisher in strategic rings. First were the ironclad monitors, then three lines of ships, followed by reserves.

At 9:00 a.m., Colonel Lamb ordered a call to arms. Knowing his need to conserve ammunition, as well as the limited range of his heavy guns, Lamb gave

FIGURE 17.1. *Bombardment of Fort Fisher* (1865). (Lithograph after a drawing by T. F. Laycock, Endicott and Co., New York .)

the order that no shot should be fired until he gave the signal. "Then, each gun that bore on a vessel could be fired every thirty minutes, and not oftener except by special order" (DFF, 362). An exception might be made if there was an attempt by any of the Federals to cross the sandbar, at which time every available gun would be trained on that one ship.

The tension finally broke, as did the silence of the morning when a flash was seen from the 230-foot ironclad USS *Ironsides*, followed by a puff of smoke. A thundering *Boom!* sent a whistling eleven-inch shell overhead from a Dahlgren cannon, exploding harmlessly behind the fort (DFF, 362). Lamb shouted his command to open the games, at which a lanyard was yanked and a perfectly aimed shot sailed from Fort Fisher into the smokestack of the side-wheel steamer USS *Susquehanna*. Beginner's luck, perhaps, but the shot foretold of a prolonged battle.

The trading of shells from the opposing forces unleashed a horrific onslaught of cannon fire from land and sea. Smoke collected on the horizon, which screened the imposing fleet from view of the fort. Admiral Porter's big guns took aim at the fort, which Godfrey Weitzel had reported to be square-shaped. Without knowing its true L-shaped design, naval officers presumed a shell that passed over the front berms might damage the rear walls. Unfortunately for the Union armada, most of the shells sailed well over the fort and splashed harmlessly into the Cape Fear River behind.

For five hours the bombardment continued relentlessly, yet Fort Fisher suffered little physical damage. Colonel Lamb's headquarters building was hit and destroyed, and a Confederate barracks and various outbuildings were set ablaze. However, the fort itself remained standing amid the hail of shot and shell that rained down all day long. "Never, since the invention of gunpowder," said Lamb, "was there so much harmlessly expended, as in the first day's attack on Fort Fisher" (DFF, 365).

Admiral Porter ordered his fleet to increase the bombardment, firing constantly at a rate of more than one hundred rounds a minute.[2] The Confederate battery returned the fire, though not anywhere near the Union's intensity. The Navy's onslaught made rebel gun emplacements dangerous duty. One Union ship trained its sights on the Confederate flag, which was mounted inside the garrison. When a well-aimed shell shattered its wooden staff, cheers rang up from the sailors as the flag fell down. Yet, despite being hit continuously, at times more than once per second, Fort Fisher was holding up amazingly well.

The Army Arrives

It was between 4:00 and 5:00 p.m. on Christmas Eve when the Army troop transports arrived on the scene. From the deck of his transport, the *Ben De Ford*, General Butler could hear the bombardment for miles away. Getting closer, he could see the incredible firepower of the naval fleet pounding the rebel land position. Porter had commenced his attack without waiting on Ben Butler and his sixty-five hundred infantrymen.[3]

The Army arrived just in time to see the sunset and the last of the first day's shells arc from the armada. About 5:30 p.m. Porter gave the order to withdraw, confident that considerable damage had been done to the rebel position. Colonel Lamb ordered a "parting shot," just to show there was still plenty of fight left inside the fort.

As soon as the Army commanders got near Porter's flagship, General Butler directed Colonel Comstock and Major General Weitzel to proceed on board the admiral's vessel and determine the result of the day's work. The two former classmates lowered themselves into a smaller cutter and steamed over to the *Malvern*. There, Godfrey was to make arrangements for gunboats to cover the infantry's landing and to procure lifeboats from the ships to use as landing vessels.[4]

Ben Butler explained that he sent Weitzel to see Porter, instead of going himself, because "as General Weitzel was to be in command of the troops on shore, I proposed that all the minor details, corresponding signals, and all that, should be arranged between Admiral Porter and General Weitzel, so that there should be no mistake in them." Cyrus Comstock was sent to lend the air of authority from General Grant, according to Butler, who added, "Also, being a member of General Grant's staff . . . he might, at least, keep up the *entente cordiale* between the army and navy."[5]

"We found the admiral in good spirits," Godfrey recalled.[6] Porter said that he had begun his attack at daylight and that the rebels "had replied with little or no spirit to his fire." According to Porter, the enemy "seemed sanguine of an easy capture of the work."[7] He felt the rebel forces were demoralized after a full day of unrelenting shelling, especially judging from the weakness of their return fire.[8]

Of course, Porter mistook the infrequent return fire as an indication of the damage he had inflicted, not realizing Colonel Lamb had restricted the batteries to just one shot every thirty minutes to conserve ammunition. Just as Ben Butler suspected, Porter had been excited about the potential of the powder boat and the damage it would do. He bragged to the two engineers, "I expected to destroy everything and take the work before the Army got here." Comstock and Weitzel were astonished at Porter's confidence in the powder boat. "He expected to destroy Wilmington—15 miles off, by [the explosion]—as well as Smithville and Fort Fisher," Colonel Comstock wrote in his diary.[9] Porter assured the two men that his officers had run the powder boat as close as possible, following a rebel blockade-runner in.

Back on board the *Ben De Ford*, General Butler eagerly received the report from Weitzel and Comstock of Porter's observations. Butler felt that given the day's events, the element of surprise was now totally lost and that the Army troops should return at once to Fort Monroe. Godfrey Weitzel strongly agreed, since the full day of bombing by the Navy fleet before an Army landing had warned the enemy, and had done little physical damage from what he could see.[10] Finally, Cyrus Comstock weighed in, proposing to land a small force in the morning, if practicable—on Christmas Day, to survey the conditions at first hand. Then they could decide on a course of action. If an assault was unsuccessful, then in no case would the Army stay. According to Comstock, all agreed to make an inspection in the morning and decide at that time whether to proceed or to abort the mission.

General Butler directed his trusted protégé to land a reconnoitering party of about five hundred men the next day, pushing up as close as possible to the fort. There, Weitzel was to ascertain its true condition and report back if it was practical to land the remainder of the troops for an all-out infantry assault.[11] "He directed me to meet the admiral the next morning at half past six o'clock and arrange details for landing the troops," Godfrey said. "He also ordered me to send five hundred men on shore, under cover of the gunboats which the admiral would detail, to make a reconnaissance of the enemy's work, and ascertain what damage had been done by the fire of the navy." If Godfrey was satisfied, then he would signal the Navy to land the remainder of his men. Weitzel had been placed in charge of the land assault by General Grant himself.[12]

Colonel Lamb's greatest fear—an attempt to cross the bar—never materialized, to his great relief and surprise. Union fleets had a reputation for such attempts, built upon Admiral Farragut, who ran the gauntlets at both New Orleans and Port Hudson. The Confederates were certain a similar attempt would be made here, the last significant seaport of the South. "One vessel inside would have ended the fight," Lamb wrote (DFF, 364). But it never happened. Instead, Admiral Porter's fleet slowly pulled anchor and moved farther away from the coast to regroup. Colonel Lamb took inventory and, to his amazement, his men suffered only twenty-three wounded, one mortally, during a day when at least ten thousand Union shots were fired (364).

Christmas Day: The Army Takes the Beach

At 6:30 a.m. on Sunday morning, children woke in nearby Wilmington and scrambled downstairs to unwrap modest presents by the fireside. It was still forty-five minutes before sunrise, and miles off the coast, Major General Weitzel and Colonel Comstock took a cutter over to the *Malvern* for their meeting with Admiral Porter (*BB*, 791). "I saw Admiral Porter and arranged with him the details for covering the landing, and also for landing the troops," Weitzel reported.[13] Godfrey delivered a letter from General Butler suggesting that the troops hit the beach as early as 8:00 a.m. and that the naval fleet should silence the Flag Pond Hill and the Half Moon batteries, so that the Army could land near them. The space between the two batteries was about two and a half miles, which gave ample room for the landing.[14]

Butler's plan was to first land five hundred men and then do a reconnaissance. "If it was found that they could hold the landing for the others," he said, "then land force enough to assault the place."[15] Porter detailed twelve gunboats and a sloop of war to cover the Army's landing, and furnished a number of other boats in addition to those Godfrey had brought, enough to carry the landing party to shore.

"I urged upon Admiral Porter, through Weitzel and Comstock, to run by the fort into Cape Fear River," Butler said, "but [Porter] said he could not do it, that there was not water enough." Ben Butler did not accept that excuse, since the Navy had four captured Confederate blockade-runners that had been converted into gunboats. These low-draft vessels had regularly skipped over the sandbar before being seized. "It might be supposed that they could go *in* where they came *out*," said Butler of the sleek steamers. Porter rejected the idea, however, claiming that the water was not high enough even for converted blockade-runners.[16]

The ominous Union fleet crept back over the horizon about ten o'clock on Christmas morning and moved into position as it had the previous day, forming a wide semicircle around Fort Fisher. The USS *Ironsides* again opened with a signal shot to break the silence at 10:30 a.m., an explosion that was faintly heard in Wilmington. The bombardment was furious, more intense and even noisier than the day before.

Grant's initial instructions to General Butler on December 6 had been to effect a landing and, if the enemy still held the fort, then to *entrench* and co-operate with the Navy in reducing the fort and capturing it. Butler interpreted

Grant's orders to mean the Army was to put its entire force onshore. Therefore, on Christmas morning, Porter resumed shelling the fort and by noon reported that the beach was clear.

The egotistic Ben Butler switched vessels from the Union steam transport *Ben De Ford* to the gunboat *Chamberlain* and took the lead. He and Colonel Comstock steamed over the waves to within eight hundred yards of the beach, with General Weitzel and the troop transports trailing close behind. The soldiers then dropped into longboats with their rifles, ammunition, and knapsacks and were rowed ashore by sailors.[17] Godfrey boarded a longboat along with his New York troops and headed west to a landing point north of the fort. "I myself went with this reconnoitring party," Godfrey said, "not caring to rely upon any other officer for information."[18]

With the Navy providing cover, Weitzel hit the beach with five hundred troops about 11:00 a.m., landing about three miles above the fort, which he found "entirely silent."[19] The lone exception was "a gun fired now and then at some small Navy boats that were apparently dragging for torpedoes, or taking soundings."[20] Weitzel's landing party consisted of men from the 112th and 142nd New York Regiments, all under the command of newly brevetted Brigadier General Newton M. Curtis.

As Godfrey and his men landed, Comstock and Butler steamed closer to shore, within about a thousand yards of the fort. There, Butler dropped Cyrus Comstock into a longboat that went ashore with a handful of troops for protection. General Butler steamed even closer to the fort, and from that distance he could make out the masts of tall ships in the Cape Fear River on the opposite side.

Generals Curtis and Weitzel were on the first boat to disembark. Within minutes, the landing spot was occupied by hundreds of bluecoats.[21] As soon as the landing was made, Weitzel ordered Curtis to push his New Yorkers down the beach as far as he could go, setting up a skirmish line within just a few yards of the walls of Fort Fisher. First, however, a group was sent in advance to take possession of some nearby woods. Once accomplished, the whole landing party moved down upon Flag Pond Hill Battery, where Curtis encountered enemy skirmishers and engaged them as the Federals struggled to secure a beach head. Overwhelmed in numbers, the rebels inside the battery quickly held out a white flag, which was snatched up by Union sailors before the infantry "moving at a double-quick, could get up to it," Weitzel said.[22] Seeing the surrender, the Navy sent in additional boats to take the prisoners off the peninsula.

General Weitzel interrogated about a dozen of the prisoners and found that they belonged to the Forty-Second North Carolina Regiment, from Kirkland's brigade of Hoke's division. This brigade was very familiar to Weitzel, as he had been fighting that division since May and knew well the strength of each company in the division. The prisoners confessed that the rest of their brigade (three regiments) was about a mile and a half to the rear, and a fourth regiment was inside the fort.

Butler and Weitzel had agreed to land the men five hundred at a time, so once the first contingent had safely landed and secured the area, the transports were sent back for five hundred more bluecoats. The second wave of troops included 150 officers and men of the Fourth U.S. Colored Troops from Paine's First Division of the Twenty-Fifth Army Corps. The landing was largely unopposed, as Colonel Lamb knew the Federals were out of range.

Seizing the rebel fort would be no easy mission for Weitzel's foot soldiers. Colonel Lamb had planted a line of subsurface explosives, dubbed "torpedoes," out in front of the northern fence line and wired to triggers within the fort. When the enemy reached that spot, the land mines would be ignited to devastate the Union troops and demoralize those who witnessed the massacre. When the second wave of Federals approached, they would face a barrage of gunfire from rebel sharpshooters mounted atop the tall sand hills as the bluecoats attempted to cross the open field in front of the fort. Those who safely evaded the rain of bullets would be confronted with an impressive wooden wall of sharpened poles more than ten feet high and planted firmly in the sandy soil. The palisade stretched across the entire peninsula, from the eastern bank of the Cape Fear River to the Atlantic Ocean. Holes cut into the wall allowed Confederates to pick off approaching Yankees at short range, from behind protection.

If Weitzel were to assault the fort from the north side, it would take several waves of men, some with axes to chop down this wall. Many soldiers would be sacrificed, but with a force of sixty-five hundred troops, this effort was necessary, no matter the initial cost.

At 2:00 p.m., Colonel Lamb braced as several of the Union frigates dared to approach the sandbar. Rather than trying to pass it, however, they lowered rowboats, and engineers attempted to measure the depth by "sounding" the bottom. The Confederates trained their guns in that direction and drove the engineers away. As with the first day, however, no attempt was made by the Navy to pass by the fort and sail into the Cape Fear River. Had Porter run any Union ships into the river, he would have trapped the rebels, since the rear of the fort was completely exposed.

Weitzel's Second Reconnaissance

After troops had landed and captured the two batteries, Ben Butler steamed in closer to a point within five hundred yards of the fort, where he met General Weitzel returning from a reconnaissance. "I have been out to the front line and seen Fort Fisher," Weitzel told him.[23] Ben Butler needed someone he trusted to give him an eyewitness account of the condition of the fort. Knowing Weitzel's youth and the importance of such a decision, Butler wanted to share the responsibility for canceling the land assault, as well as get a second opinion—one in which Grant would have to share responsibility.

Butler turned to Grant's chief engineer, Cyrus Comstock, who was also on board the *Chamberlain*. "Jump into a boat with General Weitzel," Butler said. "Pull ashore, and examine with General Weitzel, and report to me if an assault is feasible." Staring off at the fort in the distance, Butler added, "To me it does not look possible, but I am unwilling to give up." If Grant's engineer agreed with his own, Butler felt he had no choice but to follow their recommendation. As Colonel Comstock and General Weitzel pulled away in a longboat, rocking in the increasing waves, Butler's stomach sank. It was not the rolling sea, but the thought of a failed mission. The barometer had fallen half an inch, indicating a storm was approaching. "I had a vivid perception of the future which has over-taken me," he later said.[24]

Within minutes the two West Pointers were rowed roughly ashore, fully aware of the importance of their mission. Cannon fire from the fleet pounded the peninsula to the south. The whistle of shells and the concussion of the explosion added to the roar of the sea to the point that the men in the longboat could hardly hear each other.

These two young officers—academic rivals for four years, then instructors at West Point, and now soldiers in the midst of a major battle—were becoming lifelong friends. They were confronted now with a crucial decision that could make (or break) their reputations. Holding their hats with one hand and the side of the longboat with the other, the pounding waves rocked them about. Comstock and Weitzel tumbled onto the beach, having gotten soaked while landing the boat (*BB*, 794).

At the same time, the *Chamberlain*'s commander, Brigadier General Charles K. Graham, approached General Butler. Graham was in charge of the Marine Brigade's landing craft and had his concerns. "General, you have either to provide for those troops tonight on shore in some way, or get them off," Graham warned, "because it is getting so rough that we cannot land much longer." Butler recalled, "I reflected a moment before determining the course of action. A storm was coming on; the surf was rolling in; the barometer had fallen a half an inch. If we got the men on shore, it might be, and probably would be, a week before we could send any provisions to them" (*BB*, 794). He had to decide as soon as Weitzel and Comstock returned.

About this time Admiral Porter's flagship *Malvern* drew near to the *Chamberlain*. Amid the roar of the sea, the naval and Army commanders attempted to speak through trumpets. The conversation was confused, and each later reported a different understanding of what was said.

"How do you do, general?" Porter asked, almost casually. "Very well, I thank you," Butler replied. "How many troops are you going to land?" Porter inquired. "All I can," was Butler's reply. "There is not a Rebel within five miles of the fort," said Porter, adding, "You have nothing to do but to land and take possession of it," showing confidence in his bombardment's success. Butler was not convinced, but now he had Comstock and Weitzel onshore to assess the condition. "I think there is a man on shore, by the name of Weitzel, who will find out if it is so," replied Butler.[25]

Ben Butler then went inside the cabin of the *Chamberlain* and interrogated one of the captured rebel officers. Butler was known for a quick wit and even quicker temper. He was a shrewd trial lawyer whose courtroom style brought confessions out of the most rigid of witnesses. This served him well when questioning enemy prisoners to extract information about their regiment's strength, location, and plans. "What were the casualties?" he asked the frightened man. "Only two men killed," was the response, "with only one gun dismounted. Otherwise, no damage."[26]

The prisoner told Butler that two brigades from Hoke's division had arrived from General Lee, but that a few days before, when the Army transports had first arrived—with calm seas—the garrison inside Fort Fisher held only four hundred men! Now, the fort was staffed with more than one thousand troops inside the bombproofs. Butler inquired about the effects of the powder boat, and was told it had merely startled the Confederates onshore, jumping them about "like so much pop-corn on the beach," but no casualties.[27]

Once reaching shore, Cyrus Comstock and Godfrey Weitzel met up with General Curtis and Second Division commander Adelbert Ames, who had reached the position near Battery Holland. Curtis reported that he had captured nearly three hundred prisoners, including seven Confederate officers who confirmed that six thousand reinforcements under General Hoke were on their way from Wilmington. Weitzel and Curtis knew this meant the Yankees would have to work fast.

It was now about 3:00 p.m. as the Federal generals advanced south toward the fort with several hundred men from the 142nd New York. They halted about one and a half miles from the palisade and the northernmost face of Fort Fisher. There, Curtis and Weitzel organized a reconnaissance party to inch closer. They also set up a command post at the abandoned Battery Holland rebel position. The New Yorkers found success in their advance, and Curtis pushed a group of his men to within seventy-five yards of Shepherd's Battery. Weitzel would lead another portion of the 142nd himself to a position farther back than Curtis for reinforcement in case the enemy tried to attack.

Weitzel and Comstock Assess the Damage

As the sun began to drop behind the Cape Fear River at 4:30 p.m., a line of Union skirmishers advanced to the left flank of the sand fort. "I proceeded in person," Godfrey said, "accompanying the One hundred and forty-second New York, to within about 800 yards of Fort Fisher, a point from which I had a good view of the work."[28] Leaving some three hundred of the troops there, Godfrey led a line of skirmishers to within about 150 yards of the fort's northern edge.

Despite the risk, the six-foot-four Godfrey Weitzel climbed on top of a sandy knoll where he had full view of the rebel works and the ground in front of it. "I saw that the work, as a defensive work, was not injured at all, except that one gun about midway of the land face was dismounted," Weitzel reported, confirming what Butler had learned during his interrogation. To his amazement, the grassy slopes of the traverses and of the parapets did not appear broken at all by the two days of bombardment (*BB*, 816).

As he peered through his binoculars from the knoll. Godfrey counted a total of seventeen guns aimed directly toward him, with the palisade fence peeling off to the left and into the surf. Godfrey had been told by deserters about a ditch in front of the fort, about twenty feet wide and six feet deep, crossed by a bridge (*BB*, 817). "It was a stronger work than I had ever seen or heard of being assailed during this war," he said. Fort Fisher had hardly been damaged by the shell fire of the Navy.[29]

Considerable difference of opinion was developing on the beach north of the fort. General Curtis approached Cyrus Comstock and relayed a story of how some of his men had taken a flag from the fort. "He said he could take the work with 50 men," Comstock recalled, adding that "there were not more than 20 men inside."[30] That information was grossly inaccurate, of course, as there were no less than 1,450 Confederates hidden unseen inside the bomb-proofs of Fort Fisher, according to Colonel Lamb's later accounts (*BB*, 818). A land assault with just fifty men would have been a massacre if the rebels had emerged like a swarm of hornets from their nest. Based on this misinformation, however, Comstock told Curtis he should make a run at it, despite Butler's orders. If Curtis could seize the fortress, he would be justified. "If I had been in command of the forces at that point," Comstock later said, "I should have made the trial to take the fort."[31]

General Ames also encouraged Curtis to make an attempt to capture the fort. The recently brevetted Brigadier General Curtis was not about to take responsibility for this critical decision. He wanted specific orders from Grant's chief engineer. "I would have given them," said Comstock, "but before I could get to Butler, the Navy fire ceased and the fort opened heavily with artillery and musketry."[32] Comstock approached Weitzel and the two friends discussed the situation. Godfrey told his classmate that he did not think a land assault would work, to which Comstock did not reply. "I understood Colonel Comstock to agree with me perfectly, although I did not ask him," Godfrey later told a congressional inquiry panel (*BB*, 817).

It was time to communicate his assessment of the situation to General Butler. Godfrey knew the importance of this decision. "Because another officer selected by the War Department had once shown timidity, and in face of the fact that I had been appointed a major-general only twenty days before, and needed confirmation," he said, "I went back to General Butler" (*BB*, 817). With this go/no-go decision on the line, Weitzel boarded a longboat and was rowed back out to sea.

Butler Cancels the Mission

Ben Butler waited anxiously aboard the *Chamberlain*, squinting through binoculars to monitor the landing. He saw the now familiar figure of Godfrey Weitzel approaching and was eager to hear his report. The tall German was helped aboard, a bit damp from the sea spray and tracking sand onto the deck of the *Chamberlain* from his long riding boots. After saluting his commander, he reported the bad news. "As a defensive work," Godfrey said, "the fort was not injured at all. The grass slopes of the traverses and of the parapet did not appear broken in the least." Weitzel explained that even the tall wooden palisade, "seemed to me perfectly intact."[33] The Union frigate *Minnesota* had fired 1,982 shells, and another 1,569 shells were fired by the frigate *Colorado* alone. Yet the sand dunes had merely absorbed the pounding.

Weitzel explained that he had been within fifty yards of the fort and could see that Lamb's picket line "was crouched under the counterscarp of a ditch, which was so high that it covered them" (*BB*, 794). "General, it would be butchery to order an assault on that work under the circumstances," Godfrey said (817).[34] He confessed that he could not carry the work by an infantry assault, based on his firsthand assessment.

This was not the news Butler wanted to hear, expecting more damage to have occurred from the powder-boat blast and from Porter's heavy bombardment.

Godfrey added that he was concerned for the safety of the Federal troops already on shore after nightfall, since they were now sandwiched between two strong rebel positions—Fort Fisher to the south and the "Sugar Loaf" line to the north, where the rest of Kirkland's brigade had retreated. Godfrey strongly advised against any attempt to assault the fort in its present condition.

By now, Hoke's division had arrived to back up Colonel Lamb, estimated by Butler to add another 6,000 troops. In contrast, the Union had landed only between 2,100 and 2,300 men, and no more could be landed in the high surf and approaching storm. All who landed already were at risk of being killed or captured. The Federals had insufficient manpower to effectively storm the palisade.

Ben Butler then received word from Admiral Porter that the Navy had nearly exhausted its ammunition, and that he needed to go back to Beaufort to replenish. As it took Porter four days to put in his ammunition the first time, Butler presumed it would take at least that long again. Beaufort was some ninety miles away, and Butler figured it would take the Navy several days to get there and back. Adding in the days in port, the Army would be left adrift for at least a week, with only limited naval support. This weighed in favor of abandoning the mission (*BB*, 797).

Storm clouds were rolling in and landings were becoming increasingly difficult. Any supplies sent ashore to support the New Yorkers would likely be ruined in the rough surf. Butler knew that his decision would be second-guessed back in

Washington and wanted to see the conditions for himself. He ordered Captain Graham to run the *Chamberlain* close to the beach to "reconnoiter" the works. With Weitzel by his side, the two splashed their way closer as the setting sun cast the fort in near silhouette. Butler agreed with Weitzel's assessment. He made the critical decision to cancel the landing of any more troops, then directed Weitzel to reembark those already on shore.[35]

As evening approached, Godfrey was charged with the daunting task of getting more than two thousand soldiers safely off the beach. Following Butler's orders, he began the rescue mission. Weitzel was not aware of Grant's mandate of December 6, that the troops were to *entrench*. General Butler had decided to keep that part of the orders to himself.[36]

A Storm Approaches

Unaware of Butler's decision, at 5:30 p.m. Admiral Porter commenced a final surge against the sand fortress, unleashing more than two shot and shell per second, in what Lamb described as a "most furious" assault, "certainly never surpassed in warfare" (DFF, 367). Just as suddenly as it began, the naval guns were silenced. As he had done on the first day of bombardment, Colonel Lamb fired the last shot on Christmas Day, "to let our naval visitors know that we had another shot in the locker" (366).

In the darkness, General Curtis advanced a skirmish line composed of elements of the Third, 117th, and 142nd New York Regiments toward the fort. Unable to see the approaching enemy, Colonel Lamb directed some eight hundred of his men to climb down the north face of the sandy hills and take cover behind the unbroken palisade. If the Union troops that had landed to the north tried a land assault, the North Carolina boys would give them a warm welcome. An engineer stood waiting for the order to ignite the rows of buried torpedoes that would send bluecoats flying in pieces.

The tension was thick as Lamb watched from the parapet, waiting patiently for his plan to fall into place. To his amazement, however, the Federal troops did not make an assault. Butler's orders to reembark had reached General Curtis in time. The waves had grown and the rowboats were tossed about, hampering the arrival of troop transports. One man drowned in the surf upon reembarkation. "The gale was increasing," Butler recalled, "and by ten o'clock the sea got so high that I could get off no more men that night with my utmost efforts" (*BB*, 797). About seven hundred Union troops would have to spend the night bivouacked on the soggy beaches (DFF, 369).

From the day's efforts, Weitzel reported a modest loss of just one officer captured, plus the one man who drowned, and fifteen wounded, nearly all the latter by friendly fire from Porter's gunboats.[37] Colonel Lamb took in reports from his officers and was relieved to learn that only three men had been killed, with thirty-five wounded, most of them only slightly—amazing results after a brutal naval bombardment from the largest armada ever assembled in U.S. history.

Admiral David Porter sent dispatches to the Navy Department complaining bitterly of being "abandoned by the army just when the fort was nearly in our possession, and begged that our troops might be sent back again to cooperate, but with a different commander."[38] Ulysses S. Grant was embarrassed and outraged that the combined forces of the Army and the Navy, with a huge fleet of more than fifty armed ships and more than sixty-five hundred troops, could not take one Confederate position. Grant shot off a curt telegraph to President Lincoln from City Point: "The Wilmington expedition has proven a gross and culpable failure."[39]

Butler's Unbending Loyalty to Weitzel

The Christmas Day attack on Fort Fisher was a Confederate victory, due more to the high surf and impregnable sand dunes than to rebel military force. In his 1892 memoirs titled *Butler's Book*, Benjamin Butler fully exonerated Godfrey Weitzel, taking sole responsibility for canceling the mission in order to save lives. "I prevented my major-general of [the] division from making an assault on Fort Fisher by which very many of the troops of the expedition would have been slaughtered in a useless attack," Butler wrote. "I believe my withdrawal from Fort Fisher to face the calumny which has rolled its waves over me, and which I calmly looked in the face when I made my decision to withdraw my troops, was the best and bravest act of my life." Showing his affection for Godfrey, Butler added, "I feared it would destroy my friend Weitzel, and so I took pains to put before the [congressional inquiry] committee the acts which were done as if they had been done by my command" (*BB*, 1036).

Ben Butler admitted that there was but one subject on which he and General Weitzel disagreed. "As a junior officer in the regular army he has said, and I have no doubt he would have done so although against his own judgment, that he would have held on to his position. Indeed, I believe his words were those of a junior officer." Butler respected Godfrey's loyalty, noting, "Weitzel had no profession but arms, and his disobedience of orders would have ruined him in that profession" (*BB*, 814). The young general had merely followed orders, Butler said.

CHAPTER 18

The Trial of Benjamin F. Butler

With the defeat at Fort Fisher fresh on his mind, Godfrey Weitzel applied for and was granted a one-month furlough, begining January 1, 1865. He returned home to Cincinnati with plans to marry. Command of his all-black Twenty-Fifth Army Corps was temporarily turned over to Brigadier General Charles Heckman. Meanwhile, in Washington, D.C., an investigation was being called for into the failed Wilmington expedition. Weitzel and Butler would have to convince a congressional panel that they had made the right decision on Christmas Day. David Porter was already spinning the story.

In the case of Ben Butler, it was not taking slaves as "contraband," seizing sugar and cotton, stealing spoons, his infamous "Woman's Order," or the hanging of Mumford that did him in. His failure at Fort Fisher was the last straw that drove Butler out of the military for good. Washington gave him all the troops, ships, and powder boats he asked for. Why, then, had he failed? Although official military records call it merely an "inquiry," make no mistake—the congressional hearing into the decisions made off the North Carolina coast was the trial of Benjamin F. Butler.

Ben Butler Removed of Command, Again!

From his office at City Point, Ulysses S. Grant wrote on January 4, 1865, to Secretary of War Stanton, "I am constrained to request the removal of Maj.-Gen. B. F. Butler from the command of the Department of Virginia and North Carolina." Grant was reluctant to issue the order, but believed that "the good of the service" required it. "There is a lack of confidence felt in his military ability," Grant said, "making him an unsafe commander for a large army. His administration of the affairs of his department is also objectionable." Grant informed President Lincoln of his request on January 6, asking for "prompt action" in the matter.[1] That was all it took. Ben Butler's controversial military career was over about as suddenly as it had begun.

Godfrey Marries for a Second Time

It is a wonder that Godfrey found the time to meet or pursue any woman after his first wife died so tragically on Thanksgiving Day 1859 at West Point. But somewhere between his duties in Louisiana, Virginia, and North Carolina, the young general met, courted, and proposed to another lady from his hometown, Miss Louise Bogen.

Godfrey was somewhat of a loner, promoted so fast that he rose in rank above any other soldier his own age. His closest friends were, perhaps, Ben Butler, Cyrus Comstock, and George Shepley, all of whom were much older. Godfrey found the companion he desperately needed at this time in his life in Louise. She was the twenty-two-year-old daughter of a prominent German family who owned a pork-packing plant and a successful winery specializing in Catawba wines.

Godfrey had written sweet love letters to Louise from the battlefield, including this rather racey note on March 4, 1864:

My darling Louise, I have pinched your picture and it does not holler. I have bitten it and it does not holler. I have kissed it and it does not return my kisses. I have hugged it and it does not return my hug. So just consider yourself pinched, bitten, hugged and kissed. I have been dreaming about you all last night. I was back at home and had only 12 hours to stay. You and I sneaked away from the rest of the folks and went upstairs to that little front room in your house and we had such a pleasant time. But alas! It was only a dream.[2]

While on his short furlough to Cincinnati, the twenty-nine-year-old major general and Louise were married on January 13, 1865. The couple's short honeymoon produced a pregnancy, the first of three during their marriage. She would give birth on September 26, 1865—but oh, so much would happen in those next nine months. The U.S. infant mortality rate among white couples in the 1860s was 181 per 1,000 live births, a figure that suggested Godfrey and Louise might enjoy a large family. However, only one of their three babies would survive infancy.

Saying good-bye to his new wife and family back in Cincinnati, Godfrey headed back to duty in Virginia where he re-joined his newly organized Twenty-Fifth Army Corps on February 2. During the next six months, General Weitzel and his troops operated on the north side of the James River in Virginia, keeping the rebels in check. However, just five days after his return to active duty, he was summoned to Washington, D.C., by order of the United States Congress. A hearing had convened into the Fort Fisher expedition and Godfrey was slated to testify on February 7.

Fort Fisher Falls

On the same day that Godfrey and Louise were saying their vows in a Cincinnati church, General William Whiting entered Fort Fisher and made a different vow to Colonel Lamb. "Lamb, my boy," he said, "I have come to share your fate. You and your garrison are to be sacrificed." Lamb replied, "Don't say so, General. We shall certainly whip the enemy again."[3] But it was not to be. This time, the Union attack was better manned and the much smaller Confederate garrison of just seven hundred was forced to surrender after a courageous battle.

General Grant chose Major General Alfred Terry to replace the deposed Ben Butler, but kept Admiral David Porter in charge of an even larger naval fleet of 59 warships mounting 627 guns. Of course, much had been learned from the first expedition. In light of Weitzel's men being marooned on the beach during the Christmas Day assault, General Terry's troops each were supplied with three days' rations. The landing was unopposed, and eight thousand bluecoats placed under command of General Newton Curtis got safely ashore by midafternoon on January 14. Curtis was a logical choice given his knowledge of the fort from the December expedition. The Navy kept up a constant bombardment until nightfall, when the ironclads took over.[4] The barrage of fire from Porter's fleet the next day was overwhelming. As Confederate general Whiting reported, "It was beyond description, no language can describe the terrific bombardment."[5]

The assault inflicted much more damage than the Christmas Day barrage, including about 300 Confederate casualties, and knocked out more than half of the rebel guns. The next day, while 4,000 Army troops assaulted the land face of Fort Fisher, near its vulnerable western side, 2,000 sailors and marines attacked the northeast bastion. Although the initial Yankee assault that day failed, a second attack resulted in the surrender of Fort Fisher. "If hell is what it is said to be," wrote one Union sailor, "then the interior of Fort Fisher is a fair comparison. Here and there you see great heaps of human beings laying just as they fell, one upon the other." It was a pitiful sight of dead and wounded soldiers inside the sand fort.[6]

The Northern loss amounted to almost 700 soldiers, with the Navy losing an additional 200-plus killed or wounded. It was, as Godfrey Weitzel predicted— "murder"—to send the troops against the fortified position. But with a much larger infantry on the second assault, and a smaller enemy force inside, General Terry could afford to lose 700 and still have more than 7,000 remaining to finish the job. Casualties of war were a necessity to accomplish the task.

The surrender of Fort Fisher prompted a national celebration. Congress tendered its thanks to both Terry and Porter. General Grant ordered the firing of a one-hundred-gun salute at his City Point headquarters.

Ironically, it was Godfrey's rival from West Point who received the most credit. Cyrus B. Comstock was brevetted a brigadier general by Secretary of War

Stanton. In his report on the battle, General Terry said of Comstock, "I am under the deepest obligations. At every step of our progress I received from him the most valuable assistance. For the final success of our part of the operations, the country is more indebted to him than to me."[7]

A month after the surrender, Admiral Porter's gunboats sailed up the Cape Fear River where Union troops captured Wilmington on February 22, 1865. Colonel William Lamb survived both battles but spent the next seven years on crutches. General Whiting, the engineer who had helped design the fort, was wounded, taken prisoner, and died in Federal captivity, but not before giving written answers to a congressional inquiry into Ben Butler's conduct.

The Accused Testifies before Congress

In Washington, the eight-man Joint Congressional Committee on the Conduct of the War made a list of witnesses to interview about the failed Christmas Day invasion. The committee was made up of four members each from the Senate and the House and chaired by Benjamin Franklin Wade, a sixty-four-year-old Ohio senator associated with the Radical Republicans. Chairman Wade had all the official reports and accounts of the battle furnished to the committee members in advance of the hearings.

Testimony was taken under oath from Generals Butler, Grant, and Weitzel, and from Colonel Comstock as well as Admiral Porter. Ben Butler produced charts and duplicates of reports by his subordinates in an effort to prove he had been right to call off the attack on Fort Fisher, despite orders from General Grant to the contrary. It was the trial of his career, with his reputation on the line. He was well prepared.

The irony was heavy in the air. Butler had claimed the fort was impregnable and, to his embarrassment, news of the fall of Fort Fisher came during the committee hearings on January 15 with celebrating in the streets around the very building where the hearings were held. Terry and Porter were national heroes while Butler stood trial.

A confident Benjamin Franklin Butler took the witness stand two days later, wearing his decorated uniform and looking very much the part of a major general. He began with an eloquent narrative, recapping how Grant requested that then brigadier general Weitzel be sent down to Fort Fisher. He blamed the Navy for breaching military secrecy by publishing the fact that it had assembled "the largest armament in the world" with plans to take Wilmington. "This seemed to cut off all hope of surprise," Butler noted.[8] As a result, Grant postponed the expedition, which he thought would result in another prolonged siege. Butler testified at length about the "powder-boat" experiment, his idea, and its failure in Admiral Porter's hands.

When asked by Chairman Wade how it was that Butler ended up command-ing the expedition since Grant had previously chosen Weitzel, Ben Butler was delicate in his response. "I have no objection to stating it, except, as I said before, the fact that it affects a third person," he began. "General Weitzel is a very able general, but a very young man. I am anxious to see this powder experiment go on and succeed, for it is a very grave one; and I think I had better go with the expedition to take the responsibility off General Weitzel, being an older officer. To this General Grant assented."[9]

The chairman got right to the point with his next question: "To what do you attribute the failure of the expedition?" Butler gave a three-part answer. First, the delay of the Navy in Beaufort; second, the refusal of Admiral Porter to run by the fort; and third, the failure of the bombardment to silence the fort.[10] All three reasons had a common theme—they were Admiral David Porter's failures, not the Army's.

Ultimately, to get to the meat of the matter, Ben Butler acknowledged that he had relied upon Godfrey Weitzel's advice. "General Weitzel reported to me that to assault the work, in his judgment, and in that of the experienced officers of his command who had been on the skirmish line, with any prospect of success, was impossible." Supporting his junior officer, Butler added, "This opinion coincided with my own, and, as much as I regretted the necessity of abandoning the attempt, yet the path of duty was plain. Not so strong a work as Fort Fisher had been taken by assault during the war, and I had to guide me the experience of Port Hudson, with its slaughtered thousands in the repulsed assault."[11]

Butler's Protégé Testifies about His Advice

On February 7, 1865, a slightly nervous Godfrey Weitzel began his testimony be-fore the committee.[12] As Godfrey stood in his uniform of brass buttons and navy blue fabric and the two gold stars of a major general on each shoulder, he placed his left hand on the Bible, raised his right, and swore to tell the absolute truth about the events at Fort Fisher. As he settled into his wooden chair, committee members shuffled papers and focused their attention on the young officer before them. Questioning began as any other trial, led by a fellow Ohioan, Senator Ben Wade:

> WADE: We understand that you were connected with the first
>   expedition against Fort Fisher?
> WEITZEL: I was.
> WADE: Will you give us an account of that expedition from its
>   commencement until its conclusion?

Godfrey began to retell the story leading up to Christmas Day in chronological order, with frequent interruptions by the committee made up of mostly lawyers. They pried into every detail, from Weitzel's selection by General Grant, to the planning, to the day-by-day events. It was apparent that the committee was using Admiral Porter's account of the battle as a script, trying to distill fact from fiction. Godfrey based his opinion on his prior field experience in assaulting military works, naming each rebel fort he had attacked during the war. He was an expert in the topic, and he reminded the committee that he had been an instructor "on these very subjects" at West Point under Professor Mahan for three years prior to the war. He told the committee, "It would be murder to order an attack" on Fort Fisher with the number of troops he had on the beach that day. The committee pressed the young general on whether he stood by his decision, even in light of all he had learned since then. Godfrey replied affirmatively: "Yes, sir, I am fully satisfied from all I have heard since, from the result of the second attack, and everything else—I am fully satisfied that I did my duty there."

He added that after the failed mission, General Grant shared with Godfrey that he did not have much confidence in General Butler's military abilities. This intrigued the committee's chairman, Ben Wade. Leaning forward, Senator Wade asked a burning question: "Did you know of any want of concert of action or good feeling between General Butler and Admiral Porter?" Godfrey answered honestly, from years of personal observation: "I know that Admiral Porter and General Butler have been on bad terms with each other ever since the fall of New Orleans, or shortly afterwards." Godfrey painted a picture of a stubborn naval commander who held a grudge and who refused to even meet with Butler, always sending a junior officer instead.

The committee tested General Weitzel's loyalty to his mentor, Ben Butler, with this question: "Was there anything done, or omitted to be done, which you would not have done, or omitted, if you had had full command of the expedition?" Godfrey was surely aware of the damage his statement might do to his beloved commander's reputation:

> Yes, sir. If I had had the instructions that General Grant gave to General Butler I would have done one thing that General Butler did not do; I would have intrenched and remained there. I should certainly have done that. . . . There is where General Butler clearly made a mistake.

There, he had said it. Butler had disobeyed Grant's orders. Pausing for a moment, Godfrey continued, "No matter what the difficulties were, that order would have covered him from any consequences. . . . The object appeared to me to be to secure a landing, and to hold it after you had secured it."

General Grant was clear in his orders that the Navy should run past the fort, and both Weitzel and Comstock had asked Porter to do so. Had Admiral Porter done it, and entered the Cape Fear River behind, victory would have been assured. "Both of Admiral Farragut's great victories have been almost bloodless ones so far as the army was concerned," Weitzel said, "simply because he ran by the enemy's works with his fleet. A fort cannot walk off; and if you cut it off by running a fleet by it, it must fall." He concluded his testimony with this direct jab at Admiral Porter: "If such a plan had been carried out here, the navy would probably not have lost so many men as they lost in that assault, and the army would not have lost fifty men."

This prompted one final exchange between Chairman Wade and Godfrey Weitzel:

QUESTION: And the fort would have fallen just as effectually?
ANSWER: Certainly, for it would have been entirely cut off.

With that, Godfrey was dismissed from the hearing. He had faulted both Butler and Porter for not following Grant's orders; they were both to blame.

The committee heard testimony from Grant's chief engineer, Cyrus B. Comstock, on February 28, three weeks after his classmate testified. Asked about his own conclusions regarding an assault of the rebel works, Cyrus was reluctant to contradict Godfrey. "I cannot, perhaps, give a definite answer to that question," he said, "because I allow my subsequent knowledge of the work to affect my opinion, somewhat."[13]

When General Curtis revealed that his men had actually been *inside* the work and stolen a flag, Comstock had changed his view. Based on Curtis's assessment that there were no more than *twenty rebels* inside the work, Comstock believed that Curtis could surely take the fort with fifty men. In a surprising contradiction to his friend and classmate, Cyrus testified, "If I had been in command of the forces at that point, I should have made the trial to take the fort, simply because his men felt or thought they could go into the fort."[14]

However, when asked if he would have agreed with General Weitzel's assessment, based on the information Godfrey had and independent of what General Curtis had said, Comstock admitted that he would have agreed with Weitzel. "General Weitzel made an examination of the work, and reported to General Butler that in his opinion an assault upon Fort Fisher would be impracticable."[15]

The committee was influenced by the fact that General Butler had relied on the advice of these two bright West Point engineers, the top two in their class of 1855. "Both these officers were engineer officers of skill and ability, competent to judge of defensive works," the committee reported.[16]

Even Admiral Porter admitted such in his appearance at the hearing, stating that Weitzel and Comstock were "two able engineers, who said that, judging from the appearance of the place, it could not be taken by assault," but he felt they were looking at the fort from an engineering perspective only, not a military view. "They gave all the engineer reasons for not taking the place; and General

Butler himself, without landing, decided to recall his troops," Porter said. What the engineers overlooked, however, was the limited manpower inside the fort at the time. "They never made any attempt to try to find out about inside the fort."[17]

The Committee's Ruling: Not Guilty!

In reaching its final verdict on the case, the committee compared the December and January expeditions, noting that the second expedition's bombardment was far more effective in disabling almost every gun on the side of the fort where the Army made its assault. The matter was resolved, at least in the official records of the Committee on the Conduct of the War, when a unanimous report was issued through Chairman Wade: "In conclusion, your committee would say, from all the testimony before them, that the determination of General Butler not to assault the fort seems to have been fully justified by all the facts and circumstances then known or afterwards ascertained."[18]

Ben Butler had won his acquittal. Public opinion was yet another thing, however. His removal by Grant, coupled with General Terry's success, led to much criticism in the press.

Postscript

During the congressional hearings and before Godfrey was called to testify, General Butler wrote a touching letter to his friend Weitzel on January 23, 1865, from the Willard Hotel in Washington, D.C. Although such "witness tampering" would be frowned on by a Federal court today, Butler wrote:

> My Dear Weitzel: —I am afraid you have been annoyed lest I might possibly think that your advice at Fort Fisher was not such as I ought to have acted upon. Let me assure you that I have never in any moment, amid the delightful stream of obloquy which is pouring upon me, doubted the military sagacity of the advice you gave, or the propriety of my action under it. Indeed, my friend, I am glad I was there to act as a shield to a young officer in a moment of fearful responsibility, from the consequences of a proper act which might have injured him in his profession, but which cannot harm me, who have a different one. The judgment of cool reason hereafter will applaud it, but hot passion might have harmed you, as it has done me, for the hour. Indeed, it was in view of this very event that I went at all. With the invocation of every blessing upon you and yours,
>
> I am, your friend,
> BENJ. F. BUTLER, Major-General[19]

Still on leave at that time, in his hometown of Cincinnati, the newly married Godfrey Weitzel replied on January 26:

My Dear General: —I was so delighted this morning to receive your note. As the truth became developed I saw I had not made a mistake. At first, I was terribly frightened. Many of my friends and fellow-citizens here, too, at first, made long faces, and only one paper, our oldest and most respectable, the *Gazette,* stood out for you boldly as against "marking Pot Porter" as they called him. In one of his best despatches, however, Porter is compelled to acknowledge the correctness of our judgment. . . .

Yours truly, G. WEITZEL, Major-General[20]

While in Cincinnati, Godfrey learned that despite the failure at Fort Fisher, he had been nominated for another brevet of major general.[21]

CHAPTER 19

Final Days of War

The "New" Army of the James

While General Weitzel was on leave getting married and testifying, two-thirds of his new Twenty-Fifth Army Corps had stayed occupied outside Richmond, engaging in reconnaissance missions into enemy territory and light skirmishing. The other third remained near Fort Fisher, anticipating the surrender and occupation of Wilmington.

Major General Edward Ord replaced Ben Butler as overall commander of the Army of the James in early January. Ord's army assembled outside Richmond was an intimidating force, nearly thirty thousand strong, a city of black and white soldiers from the Twenty-Fourth and Twenty-Fifth Army Corps. Troops stretched along an eleven-mile line extending from Drewry's Bluff to Deep Bottom, on the Bermuda Hundred front, north of the James River. The two corps were commanded by Generals John Gibbon and Godfrey Weitzel, respectively.

General Gibbon's Twenty-Fourth Corps consisted of three divisions with forty-two infantry regiments and more than eighteen thousand men. Weitzel's Twenty-Fifth Corps was made up of three colored divisions. The first of these divisions was commanded by fellow Cincinnati native and German immigrant August V. Kautz. The Second Division was commanded by William Birney and occupied the captured Fort Harrison. Weitzel's Third Division was under the command of Brigadier General Charles J. Paine and was in North Carolina, outside Wilmington. Taken together, the Twenty-Fifth Corps contained thirty-two regiments, plus cavalry, with a strength of more than 13,600 men.

Opposite Ord's Army of the James were the strongly fortified defenses protecting Richmond, commanded by Confederate general James Longstreet.

Upon his return, Godfrey Weitzel established his field headquarters just east of the Varina Road. The far left of his two divisions was camped on the north side of the James at Fort Brady, while the left of the Twenty-Fourth Army Corps joined Weitzel's right near the Varina Road, forming the right end of the main line. The cavalry of the Twenty-Fifth Corps was placed in the front and right to monitor the roads leading into Richmond.

At three places outside Richmond, General Weitzel had constructed tall wood-frame signal towers, one hundred feet tall, to keep an eye on the rebels. One tower was built on Cobb's Hill in front of Point of Rocks on the Appomattox River; the second was constructed near the south bank of the James River, opposite Fort Brady; and the third, for Weitzel's own use, was built just a few steps north of his headquarters. These towers overlooked a large part of the enemy's lines as well as the Richmond and Petersburg pike and railroad. From the towers, observers sent regular reports about Confederate troop movements and about trains coming and going.

Grant's siege at Petersburg had begun in June 1864 and by February was in its eighth month. It was a waiting game, and each side knew that springtime would change the campaign. General Grant was certain that the increasingly desperate condition of the Confederate Army meant they would try to make an escape as soon as weather permitted. He worried each day that Lee might slip away during the night, leaving nothing but a picket line to disguise his departure. If Lee used the railroad by the way of Danville, he would leave Grant's army behind in Petersburg as the Confederates fled deeper south, thus prolonging the war for another year or more. If the conflict was going to end, this was the time. He needed to keep Lee penned in.

The Badge of the Twenty-Fifth Corps

Confidence was waning within the Confederacy, among both the military in the field and the administration in Richmond. Godfrey Weitzel was also anticipating a Northern victory. To inspire his colored troops on to the finish line, General Weitzel had a special badge designed for his Twenty-Fifth Corps. The badge was a solid blue square, tilted by 45 degrees in a diamond shape. Other corps had circles, stars, crescents, and crosses of all types to identify their fellow soldiers. General John Gibbon adopted a red heart for his Twenty-Fourth Corps. Now, the first all-black Army corps would have its own emblem.

Writing to his troops on February 20, 1865, Weitzel began, "In view of the circumstances under which this Corps was raised and filled; the peculiar claims of its individual members upon the justice and fair dealing of the prejudiced; and the regularity of the conduct of the troops which deserve those equal rights that have been hitherto denied the majority, the Commanding General has been induced to adopt the *Square* as the distinctive badge of the 25th Army Corps."[1]

Weitzel compared his comrades to some of the great armies in history, saying, "Whenever danger had been found and glory to be won, the heroes who have fought for immortality, have been distinguished by some emblem to which every victory added a new luster. They looked upon their badge with pride," he said. Urging his men of the Twenty-Fifth Corps to wear their new badge with that same honor, Godfrey concluded,

Soldiers! To you is given a chance, in this Spring Campaign, of making this badge immortal. Let History record, that on the banks of the
James, thirty thousand freemen, not only gained their own liberty, but
shattered the prejudice of the world and gave to the land of their birth,
Peace, Union and Glory.[2]

Godfrey's prediction would come true sooner than he possibly imagined.

Springtime and Movement toward Petersburg!

Grant's final assault on Petersburg was predicted to weaken the defenses of
Richmond. He gave Weitzel authority to break through the Confederate lines
defending the rebel capital when Godfrey felt the time was right. "General
Weitzel will keep vigilant watch upon his front," Grant wrote, "and if found at
all practicable to break through at any point, he will do so."[3]

It was Grant's opinion, however, that an attack by Weitzel's men would not
be feasible unless the rebel troops withdrew from their lines and entrenchments
and became largely detached. In that case, Grant told Weitzel, "it may be regarded as evident that the enemy are relying upon their local reserves, principally,
for the defense of Richmond."[4] Knowing that the local reserves were made up of
a weak collection of local residents, too old or too young to serve with Lee's Army
of Northern Virginia, they could not defend the capital city against a strong
Union advance.

In accordance with Grant's orders, three divisions of the Army of the James
moved out during the night of March 27, 1865: two white divisions of the Twenty-
Fourth Corps under command of Brigadier Generals Robert S. Foster and John
Turner, plus Birney's colored division of the Twenty-Fifth Corps, and about fifteen hundred cavalry commanded by Brigadier General Ranald S. Mackenzie.
General Weitzel stayed behind in command of all the forces that remained outside Richmond, including Charles Devens Jr.'s division of the Twenty-Fourth
Corps and Kautz's colored division of the Twenty-Fifth Corps, plus about five
hundred cavalry.[5] Camp was broken just after dark and Birney's black troops
crossed the James and Appomattox Rivers, marching to the far left of the lines of
the Army of the Potomac, near Hatcher's Run, six miles southwest of Petersburg.[6]

It was reported that Confederates had buried numerous land mines in
and around Richmond. To protect the troops and horses, General Ord advised
Weitzel that when he moved his troops, he should send his cattle and old horses
up the roads first so that they would trip any such devices before an unsuspecting Union soldier. Ord also told Weitzel to conceal his infantry movements
from the enemy by keeping his campfires going as usual in the empty camps
after they were abandoned, using old newspapers as imitation tents after the

real tents were taken down. Ord instructed Weitzel to continue with drills and parades in plain sight of the enemy to keep up the deception.[7]

The tension was apparent to everyone as the final assault on Petersburg and Richmond grew near. As General Weitzel put it, "During the six days and nights which succeeded the morning of March 28th every man in my command seemed to be fully impressed with the gravity of the situation." Gathering of information from the enemy opposite him was critical, and General Weitzel gave incentives to those who could obtain intelligence, offering special rewards to anyone bringing in Confederate prisoners and deserters. In Weitzel's words, he employed, "everything known in warfare, and all that the ingenuity of my command could devise" to get current and correct information.[8]

Advance on Petersburg

On Wednesday, March 29, 1865, Grant ordered all the troops available to advance, leaving only a small force to hold the line at Petersburg. By good fortune there had been a few days free from rain, leaving the ground dry. However, it soon began to rain, and in no time the dry roads became practically impassable for teams, and even for the cavalry.[9] Roads became like quicksand, and some of the horses and mules sank so deep that they had to be lifted out by hand. Engineers set to work building corduroy roads of parallel logs every foot of the way as they advanced, so that artillery could be pulled along without getting stuck.

There were many signs of activity in Richmond that foretold of possible evacuation. Godfrey Weitzel's old West Point schoolmate Fitzhugh Lee passed through Richmond with his Confederate cavalry, picking up two brigades on his way out of town. This left only General Martin W. Gary's cavalry brigade guarding the capital.[10]

From City Point, where a steady rain fell, an anxious President Lincoln wrote to General Weitzel asking what had been observed on his front. That evening at 8:20, Weitzel responded, "I have only heard that Fitz Hugh Lee's Cavalry passed through Richmond yesterday & at 11.25 this Morning it was seen passing Port Walthal Junction towards Petersburg at a fast gait. No movements have been observed other than the above. I expect deserters every moment & as soon as I hear anything new I will telegraph you."[11]

Shortly after midnight, General Weitzel followed up with a second message to Lincoln, saying, "A Lieutenant & 2 men have just come in from the Enemy they report no change on this front up to the time they left." Godfrey was obedient in keeping the president informed and also sent the Richmond newspaper to Lincoln, though it had no news of troop movements. General Grant authorized Phillip H. (Phil) Sheridan and his cavalry to push up the road leading to Five Forks, to "menace" the right of Lee's line.[12] His plan was to extend the Union lines to the west as far as practicable. By stretching the Confederate line, he hoped to create a weak link.

Once broken, Grant would rush through the gap. Realizing Grant's plan, Robert E. Lee sent General George Pickett with five brigades to reinforce Five Forks.

General Lee mounted his famous white horse, Traveler, and came over to superintend the defense of his right flank. Much has been written about the Battle of Five Forks in other books and the details will be spared here. Suffice it to say that the Union won the engagement, which has been called the "Waterloo of the Confederacy" due to its acceleration of the end.

With this great strategic victory at Five Forks, Grant notified President Lincoln at City Point of the success of the day. Grant later wrote, "I wanted to relieve his mind as much as I could." Grant then notified General Weitzel of the day's events, and directed him "to keep close up to the enemy, and take advantage of the withdrawal of troops from there to promptly enter the city of Richmond."[13]

The Beginning of the End

In late March, Union informants in Richmond reported to General Grant that many of the Confederate government offices were being moved from Richmond, and that the families of President Jefferson Davis, as well as the secretary of the Navy, postmaster general, and commissary general, had "gone south." Most of the Davis family furniture had been sold.[14] Lee could neither hold out in Petersburg nor protect Richmond. It was time to move the rebel government to a safer location.

Based on the large number of naval vessels assembled in the James River, spies reported that Confederate authorities feared an attempt by the Union Navy to pass upriver. For four nights in a row, three wooden gunboats and one ironclad had been sent downriver from Richmond with instructions to be scuttled and sunk to block the way if the Union fleet made any advance. The Tredegar Iron Works, which produced cannon and machinery for the Confederate war effort, was ordered to be completely closed on April 1. Though Confederate troops had normally been given rations for only one day ahead, in late March the Union spies in Richmond reported that the troops were given rations for five or six days ahead.[15] This painted a clear picture: the defenders of the rebel capital would soon be moving out.

Thursday and Friday, March 30–31, 1865: Lee's Line Weakens

Very early on the morning of March 30, Generals Edward Ord and Andrew Humphreys succeeded in capturing the entrenched rebel picket lines at their front, and Ord's troops ventured inside the enemy's earthworks. General Grant sent dispatches to all points around the Petersburg line, including Weitzel's troops on the north side of the James River, and to the president at City Point, announcing the successes of the day. Dispatches continued to pour in by the hour announcing further Union advances at various positions. The end was now surely at hand, and telegraph operators were kept busy updating the various generals. It was a great day for the North. "Lee made frantic efforts to recover at least part of the lost ground," said Grant.[16]

Outside Richmond, before noon, General Longstreet was ordered up from his position opposite Weitzel to reinforce Lee's army on the west. Grant had hoped for this very movement, as it would weaken the defenses of Richmond. As soon as Grant learned of Longstreet's withdrawal, he sent a message to Godfrey Weitzel and directed him to "keep up close to the enemy." Grant told Weitzel to have General George Hartsuff, who commanded the Bermuda Hundred front, do the same thing.[17] If either Hartsuff or Weitzel found any break in the enemy's lines, they were authorized to rush in at once. All the pieces were falling into place.

Godfrey suspected that the main action would take place farther south, between Lee and Grant at Petersburg, twenty-two miles below Richmond. But he worried that it might fall to him to launch his own attack against the network of trenches, minefields, and large-caliber artillery that guarded the eastern approaches to Richmond. Weitzel could also not rule out an offensive attack by Confederate forces.

The telegraph operator at Weitzel's headquarters was very busy all Friday morning, March 31, as multiple messages poured across the wires from Generals Grant, Hartsuff, and Devens regarding the strength and location of enemy troops. Grant wrote that prisoners captured that morning near Hatcher's Run reported their line was strongly reinforced from their left. Grant was inquisitive as to what information Weitzel had developed, asking, "What news do you get from your front?"[18] Godfrey also received a message from the Bermuda Hundred front that General Hartsuff had fresh information confirming that four brigades from Confederate general Mahone's division were still in front of Weitzel's position.

All was surprisingly quiet according to reports from all scouting parties and other reconnaissance. Yankee lookouts placed in trees at three places reported no change in enemy activity. This was a calm before the storm.

Saturday, April 1, 1865: Planning for a Suicide Mission

"Nothing unusual occurred" on Friday, Godfrey Weitzel wrote.[19] But as midnight Friday turned into predawn Saturday, "things opened lively."[20] General Grant sent a dispatch reporting that Confederate general William Mahone's division had moved during the night to Dabney's Mills. Weitzel received a similar report from General McKibben from the Bermuda Hundred that there were fewer troops in the enemy's lines than the day before. All signs indicated that at least a portion of the Southern forces were abandoning their positions to reinforce Lee at Petersburg.[21]

Substantial rebel troop movement was confirmed when Weitzel received a second telegram from Grant reporting that fresh prisoners (likely deserters) had been picked up that morning from every brigade of Confederate general George Pickett's division, and that nothing had been seen of any of the divisions commanded by Generals Charles Field, Joseph Kershaw, or Mahone.

Godfrey needed fresh intelligence regarding what had happened overnight on his own front. To test the enemy's strength, he ordered General Hartsuff to open with artillery, to be followed by an infantry attack, and see what would develop.[22] Although the artillery fire developed no response from the enemy, Weitzel was not convinced the Confederate position had been weakened. A prisoner was captured who confirmed what Godfrey suspected, that Mahone's entire division was still in his front. As a result, Hartsuff did not follow up with the infantry attack. Confirming Godfrey's assessment, General Devens's scouts reported no change in rebel troop movement.

Outside Richmond, James Longstreet had built an impressive earthworks. Although not a top student himself, Longstreet had included all the elements taught at West Point in Professor Mahan's class in one impenetrable earthwork, armed at all points with the best guns of heavy caliber.[23] In front of the high parapet, the rebels dug a deep and wide ditch protected by two parallel rows of sharply pointed "abatis" buried in the ground at an angle, eighteen inches apart. Any Federal infantry or cavalry charge would impale themselves on the wooden spikes. To prevent passage between the rows of spikes, the Confederates had buried explosive torpedoes, which would blow up under a pressure of just five to seven pounds.

In addition to the land mines, in order to further prevent a Union attack, the engineers had laid out rows of tangled trees and branches, a sort of barbed wire known as "chevaux-de-frise," in front of the double rows of abatis.[24] An assault on Longstreet's earthworks would be suicide for the first wave, requiring axes to chop through the rows of felled trees and buried spikes before even reaching the deep trench protecting the tall parapet. The worst duty was to be handed an ax instead of a gun as regiments assembled for an attack. The first wave of the colored Union infantry would be mowed down mercilessly by sharpshooters on the parapet.

Behind the intimidating fortress, Longstreet amassed a force larger than Weitzel's remaining troops. To his horror, Godfrey received orders from General Ulysses S. Grant that the Twenty-Fifth Corps was to launch an attack against Longstreet's fortified lines on Monday morning, April 3. Grant had no delusions that Weitzel's effort would succeed. The move was only to distract Longstreet and keep him "occupied." For Grant's success in holding Lee at Petersburg, it was essential that Lee not be reinforced by Longstreet, no matter the cost of Union lives.

Not simply a feint to distract attention, the Twenty-Fifth Corps was to make "a persistent and deadly assault."[25] Godfrey and his staff officers knew that they could not overtake Longstreet's lines, given the fortified position and the enemy's greater manpower. The morning's assault would result in the deaths of hundreds, perhaps thousands of his men. Black soldiers, led to the slaughter under the command of white officers.

Godfrey recalled the orders Nathaniel Banks had issued on another Sunday, nearly two years before, at Port Hudson, where more than sixteen hundred Union soldiers were killed or wounded in an attempted assault on another fortified Confederate position. Black soldiers had died there among the willows and fields, though they fought valiantly. Longstreet's position was even better protected than the approach to Port Hudson; the bloodshed would be greater; and it would be blood on Godfrey's hands.

General George Shepley said it best: "It was one of those necessities of warfare which require the sacrifice of a few to save many, the destruction of a portion of an army to insure the victory of the remainder."[26] Godfrey's mind was racing now, thinking through all of his formal training and field experience. He pulled together his engineers and key officers to plan for the assault, then directed the quartermaster to stash ten days' rations in square redoubts along the Union line. In the anticipated repulse of the Union attack, the remains of Weitzel's men would take refuge in the redoubts and try to sustain themselves until Grant could send reinforcements.

Godfrey needed to build a mock-up of Longstreet's defenses to experiment with. On Saturday afternoon, he and two of his officers assembled some artillery in a meadow near Dutch Gap. They set up a double line of spiked abatis just like Longstreet's. Again and again, Godfrey had his artillery fire various projectiles at the pointed logs, trying to find the right weapon that would clear the path for an infantry charge. They tried firing chain shot, then Parrott shells, followed by iron balls and every other available form of projectile that might knock down or destroy the spiked wall. Nothing worked.[27] Time after time, the command of "Fire!" was yelled, but when the smoke cleared, there was still no visible break or opening. Artillery had no effect. It would be left to axes after all.

Mentally and physically exhausted, weary with the dreadful responsibility that was less than twenty-four hours away, General Weitzel and his officers gave up the experiment. The only way to break down the rows of wooden obstructions was the most dangerous—by hand.

Tension continued to mount as the sun set and day turned into night. At 7:00 p.m., General Grant telegraphed that he did not think Mahone had moved after all. In order to verify Mahone's position, Weitzel again ordered Hartsuff to attack the line with infantry the next morning and ascertain Mahone's strength and position.

The night was clear, starlit, still, and beautiful.[28] But the tranquillity was lost on Godfrey Weitzel, who had the weight of the next day's suicide mission on his mind. The young general was deeply troubled with the responsibility of leading even one division of his Twenty-Fifth Army Corps into the morning's battle. His colored troops were certain to be slaughtered, and defeat was guaranteed. The men tried to rest, but anxiety was felt by every officer and soldier in the camp. By daybreak, the silence would be shattered by the blasts of cannon and the snaps of musket fire. The earth would shake and men under his command would fall in place, never to see another beautiful night like this one.

Some men wrote letters to loved ones back home, to faces they never expected to see again. Others gathered for prayer, while officers studied maps and discussed the fight to come. As the evening dragged on, hour after hour, fresh pickets came up from the reserves and passed along the line to replace their comrades of the Twenty-Fifth Corps. The "hushed sound of low voices" broke the solemn stillness for a moment as tired soldiers returned from their posts, hoping to catch whatever rest they could before daylight brought on the new assault.[29]

Unaware of the events unfolding in Richmond, the twenty-nine-year-old German general made the rounds to his officers. Godfrey Weitzel encouraged them and helped make final arrangements for the morning's assault.

Shepley's Analysis

Noticing a light, General Weitzel walked into the hut of his trusted friend and chief of staff, George Shepley, the lawyer from Maine. The two officers had become close friends during their stint in Louisiana, where Shepley had served as military governor and Weitzel as mayor. Godfrey needed a trusted adviser now to share his load. George Shepley was a handsome man, with blue eyes and a brown mustache and curly long hair that swept back from his forehead.[30] As Godfrey walked in, Shepley was plotting out schedules of the rebel troop strength of the various corps opposing them. Godfrey was quite impressed by the schedules Shepley had tacked onto the rough timber walls of his hut, and surprised at the level of detail.

"How can you be certain of your accuracy," Weitzel asked, "with so limited means of information?" The bright lawyer-turned-soldier pointed to a large tabulated sheet on the wall. "Sir," he said proudly, "by inquiring of each spy, prisoner, and deserter from the enemy respecting his company, regimental, brigade, and division commanders, and also respecting the companies on his right and left flank, I was able to compare all of the answers."[31] His chart was the result.

Weitzel's eyes brightened as Shepley continued in the dim lantern light: "I have supplemented the ignorance of some of the Rebels and corrected the falsehoods of others, verifying each by the other. By this, I have arrived at an approximately correct result." He now had Weitzel's full attention. "This is wonderful!" Weitzel exclaimed. "And that is where the lawyer comes in."[32]

Drawing a deep breath, he turned to Shepley. "I have been trying to ascertain what troops passed through Richmond yesterday," he said. "And from what part of Longstreet's line they were withdrawn." Weitzel explained that exchanged prisoners from near Richmond had been brought in regularly on a flag-of-truce steamer. Despite questioning of the released Yankees, however, Godfrey had been unable to obtain any information on the remaining troop strength in Richmond. Shepley agreed to ride at once to the landing point on the James and to interview the next load of freed prisoners. He set off at once and returned after an eventful ride, which included a bath courtesy of his horse, Charley, who decided to take a dip in a creek along the way.[33]

A Reprieve Comes in the Nick of Time

Brigadier General Edward H. Ripley summed up the thoughts of every Union man in Weitzel's camp:

> It had been a day of unusual solemnity, lying through the dragging hours in the straining suspense of waiting for the fateful word that would clash us against those fearful walls of red earth, deep ditches, impenetrable abatis, and thickly planted torpedoes, from which so many bloody assaults of columns heavier than ours had been hurled back with ease.[34]

The men were nearly assured of being wounded, if not killed, in the attempt. It was like waiting for the gallows. Just before midnight, however, a welcome dispatch arrived from General Grant. The telegraph message stated that operations on Grant's left flank had been so successful that General Weitzel could delay his attack until reinforcements could be sent from the Army of the Potomac. Weitzel was not to attack in the morning unless he felt "perfectly certain of success."[35]

What a relief! It was like a governor giving a last-minute reprieve to a death-row inmate. The heavy weight of responsibility for the planned bloodshed was lifted and Godfrey Weitzel breathed a sigh. Reading the message again, Godfrey walked out into the night. *Dank an Gott!* he thought. *Thank God!*

On General Shepley's return from his wet ride to the exchange point, he sent for Major Atherton Stevens, who commanded the picket line and would be able to get fresh reports on the strength of the rebel positions. All week long, crowds of Confederate soldiers had deserted their positions nightly, throwing away their arms and all hope for their cause. They crossed into the Union lines seeking rest, food, and safety, not wanting to fight another day.

Shepley gave orders to Major Stevens that if any enemy prisoner or deserter was brought in that night, he should be brought directly to Shepley's hut for interrogation. If no prisoners or deserters were taken by 2:00 a.m., Stevens was authorized to offer a reward of a thirty-day furlough to any picket who could

bring one in. With the furlough as a reward, Shepley felt certain he would have a
rebel to question before morning.

April 2, 1865: Evacuation Sunday

April meant the start of spring, and on Sunday morning, April 2, 1865, the air was
calm and the sun shining bright in a clear sky. The birds were beginning to twitter
in the budding trees and the fields were already green. Farmers had started plow-
ing their fields for the planting of the season's corn.[36] Flag-of-truce boats floated
lazily up and down the James River between Richmond and City Point carrying
exchanged prisoners of both armies back and forth.

Although Grant had canceled plans for Weitzel's assault against Longstreet's
fortification, Godfrey was still uncertain of the enemy's numbers and needed to
probe the lines with a small attack. After dawn, Weitzel gave General Hartsuff
orders to make an advance with one of the colored regiments. There would be
considerable loss of life, all in an effort to gain not one inch of ground, but
only to gain information on troop strength. With bayonets fixed and adrenaline
pumping in anticipation of a skirmish, Hartsuff gave the command. The black
troops climbed out from behind their earthworks and almost immediately encountered enemy fire.

With the morning sun glistening off their bayonets, a brave advance was
made. The Federals succeeded in driving back the Confederate picket line with
ease for more than half a mile, capturing six of their pickets in the process. This,
however, drew out the full force of the enemy, which, Weitzel said, "was found
not to have been diminished." Hartsuff attacked "vigorously as he was able" by
opening up with his artillery all along the enemy line to test Mahone's response.

At about 10:45 a.m., Godfrey Weitzel received word from Grant that the
Army of the Potomac had breached the Confederate trenches in front of Petersburg. Grant advised Godfrey to "keep in a condition to assault when ordered
or when you may [feel] the right time has come."[37] As the day went on, Weitzel
detected what he called "a nervousness" in the Confederate lines. Telegraphs from
City Point continued to stream in throughout the day, reporting Union success
at various locations near Petersburg. It was evident that Lee's army was suffering
substantial blows. With a break at Petersburg, Richmond could not be held.
Godfrey Weitzel would be in position to advance, perhaps as early as that night
or certainly the next morning.

Richmond Evacuates

As usual on Sunday mornings, President Jefferson Davis left his home at Twelfth
and Clay Streets to attend church service. His carriage horses slowly clip-clopped

the six blocks to St. Paul's Episcopal Church at 815 East Grace Street. Davis walked through the massive entrance portico alone, having sent his wife, Varina, and their two children on the Danville train the Friday before as a precaution.[38] He walked past the ornate Corinthian columns and through the tall doors, shaking hands with some civilians and officials. Entering the church, Davis took a seat in his family's pew beneath the high ceiling that supported the 225-foot spire. The Greek Revival–style building was known as the "Cathedral of the Confederacy" because both Confederate president Davis and General Lee attended this church when in Richmond.

There was an air of elation among the congregation based on a rumor that Lee had crushed Grant's whole front in a surprise nighttime attack. It was two weeks before Easter, and Reverend Charles Minnigerode was preaching on the Last Supper. Halfway through the service, a uniformed man entered the church from the rear doors. Heads turned as his boot-steps were heard coming down the wooden aisle. Oblivious to the stares he attracted, the messenger from the War Department stopped at the president's pew and pressed a note into Mr. Davis's hand. It was from General Lee.

The president's face flushed as he read these words: "I see no prospect of doing more than holding our position here till night. I am not certain that I can do that. . . . I advise that all preparations be made for leaving Richmond to-night."[39] Lee warned that he had to retreat at once to save his army and, more importantly, that Davis must evacuate Richmond. At once, Mr. Davis rose to his feet and left the church.

Though Dr. Minningerode continued the service, the messenger reappeared after a few minutes to summon other officials. As more and more men rose to leave the church, a wave of dread and murmuring swept through the congregation. Word of Grant's success and of Lee's telegram now began to spread throughout Richmond as church services let out. Citizens panicked to make plans for evacuation before being overrun by Union troops. President Davis called an emergency cabinet meeting and read the bleak news from Lee, ordering all cabinet members to prepare to leave town that night. Confederate troops, stationed just across from Weitzel's pickets, were instructed to quietly pull back, leaving the city defenseless.

The Night They Drove Old Dixie Down

At Petersburg, Ulysses S. Grant was so confident in the day's success that just before 5:00 p.m., he sent a message from his field position to his staff back at City Point, saying, "I think the President might come out and pay us a visit tomorrow."[40]

The sun set and the night sky became cloudy and dark, with a mysterious silence as an ominous mist settled on the earth.[41] With darkness to conceal movement of the rebel fleet, Admiral Semmes ordered all of his vessels under way to that sharp curve at Drewry's Bluff. There he would either sink the ironclads or blow them up so they would not fall into enemy hands. Once the vessels were sunk, Semmes would put the sailors on board wooden gunboats and head upriver to Manchester, just across from Richmond, where he would meet up with General Lee for a forced march to Danville.[42]

There was substantial troop movement all Sunday to reinforce Lee at Petersburg. General Weitzel received reports that about 1,400 rebel infantry, 300 cavalry, and a light battery were seen passing down the turnpike and railroad toward Petersburg. "From this and other sources of information," Weitzel said, "I felt the enemy were weakening in my front north of the James." Godfrey believed this movement would continue during the night, to some extent. This was the opening General Grant had predicted. "I ordered preparations for attack in the morning," Weitzel wrote.[43]

After Midnight: Burning Bridges

Confederate general Richard S. Ewell gave orders that all the bridges over the James River were to be destroyed to prevent an attack from the rear by the Federals. Only Mayo's Bridge, at the foot of Fourteenth Street, would be spared. Mayo's Bridge led across the river to the city of Manchester on the south side. Captain Clement Sulivane was charged to protect the bridge, and one remaining footbridge over the canal leading to it, until General Martin Gary's cavalry brigade arrived. That brigade would serve as escort to President Davis and his cabinet.

Two months prior, General Lee had instructed Ewell that it would be necessary to destroy all cotton and tobacco in Richmond if the capital were evacuated. Lee's order was in line with a Confederate statute directing the destruction of the commodities so as to avoid their capture. General Ewell issued orders to destroy the tobacco in three local warehouses only after everything that could be carried was removed. He also made plans to destroy the powder magazine. Following Ewell's orders, the key buildings were torched.[44]

General Ewell directed Captain Sulivane to assemble and command the so-called "Local Brigade," to arm the men and await further orders. When Sulivane arrived to guard Mayo's Bridge, he gazed on "the terrible splendor of the scene." He wrote, "Such a scene probably the world has seldom witnessed . . . The two cities, Richmond and Manchester, were like a blaze of day amid the surrounding darkness."[45]

Fires quickly broke out all over town. The Tredegar Iron Works caught fire and the shells stored there spiraled through the air and exploded in every direction. Many residents thought that the city was under attack, unaware that the devastation was self-inflicted by their own government and military. Thousands

FIGURE 19.1. *The Fall of Richmond, Va., on the Night of April 2d. 1865.* (Currier & Ives, New York; Library of Congress, Prints and Photographs Division, Reproduction No. LC-DIG-pga-03629.)

of residents fled across the James, hoping to escape not only the fire but the advance of the Union Army.

With the government and military now abandoning the city, Richmond erupted into plundering and looting, described by one observer as "a mad revelry of confusion." Police tried to contend with the mob and arrested a few ringleaders.

Just before midnight, Jefferson Davis stepped aboard a train that carried the vagabonds of the Confederate government—other than Judge John Campbell. As residents and soldiers continued across the Mayo Bridge, the presidential train slowly pulled away from the station and headed southwest on the only safe rail line, bound for Danville, Virginia. The Richmond and Danville Railroad had been the main supply route into Petersburg for Lee's Army of Northern Virginia. However, General George Stoneman's Union cavalry had been busy tearing up the tracks, destroying bridges and culverts, burning rail stations and water tanks. This broke the supply line, later immortalized in the song lyric "Virgil Caine is the name, and I served on the Danville train, 'til Stoneman's cavalry came and tore up the tracks again."[46]

It was the night they drove old Dixie down.

CHAPTER 20

The Fall of the Confederacy

About 5:00 p.m. on Sunday night, April 2, 1865, Weitzel's chief signal officer, Lieutenant Sylvester B. Partridge, peered through his spyglass from the observation tower near General Weitzel's headquarters. The lieutenant noticed something quite unusual in the otherwise stillness in Richmond. There was a great excitement in the streets of the city, with people rushing in and out of homes and public buildings. What Partridge did not know was that Jefferson Davis was following a recommendation from Robert E. Lee to evacuate the Confederate capital as quickly as possible. The rebel government was collapsing before his eyes. The lieutenant rapidly climbed down from the wooden ten-story tower and rushed into General Weitzel's quarters with the news. The young general was quite interested in the report.

Along the picket lines, Union officers had placed men in the treetops to peer across into the enemy camps. All seemed still as the rebel troops enjoyed the Sabbath Day in their tents. One Yankee picket recalled that "the night fell cloudy and dark as I plunged into the mysterious silence and gloom for my last night on the picket line. It passed uneventfully, as the preceding one had passed, except that blue mist settled on the earth."[1] The calmness was deceiving, as Confederate officers were already planning to pull back from the front, abandoning their lines . . . and Richmond.

News of Longstreet's Evacuation

Godfrey Weitzel was known for his calm, cool demeanor under fire, and the German rarely displayed much emotion in front of his men. But on this night, the excitement was great and he was preoccupied with plans for the day ahead. It was around midnight before he could lie down for a rest, leaving his chief of staff, General George Shepley, and his ordnance officer on guard at his headquarters.

Before 2:00 a.m. on Monday, Shepley's offer of a reward of a thirty-day furlough paid off. Major Stevens came to Shepley's hut with "a ragged specimen" of a rebel soldier in tow. Shepley quickly rose and began his lawyer's interrogation of the poor fellow. The news he was about to hear would change history:

"What regiment do you belong to?" he began.

"To the Eighteenth Georgia battalion," the young Southerner answered.

"The deuce you do!" Shepley exclaimed. "That battalion is in Custis Lee's division. You are the man of all others in the world I want to see!"[2]

Shepley's excitement rose as he glanced at his large chart on the wall. He knew from his prior analysis that Custis Lee's division occupied a point on the line that the enemy could not afford to weaken. "Where is your division?" he continued. "All I can tell you, General, is that I was out on picket," replied the prisoner, "and at one o'clock, when the relief should have come, the officer came and marched us silently inside of the parapet, and left nobody in our places."[3]

The rebel continued, "When I got in, I found my battalion marching out towards Richmond." Shepley now knew that Longstreet was abandoning his position, pulling in his pickets and moving back toward the Confederate capital. Looking through the dim light of the hut at the bearded officer, the scraggly young man continued, "So I thought I would not march any more, but would come over to you-uns."[4] George Shepley dismissed the pathetic young man, and Major Stevens took him away.

Now Shepley's excitement could hardly be contained! He alone knew that the road to Richmond was open. As he later wrote of his emotions,

Imagine the feelings of a Union officer, upon whom, in an instant, before it was known to any other person on the Union side, there flashed the conviction that Richmond was at our mercy; that we should go there the next day; and that in the stillness of that night, while the whole army was quietly sleeping, he was the sole possessor of the knowledge![5]

George Shepley immediately sent a dispatch to Brigadier General Charles Devens Jr. to have his Twenty-Fourth Army Corps ready to move at daylight. He issued the same orders to Weitzel's Twenty-Fifth Corps in anticipation that Godfrey Weitzel would agree. He then went to wake up his boss, who had finally drifted off to sleep in an adjacent hut.

Godfrey's eyes had barely closed when his slumber was suddenly interrupted by his chief of staff about 2:00 a.m. An excited George Shepley entered the wood cabin and found the lanky German general fast asleep. Shepley recalled that Weitzel was "sleeping the profound sleep of a Teuton."[6] Pulling the six-foot-four general out of his bunk, which was the only way Shepley could wake him from the deep sleep, Shepley shouted in his ear. "General, we can take Richmond this morning!" He went on to report that bright fires were seen in the direction of Richmond.[7]

Weitzel was still too groggy to comprehend the words. "General Shepley, you are dreaming," came his reply. But Shepley persisted, "Come out and put your ear to the ground, and you shall hear the tramp of Custis Lee's division on their way to Richmond." Godfrey was still skeptical, and half asleep. *The rebels abandoning their position? Could it be true?* Shepley relayed his conversation with the young deserter from Custis Lee's division and, after some discussion, Weitzel stood in the open door of his hut and wiped his eyes. Looking toward Richmond, he could see a bright light on the horizon that kept gradually increasing. Suddenly there were the unmistakable sounds of explosions. It was Admiral Semmes's flagship, the famous rebel ram *Virginia*, being blown up to prevent her falling into Union hands. The shell-rooms of his flagship had been full, and the explosion sent projectiles flying into the air over the river, with lit fuses of different lengths, exploding "by twos and threes, and by the dozen."[8] The concussions were so great that they shook houses in Richmond and echoed into the night for forty miles around.

Godfrey was now convinced. "By heavens! General, you are right!" he exclaimed. "Telegraph Devens to be ready to move by daylight!" With a smile the chief of staff replied, "I have sent orders to that effect, and received his reply, that the 24th will be ready. The 25th is ready now!"[9]

Neither Weitzel nor Shepley could have anticipated that overnight the city of Richmond would be intentionally set ablaze by withdrawing Confederates, nor that it would be up to them to save the enemy's capital, and its residents, from near total destruction. Now wide awake, Godfrey pulled on his knee-high boots and stepped outside his quarters to join Shepley and other officers who watched the glowing sky above Richmond. The men stared in disbelief through spyglasses at the fire and smoke rising above the horizon. The flames were followed by muffled explosions as the rebels destroyed key storehouses of tobacco, cotton, and ammunition, as well as the remainder of their naval fleet. The time had certainly come, and with the fall of Richmond, would surely come the fall of the Confederacy as well.

Godfrey Weitzel was very pleased at the quick work of his chief of staff. Officers began to spread the word to the weary soldiers, some of whom were already awakened by the sounds of explosions. Two more Confederate deserters were brought in by Union pickets, hoping for a furlough. The pair barely spoke English, but their interrogators understood that the men did not know where their unit was and did not know why they had not been relieved. After speaking with them, General Weitzel described them as being "Alsatian," as "they spoke poor German and worse French."[10]

Shortly thereafter, another prisoner was sent in for questioning from General Kautz's front. The prisoner was a black teamster who gave Generals Weitzel and Shepley confirmation that just after dark the rebels began making preparations to abandon their lines and that they were all now gone. Weitzel ordered an immediate forward movement of the entire picket line, which confirmed the teamster's statements.

Knowing that the moment was at hand, Godfrey directed all of his troops to be awakened and furnished with breakfast in order to prepare for the march and possible fight ahead. About 3:00 a.m., he directed the division commanders and cavalry officers to hold their men in readiness to move at daybreak, when it would be light enough to see through the mine-laden roads without risking injury.[11]

At 4:30 a.m., Major General Weitzel informed General Grant of the fires and explosions, and that he would move at daybreak. An anxious President Abraham Lincoln also received a telegram from General Weitzel that Richmond was being evacuated. After a siege of nine months, the Confederacy was against the ropes and it was time to close in for the knockout punch. Weitzel immediately gave orders to concentrate some of his brigades toward making an assault on the enemy lines if still manned. He sent word to Grant that the offensive toward Richmond had begun.

Grant responded that his efforts in Petersburg had been so successful that he would return William Birney's division of the Twenty-Fifth Corps. He added that when Weitzel received that division, he could "make a sure thing of the attack."[12] Other than that last directive from City Point, Godfrey Weitzel heard nothing further from the other side of the Appomattox during that day or evening. As it turned out later, Grant detained Birney's division in Petersburg for additional work, but Weitzel did not wait on them to make his move. He did not need that division.

At daybreak, billowing black smoke could be seen rising over the capital city and more explosions could be heard. One former slave recalled that at the break of day "a colored man" was the first to carry the news into General Weitzel's camp that President Davis and General Lee had "skedaddled."[13] It was true; Jefferson Davis had left Richmond with his cabinet members on the train to Danville. Before the day was over, Godfrey Weitzel would sleep in Davis's bed. It would be an amazing twenty-four hours.

Brigadier General Edward H. Ripley's brigade had been on picket duty Sunday night and was the first to move forward against Longstreet's protected fortress. He sent his picket line forward, followed closely by the entire brigade, ready to engage at any moment. Ripley's message that the enemy camp was a ghost town reached General Weitzel around 5:00 a.m. As his men stepped through the twisted tree limbs and through the pointed log spikes, then climbed the steep hillside, they cautiously peered over the rim of the parapet, trying to catch sight of the opposing sentinels. To their amazement, the rebel fortifications were entirely deserted![14]

Back at Weitzel's camp, the Federal officers had their horses saddled and ready to ride, impatiently awaiting the first glimpse of daylight before crossing the enemy lines. The mood was jubilant and all were exchanging congratulations.

As General Shepley stood waiting by his horse, a young lieutenant and aide-de-camp on his staff named Johnston Livingston De Peyster hurried over to Shepley with an eager personal request. "General," he blurted, "do you remember a promise made to me a few months ago, when we left Norfolk for the Army of the James?" Shepley smiled, as he knew exactly what the young man had in mind. "Yes, De Peyster," he replied. "I promised if you would bring with you and take care of my old flag that had floated over the city-hall in New Orleans, you should raise it over Richmond."[15]

De Peyster's eyes grew large. "Will you let me do it?" he eagerly asked. "Yes, go and get it," assured Shepley. "And if you will carry it to Richmond you may raise it over the Rebel capital."[16] De Peyster was off like a rabbit and quickly found the flag, then carefully strapped it to the leather pommel of his saddle. The young man's name would go down in history, including in this book, when later that day he raised the first Union flag to fly over Richmond since the secession of Virginia four years prior.

By now, the sun had begun to show its first rays in the east. Word spread like a wildfire among the officers of the two Army corps, who soon came flocking to General Weitzel's headquarters, "almost crazy with exultation" at the idea of an immediate advance on Richmond.[17] Everyone could now see the bright flames rising above the burning city and hear the explosions. Richmond was finally theirs for the taking.

In the Virginia capital, as the sun began to peek over the eastern horizon, a crowd of several thousand starving men, women, and children gathered at the corner of Fourteenth and Cary Streets, in front of the Mayo Bridge. There had been a large commissary depot at that place and the Confederate government had removed its guards and abandoned the remaining provisions. One eyewitness described the scene as the depot doors were forced open and, "a demoniacal struggle for the countless barrels of hams, bacon, whisky, flour, sugar, coffee, etc., etc., raged about the buildings among the hungry mob."[18] The flames at last reached the commissary, and what was left of the supplies was burned up inside the building, to the disappointment of the angry mob. The town was in utter chaos, at the hands of its own people and even members of the Confederate Army who roamed Main Street, drunk with liquor, smashing the plate glass of storefronts and pillaging the goods within.[19]

The Race for Richmond

An advance team of cavalry was needed to ride into Richmond and report back with fresh information. Godfrey's junior aide-de-camp and senior aide-de-camp were both named "Graves." The junior aide, Thomas T. Graves, recalled that "as soon as it was light General Weitzel ordered Colonel [Edmond] E. Graves, senior aide-de-camp, and Major Atherton H. Stevens, Jr., provost-marshal, to take a detachment of forty men from the two companies (E and H) of the 4th Massachusetts Cavalry, and make a reconnaissance." Slowly this little band of scouts was to pick their way in.[20] These two New Englanders were about to play their most significant part in the entire war in the hours to come, making history as the first Union officers to enter Richmond.

Weitzel directed Graves and Stevens to take their detachment as an advance team and try to get through the rebel lines. If successful, Weitzel directed the pair to advance at once toward Richmond and "to receive the surrender of the city, and to direct the authorities and citizens to cause all liquor to be destroyed and to preserve order until my troops arrived."[21] This was quite a task for forty men entering the enemy's capital. Graves and Stevens saluted, mounted their horses, and galloped ahead into the woods that separated the Union camp from Longstreet's earthworks.

When the dawn cast sufficient light to see, General Weitzel straddled his horse and pulled at the reins, his knee-length boots stretched out in the stirrups. He took in the moment, glancing at his loyal officers mounted to the left and the right, all waiting for his command. Behind them, the sharp-looking black troops stood eager and at attention. Finally, he gave the anticipated order, "Forward, men!" With that, the column started its historic final march toward Richmond.

Major General Weitzel ordered General Kautz's all-black First Division of the Twenty-Fifth Corps to proceed into Richmond via the Osborne Pike, with General Devens's all-white Third Division of the Twenty-Fourth Corps to take the New Market Road. He directed that the Fifth Massachusetts Cavalry ride up the Darbytown and Charles City Roads. All infantry and cavalry were directed to halt at the outskirts of the city until further orders from General Weitzel.[22] He wanted an orderly entry of Union troops into Richmond. This was no ordinary march, and Godfrey knew that each division wished to be part of it. They were to take separate roads, but all converge at the same destination just a few miles away. This was history in the making, and it needed to be handled properly.

Weitzel and his staff, comprising about forty officers, took the lead, followed by Devens's division of the Twenty-Fourth Army Corps. General Weitzel and his officers took the Osborne Pike at a gallop. Godfrey's small group quickened their pace as they passed through the five thousand black soldiers from August Kautz's division and crossed over the rebel lines in Kautz's front. Clearing the woods, Godfrey could now see Longstreet's earthworks, with its chevaux-de-frise in front, followed by double rows of abatis.[23]

The mounted group watched for buried mines, proceeding single file out of caution. General Weitzel and his officers cautiously rode around the fallen-tree obstructions and the double-rowed spikes. To their amazement, they found that Longstreet's men had been in such a hurry to retreat that they'd left the markers for the buried explosives, small squares of red cloth inserted onto split sticks in the ground, revealing each and every one of the torpedoes. The marked passages had been flagged for the pickets' own use. The result was that the safe passages were plainly visible at dawn to Weitzel and his men.[24]

The mounted Union officers carefully guided their horses through the narrow eighteen-inch space between the spiked logs and rode down into the ditch, then up onto the parapet. The incline was so steep that several of the horses lost their footing and tumbled into the ditch or rolled down the slopes, rider and all.[25]

Crossing up the hill and over the parapet, Godfrey Weitzel saw the entire rebel encampment standing just as it had the night before.[26] The Confederates did not want to alert the Union pickets to their movements and had left their tents in place, their cannons in the embrasures. The place was entirely deserted, with campfires still smoldering as if the regiments would return shortly.

The curious officers stopped for a moment in disbelief and dismounted to inspect. Everything was undisturbed. There was no time to waste, however, with Kautz's black division marching near behind, so General Weitzel's order to resume the march echoed along the line. Riding again, the horsemen trampled through the encampment and proceeded along the New Market Road. The same road had obviously been used by Longstreet's men in their escape, as evidenced by the discarded blankets, muskets, knapsacks, clothing, and about everything else that a fleeing soldier might rid himself of in order to lighten his load.

There were suddenly several heavy explosions from the direction of Richmond and the ground vibrated with each one. Horses jumped and officers pulled at the reins to hold them steady. Thick black plumes of smoke rose in the distance.[27] Weitzel continued his brisk ride toward the source of the explosions, not quite sure what to expect within the city but anxious to find out.

Shortly after General Weitzel and his staff passed through the rebel lines, they observed a party of men mounted on horseback, just a short distance away on a slight hill. Though Confederates, the men wore blue Yankee overcoats and stood perfectly still, observing Weitzel and his men. "At first it seemed as if they were a part of the cavalry detachment which I had sent ahead under Major Graves," Godfrey recalled. "But suddenly they wheeled and went off at a gallop."[28]

Godfrey immediately directed one of his staff officers, Lieutenant Charles Phillips, to take an orderly and to ride ahead to find out just who they were. The excited Phillips kicked his horse and dashed off on a run, followed close behind by the orderly. The mounted party of disguised rebel scouts turned and headed off as well, but laid a trap for Phillips not far away. Weitzel did not hear from the lieutenant until five days later when he escaped his captors and sent General Weitzel a telegraph message.

The advance team, led by Stevens and Graves, suddenly rode past General Ripley's men, followed shortly afterward by a light battery that came dashing up. "Where is the New Market Road?" demanded a young artillery officer on horseback. General Ripley knew the game and was not about to be passed up. With Ripley's brigade in sole possession of the New Market Road, and knowing there was no use for artillery, he refused to yield the road. It was now every man for himself to be the first into Richmond. As General Ripley described the scene, "The eager, crack-brained young officer in command, frenzied with the wild joy with which every heart was throbbing, seeing an open field extending some distance ahead along our left flank, rushed into it with his horses lashed into a mad gallop and tried to run in ahead of us."[29] At this challenge, the Thirteenth New Hampshire, which was at the head of Ripley's column, broke into a sharp double-quick, racing the horseman. However, the impetuous young artilleryman soon found himself trapped by a swamp at the end of the field. Embarrassed, the young man returned and fell into his proper place—in the rear.

As another Yankee regiment marched up the Charles City Road, it encountered a signboard that read "Richmond—Two Miles."[30] The goal was now so close that every man felt he could run the remaining distance, as adrenaline pumped through their bodies to quicken the pace. Not far away, on the New Market Road, General Edward Ripley rode backward and forward along his column of marching bluecoats, "exchanging congratulations with the officers, and looking down into the flashing eyes and quivering faces of the men as they glanced up" in a common joy and glory.[31]

The brigadier soaked in the scene as he drifted back and forth along the flank, sometimes just sitting still to enjoy the sight of the long column rushing by. "I sang out, as of old, but never before so exultingly, that old, old song which will never die out from the ears of the veteran until death shall close them, 'Close up, boys! Close up! No straggling in the ranks of the First Brigade to-day. Close up! Close up!'"[32]

General Weitzel and his staff galloped along the Osborne Pike toward its junction with the New Market Road. At the intersection they saw General Charles Devens's division of the Twenty-Fourth Corps marching up the New Market Road at a rapid pace. Farther to the rear of Devens, Weitzel could see Kautz's division of the Twenty-Fifth Corps coming up behind Devens, also marching at the double-quick. Weitzel and his small group rode on ahead of the advancing infantry, anxious to get to Richmond as quickly as possible.

A footrace was now in progress to see which division would enter Richmond first. The competition was among the Twenty-Fourth and the Twenty-Fifth Army Corps, one white, the other black. Both Devens and Kautz had been warned of the land mines and had proceeded cautiously as they passed through the enemy lines, though one unfortunate man was killed by a buried torpedo. When their two columns met at the junction of the Osborne Pike and New Market Road, General Devens claimed the Pike for his division, by virtue of seniority in rank. General Kautz conceded and cleverly yielded the roadway to the more senior officer. Kautz then threw caution about torpedoes to the wind and struck out straight across the fields toward Richmond, determined to beat Devens into the Confederate capital!

One of Weitzel's officers recalled that as he moved slowly up the New Market Road he saw Kautz's and Devens's men in the distance, many of them upon the double-quick, aiming to be the first in the city. "A white and a colored division were having a regular race, the white troops on the turnpike and the colored in the fields."[33]

A humorous story told by General Weitzel was of an encounter when his group approached Rocketts Landing, the steamboat landing just outside Richmond. The approaching horsemen found a solitary sentinel on post, "in a bright and gorgeous militia uniform." The frightened man said that he had been posted the night before and had never been relieved. "He had served in the old country," Weitzel said, "and seemed to me to be an Alsatian." The former "Gottfried" Weitzel knew quite well the dialect of emigrants from Alsace-Lorraine, since his family was from this same region on the German-French border, and many of his neighbors in the Over-the-Rhine area in Weitzel's hometown of Cincinnati spoke this mixture of French and German. The poor sentry was terrified as he watched the approaching Union officers on their beautiful mounts, followed by a mass of armed soldiers. Weitzel felt pity for the abandoned immigrant soldier. "I sent him home to his family," Godfrey said.[34]

The Mayor Surrenders Richmond

Just outside the city, Richmond mayor Joseph Carrington Mayo rode east in an open carriage in search of Godfrey Weitzel to deliver a note of surrender. About 6:30 a.m., as Major Stevens and Colonel Graves approached the junction of the New Market Road and the Osborne Turnpike with their advance cavalry detachment, they saw the mayor's carriage approaching, waiving a white flag of surrender. Inside was the sixty-nine-year-old mayor and a small committee of citizens. The balding mayor climbed out of the open carriage and introduced himself to Major Stevens. From inside his dark jacket that hid his round waistline, the mayor pulled an envelope addressed to the "General Commanding the United States Army in front of Richmond." Inside was a note hastily written on a piece of wallpaper.[35] The note announced the surrender of the city and sought protection for its "women and children and property."[36]

Stevens took the note and promised that he would deliver it to General Weitzel. The mayor and his party then turned their carriage around and headed back into the city, with the invading army not far behind.

After this brief delay, Stevens and Graves each gave their horses a kick and led the forty cavalrymen into the heart of the rebel capital, arriving at the city limits just before 7:00 a.m. At Rocketts Landing, Major Stevens left a sentinel posted on the road to halt all Union troops at that point, as General Weitzel had ordered. Weitzel wanted the formal entry of Union liberators to be something dignified and memorable. Godfrey knew this was a historic moment, and he planned a grand display of the Union's impressive forces. It would be a parade to showcase the North's finest soldiers and its only all-black corps.

Stevens and Graves rode faster now through Rocketts, then galloped west up Main Street, past the burning buildings and hot cinders, turning right up Governor Street all the way to Capitol Square. The forty cavalrymen peered cautiously through the smoke to spot any Confederate stragglers who might ambush them. At Capitol Square, the two officers dismounted and Major Atherton Stevens grabbed two of his cavalry's colorful guidons and rushed cautiously into the Virginia statehouse. Climbing the stairs to the rooftop, with his men watching the feat from the square below, Stevens raised the first Northern flags high above Richmond on the morning of April 3: two small flags from the squadron of the Fourth Massachusetts Cavalry, which he commanded.[37] Godfrey Weitzel reported that "their guidons were the first national colors displayed over the city" since the ordinance of secession had been adopted nearly four years before.[38]

From the western slope of Strecker's Hill, a loyal Richmond woman wept as she watched through the haze the hauling down of the Confederate flag and the running up of the Northern flag above the statehouse.[39]

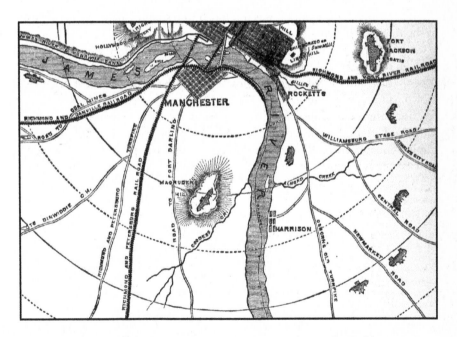

FIGURE 20.1. *The roads leading into Richmond, Virginia.* (Harper's Weekly, May 21, 1864.)

CHAPTER 21

Entry into Richmond

Weitzel Takes Richmond

Flames roared out of windows and rooftops, and two- and three-story brick walls came crashing down. Missiles and projectiles from the exploding magazines and the Confederate river fleet made for a sight like holiday fireworks. The first procession into Richmond was led by General Edward Ripley's brigade of the Twenty-Fourth Corps, which marched proudly at the head of the column with its three bands playing patriotic tunes. As company musicians played strains of "Yankee Doodle," the emotion was too much to restrain. Union troopers began to shout, cheer, and sing.

Ripley's eager brigade marched proudly up Main Street when suddenly, through the smoke and haze, crowds of dark figures materialized. Recently freed slaves pushed and shoved to get the closest look at the liberators. Their black and brown hands reached out to touch the flanks of the strong cavalry horses.

The column of white soldiers proceeded as far as the Exchange Hotel, then turned a sharp right at Governor Street and headed north another three blocks to Capitol Square.[1] There, Ripley halted his men in the open plaza where they could get fresh air away from the smoky haze that engulfed the rest of the city.

On the heels of Ripley's brigade, General Weitzel rode toward the city with a force of some nine thousand troops not far behind him. As Godfrey rode up the hill near Chimborazo Hospital, he was received by the Confederate corps of officers at the hospital, dressed in full uniform. The hospital's commandant, Dr. McCaw, asked General Weitzel for a permit for him and his officers, which was promptly granted, taking them under Union protection. Godfrey issued a verbal order that all Confederate soldiers at the hospital should be taken care of under all circumstances.

General Weitzel offered to put the commandant in the general service of the United States, so that he might issue requisitions for materials and supplies and have the same filled "as any other medical director in the United States army."[2] However, since General Robert E. Lee had not yet surrendered, Dr. McCaw respectfully declined the proffered appointment.

The scene in Richmond was a shock to the entering Union officers. Smoke poured from the raging fires, choking the men and stinging their eyes. The roar of the exploding arsenals, magazines, and warehouses filled with Ordnance Bureau explosives was "deafening and awe-inspiring," wrote one Union officer.[3] Just as Ripley's men had found, the young general inherited a city dying in its own fires. "I found the greatest confusion, pillaging and disorder reigning, and the city on fire in several places," Godfrey said. "I immediately set everyone to work to restore order and to assist in subduing the fires. I succeeded in doing this at about 2 p.m., by which time a large and valuable portion of the city had been consumed."[4]

The citizens, released prisoners, and deserters were still engaged in looting, while the suddenly free black slaves gathered in the streets to celebrate their liberation. "Now, when we entered Richmond we found ourselves in a perfect pandemonium," Godfrey wrote. "Fires and explosions in all directions; whites and blacks, either drunk or in the highest state of excitement, running to and fro on the streets, apparently engaged in pillage or in saving some of their scanty effects from the fire; it was a yelling, howling mob."[5]

Godfrey's assessment was that there were about twenty thousand people left in Richmond, half of them slaves.[6] The black population came out in droves to greet the Yankee liberators with shouts of welcome. Thousands packed each side of the street, rejoicing. Many fell upon their knees and threw their hands wildly in the air, shouting "Glory to God! Glory to God!" as tears streamed down their excited faces.[7] The soldiers had to watch their step as the black men and women threw themselves down on their hands and knees to pray in the street "in wild delirium."

The stores along Main Street had been looted overnight but were open, in contrast to the homes passed by the Federals, which were closed up with blinds tightly shut. "None of the better class of the whites were to be seen," said one Union officer, "though we occasionally saw an eye peering through the blinds."[8] Loyal Southerners stayed closed up in their homes, hidden behind doors and only peeking through lattices and blinds at the dreaded Northern soldiers marching into their town.

Finely dressed Union officers rode through the city's main streets as buildings on both sides burned with intense flames. Among them was Godfrey Weitzel's younger brother, Captain Lewis Weitzel, who served as an aide-de-camp. The two Weitzel men entered Richmond together as the greater part of the city was on fire. The air was filled with sparks and choked with black smoke. Shells exploded periodically from the burning rebel ordnance warehouses, adding an eerie sense of an ongoing battle.

The second humorous story about Weitzel's entry into Richmond was the result of his informal dress that day. Apparently some of the freed slaves mistook one of the general's staff officers for Major General Weitzel and showered him with the affection of a conquering commander by mistake. Godfrey wrote:

Major William V. Hutchings, of Roxbury, Mass., rode by my side. He was dressed in full uniform except epauletts and had the regulation equipments, &c., on his horse. He had quite a venerable and very handsome appearance. I was in undress uniform. The mob naturally supposed Hutchings to be the General, and he received the bulk of the caresses and attentions.[9]

Capital Reenactment

At 8:15 a.m., Mayor Joseph Mayo and General Weitzel enacted the symbolic handing over of Richmond. Although the mayor had surrendered the city to Major Stevens earlier that morning on the road outside of Richmond, he went through a formal surrender to Weitzel on the steps of the City Hall. The reenactment was carried out "with theatrical effect," one witness observed, as the keys of the fallen city were tendered by the town's mayor, who "begged the clemency and help of the Northern victors."[10] Thus, the city of Richmond was surrendered twice in one day.

General Weitzel then headed over to Capitol Square en route to the Virginia statehouse. One of Weitzel's aides, Thomas Graves, recalled that "entering, we found Capitol Square covered with people who had fled there to escape the fire and were utterly worn out with fatigue and fright."[11] Citizens crowded the grounds of the open square to escape the flames, saving only what they could carry. These refugees had lost or fled their homes during the night to avoid fire. The smoke was so thick in the streets that people gathered at the square just to find an open space where they could breathe. The lawn and shrubbery were black with smoke and cinders swirled in the air.

Showing the same kind disposition that won him the respect of his men, Weitzel later wrote, "Their poor faces were perfect pictures of utter despair. It was a sight that would have melted a heart of stone."[12]

At the stately white capitol building designed by Thomas Jefferson, there was "a scene of the wildest confusion." Abandoned files of Confederate government papers were scattered about the various departments, blowing about the street so thick that one Union officer said, "Our horses sank fetlock-deep in unsigned Confederate bonds and notes, letters, and documents of every kind, which covered the ground for acres."[13]

General Ripley was summoned to the capitol building where he saw a gathering of military and civilian officials on a broad landing at the head of the tall flight of steps. There stood the six-foot-four General Weitzel and staff, along with General Charles Devens with his staff. Grouped around the two generals were the sharply dressed division commanders of the Twenty-Fifth Army Corps of colored troops. Ripley recalled, "I dismounted and ascended to General Weitzel, who stood the central figure of this brilliant historical scene. I saluted and waited in innocent curiosity his orders, unsuspecting the distinguished honors the First Brigade was to receive at his hands."[14]

"I have sent for you, General Ripley," Weitzel said, "to inform you that I have selected you to take command of this city and your brigade as its garrison." Ripley was stunned. His was not only the first full brigade to enter the city, but now was given charge of securing it. Dismissing Ripley, Weitzel added, "I have no orders further to communicate, except to say that I wish this conflagration stopped, and this city saved if it is in the bounds of human possibility."[15]

In words that could have come from Ben Butler himself, Weitzel added, "And you have carte blanche to do it in your own way." Ripley had but one request from the young general. He requested that all of the other troops be withdrawn entirely from the city so that Ripley could control the situation. General Weitzel pondered the request for a moment, staring off at the smoldering city as he stroked his long beard. "Agreed," he said, and issued an order to an aide that all of the other division commanders march their troops through the city once and then go into camp just outside. To prevent any looting or harassment of the Richmond residents, Weitzel ordered that no passes be granted for entry back into the city once the parade had passed through.[16]

General Weitzel himself set up his military headquarters in the Senate Chamber of the Virginia capitol building. Meanwhile, an anxious Lieutenant Johnson L. De Peyster climbed to the top of the building with Major Atherson H. Stevens, an American flag clutched in the lieutenant's hands. They lowered the two guidons from the masthead and replaced them with the Stars and Stripes in fulfillment of General Shepley's promise.

The Telegram Read Round the World

Godfrey had important news to share, and he needed to send an urgent message to General Grant. He walked down the capitol steps and went across the road to the governor's mansion, where he ordered an aide to write a dispatch to General Grant announcing the Twenty-Fifth Corps' triumphant entrance into Richmond. Weitzel's telegraph corps did not have wire enough to carry the lines into the city, and the nearest station was about three miles away. The message was taken off the wires at City Point and sent to the War Department in Washington, and from there to the rest of the Northern states.

Weitzel's telegraph sparked spontaneous celebrations when read in cities like New York, Boston, Washington, and Philadelphia. Within twenty-four hours, the message was quoted in every Union newspaper, turning Godfrey Weitzel into a national hero. In one short paragraph he tried to convey the success of the day and the scene in Richmond:

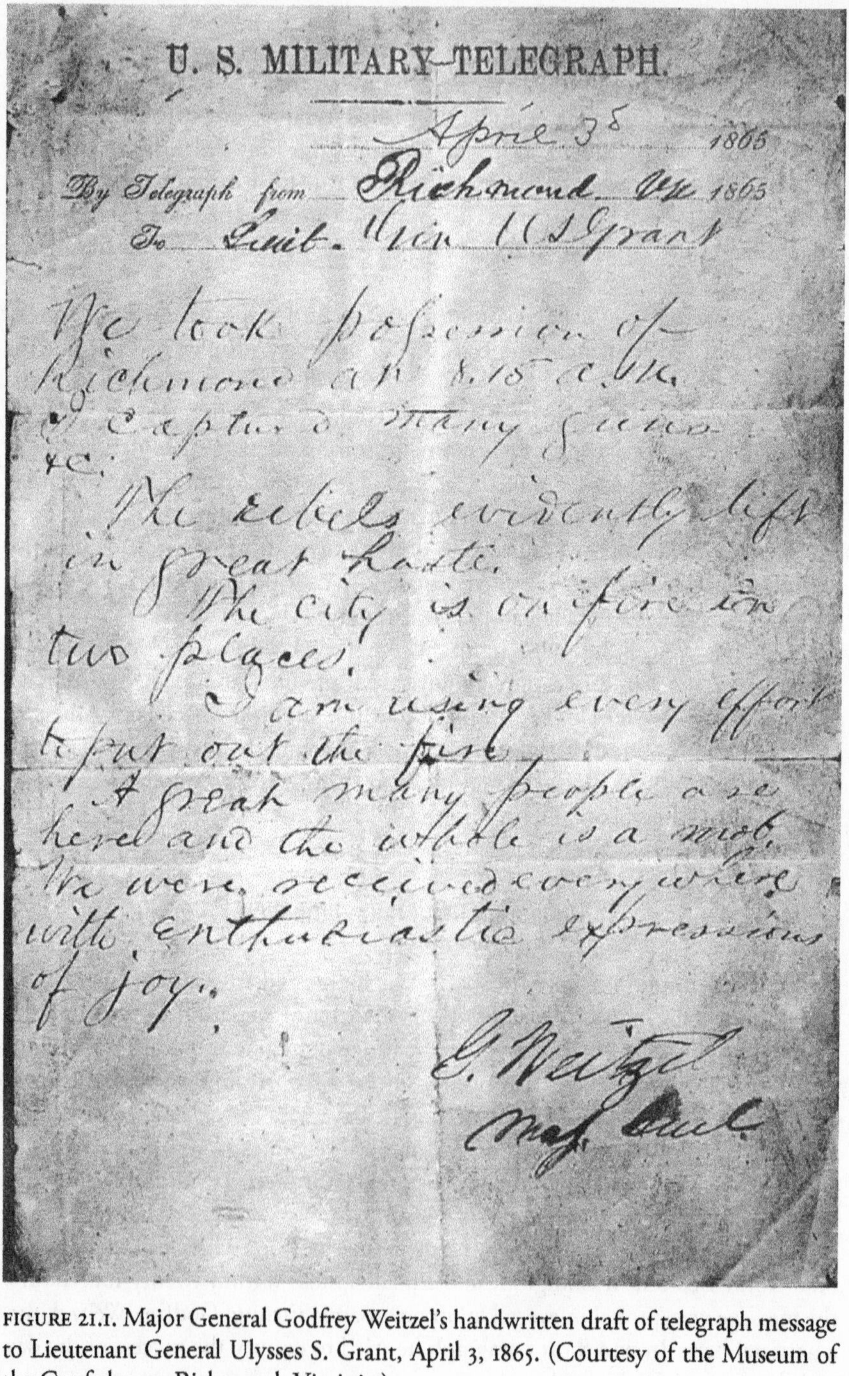

FIGURE 21.1. Major General Godfrey Weitzel's handwritten draft of telegraph message to Lieutenant General Ulysses S. Grant, April 3, 1865. (Courtesy of the Museum of the Confederacy, Richmond, Virginia.)

We took possession of Richmond at 8:15 a.m. I captured many guns &c.
The rebels evidently left in great haste. The city is on fire in two places.
I am using every effort to put out the fire. A great many people are here
and the whole is a mob. We were received everywhere with enthusiastic
expressions of joy.[17]

General Weitzel sent the dispatch to General Grant in Petersburg by cavalry courier. Oddly, Grant did not get the message, nor realize that Weitzel had
occupied Richmond, until 2:00 p.m. on April 3. It seemed that everyone else in
the nation was aware of the capture of Richmond except the commander of the
Union Army! Godfrey concluded that the delay was between City Point and
General Grant's headquarters, and not the fault of Weitzel or his courier.[18]

Securing the Rebel Capital

Richmond was still a very dangerous city. First was the blazing fire that threatened to destroy the entire city if not checked. Next was the very real risk of
enemy deserters or sympathizers lurking in the shadows to ambush unsuspecting
Federals. Godfrey Weitzel issued orders upon arriving at the Virginia statehouse
announcing the occupation of Richmond in the name of the United States government. He established marshal law and appointed his trusted friend, General
George F. Shepley, as military governor—reprising a role he played back in New
Orleans.

From an abandoned desk inside the Virginia capitol building, the young
general dictated an order assuring the residents of Richmond that he had come
"to restore them the blessings of peace, prosperity and freedom, under the flag of
the Union." He warned them to stay in their houses and off the streets.[19]

Fighting the Fire

Godfrey then turned his attention to the effort of extinguishing the blaze that
threatened the city and choked the air. He ordered a company of the First New
York Volunteer Engineers to assist General Ripley in the monumental task.[20]
Godfrey also assigned his younger brother and aide-de-camp, Captain Lewis
Weitzel, to work with Ripley to round up local men to help control the spreading fires. Details were at once made to scour the city and press into service every
able-bodied man, white or black, in extinguishing the flames.[21]

The blaze continued to spread east along Main Street but was checked by the
blowing up of the Traders' Bank about noon.[22] As Ripley's crews spread around
the city, the majority of the flames gradually died out with no more material

FIGURE 21.2. *The Federal Army Entering Richmond, Va., April 3, 1865.* (From Frank Leslie, *Famous Leaders and Battle Scenes of the Civil War*, New York [1896].)

upon which to feed. It was not until almost 4:00 p.m. that the last of the flames were snuffed out and, according to Weitzel, "perfect order restored."[23]

"We came near being burned out," Lizzie Ewell wrote her uncle the general a few days later. "This house caught [fire] & was on fire in six places at once. If it hadn't been for the exertions of the Yankees, the city would have been all gone."[24]

Protecting the Lee Residence

As Captain Lewis Weitzel was riding through the city, he was hailed down by a black servant in front of a brick house at 707 E. Franklin Street, toward which the fire seemed to be moving. The servant told Captain Weitzel that his mistress wished to speak to him. Lewis Weitzel dismounted and entered the three-story brick house, where he was met by one of the homeowner's daughters. She stated that her mother was an invalid and confined to bed. As the fire seemed to be approaching, the daughter asked for his assistance. Captain Weitzel was unaware he was speaking to a Confederate general's daughter and that the invalid woman was none other than Mary Custis Lee, the wife of Robert E. Lee.[25]

Recalling that his older brother knew General Lee from his days at the Academy, and had often heard Godfrey speak "in high terms of him and his family," Captain Weitzel responded promptly. He located the nearest regimental commander, who furnished a corporal, two men, and an ambulance. Lewis Weitzel ordered the corporal to remain near the Lee house and if there was any serious danger, to remove Mrs. Lee. These men remained on duty guarding the Lee family until the danger of the fire was over. Though none of the guards at the Lee home were black troops, this story was later twisted, with rumors that Godfrey had placed colored troops on guard at the residence, to the humiliation and horror of the Lee family.[26]

Nightfall, April 3, 1865, at the Davis Mansion

After an incredible day of organizing troops, taming fires, and restoring order in Richmond, the exhausted young general turned his attention to personal needs, a place to sleep and eat. Godfrey inquired of his staff officers and learned from the early reconnaissance of the city by Colonel Graves that a three-story mansion on the corner of Twelfth and Clay Streets had been set aside for his use by none other than the Confederate executive himself. The Davis housekeeper, Mary O'Melia, told Colonel Graves that she was under instructions from President Jefferson Davis that the Confederate White House was to be surrendered "for the occupancy of the commanding officer of the federal troops which might occupy the city."[27]

Intrigued, the twenty-nine-year-old major general and his chief of staff, George Shepley, rode their horses the four short blocks from Capitol Square to the Davis home. There, the pair set up living quarters in the mansion, which had been occupied less than twenty-four hours earlier by Jefferson Davis. Upon arrival, Godfrey learned that in addition to the housekeeper, a few of the family servants had remained behind. Walking through the house, Weitzel found that "the supplies in the larder were very scant, but everything else in the house was in good order and furnished elegant quarters for my staff and me." The two men dined on a meal that had been prepared for Davis by his servants, but which the president had neglected to eat in his hasty retreat.[28]

Prior to the war, George Shepley had known Secretary Jefferson Davis, and had even entertained him at Shepley's New England home when Davis "had been making Union speeches in Maine." Mr. Davis frequently urged his friend Shepley to come visit him at his plantation in Mississippi. While dining on Davis's abandoned meal, Shepley chuckled and thought it rather inhospitable for his host not to wait "and preside at the breakfast he had prepared for me."[29] The excitement of the day gave Shepley and Weitzel a hearty appetite and they devoured the feast.

Jefferson Davis had left his desk and personal office in neat order, despite his rush to vacate the place. Godfrey settled into the president's chair and desk, wondering where Davis might be at that very moment. The rebel president would be on the run for the next month, and his next permanent residence would be in shackles at Fort Monroe, charged with treason.

Opening a drawer of Jeff Davis's wooden desk, General Weitzel found a handwritten letter from his old friend Robert E. Lee, written to Confederate secretary of war Breckinridge, dated the previous October. It foretold of the coming end of the Confederacy. Godfrey opened the envelope and slid out the crisp paper inside. Unfolding the letter, he read Lee's confidential assessment of his army's condition: "It must be apparent to everyone that [the military condition of the country] is full of peril and requires prompt action." Lee also privately acknowledged the "superior numbers and resources of the enemy." His letter had been read to the Confederate Senate in secret session. Weitzel took from the letter that "Lee frankly and clearly showed that their cause was lost, and, I think, advised [Breckinridge] to make the best terms they could." Godfrey sent the letter by courier to Secretary Stanton.[30]

Nearby, the officers of the occupying army gathered in a large building close to the former Davis executive mansion. When Godfrey Weitzel entered at last there was applause and three cheers for their beloved young commander. General Shepley described the scene as a virtual "love-feast, to celebrate the fall of Richmond."[31]

As the officers shook hands and drank toasts to their commanders, Lincoln, Grant, Butler, and Weitzel, one officer read some of the dozens of congratulatory dispatches that had poured in from all over the North. When the revelry died down, Weitzel and Shepley rode back to the Davis mansion to retire for

FIGURE 21.3. President Lincoln enters Richmond, April 4, 1865. (From *Harper's Weekly*, February 24, 1866.)

the night. Entering the tall front door on the north side of the house, the pair thought of the men who had passed through this same doorway during the past four years. Generals including Lee, Beauregard, and Breckinridge, the entire rebel cabinet, spies, couriers, and foreign emissaries. Less than a day before, old Jeff Davis himself had walked out this door on his way to the train station. Yes, this was a day and a night to remember.

CHAPTER 22

Lincoln in Richmond

Richmond was not quite tamed by the next morning. The Fifth Massachusetts Cavalry patrolled the dirt roads around the city, arresting thirty ragged Confederates.[1] It was Tuesday, April 4, 1865, and as the city awoke to its first full day of Union occupation, telegraph machines began buzzing with a flurry of messages from the War Department and General Grant. The mood of the nation and its leaders was reflected in the messages, one of which was titled simply: "THE END. Our Details of the Decisive Contest of Sunday—WHAT GRANT HAS ACCOMPLISHED—The Destruction of Lee's Army." Godfrey Weitzel was an overnight hero for accomplishing Ben Butler's long-sought goal: the capture of Richmond. He sent reports to the State Department, which was hungry for details. In an understatement, Godfrey wrote, "Nothing new here. The fires are out and perfect quiet reigns."[2]

With the fires out and Federal troops standing guard at various points within and outside the city, Weitzel set about the business of taking inventory and running the initial governance of the city. His "inventory" included 1,000 "well" prisoners and 5,000 "wounded" found in the hospitals, plus 500 pieces of artillery and 5,000 stands of arms. Confederate stragglers were being hauled in by the hundreds between Petersburg and Richmond, with General Sheridan alone picking up 1,200 prisoners.

Defeat was now inevitable, and desertions added to Lee's problems. Grant reported, "In every direction I hear of rebel soldiers pushing for home, some in large, some in small squads, and generally without arms." Grant was relentless, however. "I shall continue the pursuit as long as there appears to be any use in it," he said. General Grant informed Stanton that his army was "pushing forward in the hope of overtaking or dispersing the remainder of Lee's army. . . . Their losses have been very heavy. Houses through the country are nearly all used as hospitals for wounded men."[3]

Weitzel Becomes a Mayor—Again

From the moment of his triumphal entry into Richmond, Godfrey said, "I was mainly engaged in restoring the wheels of government, and in taking care of the destitute."[4] He received a telegraph from General Ord, the commanding general of the Department of North Carolina and Virginia, which read, "You are appointed Governor of Richmond, and in my absence will act as commander of the Dept. in all matters which require prompt action. . . . Be your own Treasury agent."[5]

The appointment of Weitzel as top government official in Richmond was akin to being named mayor, a selection that was specifically approved by General Ulysses S. Grant. Ord directed the newly appointed military mayor, Godfrey Weitzel, to seize what tobacco had not been destroyed and use the funds to feed the poor residents of the city. He instructed Godfrey to allow food and necessary supplies to come into the city and to start utility services, including gas and water companies. Not to be overlooked in Ord's message, Godfrey was also appointed temporary commander of the Department of North Carolina and Virginia.

The next order of business was to restore law and order. General Ord instructed Weitzel to "register the white men. Appoint a military commission for the punishment of offences against law or order. Organize a police force . . . and protect all inhabitants in their property who come forward and take the oath of allegiance." Ord warned against allowing alcohol to be sold, fearing that the residents, and perhaps even the troops, might imbibe too much. "Allow loyal men to open hotels, but not grog shops," he wrote.[6]

Based on Ord's instructions, General Weitzel issued orders that "all loyal persons" could keep open public hotels and restaurants with restrictions imposed by the provost marshal, but that "bar rooms" and other places selling alcohol were to remain closed, under penalty of fine and imprisonment.[7]

Farragut in Town

Godfrey Weitzel and Admiral David G. Farragut had become well acquainted during the 1862 occupation of New Orleans. They had also cooperated in the capture of Port Hudson one year later. It was a welcome surprise when, on the morning of April 4, the accomplished and renowned admiral called on Godfrey at the Davis mansion. Godfrey was delighted to greet his old friend.

It is fitting that Godfrey Weitzel wrote of David "Damn the Torpedoes" Farragut's visit, "As soon as he heard that Richmond had fallen he came up the river, regardless of torpedoes, landed at Varina, and rode into the city." Farragut greeted Weitzel with hearty congratulations and a broad grin, knowing that the four-year war was finally nearing an end. Godfrey observed that Farragut "looked even happier and younger than he did after New Orleans fell."[8] The admiral was not the only surprise guest to call on General Weitzel that day.

Abraham Lincoln Arrives!

From City Point, an anxious Abraham Lincoln had planned to see Richmond as soon as it was in Union hands. His wait had finally come to an end. Despite warnings from Secretary of War Stanton, President Lincoln was determined to see the capital and to greet the people of Richmond, telling Stanton, "I will take care of myself." Lincoln was quoted as saying, "Thank God that I have lived to see this! It seems to me that I have been dreaming a horrid dream for four years, and now the nightmare is gone. I want to see Richmond."[9]

On the morning of April 4, just one day after Weitzel seized the blazing Confederate capital, the presidential party of Lincoln and his son Thomas (or "Tad," short for *tadpole*) steamed out of City Point aboard the *River Queen*. Tad was born April 4, 1853—and today was his twelfth birthday. The president was not about to leave his youngest son behind. Their destination was to meet Admiral David Porter's fleet in the James River, then proceed to Richmond.[10] The captain of the *River Queen* asked the president to move to the safety of the upper deck as the vessel neared Drewry's Bluff, while others stood on the bow and looked for torpedoes. Porter was waiting and when the president arrived, Mr. Lincoln and his son transferred to Porter's flagship, the *Malvern*, and the group steamed toward the fallen city.

The trip upriver was blocked at times by dead horses, abandoned barges, and broken ordnance that littered the river. Porter's ship eventually ran aground on a sandbar and the admiral transferred the Lincolns to his captain's gig, a barge rowed by twelve sailors as oarsmen—which Mr. Lincoln called "his buggy."[11] To give more speed, the rowboat was towed by a small steam tug. Remarking on their transfer to a smaller vessel, President Lincoln mused to Admiral Porter:

> Admiral, this brings to mind a fellow who once came to me to ask for an appointment as minister abroad. Finding he could not get that, he came down to some more modest position. Finally he asked to be made a tide-waiter. When he saw he could not get that, he asked me for an old pair of trousers. But tis well to be humble.[12]

The rowboat carried the president to the eastern edge of Richmond until it could go no farther due to clustered rocks in the stream. President Lincoln came onshore at Rockett's Landing about 9:00 a.m., with no fanfare or official reception.[13] Godfrey Weitzel had received a telegram from City Point that President Lincoln had departed on the *Malvern* and was headed toward Richmond. The probable time of arrival was given. Weitzel made quick preparations to receive the president and ordered his ambulance to be ready in sufficient time to meet Lincoln when he disembarked at the appointed hour. But Admiral Porter made better time in coming up the James River than Godfrey expected. Weitzel was terribly embarrassed that he was in his office at the Virginia capitol and not present to greet President Lincoln, and that no military escort had been provided.

After the boat was made fast, President Lincoln and his young son walked onto the shore and "started off uptown," surrounded by a Marine guard of twelve sailors.[14]

One of the president's bodyguards recalled that "the shore for some distance before we reached Richmond was black with Negroes. They had heard that President Lincoln was on his way—they had some sort of an underground telegraph, I am sure. They were wild with excitement, and yelling like so many wild men, 'Dar comes Massa Linkum, de Sabier ob de lan'—we is so glad to see him!' "[15] Lincoln was quite embarrassed at the attention, especially when one yelled, "Bress de Lawd, dere is de great Messiah! He's bin in my heart fo' long yeahs. Glory, hallelujah!" Some fell on their knees as the president approached. "Don't kneel to me," a humbled Lincoln said. "You must kneel to God only and thank Him for your freedom."[16]

With six sailors in front of the president and six at the rear, plus Admiral Porter and Captain Charles Penrose on one side and Tad and another officer on the other, the party proceeded on foot to General Weitzel's new residence at the Confederate White House, some two miles away uphill.

Even though Weitzel had established a relative degree of order, Lincoln's two-mile stroll through the streets of Richmond put the United States president at great personal risk. His twelve-man guard detail could provide only limited protection from would-be assassins who might lurk in the windows and doorways of the city streets. But for the dozen sailors armed with small carbines, Admiral Porter, a naval captain, and the president's personal bodyguard, William Crook, Mr. Lincoln had no protection. As word spread, flocks of newly freed slaves rushed to the street to catch a glimpse of the president, seeking to touch his hand in their excited state.

Abraham Lincoln was so anxious to see Richmond that he often strode ahead of his bodyguards in his long black coat and tall silk hat, and the marine guard followed instead of preceded the president. Lincoln's presence in the city made his bodyguards nervous, watching each outstretched hand for the point of a blade or the barrel of a handgun.

Lincoln's visit to the fallen Confederate capital was an event unprecedented in history. Two of Lincoln's earliest biographers wrote, "Never in the history of the world did the head of a mighty nation and the conqueror of a great rebellion enter the captured chief city of the insurgents in such humbleness and simplicity."[17] It was as if George W. Bush had strolled into Baghdad the day after Saddam's statue was toppled, with his daughter Jenna at his side.

The president walked "with his usual long, careless stride, and looking about with an interested air and taking in everything."[18] The nightmare was over . . . he wanted to see Richmond! It was a warm spring day, and the town's streets were dusty, with the large crowd kicking up dirt as it grew. "The atmosphere was suffocating," said one bodyguard, and Lincoln removed his hat to fan his perspiring face. "He looked as if he would have given his presidency for a glass of water," said Admiral Porter.[19]

When one of Weitzel's aides saluted the president, Lincoln remarked, "Is it far to President Davis' house?" The aide, Thomas T. Graves, offered to accompany Mr. Lincoln to the Confederate White House. General George Shepley was on horseback and happened to be riding down the street when he saw an excited crowd moving toward him. Not knowing what caused such a gathering, Shepley dispatched his orderly to investigate. The orderly scampered off and soon caught a glimpse of the six-foot-four commander in chief, with his trademark stovepipe hat bobbing above the crowd. He returned to Shepley and blurted out, "General, they say it is the president!" Shepley kicked his spurs into old Charley and rode immediately toward the mob. To his amazement, he saw the tall, thin figure of Abraham Lincoln at the head of the procession, leading Tad by the hand.[20]

General Shepley dismounted and walked up to greet President Lincoln. Mistaking Shepley for Weitzel, Lincoln said, "Hullo, General! Is this you? I was walking 'round to find headquarters" (ICR, 26). After identifying himself, Shepley dispatched his orderly to rush an urgent message to General Weitzel at the capitol building that the president was in town! He then joined the procession and led Mr. Lincoln and his entourage to the former Jefferson Davis home, now occupied by Godfrey Weitzel and staff.

Lincoln at the Confederate White House

The procession of excited slaves followed Abraham Lincoln to the corner of Twelfth and Clay Streets, where it came to a halt in front of the Davis home. General Shepley introduced President Lincoln to the crowd that had gathered there, which gave a rousing cheer. The president acknowledged them "by a few simple, sensible, and kindly words," and then entered the Confederate White House (ICR, 26).

In Godfrey Weitzel's words, "I was therefore very much surprised to hear, just about the time I intended to get into my ambulance, that the president was already at my quarters. I drove over as hastily as possible and found the report correct. It seems that the *Malvern* came up quicker than was expected, and, not finding any one at the landing to meet him, the president started on foot." After his long walk from the river landing to the Davis mansion, Lincoln was pale, sweating, and exhausted. His first words on arrival were, "I wonder if I could get a glass of water."[21]

President Lincoln was shown into the reception room by General Weitzel's aide, Thomas Graves, and provided a glass of water. Graves informed Mr. Lincoln that the Davis housekeeper had said the room was President Davis's personal office. Seating himself in the chair behind the impressive desk, Lincoln remarked, "This must have been President Davis' chair." Then, crossing his long legs, he looked far off with a serious, dreamy expression. After a thoughtful pause, he asked Graves, "Is the housekeeper in the house?" "No, Mr. President, she has left," came the reply. Upon learning that they were alone, Lincoln "jumped up" and said with a boyish manner, "Come, let's look at the house!" With that, the president and his guide "went pretty much over it."[22]

Graves repeated all that the housekeeper had told him and Lincoln "seemed interested in everything," soaking in the details. As the pair came down the staircase, General Weitzel rushed through the front door, "in breathless haste," embarrassed that he was not present at the dock or at the Davis mansion to greet the president on his historic visit.[23]

Godfrey made profuse apologies and then the two men got down to business. At once President Lincoln's face lost its boyish expression, realizing that his official duty must be resumed.[24] The president had a light lunch in Mr. Davis's office while Generals Weitzel and Shepley went over the details of the Union's entry into Richmond and shared information they had gathered from the locals.

The *New York Herald* reported that during the lunch meeting, Generals Shepley and Weitzel relayed their conversations with "several prominent secessionists," and that the president listened patiently. Lincoln agreed to meet with the locals on the condition that "I shall have one friend, with the same liberty to them." Lincoln selected Godfrey Weitzel as his "one friend" to join him as an eyewitness during the meetings with the Southern representative and his designee.[25]

Judge Campbell Pays a Visit

One of the "prominent secessionists" who had sought out General George Shepley for an audience was Judge John A. Campbell, the former justice of the U.S. Supreme Court. The judge knew General Shepley, a trial lawyer, who argued a case in 1855 before the U.S. Supreme Court in which Campbell wrote the majority opinion.[26] As the assistant secretary of war, John Campbell had overseen the Confederate practice of conscription of Southern men into military service. Serving as a quasi-administrative judge, he reviewed draft exemptions, property seizures, and military arrests. Even in that role, Campbell was a moderate, interpreting regulations leniently and helping individuals in trouble.[27]

Judge Campbell had long since made up his mind that the cause of the South was "hopeless."[28] He had written a formal memorandum to Jefferson Davis immediately after the Hampton Roads "peace conference," urging him and the Confederate Congress to take immediate steps to stop the war and restore the Union. Campbell agreed that if he could be used in the restoration of peace and order, he would gladly undertake any task that might be desired of him.

As a result, Campbell remained in Richmond after the rebel government pulled out so that he could assist in the negotiations that would certainly follow with Union officials. The judge wished to help mediate the dispute between North and South.

George Shepley said that Judge Campbell "came to me as an old friend, and solicited the favor of an interview with the president" (ICR, 26). The Union officer took the request directly to President Lincoln, who agreed to a meeting with Campbell and his "one friend." The judge selected Confederate general Joseph R. Anderson to accompany him, as Anderson had also skipped the train to Danville. General Weitzel ushered the group into the parlor of the Davis mansion and closed the doors, posting sentries at the entrance with instructions not to disturb the meeting. At Lincoln's special request, General Weitzel remained present. President Lincoln was not so much concerned for his safety in these meetings but rather wanted an eyewitness who could support Lincoln's version of the conversation.

Godfrey Weitzel recalled that during the closed-door meeting in the Davis parlor, "Mr. Lincoln insisted that he could not treat with any rebels until they had laid down their arms and surrendered; and that if this were first done, he would go as far as he possibly could to prevent the shedding of another drop of blood." Lincoln said that he and the good people of the North "were surfeited with this thing" and wanted it to end as soon as possible.[29]

During the meeting, Judge Campbell appealed "to the kind, generous, and forgiving nature of Lincoln, who was only too ready to concede everything to a fallen foe" (ICR, 27). Campbell pitched a novel idea to the president. He assured Mr. Lincoln that if he would allow the Virginia legislature to meet in Richmond, "it would at once repeal the ordinance of secession and that then General Robert E. Lee and every other Virginian would submit."[30] With their home state once again part of the Union, there would be nothing left to fight for. "This would amount to the virtual destruction of the Army of Northern Virginia and eventually to the surrender of all the other rebel armies," Campbell explained, "and would ensure perfect peace in the shortest possible time."[31] Lincoln was intrigued, and he listened carefully.

Judge Campbell's suggestion was a way for Lee to save face and to end the conflict—at least in Virginia—without further loss of life. Campbell succeeded in convincing Lincoln of the feasibility of the peace plan, primarily on the basis "that it would save the effusion of much blood" (ICR, 27).

Abraham Lincoln wanted to consider the idea overnight. He ended the meeting by proposing another meeting with Campbell the next day. President

Lincoln suggested that Campbell invite the most influential citizens left in Richmond to this second meeting. Judge Campbell and General Anderson rose and shook hands with Lincoln and General Weitzel, agreeing to arrange for the follow-up meeting.

After leaving the Davis house, Judge Campbell sent invitations to six or seven of Richmond's finest men. Surprisingly, only one responded, a prominent local lawyer named Gustavus A. Myers, one of Campbell's closest friends in Richmond. He must have been intrigued at what the Northern president would have to say about restoration of the Union and reconstruction of the South. Myers agreed to be Campbell's "second" at the follow-up meeting with Lincoln and Weitzel.[32]

The Carriage Ride around Richmond

After the Confederate judge and general had left, President Lincoln and General Weitzel exited the mansion and boarded a horse-drawn carriage for a casual ride through the city. Weitzel's aide, Thomas Graves, also accompanied them, as did a guard of cavalry. The president's new confidant, Godfrey Weitzel, sat across from Mr. Lincoln as the three men rode through the crowded streets of Richmond. They took in various points of interest, including the burned district and then the prisons, stopping only at the Virginia statehouse to get a firsthand look at Thomas Jefferson's architectural masterpiece, and the place the Confederate legislature had met.

One eyewitness among the excited crowd reported, "Here, as he ascended the steps, while the Star Spangled Banner was waving gaily above the roof, was presented a scene correspondents might well portray in colors and in language befitting the glorious nature of the event."[33]

General Weitzel described the reception of the president by the local black population along the streets as "enthusiastic in the extreme." Hundreds of women tossed their hands high in the air, and then bent down to the ground, weeping for joy. The display was like nothing Lincoln had ever seen. Some of these freed slaves shouted songs of deliverance. One in particular was an old plantation refrain that prophesied the coming of a deliverer from bondage. The mob shouted, "God bless you, Father Abraham!" through their tears of joy (ICR, 28).

As the carriage bumped along, smoke wafted over the blackened business district with a prevalent smell of burnt wood. The president wanted to see the Libby Prison and the other infamous prison, Castle Thunder. The two prisons had escaped the fire and were promptly filled with hundreds of rebel prisoners of war who had been captured. Union soldiers stood guard outside the brick walls of the massive buildings.

"Let 'Em Up Easy"

It was during this carriage ride that the young general discussed with Lincoln how to handle the local residents, former officials, and rebel officers and troops who had been captured. As Godfrey Weitzel recalled that poignant meeting, "I had considerable conversation with him in regard to the treatment of the conquered people." President Lincoln replied in his country manner that he did not wish to give any orders on that subject, but, added, 'If I were in your place I'd let 'em up easy, let 'em up easy."[34]

After dropping General Weitzel back at the Davis mansion, General Shepley and Admiral Porter boarded the carriage and took President Lincoln back to the riverbanks where Porter's ship, the *Malvern*, was docked. An immense crowd of Richmond's black population poured onto the streets and sidewalks, following the carriage and calling upon the president "with the wildest exclamations of gratitude and delight" (ICR, 28).

As Shepley characterized Lincoln's impact on the freed slaves, "He was the Moses, the Messiah, to the slaves of the South." The president studied intently all the various shades of brown and black skin among the well-wishers. George Shepley recalled that Mr. Lincoln looked into the faces of the people, "attentively, with a face expressive only of a sort of pathetic wonder" (ICR, 28).

At one point during the ride, Lincoln turned close to Shepley and remarked "on the great proportion of those whose color indicated a mixed lineage from the white master and the black slave." Lincoln said the varying skin tones reminded him of some little story of his life in Kentucky, "which he would smilingly tell" (ICR).

On the way back to the *Malvern*, the presidential carriage made an unlikely stop at the Richmond home of Confederate general George Pickett. As an Illinois lawyer, Lincoln had helped with young George Pickett's application to West Point in 1841 due to Lincoln's friendship with Pickett's uncle, a Richmond lawyer. Introducing himself to Mrs. Pickett as "George's old friend," the president kissed their infant son and reportedly said: "Tell your father, rascal, that I forgive him for the sake of your mother's smile, and your bright eyes."[35]

After leaving the Pickett home, General Shepley accompanied Lincoln and Admiral Porter to the *Malvern*, bade them farewell, and watched as the pair boarded the ship. With the president on board, at 4:35 p.m. that afternoon, the *Malvern* anchored in the James River, safely off of Rocketts Landing, and fired a thirty-five-gun salute in President Lincoln's honor and to mark the capture of Richmond.[36]

Day Two of Lincoln's Visit

At 7:00 a.m. on Wednesday, April 5, Judge John Campbell and his friend Gustavus A. Myers were escorted by General Godfrey Weitzel down to the

James River where the *Malvern* had once again docked. Campbell recalled that President Lincoln "was prepared for the visit and spoke with freedom and apparent decision."[37]

According to Myers's account of the meeting, President Lincoln "said that he was thinking over a plan by which the Virginia Legislature might be brought to hold their meeting in . . . Richmond." The purpose of the meeting was to "see whether they desired to take any action on behalf [of Virginia] in view of the existing state of affairs," recalled Myers.[38]

As to the terms of surrender, which Judge Campbell called "terms of settlement," as if this were the resolution of a court dispute, Campbell had received Lincoln's written and unconditional terms. Lincoln stated "as indispensable conditions of a settlement" three terms: (1) the restoration of the authority of the United States over the whole of the state; (2) the cessation of hostilities by the disbanding of the Army; and (3) that there should be no receding on the part of "the Executive" from his position on the slavery question. By "the Executive," Lincoln meant himself, who would not recede from his stated position on the subject of slavery, "so far as it had been declared in messages, proclamations and other official acts."[39] After permitting Campbell and Myers to read his memorandum on peace terms, Lincoln spoke of how sad he was to see the South so utterly destroyed.[40]

The Southern jurist held the legal opinion that "if the proclamation of the President be valid as law [on the issue of emancipation], it has already operated and vested rights." Campbell felt that by re-joining the Union, Virginia would have to accept presidential rulings as the law of the nation. In a subsequent letter to Weitzel, Judge Campbell made his interpretation of the law clear, stating, "The acceptance of the Union involves acceptance of his proclamation, if it be valid in law."[41]

However, according to Campbell, the president had indicated that although his position would not change, "this would not debar action by other authorities of the government." The implication was that Congress could determine the issue of slavery, even overruling Lincoln's January 1863 Emancipation Proclamation.

At the conclusion of their meeting, Mr. Lincoln directed General Weitzel to grant passes to the members of the current legislature of Virginia with permission to meet in Richmond. Campbell misinterpreted Lincoln's intent, reading into it both "legislative recognition" of the rebel Virginia legislature as well as a peace settlement, an intention not contemplated by the president.

Lincoln expressed no opinion in his meetings with Judge Campbell, nor afterward, as to the possible penalties that would be imposed upon military or government officials who had supported the Confederate cause. To the contrary, Lincoln told Campbell, "There were scarcely any one who might not get a discharge for the asking." Campbell had pressed the president during their meeting in Richmond for a suspension of the hostilities, or as the judge characterized it, "an armistice." Lincoln told Judge Campbell only that he would "consider the subject."[42]

At the conclusion of the meeting, Campbell and Myers left the *Malvern* and returned to the city with General Weitzel and his military escort, while Admiral Porter's sailors prepared the *Malvern* for the trip south to City Point. As Godfrey recalled it, "After the second interview, Mr. Lincoln told me that he would think over the whole matter carefully and would probably send me some instructions from City Point on the next day."[43]

Shepley's Warning

Upon returning to the city, Godfrey Weitzel met with his trusted friend and adviser George Shepley in the Confederate White House. Godfrey promptly informed Shepley of the meeting on the *Malvern* and of Lincoln's order regarding the Virginia legislature. "General," a startled Shepley asked, "may I see a copy of the President's order?" Weitzel replied, "I have no written order," to which Shepley responded, "You are not safe without one" (ICR, 27).

"Why do you say so?" asked Weitzel. Shepley, a former trial lawyer, was savvy in issues of politics, where Weitzel had no training or experience. "Because," Shepley explained, "this order will be revoked as soon as the president reaches Washington and confers with his cabinet. More, the cabinet will deny that any such order ever was issued" (ICR, 27).

Godfrey Weitzel was puzzled. The meetings with Campbell and Lincoln had gone so well and made so much sense as a way to end the conflict by political means without more bloodshed in the field. "Why so?" asked Weitzel. "Because this is madness," Shepley blurted. "By this shrewd move of Judge Campbell the Rebel legislature, assembled under the new constitution recognizing the Confederacy, will covertly gain recognition as a legal and valid legislature, and creep into the Union with all its rebel legislation in force, thus preserving all the peculiar rebel institutions, including slavery" (ICR, 27). Godfrey had not considered this possibility.

Shepley could foresee how this would all play out. He continued, "They will get, as the price of defeat, all they hoped to achieve as the fruits of victory. The thing is monstrous!" Now quite excited, George Sheply concluded, "The cabinet will swear that you have misunderstood the verbal order, or willfully misinterpreted it." Shepley was not only a smart lawyer, but loyal to his much younger friend, the twenty-nine-year-old Weitzel. His voice lowered and he leaned in closer to Weitzel to get his full attention. "I wish, for your sake, you had the order in writing" (ICR, 27).

Weitzel was also loyal, but to his president and his country, and he would follow orders despite any political outfall. "I am a soldier," Godfrey responded, "and do as I am ordered." Shepley replied, "Right, General. Issue to me the order for the safe conducts [of the legislature], and I will obey it" (ICR, 27). At that,

General Weitzel sat down at Jefferson Davis's old wooden desk and wrote out the form of safe conduct, or pass (ICR, 27):

> By command of the president of the United States, safe conduct through the lines of the army is hereby granted to, a member of the so-called legislature of Virginia, from his place of abode in Virginia to Richmond, and while going to, remaining in, and returning from Richmond, and during the meeting of the so-called legislature. If this permission be used for the furtherance or utterance of treason against the United States in any form, this safe conduct will be void and its protection withdrawn.
>   By command of GODFREY WEITZEL,
>   Major-General.

Shepley took Weitzel's handwritten order to the printer and had copies made. He took the printed copies to Weitzel, letting him know that the passes were ready for the members of the legislature, and that "notice has been publicly given that they can have them." Then, as a political warning once again to his friend, Shepley said, "I have obeyed orders and so have you." Pausing for a moment, Shepley continued, "I am afraid, General, as most of the gentlemen for whom these papers are intended are scattered over Virginia, and between us and them are the lines of two contending armies, not many of the passes will be delivered before this order is revoked from Washington, and before General Grant has solved the question for them. At the rate he is now progressing, he will soon withdraw the Virginia troops from the field without the help of a Rebel legislature" (ICR, 27). Of course, Shepley was right on both points.

General Weitzel returned to Rockett's Landing that morning after 10 a.m. to bid the president farewell.[44] The *Malvern* departed ninety minutes later with a marine guard and the president and his son on board.[45] The ship steamed down the James River toward Drewry's Bluff, then headed back to General Grant's headquarters at City Point where Mrs. Lincoln and Mrs. Weitzel were soon to arrive.

As Porter's flagship steamed east, President Lincoln began to think of the potential problems he had created for Godfrey Weitzel in issuing such a controversial order. From his cabin aboard the *Malvern*, the president wrote out a letter to General Weitzel with the exact same terms as Lincoln had given Weitzel verbally.

When Godfrey Weitzel returned to the Davis mansion later that night, the Richmond Armory Band serenaded him with strains of "The Star-Spangled Banner." It was his second night in the Davis house in the heart of the rebel capital. Having spent two days with President Lincoln and seeing firsthand the end days of the war, he drifted off to sleep in peace. The call for the Virginia legislature to meet would be published in the morning. All hell was about to break loose.

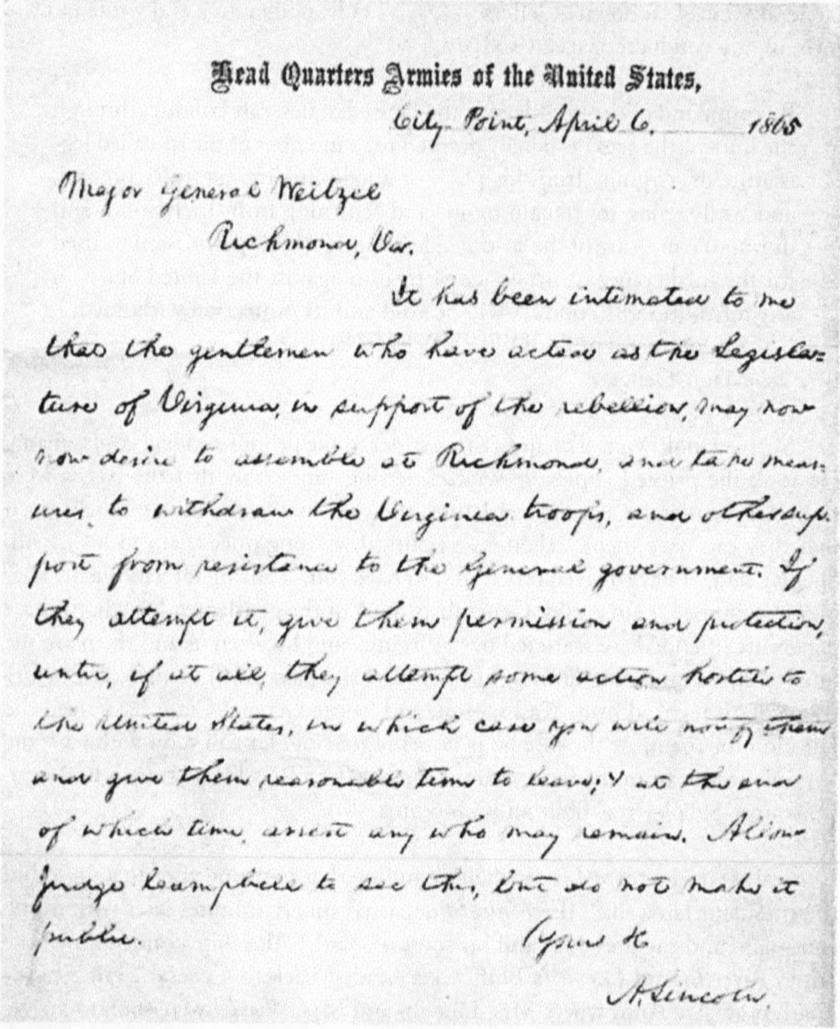

Head Quarters Armies of the United States,

City Point, April 6. _____ 1865

Major General Weitzel
    Richmond, Var.

    It has been intimated to me that the gentlemen who have acted as the Legislature of Virginia, in support of the rebellion, may now now desire to assemble at Richmond, and take measures to withdraw the Virginia troops, and other support from resistance to the General government. If they attempt it, give them permission and protection, until, if at all, they attempt some action hostile to the United States, in which case you will notify them and give them reasonable time to leave; & at the end of which time, arrest any who may remain. Allow Judge Campbell to see this, but do not make it public.

        Yours &c

        A. Lincoln.

FIGURE 22.1. President Lincoln's letter to Major General Godfrey Weitzel, written on board the *Malvern* on the way home from Richmond, April 6, 1865. (Library of Congress, Abraham Lincoln Papers, Ser. 3, General Correspondence, 1837–1897.)

CHAPTER 23

Political Troubles

The joy of the April 3 triumphal entry into Richmond was soon overshadowed for Godfrey Weitzel, who found himself in the middle of a political controversy just days later. West Point had not prepared him for life as a politician, and the military mayor of Richmond found that his fame was short-lived.

Feeding the Refugees

General Weitzel made sure that the poor people of Richmond had been fed from the first day of the Union occupation. He used captured Confederate rations as well as supplies that were donated by the agents of the Sanitary and Christian Commissions. General Shepley issued orders on April 5 to assist the "destitute families" and other refugees who stayed behind, permitting "loyal persons" to bring supplies into Richmond for aid of the refugees and the Army. Food was handed out at an office set up at Tenth and Capitol Streets.

Although he was following the president's orders to treat the residents with dignity and humanity, Godfrey Weitzel's compassion did not meet with approval from Secretary of War Edwin M. Stanton, who preferred a more punitive approach to handling the defeated Southerners.

The Secretary of War Weighs In

Edwin McMasters Stanton was one of the most unusual-looking men in Lincoln's cabinet. He swooped his hair from the left to the right in an effort to conceal a balding head. Thin wire-rimmed glasses were perched snuggly on his long nose. Like Lincoln, Stanton shaved only his upper lip and let his gray-streaked beard dribble down nearly twelve inches to the middle of his shirt. As Secretary of War, Stanton's office was adjacent to the White House in the stately War Department Building at Seventeenth and Pennsylvania. The building had several large white columns supporting the entry portico. After the war, the building was demolished in 1879 to make way for what is now called the "Old Executive Office Building," but its columns were salvaged and stored. The entry columns were later used to construct three impressive entry gates at Arlington Cemetery on the former property of Robert E. Lee—one gate would be dedicated to Godfrey Weitzel.

Stanton sent an informant to Richmond, his assistant secretary of war, Charles Dana. On his arrival, Dana told General Weitzel that he had no intention or desire to provide any instructions on how to deal with the local population, claiming that he was there purely as an observer, "only to look on and report."[1] Dana was not only Stanton's eyes and ears, but he also gave daily reports to the *New York Tribune* about affairs in Richmond.

In compliance with Stanton's instructions, Godfrey kept statistics on the aid he distributed, reporting daily on the two to three thousand rations distributed in the first four days after the occupation. These figures did not include the amount distributed in local hospitals.

Lincoln's Letter Arrives

On April 6, Godfrey received a handwritten letter from the president marked "Confidential." It was delivered by no ordinary courier, but by a United States senator, Morton S. Wilkinson of Minnesota, one of the many Northern officials who streamed into Richmond in the days after its fall. Lincoln's letter, written onboard the *Malvern*, was sent from Grant's headquarters at City Point before the president left for Washington. It read as follows:

> April 6, 1865
> Major General Weitzel
> Richmond, Va.
>
> It has been intimated to me that the gentlemen who have acted as the Legislature of Virginia in support of the rebellion may now desire to assemble at Richmond and take measures to withdraw the Virginia troops and other support from resistance to the General Government. If they attempt it, give them permission and protection, until, if at all, they attempt some action hostile to the United States , in which case you will notify them and give them reasonable time to leave; and at the end of which time, arrest any who remain. Allow judge Campbell to see this, but do not make it public.
>
> Yours &c. ,
> A. Lincoln[2]

Just as Lincoln directed, the president's handwritten letter was shown to Judge John Campbell that same day. At their meeting, Weitzel told Campbell that he would issue whatever orders were necessary, and that he would also furnish all necessary transportation for the legislators to meet in Richmond. In addition to the state legislators, Weitzel assured Campbell that the governor, the lieutenant governor, and the "public men of the State" would also be permitted to meet.[3]

Abraham Lincoln did not appreciate the Northern reaction to his agreement with Judge Campbell. Writing to General Grant on April 6, the president stated that he had written to Weitzel about convening "the rebel legislature of Virginia," but added, "I do not think it very probable that anything will come of this."[4]

Godfrey Weitzel's best friend and chief of staff, George Shepley, foresaw the backlash that might occur and the political damage to young Weitzel if the situation was not handled properly. Knowing the likely reaction in Washington, Shepley asked, "General, are you doing this on your own responsibility?" Others might read Weitzel's invitation as premature, since Virginia was still a Confederate state and Lee's Army of Northern Virginia was fighting against Grant not far away.

Weitzel responded confidently that he was not acting on his own accord, but had orders from the president himself, confirmed in the letter he had just received. Shepley asked to see the president's letter. After reading it carefully, Shepley looked up at Godfrey and said, "General, this is a political mistake. Don't you lose that letter, for if you do, your Major General's commission may not be worth a straw!"

General George Strong later said that Lincoln's written confirmation of his direction to Weitzel "shows the kindness and sense of justice. . . . The written order was sent purely for Weitzel's protection, that the responsibility for the act might rest on the president's own shoulders, and no one else might suffer."[5] Godfrey Weitzel wrote many years later, on reflection, that "the history of the letter from Mr. Lincoln directing me to permit the assembling of the Virginia Legislature, and its subsequent revocation, is so intimately bound up with the history of my brief occupation of the city."[6] Godfrey held tight to Lincoln's letter on Shepley's advice.

Not only did President Lincoln confirm in writing the orders he gave to Godfrey Weitzel, but that same day Lincoln wrote a second letter, this one to General Grant, confirming that he had put into Judge Campbell's hands "an informal paper"—a third paper—that included Lincoln's propositions for General Lee's surrender. According to Lincoln, his note to Campbell added that confiscated property would be returned to the people of any state, "which will now promptly and in good faith withdraw its troops and other support from resistance to the government."[7]

Lincoln wrote that when they met, Judge Campbell felt it was possible that the Virginia legislature would vote to withdraw its troops. Lincoln confirmed to Grant, "I addressed a private letter to General Weitzel with permission for Judge Campbell to see it, telling him that if they attempt this, to permit and protect them, unless they attempt something hostile to the United States."[8]

Judge Campbell confirmed that, in fact, Lincoln's letter had been received by him on Thursday, April 6, and "it authorized General Weitzel to grant a safe conduct to the Legislature of Virginia to meet at Richmond, to deliberate and to return to their homes at the end of their session."[9]

However, Campbell's idea for the legislative session was different from Lincoln's plan. In Lincoln's mind, the only objective was that Virginia re-join the Union and lay down her arms. However, Campbell felt that the object of the invitation was for the government of Virginia "to determine whether they will administer the laws in connection with the authorities of the United States," a purpose that did not clearly require re-joining the Union or ceasing hostilities. Campbell wrote to a friend, "I understand from Mr. Lincoln, if this condition be fulfilled that no attempt would be made to establish or sustain any other authority."[10]

General Weitzel should have been adequately protected, with a total of *three* letters written by the United States president himself to validate the orders: one to Grant, one to Campbell, and one to Weitzel. But the political winds were about to change, and the voice of Abraham Lincoln would soon be silenced by an assassin's bullet. Godfrey Weitzel's world was about to be turned upside down.

Reaction in Washington

Immediately some members of the Virginia legislature wrote out a call for a meeting in Richmond and had it published in their own local papers. This call, however, went very much further than Mr. Lincoln had contemplated. He had not authorized a meeting of a recognized legislative body, but only the group that "called itself the Legislature of Virginia." Even Weitzel's printed order referred to "the *so-called* legislature of Virginia." When the morning's Richmond *Whig* newspaper carried a report, under the headline "Address to the People of Virginia," with Weitzel's invitation to the former rebel legislators, the rabid Republicans in Washington, D.C., went ballistic. "We were all thunderstruck," radical Indiana Republican congressman George W. Julian wrote upon reading about Weitzel's order.[11]

Edwin Stanton saw the published invitation in the Southern papers the next day and personally took the liberty of countermanding the order. As General Grant put it accurately, "This was characteristic of Mr. Stanton. He was a man who never questioned his own authority, and who always did in war time what he wanted to do."[12]

Ohio senator Benjamin Wade, who had presided over the Fort Fisher inquiry, flew into a rage over the invitation. "I never before saw such force and fitness in Ben Wade's swearing," said Congressman George Julian.[13] The enraged Senator Wade promptly canceled a trip to Charleston and decided to return at once to Washington to meet with his fellow radicals and put an end to this nonsense. But no action was needed by Wade or the others, as Lincoln himself would cancel the invitation.

After the Lincolns returned to Washington on April 9, the president met with Secretary Stanton and other members of his cabinet. Under pressure from his advisers, Lincoln agreed to revoke his instructions, although Godfrey Weitzel did not receive any such notice from the president until three days later, on April 12 .

The Political Fallout Begins

Just as General Shepley had feared, once back in Washington, the president's loyal advisers began to spin the story that Lincoln had never issued such an order. By denying the order, they tried to cover what they felt was Lincoln's blunder, protecting their president. Blame was thrown entirely on young Godfrey Weitzel, an inexperienced officer whose loyalty to the Union flag was even called into question. Northern newspapers pounced on the story, reporting that the action had originated solely with twenty-nine-year-old Weitzel. Some writers even went so far as to attribute the order to Weitzel's alleged sympathy for the rebels.[14]

General George Strong wrote that "a high government official" stated confidently that Lincoln had "bitterly condemned the acts of General Weitzel and his officers in Richmond" in attempting to assemble the rebel legislature of Virginia.[15] The official, most likely Secretary Edwin Stanton, did not know that both Generals Grant and Weitzel, as well as Judge Campbell, had written proof of Lincoln's direction.

About sixty-four miles southwest of Richmond, General Phil Sheridan's Union forces attacked the rear of Robert E. Lee's column at Sayler's Creek, inflicting more than seven thousand casualties and taking several thousand prisoners. Among the captives were at least six Confederate generals, plus two hundred wagons and much-needed supplies. The Army of Northern Virginia was being slowly decimated as it headed toward Appomattox.

That evening, General Grant forwarded to Lincoln a telegram from Sheridan reporting the day's success. Sheridan wrote, "If the thing is pressed I think that Lee will Surrender."[16] Lincoln's response was firm: "Let the thing be pressed."[17]

A Series of Controversies

Back in Richmond, on April 7, Judge Campbell urged General Weitzel that "the legislature of Virginia be immediately convened" and that a similar offer be made to the legislature of South Carolina, "and that it be invited to send commissioners to adjust the questions that are supposed to require adjustment." Campbell also wrote to General Joseph R. Anderson, who had participated in the first meeting with Lincoln at the Davis mansion. Campbell stated that he'd had two meetings with President Lincoln since the evacuation and that General Weitzel had agreed with President Lincoln that there would be no requirement of an oath of allegiance from the citizens of Richmond! Campbell understood that although Lincoln did not promise universal amnesty, that was the implication of the president if peace was to be declared.[18]

Judge Campbell had come to trust Godfrey Weitzel after their meetings and wrote, "I believe that full confidence may be placed in General Weitzel's fulfillment of his promises to afford facilities to the Legislature, and that its members may return after they have concluded their business, without interruption."[19]

Campbell wrote a handbill titled "To the People of Virginia," which was published in the *Richmond Whig* to notify all Virginia legislators that a general meeting had been scheduled for April 25 to discuss "the restoration of peace to the state of Virginia, and the adjustment of questions involving life, liberty and property that have arisen in the state as a consequence of the war."[20] It was endorsed by a list of thirty-five men including Mayor Joseph Mayo, Judge Campbell, and certain members of the Virginia Legislature.[21] By Friday, April 7, five members of the Virginia legislature had arrived in Richmond and met to consider the written propositions that the president had given to Judge Campbell.[22]

That night, Charles Dana met with Godfrey Weitzel about another pressing topic—Palm Sunday church services in Richmond. Dana had asked General Weitzel what he was going to do about opening the churches for services. According to Dana, Weitzel responded "that all were to be allowed to be opened on condition that no disloyalty should be uttered and that the Episcopal ministers would be required to read the prayer for the President." Dana told him "this was all right."[23] What appeared to be a simple topic was about to blossom into a complex nightmare for Godfrey. Mixing politics and religion has a history of division, worldwide. The division was about to take root in Richmond, with Godfrey Weitzel at the epicenter.

Saturday, April 8, 1865

On Saturday morning, Charles Dana attended another meeting with Generals Weitzel and Shepley, plus a committee of prominent citizens and the few members of the state legislature who had returned. Weitzel and Shepley made it clear to the Southerners that no propositions could be entertained that involved a recognition of the Confederate authorities. Dana said that the committee was also informed, "that if they desired to prepare an address to the people, advising them to abandon hostility to the Government at once, and begin to obey the laws of the United States, they should have every facility for its circulation through the State, provided, of course, that it met the approval of the military authorities."[24]

The two Union generals agreed to give safe passage to the committee out-side the lines of Richmond for the sole purpose of visiting prominent citizens in different parts of the state and inducing them to take part in a convention. How-ever, they made it clear that the meeting in Richmond would be only to consider the restoration of the authority of the United States government.[25] Weitzel and Shepley advised that if the Virginians could not find transportation for the jour-ney, horses would be loaned to them.

Opening the Churches for Palm Sunday

As the Sabbath approached, the question about opening the churches on Sunday remained open. April 9 was Palm Sunday, and the good Christians of Richmond wanted to be able to attend their regular places of worship. Since 1863, Episcopal ministers in all the Southern states had officially included a prayer for "the Pres-ident of the Confederate States, and all others in authority."[26] Would General Weitzel order the ministers to change the prayer, and to substitute "the President of the United States"? Dana felt that he should. When Judge Campbell heard of this, he used all his influence with Weitzel and Shepley to get them to agree that no prayer—loyal to either the North or the South—be required.

General Shepley sought out Charles Dana to ask that the order be relaxed so that the clergy should be required only "not to pray for Davis." Dana declined, however, to give any orders on the subject, since he had received none from Washington. "General Weitzel must act in the matter entirely on his own judg-ment," Dana replied.[27]

Meeting with Richmond's Clergy

The first Sunday following the fall of Richmond was now just a day away, and the pastors of Richmond were planning their sermons. Could the residents be ordered to pray for the enemy, instead of their own brothers, fathers, and uncles in arms? On Saturday afternoon, April 8, Dr. Charles Menningerode of St. Paul's Episcopal Church and several other ministers of Richmond called upon Gen-eral Weitzel. Godfrey told the anxious ministers, of course, to hold their regular Sunday services. As to what prayers they should say, General Weitzel told the group that no expression would be allowed in any part of any church service, whether in the form of prayer, preaching, or singing, "which in any way implied a recognition of any other authority than that of the United States, or gave any countenance to the rebellion."[28]

He warned the clergymen that any prayers for the rebel government, its officials, or for the success of the rebellion would be considered as treason and punished as such. In particular, General Weitzel said that the normal prayer used in the Richmond Episcopal churches for the president "of the Confederate States, and all others in authority" must be omitted. As to the topic of Sunday's sermons, Godfrey gave no orders as to what should be preached or prayed for, but only as to what was prohibited. Charles Dana attended the meeting with the preachers and he quickly reported back to Stanton that Weitzel had not ordered a prayer for Lincoln, nor for the United States. This furthered Stanton's belief that Weitzel was the wrong man for Richmond.

Edwin Stanton wanted an order that the people of Richmond pray for the president "of the United States," Abraham Lincoln. However, Lincoln's direction to "let 'em up easy" was interpreted by Godfrey as not to be a stickler in the little things. He would allow the pastors of Richmond to conduct services as they wished, only on the condition that they said a prayer for peace for the nation.

Stanton's Rebuke

Charles Dana reported to Stanton that on Saturday evening General Shepley asked that the order regarding church prayer "might be relaxed, so that the clergy would only be required not to pray for Jeff Davis." Shepley told Dana that this was what had been decided by General Weitzel. Dana also reported to Stanton that Judge Campbell had urged that a loyal prayer to the Union president should not be required, and that Weitzel had consented. Dana told Stanton, "It shakes a good deal my confidence in Weitzel." In response to Dana's report, Stanton sent a telegraph to General Weitzel with a condemnation for his actions: "If such has been your action it is strongly condemned by this Department . . . you are directed immediately to report by telegraph your action in relation to religious services in Richmond . . . and also to state what took place between you and Mr. Campbell on the subject."[29]

General Weitzel replied that his orders in relation to religious services in Richmond were only verbal, and were applicable alike to all religious denominations. "They were, in substance, that no expression would be allowed in any part of the church service . . . which in any way implied a recognition of any other authority than that of the United States." Stanton had to decide who was telling the truth, his trusted spy and assistant secretary of war, Charles Dana, or the young general Godfrey Weitzel.

Major General Jacob Dolson Cox, former commander of the Twenty-Third Army Corps, wrote that "Mr. Stanton's habit of impetuous action without reflection, upon first impressions and imperfect knowledge, was notorious, as was his constitutional inability to admit that he had been in the wrong." Once aroused, Stanton was "a fierce combatant," Cox wrote.[30] Edwin Stanton would get his way, and soon. General Weitzel would be removed from Richmond as his way of revenge.

Palm Sunday, April 9, 1865

Charles Dana was downstairs at the Spotswood Hotel on Sunday morning when he heard his name called. He turned to see Andrew Johnson, the vice president of the United States, who had traveled to Richmond. Johnson whisked Dana aside and gave him a twenty-minute lecture that whatever the terms of surrender were, there had to be some punishment for the Confederates. "He insisted that their sins had been enormous, and that if they were let back into the Union without any punishment, the effect would be very bad," Dana recalled. "They might be very dangerous in the future," the vice president said.[31]

Just a few blocks away, the churches opened their doors to the heartbroken refugees of Richmond. A few Union officers attended services. One such officer attended the Episcopal church service and reported to General Weitzel that prayers were offered only "for those in authority," with no references to Davis. Godfrey learned that similar prayers were offered in other Episcopal churches in Richmond and that "all present understood them to refer to *our* government."[32] This would not satisfy Edwin Stanton, however.

Surrender at Appomattox

Some ninety-two miles from Richmond, General Robert E. Lee and his diminishing army of just over 28,000 weary men confronted General Grant's force of 120,000 bluecoats. Faced with the inevitable, Lee made the most difficult decision of his life and sent word to Grant that he would meet him in a farmhouse at the village of Appomattox Courthouse to surrender his army, thereby ending the conflict. "Then there is nothing left for me to do but go and see General Grant," Lee told his staff that day. "And I would rather die a thousand deaths."[33]

The surrender occurred on Palm Sunday, April 9, 1865, just six days after General Weitzel had occupied the rebel capital. As the terms of surrender were written out at Appomattox and church bells rang in Richmond, a steamer made its way up the James River from City Point. On board was a special guest—Louise Weitzel—who had made her way to Richmond to see her heroic husband. It was a welcome visit by a friendly face amid all the controversy and stress of the past week.

Louise moved into the presidential mansion where General and Mrs. Weitzel spent the night in the bed formerly occupied by President Jefferson Davis and his wife, Varina.[34] Louise was three months pregnant at the time and showing a slightly rounded belly. Godfrey welcomed her kind face and warm embrace. They were awakened about 5:40 a.m. on Monday morning by gunfire. It was not the enemy, but the Union naval fleet anchored off Richmond, firing a salute to General Grant and to the surrender of Lee's army. A thirty-five-gun salute blasted from each vessel in the early dawn, rattling windows in the city.[35] Soon, the news of Lee's surrender spread throughout Richmond. "It produced a deep impression," Charles Dana recalled.[36]

Outfall Over Prayer and the Virginia Legislature

On Monday afternoon, Dana reported to Edwin Stanton that General Weitzel had not required the Episcopal ministers to offer a prayer for the "President of the United States." The War Department, already unhappy with Weitzel's "liberal" treatment of the people of Richmond, found his conduct totally unacceptable. The irate secretary of war denounced Godfrey Weitzel for his disobedience and fired off a blistering reprimand. To Stanton, the president's leniency toward the residents of Richmond had been returned with an "indefensible" insult.[37]

Godfrey replied to Secretary Stanton that in all he had done during the past week, he had followed the advice of the president. "I have intended to show him the greatest respect, instead of any disrespect," he wrote. Weitzel's chief of staff, General Shepley, had met personally with Assistant Secretary Dana and, according to Weitzel, he "distinctly understood him to authorize and sanction my course upon the subject." Stanton replied, "Your explanation in regard to the omission of prayers for the President in the city of Richmond is not satisfactory." Stanton would not tolerate anything less than a specific prayer for President Lincoln in all Richmond churches the following Sunday. "Officers commanding in Richmond are expected to require from all religious denominations in that city to regard those rituals in no less respect for the President of the United States than they practiced towards the rebel chief, Jefferson Davis, before he was driven from the Capitol," Stanton ordered.[38]

Godfrey was likely coached in his careful response by his friend, adviser and lawyer George Shepley. General Weitzel wrote back claiming that he had not fully explained his orders on the issue of prayer, due to the confidential nature of the meetings with the president and Judge Campbell. His direction to the Richmond ministers was the same, that regardless of religious denomination, they could not pray or preach in support of the Confederacy or its success. Godfrey requested permission to reveal all such communications so that Stanton could judge his conduct correctly in regard to churches and prayers. He wrote, "Not having had authority to divulge these things, I am convinced my action had been judged incorrectly."[39]

The very idea of ordering ministers, priests, and rabbis to say any specific prayer seemed absurd to Godfrey Weitzel. After some checking, Godfrey learned that in neither Charleston, New Orleans, Norfolk, or Savannah, nor in any other captured city, were the Episcopal churches required at first to adopt the form of prayer for the president of the United States. The young general asked Stanton, "Do you desire that I should order this form of prayer to be used in the Episcopal, Roman Catholic, Hebrew, and other churches where they have a prescribed liturgy and form of prayer?" Stanton replied in the affirmative, repeating his reprimand of the (in his mind) impetuous young officer.[40]

Edwin Stanton was quickly concluding that Godfrey Weitzel was the wrong man to be in charge of Richmond, too young and inexperienced in political matters.

The President Comes to Godfrey's Aid

President Abraham Lincoln had grown fond of young Godfrey Weitzel during their time together in Richmond. Apparently the exchange of telegraphs regarding church prayer crossed the president's desk, and on Wednesday, April 12, Mr. Lincoln weighed in. He wrote to Godfrey that it appeared from all he'd heard and read that Weitzel was handling things just fine. "I have seen your dispatch to [Stanton] about the matter of prayers," Lincoln wrote. "I do not remember hearing prayer spoken of while I was in Richmond, but I have no doubt that you have acted in what appeared to you to be the spirit and temper manifested by me while there."[41]

Abraham Lincoln was more interested in the status of the call to meet of the Virginia legislature. He asked Weitzel, "Is there any sign of the rebel legislature coming together on the understanding of my letter to you? If there is any such sign inform me what it is. If there is no such sign you may withdraw the offer." Even before receiving this message, Godfrey had determined that the surrender at Appomattox made the meeting of the Virginia legislature moot. He wrote the next day to Secretary Stanton that the surrender of Lee's army "removed the necessity for further conference." He asked the secretary of war, "Shall I stop it?" Lincoln's message, two days later gave him that answer: "Withdraw the offer."[42]

The political winds were not blowing in Godfrey Weitzel's favor. While it is often said that a man cannot serve two masters, Godfrey felt that he was trying to "satisfy four different commanding officers—two soldiers and two civilians." The directions from his military superiors, Ord and Grant, coupled with the mixed orders from Lincoln and Stanton, had placed the young general in a no-win position. He had no similar difficulties while serving as acting mayor of New Orleans, where there was no hourly telegraphic communication with Washington and Edwin Stanton, nor any spies like Charles Dana reporting his every move. But Richmond was, in his words, "too near Washington and in telegraphic communication with it."[43] He was anxious to get back to the field and, the next day, he got his wish.

At 3:00 p.m. on April 12, Godfrey replied to President Lincoln with words reflecting the shared views of the two men. "You spoke of not pressing little points," Godfrey wrote, "You said you would not order me, but if you were in my place you would not press them. The passports have gone out for the legislature, and it is common talk that they will come together."[44] The president came to Godfrey's rescue at 6:00 p.m. that same day, officially rescinding permission for the Virginia legislature to meet. President Lincoln wrote to Godfrey:

> I have just seen Judge Campbell's letter to you of the 7th. He assumes, it appears to me, that I have called the insurgent Legislature of Virginia together, as the rightful Legislature of the State to settle all differences with the United States. I have done no such thing. I spoke of them not as a Legislature of Virginia in support of the rebellion, I did this on purpose to exclude the assumption that I was recognizing them as a rightful body. I dealt with them as men having power *de facto* to do a specific thing, to wit: "To withdraw the Virginia troops and other support from resistance to the general government," for which, in the paper handed to Judge Campbell, I promised a special equivalent, to wit "A remission to the people of the State, except in certain cases, of the confiscation of their property." I meant this, and no more. Inasmuch, however, as Judge Campbell misconstrues this, and is still pressing for an armistice contrary to the explicit statement of the paper I gave him, and particularly as General Grant has since captured the Virginia troops, so that giving a consideration for their withdrawal is no longer applicable, let my letter to you and the paper to Judge Campbell both be withdrawn or countermanded, and he be notified of it. Do not now allow them to assemble, but if any have come allow them safe return to their homes.
>
> A. LINCOLN[45]

This was Lincoln's last message to Weitzel. The president, whom Godfrey had guarded at his inauguration in 1861, was assassinated just two days later at Ford's Theater on April 14, 1865, by John Wilkes Booth, a Southern sympathizer.

For the remainder of their lives, both Judge Campbell and General Weitzel maintained that Lincoln had officially sanctioned the meeting of the Virginia legislature. Godfrey Weitzel promptly turned the matter over to his superior officer, General Ord, who arrived at Richmond and was prepared to take over command.

Godfrey Is Removed from Richmond

On Thursday, April 13, Major General Godfrey Weitzel was officially removed from Richmond. Stanton had not wanted either Weitzel or Shepley in command there from the start. Shepley had been made governor, reprising his role from Louisiana, and Stanton associated them both with Ben Butler and trusted neither. "I would greatly prefer some other person than Shepley for military governor," Stanton wrote to Grant on April 5. "Please remove him immediately and appoint some good man of your own selection, who has not been connected with Butler's administration."[46]

Specifically as to Godfrey Weitzel, he was too young and inexperienced in Stanton's mind to be in command at Richmond. "Had not Weitzel better have duty elsewhere than Richmond?" he asked Grant.[47] Stanton criticized Weitzel for his aid to Richmond refugees, the call of the Virginia legislature, and the handling of church prayer. It was time for new leadership in Richmond.

The official revocation of Weitzel's call to the Virginia legislature, coupled with his removal from Richmond, sent a message to the North that the young general had blundered in his handling of the local affairs in Richmond. Godfrey lamented, "I was paraded in some papers, and in one even published in my own home, as a flunky." In his opinion, the cancellation of the call was only natural, "since Lee had surrendered on April 9, and the original permission was granted simply to disband that army, there was no longer any use for the legislature."[48]

Thinking back years later, Godfrey Weitzel speculated that had Lee not been forced to surrender, Lincoln's plan for the Virginia legislature to meet and to rescind the order of secession would have brought about a political end to the war, not a military end. He wrote, "It seems to me that if General Grant and his subordinate commanders had not pushed matters so much, the legislature would have been allowed to meet, and Mr. Lincoln's permission would have been held as another proof of his great wisdom."[49] But that was not to be.

CHAPTER 24

Good Friday—Black Friday

April 14, 1865, was a day of infamy, a day of cheers, of somber reflection, and of horror. For Godfrey Weitzel, it was a day of emotional highs and lows, lower than he could ever imagine. It was his last day in command of his post at Richmond. It was Good Friday.

Weitzel Forced Out of Richmond

Early Friday morning, President Lincoln held a cabinet meeting in Washington. Treasury Secretary Hugh McCulloch noted that he had never seen the president so cheerful and happy. Godfrey Weitzel was also happy that day, since he was relieved of command in Richmond, an assignment that had been as remarkable as it was stressful. Godfrey attributed his removal not so much to his flap with Secretary Stanton over church prayers, but to the aristocrats of the "first families of Virginia" who wished to be rid of his company of black soldiers. His reassignment was not welcomed by all the residents of Richmond, however, many of whom respected the way in which he had carried out the occupation. The Federally controlled *Richmond Whig* reported the local sentiment: "During his short administration of the duties of this military post, [Weitzel] won many friends, who would regret his retirement the more were they not entirely satisfied of Gen. Ord's great fitness and capacity for the post."[1]

Unlike Ben Butler, Godfrey had never sought out fame or fortune. He had his fill and wished for no more notoriety. He had watched for years as the press viciously attacked his mentor, and now they were starting in on Butler's protégé. Weitzel had been labeled by the media as a "flunky" because he held a review in Richmond of Charles Devens's division, but not of August Kautz's. In truth, a review was ordered for both divisions, but in order not to deplete the lines completely, Weitzel ordered Devens's review one day and Kautz's another. Although Devens and his division had their formal review, Kautz's never materialized because Weitzel was removed and ordered to move south with his Twenty-Fifth Corps before their review took place.[2]

More stinging to Godfrey, however, was that he had been defamed in his hometown of Cincinnati with rumors that he was being removed for incompetence. The same day that Lee rode into Richmond and Weitzel rode out, Virginia newspapers published the formal revocation of the call for the state legislature. A rumor was spread, and generally believed, that the young general was removed for issuing that ridiculous invitation in the first place. As Godfrey recalled:

> Advantage of this was taken to fan the east and south winds which had been blowing for me during some time, and against which I had been cautioned by warm friends who were more solicitous about my welfare than I was myself. It fanned these breezes so strongly that even the fair and just mind of General Grant nearly became tainted, and a false reputation for myself and corps was nearly started.[3]

Weitzel had explained the whole legislature debacle to General Grant, who believed Weitzel's account of the story, having seen Lincoln's letter of April 6. According to Godfrey, General Grant "made everything all right, and as the officers of my corps got a fair share of honor in the re-organization of the regular army, I did not consider it necessary to say anything more, either officially or publicly."[4]

After congratulating General Ord on his appointment and briefing him on the situation, Major General Weitzel walked out of the former Davis residence for the last time and mounted up. He mobilized his black troops and marched them south in the direction of Petersburg, where he had been ordered to bring together all the divisions of his Twenty-Fifth Corps from their various stations in Virginia. Standing high in the saddle, Godfrey took a last look at the conquered city, gave a nod to his officers, and led his colored foot soldiers out of Richmond.

Outside Petersburg, the Twenty-Fifth Corps halted for temporary posting at a dirty camp with a polluted stream for water. There, he was ordered to hold his troops ready to move in the direction of North Carolina with the Sixth Army Corps and cavalry, all under the command of General Philip Sheridan. "I was delighted to get out of Richmond and get back to real military duties," Godfrey said.[5]

The President Is Murdered

President Abraham Lincoln and his wife, Mary, decided it was time to get back to normalcy by attending a play. The three-act comedy *Our American Cousin* was playing at Ford's Theatre on Tenth Street in Washington, D.C. It would be a well-deserved break from the stress of the war and the celebrations of the past two weeks.

Maryland native John Wilkes Booth had been planning to overthrow the government by killing President Lincoln and Vice President Andrew Johnson on the same night, as well as Secretary of State William Seward. Newspapers erroneously reported on April 14 that General and Mrs. Grant would accompany the Lincolns to the theater, and Booth delighted in the opportunity to kill Grant as well. However, the Grants declined the Lincolns' offer, as did several others until a young officer, Major Henry Rathbone, and his fiancée, accepted.

Lincoln's carriage was late arriving at the theater, and when the president and First Lady were spotted walking to the presidential box about 8:30 p.m., the play stopped and the orchestra struck up "Hail to the Chief," to the sustained applause of the largely military audience of more than one thousand.[6] About thirty minutes later, John Wilkes Booth arrived at the theater's back door. When the play reached a comedic high-point, Booth entered the rear of the presidential box and fired his derringer pistol point-blank into the back of Lincoln's large head. The president slumped over.

General Lee Returns Home

Just eleven days after the triumphant Union entry into Richmond, a more solemn entry was made by another general. Robert E. Lee returned home on his trusted horse Traveler, having concluded the surrender at Appomattox. Lee turned down an offer to have Union cavalrymen escort him home to Richmond, where his wife and daughter lived. Nonetheless, out of respect, twenty-five mounted Yankees escorted the stately Confederate general a short distance from Appomattox. From there, Lee and his small staff continued their journey home unescorted on April 12, three days after the surrender.

The news of Lee's arrival spread ahead of him, from town to town, where he was greeted as he passed and provided with food and shelter. His son "Rooney" Lee joined the group along the way, which had by now grown to twenty horsemen headed for Richmond. After a slow two-day ride, General Lee arrived in Richmond. The hero of the Confederacy had returned home.

Prior to his departure from the Davis mansion, word reached Godfrey Weitzel that his former superintendent had arrived in town. Weitzel summoned his aide Thomas T. Graves into a private room in the Davis home. Godfrey presumed that General Lee would have been accompanied home by his nephew, Fitzhugh Lee, who had been reported to be with his uncle at Appomattox. Confederate currency was now worthless paper, and Godfrey's heart went out to the man who had shown him such kindness as a cadet. Taking out a large, well-filled pocketbook of U.S. currency, Weitzel turned to Graves and said, "Go to General Lee's house, find Fitzhugh Lee, and say that his old West Point chum Godfrey Weitzel wishes to know if he needs anything." Handing the stuffed wallet to

Graves, Godfrey continued, "Urge him to take what he may need from that pocket-book."[7] The aide took the leather wallet, saluted his commanding officer, and exited the former Confederate White House, where he mounted his horse and rode the nine blocks to Lee's home.

Upon reaching the three-story brick house on Franklin Street, Graves saluted the guards posted there and knocked on the front door. After a few moments, the bearded Fitzhugh Lee came to the door, still dressed in his Confederate uniform. Graves introduced himself and was invited in. The gracious younger Lee showed the aide into the family's parlor with double doors, explaining that the servants had all left. The aide repeated General Weitzel's generous offer, pulling out the wad of greenbacks. "Fitz" Lee was touched by the gesture from his former schoolmate and friend. "He was so overcome by Weitzel's message," Graves recalled, "that for a moment he was obliged to walk to the other end of the room" to regain his composure. Fitz then excused himself, and passed into the inner room, where Graves noticed the elder Robert E. Lee sitting in a stuffed chair with a "tired, worn expression upon his face." General Lee's nephew knelt beside the chair and placed a hand upon his uncle's knee, repeating the words from the Union aide in the parlor. Robert E. Lee nodded and spoke quietly to his nephew for a moment.[8]

After a few minutes, Fitz Lee came back to the parlor, "and in a most dignified and courteous manner sent his love to Godfrey Weitzel, and assured him that he did not require any loan of money." However, General Lee did have a request for General Weitzel: "If it would be entirely proper for Godfrey Weitzel to issue a pass for some ladies of General Lee's household to return to the city," Fitzhugh said, "it would be esteemed a favor." Graves was told that if the request for passes would in any way embarrass General Weitzel, on no account would they request the favor. Thomas Graves understood, shook hands, and returned the pocketbook to Godfrey at the Davis mansion. He repeated the scene to the waiting General Weitzel, including the request for the necessary passes. "It is needless to state," Graves said, "that the ladies were back in the house as soon as possible."[9]

Upon arrival in Petersburg, Godfrey Weitzel received new orders. He was to commence preparations for the transfer of his Twenty-Fifth Army Corps to the Texas-Mexico border, where he would serve out the remainder of his volunteer service. Godfrey and his division commanders organized their men and obtained supplies for redeployment.

Clearing Godfrey's Name

In late April, Louise Weitzel re-joined her husband at his camp outside Petersburg. She brought word from Cincinnati of rumors regarding Godfrey's removal from Richmond and encouraged him to do something to clear up the false accusations. On April 27 Godfrey wrote a letter to influential family friend Judge Bellamy Storer, the former congressman who had supported Godfrey's appointment to

FIGURE 24.1. General Robert E. Lee on his return home to Richmond, April 1865. (Photograph by Mathew Brady, Library of Congress, Prints and Photographs Division, Reference No. LC-DIG-cwpbh-03115 DLC.)

West Point. Godfrey asked the judge to help clear his name in the local community and "to have the truth stated in all the papers in Cincinnati, both English and German."[10] He wrote,

> My dear Judge, I have been much distressed by letters which I have received from home and all parts of the country. The writers all think I called together the "persons composing the late Virginia Legislature" on my own responsibility and think I made a mistake or blunder. My

mother writes me that in Cincinnati, I have been called a friend of the rebels! All believe that in consequence of this act I was removed from command at Richmond.[11]

Godfrey continued, "I was not removed from Richmond. Any person who has the least knowledge of military matters can see how it was."[12] It was only because General Ord was unavailable that Weitzel was temporarily left in command of the troops outside Richmond in the first place. By that stroke of fate, it was Godfrey's detachment that was the first to enter Richmond, and the responsibility fell to him to set up command of the Federal occupation forces there. Ord had gone west with Grant, chasing Lee's Army of Northern Virginia, but once Lee surrendered on April 9, Ord had simply returned to his headquarters and reassumed his command. As a result, Godfrey's temporary command was terminated and he went back to his Twenty-Fifth Army Corps, which was ordered to concentrate near Petersburg. It was that simple.

Godfrey clarified to Judge Storer that "everything of importance I did at Richmond was in accordance with written orders from my superiors. I was blamed, censured, or found fault with by no one. But enemies of mine have so perverted this peculiar combination of circumstances." He closed his letter by saying, "I do not wish to be maligned in this manner."[13] Judge Storer was not only a lawyer and professor in the Cincinnati Law School, but a sitting judge of the superior court of Cincinnati. He set to work correcting the record in the Over-the-Rhine neighborhood.

The *New York Times* came to Godfrey's aid in an article that attempted to defuse the vicious rumors. Regarding General Weitzel's removal, the *Times* reporter in Richmond wrote that it was "the faculty of malicious invention for a newsmonger to pervert it into a censure of Gen. Weitzel's conduct." The article continued that it was not the calling together of the Virginia legislature that led to his replacement by General Ord, and "the statement that his doing so was the cause of his removal, is simply a mischievous falsehood." Referring to those who sought to tarnish Weitzel's good name, the article closed, "The mischief-makers here need the closest sort of watching. They are more dangerous, for the time than the disjointed bands of insurgents that still wear the ragged livery of JEFF. DAVIS."[14]

Arrest and Imprisonment of Justice Campbell

Back in Richmond, a vengeful Edwin Stanton was still investigating Lincoln's murder and made an unlikely arrest in the middle of the night. After Lincoln's assassination, radical Republican leaders in the North became eager to punish the South and to implicate its leaders in the plot. Loyal Unionists began to suspect any Southern leader as a coconspirator. By Edwin Stanton's orders, numerous arrests were made of Confederate civil officers who were held as prisoners of war. Some in the Northern press were calling for the lynchings of Lee and Davis and, perhaps, other members of the rebel government.

A grand jury convened in Norfolk, Virginia, indicted Robert E. Lee for treason. Had it not been for the intervention of General Ulysses S. Grant, Lee might have been tried and imprisoned, or even hanged. Jefferson Davis was eventually captured on May 10 in Irwinsville, Georgia, and was held for two years at Fort Monroe. He was never brought to trial and was eventually released on bail. Even the peacemaker, Judge John Campbell, became a target of the conspiracy investigation into the assassination at Ford's Theatre.[15]

Campbell said this paranoia "naturally aroused wild and improbable suspicions as to the extent of the conspiracy."[16] At 10:00 p.m. on May 22, as John and Anne Campbell relaxed at their Richmond home, armed Federal soldiers knocked on their door. The former U.S. Supreme Court justice was promptly arrested, iron restraints placed on his hands and feet, and led from his home like a common criminal—with no explanation of his offense. His wife was terrified, fearing for her husband's fate and fully aware that Confederate officials were being rounded up and imprisoned.

Campbell was taken to the docks on the James River, where he was transferred to a small room onboard the Army gunboat USS *Mosswood*. He remained confined in his floating prison on the steamer for the next week without being charged with any crime. For a former U.S. Supreme Court justice, this was not only an indignity but a violation of his civil rights as a citizen. All the while he believed that his imprisonment was simply due to his role as assistant secretary of war in the Confederacy. From his floating prison, Campbell wrote a lengthy letter to President Johnson requesting amnesty. He also wrote to his wife, Anne, attempting to assure her that he was in no discomfort and was exercising regularly.[17]

Campbell was later transferred to a prison cell at Fort Pulaski, an island just off the Georgia coast. Supreme Court Justice Benjamin Curtis and other friends petitioned the president and finally convinced Andrew Johnson to release Judge Campbell from the Federal island prison. The president issued the release order on October 11, nearly five months after the judge had been seized from his home. At this point, however, Campbell was bankrupt, both financially and politically. His home, property, and reputation had all been destroyed. He and Anne moved to New Orleans, where he set up a law practice with his son, Duncan.[18] Campbell pondered "what the course of Mr. Lincoln would have been had his life been spared."[19] He closed his law practice in 1886 and died three years later, on March 12, 1889, at the age of seventy-seven.

CHAPTER 25

Postwar Life of the Young General

Banished to Mexico!

Foreign governments had seized on an opportunity during America's Civil War to take advantage of the distraction of the United States. In December of 1861, an allied force made up of the governments of France, Great Britain, and Spain landed at Vera Cruz, Mexico, to protect their interests over debts owed by that country. President Benito Juárez negotiated with the foreigners and promised to resume debt payments. In reliance on the Mexican president's word, British and Spanish troops began to withdraw from Mexico in April 1862. The French, however, did not leave. Instead, France's ruler Louis Napoleon sent reinforcements to Mexico. This "Napoleon," who proclaimed himself "Napoleon III," was the nephew of Napoleon Bonaparte.

On May 5, 1862, the Mexicans won a victory over the French, which is still celebrated annually as Cinco de Mayo, but the French military advanced on Mexico City from Vera Cruz and began an occupation. President Juárez was forced to retreat in exile, while France's emperor Napoleon III installed an Austrian archduke named Maximilian von Habsburg as "Emperor Maximilian I of Mexico." The United States was deeply concerned about France's motives, suspecting that Napoleon III did not intend to stop at the Rio Grande. As a result, with the American Civil War now essentially over, the U.S. Departments of State and War turned their focus to the French threat in Mexico. General Grant ordered General Philip Sheridan to the Rio Grande to aid in expelling the French. Grant appointed Sheridan the commander of the Military Division of the Southwest, and General Godfrey Weitzel was given command of the District of the Rio Grande. Sheridan promptly organized an enormous flotilla headed for Texas, which included Godfrey Weitzel's all-black Twenty-Fifth Army Corps. The flotilla of more than thirty-three thousand soldiers was perhaps the largest in military history at that time. Major General M. C. Meigs said of the armada, "No great nation ever before put such a transport fleet on the ocean."[1] Though weary from four years of war, Weitzel dutifully boarded a steamer out of Hampton Roads, Virginia, and headed south to Texas in June 1865. There he set up a headquarters at Brazos Santiago, near the south end of what is now Padre Island.

The Union's show of force along the Rio Grande achieved its intended effect, and in September 1865 the United States minister in Paris, John Bigelow, obtained a tentative statement from the French that they intended to withdraw from Mexico. While the news was welcomed by Godfrey Weitzel and his soldiers who were sweating in the hot Texas sun, another telegraph brought tragic personal news to General Weitzel at his headquarters. The honeymoon pregnancy of his bride, Louise Bogen, had ended in the death of Godfrey's only son. The infant was stillborn in Cincinnati on September 26, 1865. Louise had named the baby boy after her husband, Godfrey Weitzel Jr.

With the French expelled from Mexico, on January 8, 1866, Weitzel's Twenty-Fifth Army Corps of all black troops was discontinued, the very last Army corps mustered out of service from the Civil War. Major General Weitzel sailed home in February and was personally mustered out of the U.S. Volunteers on March 1, 1866, at age thirty. It was time to go home to his wife, and time to find a new occupation. His days on the battlefield and as a reluctant politician were over, to his relief. Writing years later about his removal from Richmond, Godfrey said: "I was as happy only once afterwards, and that was when I was relieved on the Rio Grande in February of the next year."[2]

Despite all of his promotions and brevets in the Volunteer Army, Godfrey abandoned his title of major general of the U.S. Volunteers and reverted to his former rank of captain of engineers in the regular Army.[3] On August 8, 1866, however, he was promoted to full major.[4] Major Godfrey Weitzel spent the next sixteen years in the service of the Corps of Engineers, designing locks, dams, lighthouses, and harbors on the rivers and Great Lakes.

Reconstruction in the South; Construction in the North

Even though Godfrey Weitzel had a distinguished military career in the Volunteer Army, his postwar career in civil engineering was equally impressive. As new president Andrew Johnson began to reconstruct the former Confederate States, the Army's Corps of Engineers turned its attention to engineering projects in the North. Godfrey Weitzel was appointed to several engineering boards and commissions in the Midwest and the Northeast, as well as being named a trustee of the Cincinnati Southern Railroad.[5] He was challenged with many substantial engineering assignments that included improving the shipping lanes on the Cumberland, Ohio, Tennessee, Wabash, and Mississippi Rivers.

On February 16, 1868, Godfrey and Louise celebrated the healthy birth of a daughter, Blanche Celeste Weitzel. The couple was joyous after having lost their first baby, Godfrey Jr., during childbirth. Their joy was brief, however, when the newborn baby girl contracted the measles. Godfrey knew the devastating effect that measles had had on both armies during the Civil War, where an estimated 75,000 soldiers contracted the disease in the close confinements and abysmal sanitary conditions of the camps, with 5,000 men dying from simple measles.[6] Although the effects of measles were only temporary for most adults, measles was often deadly among infants. Young Blanche succumbed to the disease and died on April 5, 1868. Her grief-stricken parents buried their daughter in Cincinnati next to their infant son. In a span of just a few years, Godfrey Weitzel had lost his father, a wife, and now two children, almost more than a thirty-two-year-old man could bear. But duty called, and despite a broken heart, Godfrey returned to his work with the same effort he had used when leading brigades into battle.

A New President, New Controversies

On February 24, 1868, the House voted 127 to 47 to file Articles of Impeachment against Andrew Johnson. The president was tried by the Senate in the spring of 1868 and acquitted by just one vote. The chief prosecutor in the trial, who gave a three-hour opening statement, was none other than the newly elected representative from Massachusetts, Benjamin F. Butler. The fall of 1868 brought another presidential election, and the Union could not wait to elect its hero, Lieutenant General Ulysses S. Grant, as president. On November 3 Grant became the eighteenth president of the United States. Even though he had no political experience, the forty-six-year-old Grant won the nation's highest office, the youngest U.S. president at that time.

With so many former military leaders now wearing civilian clothes, government offices under Grant's administration were filled with war veterans. Grant's two terms as president were plagued with accusations of favoritism as he doled out many posts to friends and political contributors rather than taking recommendations of party officials. One of the Army veterans who received a government job was Godfrey Weitzel's brother, Captain Lewis Weitzel, whom Grant appointed as a collector of internal revenue for the First Congressional District of Ohio. Less than two years later, President Grant nominated Lewis Weitzel for the position of assessor of internal revenue for the same district.[7] It was during his time as a tax assessor that Lewis Weitzel got caught up in a conspiracy known as the "Whiskey Ring" of 1875. There were allegations of kickbacks on taxes from alcohol distilleries, claims that involved several revenue collectors in Grant's administration. Some even alleged that the whole Grant administration was in on the ring.[8] Despite the charges, Lewis Weitzel ran for the Ohio House of Representatives in 1878.[9] When his political opponents tried to tarnish the Weitzel name, Godfrey wrote to fellow Ohioan and then president Rutherford B. Hayes seeking the president's intercession on Lewis's behalf. Godfrey pleaded with Hayes to take action "in the infamous raid that is in progress on my brother at the instigation of politicians of Hamilton County, Ohio."[10] The intervention paid off, and despite the alleged ties to the "ring," Lewis Weitzel was elected in 1878 to the Ohio House of Representatives.[11] He went on to become a state senator in the Ohio legislature, serving from 1882 to 1884.

Engineer of the Eleventh Lighthouse District—Detroit

The year before Grant's election as president, Godfrey Weitzel was ordered to Louisville to complete the survey authorized by Congress for the ship canal around the Falls of the Ohio River.[12] The project was of great interest to Godfrey, having grown up along the Ohio River, and he promptly traveled to Louisville and began surveys for the partially finished Louisville Canal. He surprised everyone when he recommended that an additional and larger canal, 110 feet wide and 400 feet long, be constructed on the Indiana side of the river.[13] Weitzel also recommended construction of a dam across the falls to increase the depth of the Louisville harbor by three feet, a precaution to prevent boats from wrecking when attempting to enter the canal.[14] He commenced the enlargement of the Louisville Canal in September 1868 and oversaw the construction of what was considered a major civil engineering breakthrough.[15] In order to be close to his work, Godfrey and Louise moved to New Albany, Indiana, just across the Ohio River from Louisville, Kentucky, overlooking the Falls of the Ohio and the Louisville Canal. From there, he could easily oversee the construction operations.

The success of Godfrey's work on the Ohio River made him a popular engineer who was sought out to serve on various regional boards for bridges and canals across the nation's waterways. In 1873, he was appointed to at least five different engineering boards to conduct studies in Michigan, Missouri, Nebraska, New York, and Pennsylvania. In his spare time, Godfrey translated several German engineering books into English.[16] The greatest postwar honor Weitzel received was his promotion in 1873 to engineer of the Eleventh Light House District. Major Weitzel was to oversee a region that included Lakes St. Clair, Huron, Michigan, and Superior. With so many engineering projects to his credit, from ten-story observation towers, to pontoon bridges, to the Louisville Canal, Godfrey Weitzel left his mark on the world with his designs for more simple structures—lighthouses on the Great Lakes. As an engineer for the Eleventh Light House District, Godfrey Weitzel was responsible for the design and construction of at least six impressive lighthouses on the Great Lakes at McGulpin's Point, Eagle Harbor, Spectacle Reef, White River, Saginaw River, and Sand Island, some of which survive today.

His most difficult engineering challenges came, however, when District Engineer Weitzel was placed in charge of improvements to the St. Clair and

St. Mary's Rivers, the harbors of the Sable and Cheboygan, the construction of a harbor of refuge on Lake Huron, and the enlargement of the St. Mary's Falls Canal.[17] He and Louise moved to Detroit and rented a lovely house from a local doctor on scenic Jefferson Avenue. Godfrey was delighted upon his arrival in Michigan to encounter his old pal from West Point, Cyrus B. Comstock, who was, ironically, also stationed there to conduct a survey of the Great Lakes. The two classmates from West Point seemed inseparable throughout their careers, and must have often reminisced about their days at the Academy, Benny Havens' Tavern, and all the boys who went on to become generals during the war. Godfrey Weitzel often consulted with Comstock on matters of engineering design such as foundations and soil pressure.[18] Cyrus Comstock's wife, Elizabeth Blair, the daughter of Lincoln's former postmaster general, had died in Detroit during childbirth, as did her baby girl.[19] Unlike Godfrey, however, Cyrus Comstock never remarried.

While living in Detroit, Louise Weitzel bore the couple's third child, a daughter named Irene, born on April 11, 1876. She was the last and only surviving child of Godfrey Weitzel, and she lived to the age of sixty. Her father worked day and night on the engineering projects, poring over drawings and reading texts. The eyestrain eventually caught up with Godfrey, and in February 1878, he applied to the chief of engineers for a four-month medical leave of absence, to go abroad to Europe or, as he called it, "to go beyond the sea."[20] Godfrey argued that "during the last six years I have had but one leave. Its duration was ten days." His request was promptly granted, and Major Weitzel borrowed money to make the trip and seek treatment for his eyes.[21]

On his return, Godfrey embarked upon the largest engineering project of his career, a new, deeper lock at the St. Mary's Falls Canal.[22] The waterfall of the St. Mary's River is better known as Sault (pronounced "Soo") St. Marie, where the river falls twenty-one feet from Lake Superior on the U.S.-Canada border. This would be Godfrey Weitzel's most noteworthy project, even greater than the one at the Ohio River Falls. It was his innovative design for a canal lock on the St. Mary's River that would bear his name. The massive sixteen-foot-deep, $2.4 million "Weitzel Lock" was the largest of its kind in the world at the time it was opened in 1881. The lock continued in operation until 1943, when the Corps of Engineers replaced the Weitzel Lock with the 800-foot-long by 31-foot-deep "McArthur Lock."

Declining Health and Move to Philadelphia

Godfrey wrote to the assistant surgeon general on March 31, 1882, stating that "something was wrong in my throat."[23] A local doctor examined Major Weitzel and told him that he had a severe problem with the larynx with polypus

FIGURE 25.1. Postwar photo of Godfrey Weitzel, age thirty-seven. (From James Landry, *Cincinnati Past and Present*, 334.)

developing, possibly brought on by exposure on the freshwater lakes. The cash-poor Weitzel asked if he could be reimbursed for his medical expenses. Due to the cold and damp conditions on the Great Lakes and declining health, the Army Corps of Engineers reassigned Godfrey to lighter duty in Philadelphia. With Godfrey's poor health from chronic chest and nasal congestion, the Weitzels began to pack belongings for their last move.[24] In late April 1882, he petitioned Congress for a promotion that would result in a modest salary increase, claiming he had been passed over for promotion since the war—"a very severe punishment." He wrote, "I commanded an Army Corps during 18 months of the war. I am the only Corps Commander who has not long ago been promoted. . . . Why am I thus punished? No one can give a good reason for it."[25] He asked that the matter be laid before the president for consideration. Major Weitzel received his promotion on June 23, 1882, when he was elevated to the rank of lieutenant colonel.

With his orders to relocate to Philadelphia, Lieutenant Colonel Weitzel was subsequently appointed a member of that city's harbor commission advisory board.[26] His friends and coworkers in Michigan were sad to see Godfrey, Louise, and Irene leave, but many knew that given Godfrey's declining health, the move was for the best for his family, personally and professionally. On July 26, 1882, the night before his move from Detroit, a large banquet was held in Weitzel's honor. However, soon after Godfrey and Louise arrived in the City of Brotherly Love, his health became so poor that he had to take two months' leave from his work to recover.[27] He would be plagued by sickness for nearly two years.

Godfrey Weitzel continued to struggle with congestion, easily contracting colds with changes in the weather. Late in 1883, he developed a severe cold that he just could not shake. By early January 1884, he developed jaundice with a loss of appetite, impaired digestion, and great debility. Although treated by local physicians, Weitzel's jaundice intensified, and he became weaker and lost weight. Godfrey's condition rapidly deteriorated into typhoid symptoms, with profuse sweating and intestinal pains. In February, Godfrey began to experience chills from a low-grade fever. He lacked the energy to perform even moderate tasks, and also suffered from severe headaches. Then he developed a cough—the onset of typhoid fever, and he was confined to bed in early March 1884.

The illness known simply as "typhoid" was usually caused by sewage leaking into water wells, transmitting salmonella bacteria into food or water. Water quality was very poor in some parts of the city, and about five miles from Godfrey's house on Thirty-Sixth Street was the Aramingo Canal. The Philadelphia Water Department described the canal "as an open sewer clogged with filth" that had been used for industrial waste. Newspaper reports from that era said the water was ink-black and smelled horrible. City officials blamed the Aramingo Canal for outbreaks of typhoid fever and malaria. There was no cure for the disease at that time, and the spread of disease was such a threat that Congress introduced a bill in March 1884 titled "A Bill to Protect the Public Health," which created a United States Board of Health. That same year, Theodore Roosevelt's mother and Thomas Edison's wife both died of typhoid.

Listless and weak, Godfrey remained confined to bed in his Philadelphia home while Louise tended to him as their seven-year-old daughter watched on. Modern antibiotics were not available, and Godfrey's doctors could do no more than treat his symptoms and give him drugs to make him more comfortable. Fevers that peaked from infection in the blood stream at 104°F brought on delirium, and Louise tried her best to comfort her husband with cold compresses and water. Near the end of the third week, Godfrey's fever broke and Louise hoped that her husband would begin to recover. However, the reduced temperature only signaled that the typhoid was entering its final stage.

Death of the Young General

After a month of struggling with typhoid, Godfrey Weitzel died from complications at his home in Philadelphia on March 19, 1884. His remains were taken by train to his elderly mother in Cincinnati for burial. Louise and Irene accompanied Godfrey's body by train as it returned to his boyhood home. Though Godfrey had told Louise that he wanted a private funeral, the city could not hold back its emotion for its adopted native son, the famous engineer and military hero who had grown up in the town's Over-the-Rhine neighborhood. Awaiting the arrival of the remains at the train station was the First Regiment of the Ohio National Guard and fellow members of the Cincinnati Society of Ex-Army and Navy Officers. The somber procession accompanied the body to the residence of Godfrey's brother, State Senator Lewis Weitzel, on West Ninth Street.

Shortly after noon, a military assembly made up of the Ohio National Guardsmen, plus the Veteran Guards, as well as various posts of the Grand Army of the Republic (or "GAR") gathered at Senator Weizel's home where the family visitation had been held. From his brother's house, Godfrey's remains were escorted a few blocks to the English Lutheran Church on Elm Street between Ninth and Court Streets. The newspaper reported, "Long before the hour appointed the church was filled with people." Godfrey Weitzel's remains were carried from the hearse into the church by a squad of enlisted Army soldiers. The casket was covered in black velvet, on which lay a simple gold inscription that read "General G. Weitzel, Died March 19, 1884, in the 49th year of his age." Following the church service, the casket made its way to Spring Grove Cemetery in a horse-drawn hearse. All along the procession route, thousands of citizens lined the streets to pay homage to the famous military officer. In an article titled "General Godfrey Weitzel, Imposing Funeral Services—Thousands of People Do Him Honor," Cincinnati's newspaper described the spectacle as the largest gathering seen for a funeral in many years. "His friends in private life, his comrades in war, and citizens generally of this city of his youth, felt that they must pay a last tribute to him they had known and loved so well," the article said.

Godfrey was buried in the plot of his in-laws, Peter and Wilhelmina Bogen. His wife, Louise, was buried by his side in 1927. Their only surviving child, Irene Weitzel-Nye, was buried just to the right of her parents nine years later, in 1936.[28]

The *Cincinnati Commercial Gazette* honored Godfrey Weitzel with these appropriate words: "In private life he was one of the most diffident and unassuming men. He was quiet in all his ways, and plain and practical in the discharge of all his duties. In his death the army and the Corps of Engineers loses one of its most capable officers, and society one of its best citizens." Not surprising, considering Godfrey's humility in life, the grave site of this military hero has no statue, no fancy urn, nothing but a small slab in the ground. It is a simple marker, difficult even to locate among the Peter Bogen plot. Etched into the stone are the words "Godfrey Weitzel, 1835–1884." Years later, it appears as if someone has carved the word *General* above his name, as an afterthought.

The body of this brilliant young general, who seized Richmond and designed impressive structures along the Great Lakes, lies in a forgotten and hard-to-find family plot. However, the U.S. Army did not forget this man's contributions to military and engineering efforts, nor his career of service. Perhaps even more fitting, Godfrey's "monument" lies not in Cincinnati, but on the land once owned by his superintendent, Robert E. Lee—Arlington Cemetery. Major General Weitzel was not honored with a statue, but by the naming of one of the major roads through the north portion of Arlington Cemetery in Arlington, Virginia, as "Ord & Weitzel Drive."

The Ord-Weitzel Gate

"It is sweet and glorious to die for the Fatherland." So read the phrase translated from a ode by the Roman poet Homer (Dulce et Decorum est) that was etched onto two large iron gates dedicated to Major Generals Edward Ord and Godfrey Weitzel at Arlington Cemetery. "The Ord-Weitzel Gate" consisted of two white columns from the old War Department Building, set about eight feet high on stone bases. The marble columns were inscribed with "Ord" on the south column and "Weitzel" on the right-hand column, to the north. The two columns were capped with curled ionic capitals supporting urns, and an iron gate of double doors was hinged between them. However, after a major land acquisition was made by the government, Arlington Cemetery was expanded to the east in the 1960s, and the Ord-Weitzel Gate was considered to be no longer needed. Although the tall white columns were torn down, today the northernmost entry to the cemetery is still called "Ord and Weitzel Gate."

FIGURE 25.2. Ord and Weitzel Gate (as originally constructed), Arlington Cemetery, Virginia. (Library of Congress, Prints and Photographs Dept., Reproduction No. LC-D4-500356.)

Postscript

From his modest immigrant roots, Godfrey Weitzel rose to the top of his class at West Point, helped plan the assault on New Orleans where he briefly served as its mayor, and, under the mentorship of Ben Butler, rose to the rank of major general of Volunteers. Fate placed him in command of troops outside Richmond in early April 1865 and as President Lincoln's only reliable witness to negotiations aimed at ending the war. Well known to P. G. T. Beauregard, Robert E. Lee, Fitzhugh Lee, Ben Butler, David Farragut, Ben Butler, John Campbell, David Porter, Abraham Lincoln, and Ulysses S. Grant, the young general rubbed shoulders with the legendary officers and leaders on both sides of the conflict. With this book, perhaps Godfrey Weitzel will be recognized by future generations as one of the key players in the Civil War and his memory given the honor he is due.

Notes

Epigraph: Verse from the postwar song titled "At Eight in the Morning," Charles Haynes, words; J. E. Haynes, music (Chicago: H. M. Higgins, Chicago, 1865).

Prologue

1. George F. Shepley, "Incidents of the Capture of Richmond," *Atlantic Monthly* 46, no. 273 (July 1880): 27.

2. Godfrey Weitzel, "Entry of the United States Forces into Richmond, April 3, 1865," in *Letter Book of Gen. G. Weitzel*, vol. 1, 1881, Cincinnati Historical Society Library.

3. Shepley, "Incidents," 26.

4. Weitzel, "Entry."

5. *New York Herald*, 9 April 1865.

Chapter 1: Over-the-Rhine

1. Christian B. Keller, *Chancellorsville and the Germans: Nativism, Ethnicity, and Civil War Memory* (New York: Fordham University Press, 2007), 3.

2. Joseph R. Reinhart, Kentucky's German-Americans in the Civil War, http://kygermanscw.yolasite.com.

3. Lt. G. Weitzel to Capt. G. W. Cullum, 11 September 1859, U.S. Military Academy.

4. Merlin E. Sumner, ed., *The Diary of Cyrus B. Comstock* (Dayton, OH: Morningside House, 1987), 194.

5. Confirmed with the registration officer for the town of Winzeln, Germany, where Gottfried Weitzel's birth certificate is found in the town's official birth records. Ulf Kolbenschlag to this author, 14 October 2004, author's private collection.

6. Ibid.

7. C. S. Williams, *Williams' Cincinnati Directory City Guide and Business Mirror* (Cincinnati, OH: C. S. Williams), 111, 413.

8. James Landry, *Cincinnati Past and Present: Its Industrial History, as Exhibited in the Life-Labours of Its Leading Men* (Cincinnati: Joblin, 1872), 336.

9. G. Weitzel to Pres. Rutherford B. Hayes, 14 May 1878, *Letter Press Volumes of Gen. G. Weitzel*, vol. 1, p. 115, Cincinnati Historical Society Library.

10. James L. Morrison, *"The Best School": West Point, 1833–1866* (Kent, OH: Kent State University Press, 1998), 27.

11. Ibid., 4.

12. George C. Strong, *Cadet Life at West Point: By an Officer of the United States Army* (Boston: Burnham, 1862), 31–32.

13. Henry Roedter to Rep. David Tiernan Disney, 16 August 1859, National Archives.

14. Strong, *Cadet Life*, 43–44.

15. Sumner, *Diary*, 9.

16. Williams, *Williams' Cincinnati Directory*, 111, 413.

Chapter 2: Welcome to West Point

1. Merlin E. Sumner, ed., *The Diary of Cyrus B. Comstock* (Dayton, OH: Morningside House, 1987), 86.

2. John Grant, James Lynch, and Ronald Bailey, *West Point: The First 200 Years* (Guilford, CT: Globe Pequot Press, 2002), xiv.

3. Ibid., 4.

4. George C. Strong, *Cadet Life at West Point: By an Officer of the United States Army* (Boston: Burnham, 1862), xvi.

5. James L. Morrison, *"The Best School": West Point, 1833–1866* (Kent, OH: Kent State University Press, 1998), 3.

6. Ibid., 64.

7. Ibid., 72.

8. Sumner, *Diary*, 10.

9. Ibid.

10. Strong, *Cadet Life*, 52.

11. Ibid., 53.

12. Ibid., 57–58.

13. Ibid., 120.

14. Morrison, *Best School*, 65.

15. Strong, *Cadet Life*, 65; Morrison, *Best School*, 65.

16. Morrison, *Best School*, 65; John C. Waugh, *The Class of 1846: From West Point to Appomattox; Stonewall Jackson, George McClellan and Their Brothers* (New York: Random House, 1994), 12.

17. Waugh, *Class of 1846*, 12.

18. Strong, *Cadet Life*, 121.

19. Sumner, *Diary*, 15.

20. Semi-Annual Roll of Cadets, 1840–1861, September 1851, U.S. Military Academy.

21. Book of Delinquencies, U.S. Military Academy, West Point, New York, 1851–1852.

22. Sumner, *Diary*, 10.

23. Ibid.

24. Ibid., 37.

25. Ibid., 51.

26. Ibid., 18.

27. Waugh, *Class of 1846*, 37–38.

28. U.S. Military Academy Staff Records, vol. 5, 1851–1854.

29. Report of the Progress, Aptitude and Habits, January 1852, pp. 129–30, U.S. Military Academy Staff Records, vol. 5, 1851–1854.

30. 24 July—1 demerit; 11, 19, and 21 October 1851—2 demerits each; Book of Delinquencies, U.S. Military Academy.

31. General Merit Roll of the Fourth Class, June 1852, p. 193, U.S. Military Academy Staff Records, vol. 5, 1851–1854.

32. Strong, *Cadet Life*, 209.

33. Register of Merit, 1836–1853, vol. 2, U.S. Military Academy.

34. Sumner, *Diary*, 161–62.

Chapter 3: No Longer a Plebe

1. Merlin E. Sumner, ed., *The Diary of Cyrus B. Comstock* (Dayton, OH: Morningside House, 1987), 96.

2. Ibid., 114.

3. Ibid.

4. Roll of the Third Class in Mathematics, 12 January 1853, p. 255; 6 June 1853, p. 283, U.S. Military Academy Staff Records, vol. 5, 1851–1854.

5. Roll of the Third Class in French, 18 January 1853, p. 265; 15 June 1853, p. 296, U.S. Military Academy Staff Records, vol. 5, 1851–1854.

6. James L. Morrison, *"The Best School": West Point, 1833–1866* (Kent, OH: Kent State University Press, 1998), 55.

7. Roll of the Third Class in Drawing, 19 January 1853, p. 267; 18 June 1853, p. 313, U.S. Military Academy Staff Records, vol. 5, 1851–1854.

8. Roll of the Third Class in Mathematics, U.S. Military Academy Staff Records, vol. 5, 1851–1854, Archives U.S. Military Academy.

9. James Robbins, *Last in their Class: Custer, Pickett and the Goats of West Point* (New York: Encounter Books, 2006), 129.

10. General Merit Roll of the Third Class, June 1853, p. 326, U.S. Military Academy Staff Records, vol. 5, 1851–1854.

11. Sumner, *Diary*, 137–38.

12. Roll of the Second Class in Philosophy, 7 January 1854, p. 357; Roll of the Second Class Arranged According to Merit in Chemistry, 13 January 1854, p. 363, U.S. Military Academy Staff Records, vol. 5, 1851–1854.

13. General Merit Roll of the Second Class, June 1854, p. 421, U.S. Military Academy Staff Records, vol. 5, 1851–1854.

14. Morrison, *Best School*, 72–73.

15. Sumner, *Diary*, 151.

16. Ibid.

17. Morrison, *Best School*, 77.

18. Post Orders, vol. 4, 13 November 1852 to 30 September 1856, U.S. Military Academy, West Point, New York; Special Orders No. 37, 22 December 1854, p. 236.

19. Ibid., 237.

20. Ibid.

21. Ibid.; Special Orders No. 157, 29 December 1854, p. 238.

22. Sumner, *Diary*, 168.

23. John C. Waugh, *The Class of 1846: From West Point to Appomattox; Stonewall Jackson, George McClellan and Their Brothers* (New York: Random House, 1994), 39.

24. Evans J. Casso, *Francis T. Nicholls: A Biographical Tribute* (Thibodaux, LA: Nicholls College Foundation, 1987).

25. *Boston Morning Post*, 3 May 1952.

26. Morrison, *Best School*, 98.

27. Sumner, *Diary*, 166.

28. Ibid., 178.

29. Ibid., 167.

30. First Class Arranged According to Merit in Engineering, 4 June 1855, p. 47; First Class Arranged According to Merit in Infantry Tactics, 12 June 1855, p. 56; First Class Arranged According to Merit in Artillery, 13 June 1855, p. 59; First Class Arranged According to Merit in Cavalry Tactics, 14 June 1855, p. 61.

31. First Class Arranged According to Merit in Horsemanship, June 1855, p. 65.

32. Cadets of the First Class Recommended for Promotion to Mounted Cavalry, June 1855, p. 70.

33. Sumner, *Diary*, 204.

34. Ibid., 205.

35. Ibid., 206.

36. Morrison, *Best School*, 110.

37. General Merit Roll of the First Class in June 1855, p. 62.

38. Members of the First Class Recommended for Promotion in the Corps of Engineers, June 1855, p. 66.

39. Post Orders, vol. 4, 13 November 1852 to 30 September 1856, U.S. Military Academy; Special Orders No. 97, 15 June 1855, p. 294.

Chapter 4: Early Career in New Orleans

1. Lt. G. Weitzel to Capt. G. W. Cullum, 11 September 1859, U.S. Military Academy.

2. Returns of the Corps of Engineers, April 1832–December 1916, M851/Roll 2, National Archives.

3. George F. Shepley, "Incidents of the Capture of Richmond," *Atlantic Monthly* 46, no. 273 (July 1880): 22.

4. Frances P. Keyes, *Madame Castel's Lodger* (New York: Farrar, Straus, 1962), 198.

5. Ibid., 196.

6. Returns of the Corps of Engineers, April 1832–December 1916, M851/Roll 2, National Archives.

7. Keyes, *Madame Castel's Lodger*, 198.

8. Lt. G. Weitzel to Capt. G. W. Cullum, 11 September 1859, U.S. Military Academy.

9. Merlin E. Sumner, *The Diary of Cyrus B. Comstock* (Dayton, OH: Morningside House, 1987), 215.

10. Special Orders No. 821, Returns of the Corps of Engineers, April 1832–December 1916, M851/Roll 2, National Archives.

11. G. Weitzel to C. Comstock, 1 January 1859.

12. Ibid.

13. Ibid.

14. George A. Custer, "War Memoirs," *Galaxy* 21, no. 4 (April 1876): 449.

15. Sumner, *Diary*, 221; Special Orders No. 155, 2 September 1859, p. 282; Post Orders No. 5, 1 December 1856–23 February 1861, U.S. Military Academy; see also Lt. G. Weitzel to Capt. G. W. Cullum, 11 September 1859, U.S. Military Academy.

16. National Academy of Sciences, *Biographical Memoirs*, vol. 2, *Cyrus Ballou Comstock* (Washington, DC, 1911), 200.

17. Special Orders No. 178, 23 October 1859, Returns of the Corps of Engineers, April 1832–December 1916, M851/Roll 2, National Archives.

18. Special Orders No. 187, 25 October 1859, p. 300; Post Orders No. 5, 1 December 1856–23 February 1861, U.S. Military Academy.

19. "Bedauernswerthes Unglüd," *Cincinnati Volksfreund*, 25 November 1859.

20. Special Orders No. 202, 26 November 1859, p. 308; Post Orders No. 5, 1 December 1856–23 February 1861, U.S. Military Academy.

21. Sumner, *Diary*, 223.

22. *Cincinnati Daily Gazette*, 25 November 1859.

23. Special Orders No. 243, 14 December 1859, Returns of the Corps of Engineers, April 1832–December 1916, M851/Roll 2, National Archives.

24. General Orders No. 17, 2 July 1860, Returns of the Corps of Engineers, April 1832–December 1916, M851/Roll 2, National Archives.

25. Custer, "War Memoirs," 449.

26. Maj. P. G. T. Beauregard to Maj. J. G. Barnard, 2 October 1860, Tulane University, Manuscripts Dept., Jones Hall, Item 240 (Beauregard Papers, 1858–1860).

27. Ibid.

28. Sumner, *Diary*, 224.

29. Maj. P. G. T. Beauregard to Sec. H. Cobb, 21 November 1860, Tulane University, Manuscripts Dept., Jones Hall, Item 240 (Beauregard Papers, 1858–1860).

30. Sumner, *Diary*, 225.

31. James L. Morrison, *"The Best School": West Point, 1833–1866* (Kent, OH: Kent State University Press, 1998), 127.

32. Special Orders, 2 January 1861, Returns of the Corps of Engineers, April 1832–December 1916, M851/Roll 2, National Archives.

33. Sumner, *Diary*, 227.

34. Orders No. 3, 7 January 1861, p. 400, Post Orders No. 5, 1 December 1856–23 February 1861, U.S. Military Academy.

35. Sumner, *Diary*, 227.

36. H. Robert Cowley and Thomas Guinzburg, eds., *West Point: Two Centuries of Honor and Tradition* (New York: Warner, 2002), 83.

37. Sumner, *Diary*, 227.

38. Ibid.

Chapter 5: Lincoln's Inauguration and War Begins

1. *New York Times*, 18 February 1861.

2. *The Papers of Jefferson Davis*, vol. 7, pp. 45–51, transcribed from the *Congressional Journal*, vol. 1, pp. 64–66.

3. Merlin E. Sumner, ed., *The Diary of Cyrus B. Comstock* (Dayton, OH: Morningside House, 1987), 228.

4. *Harper's Weekly*, 16 March 1861, 166.

5. Ibid.

6. Jessie A. Marshall, ed., *Private and Official Correspondence of Gen. Benjamin F. Butler* (Norwood, MA: Plimpton Press, 1917), 43.

7. *Harper's Weekly*, 16 March 1861, 166.

8. Ibid.

9. Sumner, *Diary*, 229.

10. Ibid.

11. Brig. Gen. P.G.T. Beauregard's aide-de-camp's message to Major Robert Anderson, 12 April 1861.

12. Richard S. West, Jr., *Lincoln's Scapegoat General: A Life of Benjamin F. Butler, 1818–1893* (Boston: Houghton Mifflin, 1965), 42.

13. David D. Ryan, ed., *A Yankee Spy in Richmond: The Civil War Diary of "Crazy Bet" Van Lew* (Mechanicsburg, PA: Stackpole Books, 2001), 32.

14. West, *Lincoln's Scapegoat*, 61.

15. Ibid., 73.

16. Ibid., 81.

17. Ibid., 82.

18. Ibid., 84.

19. Marshall, *Private and Official*, 43.

20. Department Letter,14 October 1861; Special Orders No. 279, 15 October 1861, Returns of the Corps of Engineers, April 1832–December 1916, M851/Roll 2, National Archives.

21. Spring Grove Cemetery, Cincinnati, Ohio, Section 30, Lot 91.

Chapter 6: From Cincinnati to New Orleans

1. Jean H. Baker, *Mary Todd Lincoln: A Biography* (New York: Norton, 1989), 157.

2. Dept. Letter, 14 October 1861; Special Orders No. 279, 15 October 1861, Returns of the Corps of Engineers, April 1832–December 1916, M851/Roll 2, National Archives.

3. *Louisville Anzeiger*, 11 October 1861.

4. Special Orders No. 312 (HQA), 23 November 1861, Returns of the Corps of Engineers, April 1832–December 1916, M851/Roll 2, National Archives.

5. Journal of the Executive Proceedings of the U.S. Senate, 27 February 1863.

6. David D. Porter, *The Opening of the Lower Mississippi* (New York: Yoseloff, 1956), 22.

7. James P. Duffy, *Lincoln's Admiral: The Civil War Campaigns of David Farragut* (Hoboken, NJ: Wiley, 1997), 52.

8. Porter, *Opening*, 23.

9. Duffy, *Lincoln's Admiral*, 49.

10. Porter, *Opening*, 23.

11. Ibid., 25.

12. Ibid., 26.

13. Richard S. West, Jr., *Lincoln's Scapegoat General: A Life of Benjamin F. Butler, 1818–1893* (Boston: Houghton Mifflin, 1965), 119 .

14. *Journal of the Executive Proceedings of the U.S. Senate*, 6 May 1858.

15. Special Orders No. 37, 19 February 1862, Returns of the Corps of Engineers, April 1832–December 1916, M851/Roll 2, National Archives.

16. George N. Carpenter, *History of the Eighth Regiment Vermont Volunteers, 1861–1865* (Boston: Deland and Barta, 1886), 153.

17. Benjamin F. Butler, *Butler's Book: Autobiography and Personal Reminiscences of Major-General Benjamin F. Butler* (Boston: Thayer, 1892), 355–56.

18. Jessie A. Marshall, ed., *Private and Official Correspondence of General Benjamin F. Butler* (Norwood, MA: Plimpton Press, 1917), 188.

19. James R. Soley, "Early Operations in the Gulf," in *Battles and Leaders of the Civil War*, ed. Robert U. Johnson and Clarence C. Buel (New York: Century, 1884, 1887–88), 2:13.

20. West, *Lincoln's Scapegoat*, 117.

21. Ibid., 121.

Chapter 7: The Capture of New Orleans

1. Richard S. West, Jr., *Lincoln's Scapegoat General: A Life of Benjamin F. Butler, 1818–1893* (Boston: Houghton Mifflin, 1965), 123.

2. Ibid., 358–59.

3. Benjamin F. Butler, *Butler's Book: Autobiography and Personal Reminiscences of Major-General Benjamin F. Butler* (Boston: Thayer, 1892), 359.

4. Hans L. Trefousse, *Ben Butler: The South Called Him Beast!* (New York: Twayne, 1957), 100.

5. David D. Porter, *The Naval History of the Civil War* (Mineola, NY: Dover, 1998), 230–31.

6. *Harper's Weekly*, 24 May 1862, p. 327.

7. Porter, *Naval History*, 230–31.

8. *Harper's Weekly*, 24 May 1862, p. 327.

9. Butler, *Butler's Book*, 360.

10. Testimony of Maj-Gen. Godfrey Weitzel, *Report to the Joint Committee on the Conduct of the War, at the Second Session, Thirty-Eighth Congress* (7 February 1865).

11. Butler, *Butler's Book*, 361.

12. West, *Lincoln's Scapegoat*, 125.

13. Ibid.

14. Porter, *Naval History*, 180.

15. Butler, *Butler's Book*, 365.

16. Ibid.

17. *Harper's Weekly*, 24 May 1862, p. 327.

18. Butler, *Butler's Book*, 366.

19. *Harper's Weekly*, 24 May 1862, p. 327.

20. West, *Lincoln's Scapegoat*, 126.

21. James P. Duffy, *Lincoln's Admiral: The Civil War Campaigns of David Farragut* (Hoboken, NJ: Wiley, 1997), 22.

22. *Harper's Weekly*, 24 May 1862, p. 327.

23. Butler, *Butler's Book*, 438.

24. West, *Lincoln's Scapegoat*, 127.

25. Butler, *Butler's Book*, 439.

26. Ibid.

27. Ibid., 365.

28. Jessie A. Marshall, ed., *Private and Official Correspondence of Gen. Benjamin F. Butler*, vol. 2 (Norwood, MA: Plimpton Press, 1917), 43.

29. George N. Carpenter, *History of the Eighth Regiment Vermont Volunteers, 1861–1865* (Boston: Deland and Barta, 1886), 153.

Chapter 8: Occupation of the Crescent City

1. Elizabeth J. Doyle, "Civilian Life in Occupied New Orleans, 1862–65" (PhD Diss., Louisiana State University, 1955), 1.

2. Ibid., 3.

3. Benjamin F. Butler, *Butler's Book: Autobiography and Personal Reminiscences of Major-General Benjamin F. Butler* (Boston: Thayer, 1892), 374 (hereafter cited in text as *BB*).

4. Homer B. Sprague, *History of the Thirteenth Infantry Regiment of Connecticut Volunteers during the Great Rebellion* (Hartford, CT: Lockwood, 1867) 52.

5. G. Weitzel to M. D. Fairex, 25 June 1881, *Letter Press Volumes of Gen. G. Weitzel*, vol. 1, p. 578, Cincinnati Historical Society Library.

6. Sprague, *History of the Thirteenth Infantry*, 52.

7. Ibid., 54.

8. Special Orders No. 179, 10 July 1862, in *Private and Official Correspondence of Gen. Benjamin F. Butler*, vol. 2 (Norwood, MA: Plimpton Press, 1917), 57.

9. Marshall, *Private and Official*, 426.

10. United States War Department, *The War of the Rebellion: A Compilation of the Official Records of the Union and Confederate Armies* (Washington: Government Printing Office, 1894–1922), Ser. 2, Vol. 5, pp. 795–97 (hereafter cited in notes as O.R.).

11. S. E. Howard, "Eighth Vermont Infantry Regimental History," Vermont-CivilWar.Org Database, http://vermontcivilwar.org/units/8/history.php.

12. Sprague, *History of the Thirteenth Infantry*, 58.

13. Ibid., 50.

14. Doyle, "Civilian Life," 259.

15. Sec. E. M. Stanton to Gen. B. F. Butler, 23 June 1862, Item MSS 154, Historic New Orleans Collection, Williams Research Center.

16. Marshall, *Private and Official*, 59.

17. John C. Breckinridge, address at Bowling Green, Kentucky, 8 October 1861.

18. *Journal of the U.S. Senate*, 4 December 1861, Library of Congress.

19. Marshall, *Private and Official*, 168.

20. Ibid., 159.

21. Ibid., 158.

22. Ibid., 159.

23. O.R., Ser. 1, Vol. 15, p. 51.

24. Marshall, *Private and Official*, 170.

25. George N. Carpenter, *History of the Eighth Regiment Vermont Volunteers, 1861–1865* (Boston: Deland and Barta, 1886), 153.

26. Carpenter, *History of the Eighth Regiment*, 41.

27. Marshall, *Private and Official*, 147.

Chapter 9: The Lafourche Campaign

1. Benjamin F. Butler, *Butler's Book: Autobiography and Personal Reminiscences of Major-General Benjamin F. Butler* (Boston: Thayer, 1892), 495.

2. Jessie A. Marshall, ed., *Private and Official Correspondence of Gen. Benjamin F. Butler*, vol. 2 (Norwood, MA: Plimpton Press, 1917), 43 (hereafter cited in text as *POC*).

3. Return for August 1862, Returns of the Corps of Engineers, April 1832–December 1916, M851/Roll 2, National Archives.

4. Butler, *Butler's Book*, 495.

5. G. Weitzel to M. D. Fairex, 25 June 1881, *Letter Press Volumes of Gen. G. Weitzel*, vol. 1, p. 578, Archives of the Cincinnati Historical Society Library.

6. Homer B. Sprague, *History of the Thirteenth Infantry Regiment of Connecticut Volunteers during the Great Rebellion* (Hartford, CT: Lockwood, 1867), 74.

7. Ibid., 75.

8. John W. De Forest, *A Volunteer's Adventures: A Union Captain's Record of the Civil War*, ed. James H. Croushore (New Haven, CT: Yale University Press, 1946), 53.

9. Richard H. Steckel, "A History of the Standard of Living in the United States," EH.Net Encyclopedia, ed. Robert Whaples, July 22, 2002, http://eh.net/encyclopedia/?article=steckel.standard.living.us.

10. De Forest, *Volunteer's Adventures*, 54.

11. Ibid.

12. Elliot G. Storke, *History of Cayuga County, New York* (Syracuse, NY: Mason, 1879), 126.

13. Sprague, *History of the Thirteenth Infantry*, 75.

14. Hans L. Trefousse, *Ben Butler: The South Called Him Beast!* (New York: Twayne, 1957), 100.

15. Sec. E. M. Stanton to Gen. B. F. Butler, 23 June 1862, Item MSS 154, Historic New Orleans Collection, Williams Research Center.

16. Sprague, *History of the Thirteenth Infantry*, 78.
17. O.R., Ser. 1, Vol. 19, p. 141.
18. Butler, *Butler's Book*.
19. *New York Times*, 3 November 1862.
20. Ibid.
21. Ibid.
22. Ibid.
23. De Forest, *Volunteer's Adventures*, 53.
24. *New York Times*, 27 October 1862.
25. O.R., Ser. 1, Vol. 19, p. 326.
26. O.R., Ser. 1, Vol. 15, p. 166.
27. *New York Times*, 5 November 1862.
28. Ibid.
29. Ibid., 8.
30. Elliot G. Storke, *History of Cayuga County, New York* (Syracuse, NY: Mason, 1879), 126.
31. Sun-tzu, *The Art of War* (New York: Barnes and Noble, 2003), 12.
32. *New York Times*, 27 October 1862.
33. Sprague, *History of the Thirteenth Infantry*, 78.
34. F. S. Twitchell letter, Item MSS 282, Historic New Orleans Collection, Williams Research Center.
35. *New York Times*, 27 October 1862.
36. O.R., Ser. 1, Vol. 15, p. 176.
37. Sprague, *History of the Thirteenth Infantry*, 79.
38. Ibid., 81.
39. O.R., Ser. 1, Vol. 15, pp. 167–70.
40. *New York Times*, 17 November 1862.
41. O.R., Ser. 1, Vol. 15, pp. 167–70.
42. De Forest, *Volunteer's Adventures*, 55.
43. Sprague, *History of the Thirteenth Infantry*, 82.
44. De Forest, *Volunteer's Adventures*, 56.

Chapter 10: Fighting in the Bayous

1. Homer B. Sprague, *History of the Thirteenth Infantry Regiment of Connecticut Volunteers during the Great Rebellion* (Hartford, CT: Lockwood, 1867), 82.
2. John W. De Forest, *A Volunteer's Adventures: A Union Captain's Record of the Civil War*, ed. James H. Croushore (New Haven, CT: Yale University Press, 1946), 56.
3. Sprague, *History of the Thirteenth Infantry*, 80.
4. De Forest, *Volunteer's Adventures*, 56.
5. Ibid.
6. Elliot G. Storke, *History of Cayuga County, New York* (Syracuse, NY: Mason, 1879), 127.
7. Sprague, *History of the Thirteenth Infantry*, 79.
8. De Forest, *Volunteer's Adventures*, 57.

9. Ibid., 56.

10. Sprague, *History of the Thirteenth Infantry*, 80.

11. Ibid., 82.

12. Ibid.

13. Ibid., 83.

14. O.R., Ser. 1, Vol. 15, pp. 167–70.

15. De Forest, *Volunteer's Adventures*, 58; Sprague, *History of the Thirteenth Infantry*, 83.

16. O.R., Ser. 1, Vol. 15, pp. 167–70.

17. Sprague, *History of the Thirteenth Infantry*, 84.

18. Ibid.

19. Ibid., 87.

20. Ibid.

21. De Forest, *Volunteer's Adventures*, 61.

22. Ibid.

23. F. S. Twitchell letter, Item MSS 282, Historic New Orleans Collection, Williams Research Center.

24. Sprague, *History of the Thirteenth Infantry*, 87.

25. Ibid., 88.

26. Ibid., 89.

27. De Forest, *Volunteer's Adventures*, 62.

28. Ibid., 62.

29. Ibid., 62, 63.

30. Sprague, *History of the Thirteenth Infantry*, 89.

31. Twitchell letter (see note 23 above).

32. De Forest, *Volunteer's Adventures*, 67.

33. Twitchell letter (see note 23 above).

34. De Forest, *Volunteer's Adventures*, 69, 70.

35. Ibid., 69.

36. Ibid., 67.

37. Sprague, *History of the Thirteenth Infantry*, 91.

38. Ibid.

39. George N. Carpenter, *History of the Eighth Regiment Vermont Volunteers, 1861–1865* (Boston: Deland and Barta, 1886), 154.

40. Sprague, *History of the Thirteenth Infantry*, 24.

41. Jessie A. Marshall, ed., *Private and Official Correspondence of Gen. Benjamin F. Butler*, vol. 2 (Norwood, MA: Plimpton Press, 1917), 490.

42. Twitchell letter (see note 23 above).

43. Sprague, *History of the Thirteenth Infantry*, 92.

44. O.R., Ser. 1, Vol. 15, pp. 167–70.

45. Marshall, *Private and Official*, 427.

46. O.R., Ser. 1, Vol. 15, p. 170.

47. Marshall, *Private and Official*, 430.

48. Ibid., 429.

49. O.R., Ser. 1, Vol. 15, pp. 167–70.

50. Marshall, *Private and Official*, 439.

51. O.R., Ser. 1, Vol. 15, pp. 167–70.

52. Carpenter, *History of the Eighth Regiment*, 15.

53. S. E. Howard, "Eighth Vermont Infantry Regimental History," Vermont CivilWar.Org Database, http://vermontcivilwar.org/units/8/history.php.

54. O.R., Ser. 1, Vol. 15, p. 171.

55. O.R., Ser. 1, Vol. 15, p. 164.

56. Marshall, *Private and Official*, 461.

Chapter 11: Commanding Black Troops

1. Benjamin F. Butler, *Butler's Book: Autobiography and Personal Reminiscences of Major-General Benjamin F. Butler* (Boston: Thayer, 1892), 495.

2. Ibid., 496–97.

3. O.R., Ser. 1, Vol. 15, p. 171.

4. Butler, *Butler's Book*, 497.

5. O.R., Ser. 1, Vol. 15, p. 164.

6. Ibid.

7. Ibid.

8. David D. Ryan, ed., *A Yankee Spy in Richmond: The Civil War Diary of "Crazy Bet" Van Lew* (Mechanicsburg, PA: Stackpole Books, 2001), 33.

9. Butler, *Butler's Book*, 496–97.

10. O.R., Ser. 1, Vol. 15, p. 172.

11. O.R., Ser. 1, Vol. 15, pp. 164–66.

12. Butler, *Butler's Book*, 499.

13. John D. Winters, *The Civil War in Louisiana* (Baton Rouge: Louisiana State University Press, 1991), 307.

14. Joseph T. Glatthaar, *Forged in Battle: The Civil War Alliance of Black Soldiers and White Officers* (Baton Rouge: Louisiana State University Press, 1990), 156–57.

15. Butler, *Butler's Book*, 498.

16. Dudley Taylor Cornish, *The Sable Arm: Negro Troops in the Union Army, 1861–1865* (New York: Norton, 1966), 281.

17. Proclamation of Confederate President Jefferson Davis, 23 December 1862; O.R., Ser. 2, Vol. 5, pp. 795–97.

18. James M. McPherson, *Tried by War: Abraham Lincoln as Commander in Chief* (New York: Penguin, 2008), 151.

19. Jessie A. Marshall, ed., *Private and Official Correspondence of Gen. Benjamin F. Butler*, vol. 2 (Norwood, MA: Plimpton Press, 1917), 554.

20. Ibid., 556.

21. Ibid., 339.

22. Chester G. Hearn, *When the Devil Came Down to Dixie: Ben Butler in New Orleans* (Baton Rouge: Louisiana State University Press, 1997), 105.

23. Ad placed by Richard Yeadon, of Charleston, South Carolina, 1 January 1863.

24. O.R., Ser. 2, Vol. 5, pp. 795–97.

25. Ibid.

26. Ibid.

27. Ibid.

28. Marshall, *Private and Official*, 571.

29. Butler, *Butler's Book*, 549–50.

30. Ibid., 550.

31. Ibid.

Chapter 12: Destroying The *J.A. Cotton*

1. O.R., Ser. 1, Vol. 15, p. 641.

2. Joseph T. Glatthaar, *Forged in Battle: The Civil War Alliance of Black Soldiers and White Officers* (Baton Rouge: Louisiana State University Press, 1990), 36.

3. O.R., Ser. 1, Vol. 15, p. 234.

4. O.R., Ser. 1, Vol. 19, p. 539.

5. S. E. Howard, "Eighth Vermont Infantry Regimental History," VermontCivil War.Org Database. http://vermontcivilwar.org/units/8/history.php.

6. O.R., Ser. 1, Vol. 19, p. 520.

7. Ibid., pp. 494–95.

8. Ibid., p. 518.

9. *Harper's Weekly*, 14 February 1863, 103.

10. O.R., Ser. 1, Vol. 19, p. 516.

11. Ibid., p. 523; *Houston Tri-Weekly Telegraph*, 2 February 1863.

12. O.R. Ser. 1, Vol. 19, p. 552.

13. Ibid., p. 522.

14. Ibid.

15. *Harper's Weekly*, 14 February 1863, 103.

16. Leland R. Johnson, *The Falls City Engineers: A History of the Louisville District, Corps of Engineers, United States Army, 1970–1983* (Louisville, KY: U.S. Army Corps of Engineers, 1975), 122.

17. O.R., Ser. 1, Vol. 19, p. 516.

18. Ibid., pp. 519–20.

19. Ibid., p. 518.

20. *Harper's Weekly*, 14 February 1863, 103.

21. Howard, "Eighth Vermont Infantry."

22. Howard, "Eighth Vermont Infantry."

23. O.R., Ser. 1, Vol. 19, p. 523, *Houston Tri-Weekly*, note 11, above.

24. Ibid.

25. Howard, "Eighth Vermont Infantry. "

26. O.R., Ser. 1, Vol. 19, p. 520.

27. Ibid., pp. 519–20.

28. Ibid, p. 523, *Houston Tri-Weekly Telegraph*, note 11, above.

29. O.R., Ser. 1, Vol. 19, pp. 517–18.

30. Ibid., p. 233.

31. Return for March 1863, Returns of the Corps of Engineers, April 1832–December 1916, M851/Roll 2, National Archives.

32. Homer B. Sprague, *History of the Thirteenth Infantry Regiment of Connecticut Volunteers during the Great Rebellion* (Hartford, CT: Lockwood, 1867), 99.

33. Jessie A. Marshall, ed., *Private and Official Correspondence of Gen. Benjamin F. Butler*, vol. 2 (Norwood, MA: Plimpton Press, 1917), 587.

34. Marshall, *Private and Official*, 593.

35. A. Lincoln to E. Stanton, 23 January 1863, in Roy P. Basler, ed., *Collected Works of Abraham Lincoln*, vol. 6 (New Brunswick, NJ: Rutgers University Press, 1953), 76–77.

36. John W. De Forest, *A Volunteer's Adventures: A Union Captain's Record of the Civil War*, ed. James H. Croushore (New Haven, CT: Yale University Press, 1946), 82.

37. Sprague, *History of the Thirteenth Infantry*, 101.

38. De Forest, *Volunteer's Adventures*, 86.

39. Ibid.

40. Ibid., 88.

41. Ibid.

42. Ibid, 89.

43. Ibid.

44. Sprague, *History of the Thirteenth Infantry*, 110.

45. De Forest, *Volunteer's Adventures*, 91.

46. O.R., Ser. 1, Vol. 26, p. 10.

47. De Forest, *Volunteer's Adventures*, 91.

48. Sprague, *History of the Thirteenth Infantry*, 101.

49. Ibid., 92.

Chapter 13: Battle of Port Hudson

1. O.R., Ser. 1, Vol. 26, p. 11.

2. John W. De Forest, *A Volunteer's Adventures: A Union Captain's Record of the Civil War*, ed. James H. Croushore (New Haven, CT: Yale University Press, 1946), 100.

3. Ibid.

4. De Forest, *Volunteer's Adventures*, 101.

5. From *The Papers of Jefferson Davis*, vol. 8, 565–84, transcribed from the *Memphis Appeal*, 29 December 1862.

6. Homer B. Sprague, *History of the Thirteenth Infantry Regiment of Connecticut Volunteers during the Great Rebellion* (Hartford, CT: Lockwood, 1867), 103.

7. George N. Carpenter, *History of the Eighth Regiment Vermont Volunteers, 1861–1865* (Boston: Deland and Barta, 1886), 112.

8. O.R., Ser. 1, Vol. 26, p. 92.

9. Ibid., p. 505.

10. Ibid., p. 506.

11. DeForest, *Volunteer's Adventures*, 105.

12. Richard B. Irwin, *History of the Nineteenth Army Corps* (Fairford: Echo Library, 2009), 97.

13. O.R., Ser. 1, Vol. 26, p. 93.

14. Irwin, *History of the Nineteenth Army Corps*, 98.

15. Carpenter, *History of the Eighth Regiment*, 114.

16. De Forest, *Volunteer's Adventures*, 105.

17. Ibid.

18. Irwin, *History of the Nineteenth Army Corps*, 98.

19. Ibid., 97.

20. Ibid.

21. Ibid., 98.

22. De Forest, *Volunteer's Adventures*, 108.

23. Irwin, *History of the Nineteenth Army Corps*, 98.

24. De Forest, *Volunteer's Adventures*, 111.

25. Ibid., 112.

26. Irwin, *History of the Nineteenth Army Corps*, 101.

27. O.R., Ser. 1, Vol. 26, p. 506.

28. Carpenter, *History of the Eighth Regiment*, 115.

29. Ibid, p. 114.

30. Ibid.

31. S. E. Howard, "Eighth Vermont Infantry Regimental History," Vermont CivilWar.Org Database, http://vermontcivilwar.org/units/8/history.php.

32. De Forest, *Volunteer's Adventures*, 114.

33. Christian A. Fleetwood, *The Negro as a Soldier* (Washington, DC: Cook, 1895).

34. P. F. DeGournay, "The Siege of Port Hudson," *New Orleans Weekly Times*.

35. O.R., Ser. 1, Vol. 26, p. 512.

36. Ibid., pp. 119–20.

37. Ibid., p. 109.

38. Sun-tzu, *The Art of War* (New York: Barnes and Noble, 2003), 9.

39. O.R., Ser. 1, Vol. 26, p. 109.

40. De Forest, *Volunteer's Adventures*, 116.

41. O.R., Ser. 1, Vol. 26, p. 131.

42. DeForest, *Volunteer's Adventures*, 133.

43. Ibid.

44. Carpenter, *History of the Eighth Regiment*, 123.

45. De Forest, *Volunteer's Adventures*, 133.

46. Ibid., 133, 134.

47. Irwin, *History of the Nineteenth Army Corps*, 113.

48. Ibid.

49. William H. Barnes, *The Fortieth Congress of the United States: Historical and Biographical*, vol. 2 (New York: Perine, 1870), 120.

50. DeForest, *Volunteer's Adventures*, 135.

51. Ibid., 136.

52. Carpenter, *History of the Eighth Regiment*, 124.

53. Howard, "Eighth Vermont Infantry."

54. Edward Cunningham, *The Port Hudson Campaign, 1862–1863* (Baton Rouge: Louisiana State University Press, 1963), 117.

55. O.R., Ser. 1, Vol. 26, p. 119.

56. James P. Duffy, *Lincoln's Admiral: The Civil War Campaigns of David Farragut* (Hoboken, NJ: Wiley, 1997), 3.

57. De Forest, *Volunteer's Adventures*, 145.

58. O.R., Ser. 1, Vol. 26, p. 626.

Chapter 14: Thibodeaux and the Sabine Pass

1. Richard B. Irwin, *History of the Nineteenth Army Corps* (Fairford: Echo Library, 2009), 251.

2. George N. Carpenter, *History of the Eighth Regiment Vermont Volunteers, 1861–1865* (Boston: Deland and Barta, 1886), 137.

3. John W. De Forest, *A Volunteer's Adventures: A Union Captain's Record of the Civil War*, ed. James H. Croushore (New Haven, CT: Yale University Press, 1946), 150.

4. Ibid.

5. Irwin, *History of the Nineteenth Army Corps*, 251.

6. De Forest, *Volunteer's Adventures*, 56.

7. Ibid., 252.

8. Irwin, *History of the Nineteenth Army Corps*, 143.

9. De Forest, *Volunteer's Adventures*, 252.

10. O.R.N., Ser. 1, Vol. 26, p. 230.

11. Ibid., p. 214.

12. Irwin, *History of the Nineteenth Army Corps*, 253.

13. Ibid.

14. Ibid., 142.

15. Ibid., 256.

16. Carpenter, *History of the Eighth Regiment*, 137.

17. Irwin, *History of the Nineteenth Army Corps*, 147.

18. Ibid., 148.

19. James M. McPherson, *Tried by War: Abraham Lincoln as Commander in Chief* (New York: Penguin, 2008), 188.

20. Edward T. Cotham, Jr., *Sabine Pass: The Confederacy's Thermopylae* (Austin: University of Texas Press, 2004), 5.

21. Ibid., 150.

22. Benjamin F. Butler, *Butler's Book: Autobiography and Personal Reminiscences of Major-General Benjamin F. Butler* (Boston: Thayer, 1892), 466–67.

23. Cotham, *Sabine Pass*, 12–13.

24. Ibid., 30.

25. Ibid., 30–31.

26. O.R., Ser. 1, Vol. 15, p. 237.

27. O.R.N., Ser. 1, Vol. 19, pp. 431–32.

28. Ibid., p. 525.

29. Ibid., p. 539.

30. Ibid., p. 618.

31. O.R., Ser. 1, Vol. 26, p. 288.

32. O.R., Ser. 1, Vol. 38, pp. 299–300.

33. Cotham, *Sabine Pass*, 104.

34. Ibid.

35. Ibid.

36. Ibid., 108.

37. O.R., Ser. 1, Vol. 38, pp. 298–99.

38. Ibid., pp. 299–300.

39. Ibid., pp. 298–99.

40. Cotham, *Sabine Pass*, 109.

41. Ibid., 115, 116.

42. O.R., Ser. 1, Vol. 38, pp. 299–300.

43. Cotham, *Sabine Pass*, 121.

44. Ibid., 131.

45. Ibid., 132, 133.

46. O.R., Ser. 1, Vol. 38, pp. 298–99.

47. Ibid., pp. 299–300.

48. O.R.N., Ser. 1, Vol. 26, p. 293.

49. O.R., Ser. 1, Vol. 38, pp. 299–300.

50. Ibid., pp. 298–99.

Chapter 15: Reunited: Drewry's Bluff and the Spring Campaign of 1864

1. John D. Winters, *The Civil War in Louisiana* (Baton Rouge: Louisiana State University Press, 1991), 296.

2. O.R., Ser. 1, Vol. 38, pp. 299–300.

3. John W. De Forest, *A Volunteer's Adventures: A Union Captain's Record of the Civil War*, ed. James H. Croushore (New Haven, CT: Yale University Press, 1946), 154.

4. Benjamin F. Butler, *Butler's Book: Autobiography and Personal Reminiscences of Major-General Benjamin F. Butler* (Boston: Thayer, 1892), 897 (hereafter cited in text as *BB*).

5. O.R., Ser. 1, Vol. 26, p. 837.

6. O.R., Ser. 1, Vol. 53, p. 592.

7. Napier Bartlett, *A Soldier's Story of the War: Including the Marches and Battles of the Washington Artillery, and of Other Louisiana Troops* (New Orleans: Clark and Hofeline, 1874).

8. Richard S. West, Jr., *Lincoln's Scapegoat General: A Life of Benjamin F. Butler, 1818–1893* (Boston: Houghton Mifflin, 1965), 232.

9. O.R., Ser. 1, Vol. 51, p. 1161.

10. E.O.C. Ord (21 July–4 September); John Gibbon (4–22 September); E. O. C. Ord (22–29 September); Charles A. Heckman (29 September–1 October).

11. *Harper's Weekly*, 21 May 1864.

12. Godfrey Weitzel to Louisa Bogen, 8 May 1864.

13. Asa W. Bartlett, *History of the Twelfth Regiment: New Hampshire Volunteers in the War of the Rebellion* (Concord, NH: Evans, 1897), 188–92.

14. Ibid.

15. Godfrey Weitzel letter to Louisa Bogen, 21 May 1864.

16. Bartlett, *History of the Twelfth Regiment*, 188–92.

17. West, *Lincoln's Scapegoat General*, 237.

18. *Janesville (WI) Daily Gazette*, 2 July 1864.

19. West, *Lincoln's Scapegoat General*, 237.

20. Godfrey Weitzel to Louisa Bogen, 21 May 1864.

21. Merlin E. Sumner, ed., *The Diary of Cyrus B. Comstock* (Dayton, OH: Morningside House, 1987) , 272.

22. Ibid., 277.

23. Ibid.

24. Ibid.

25. Sumner, *Diary*, 283.

26. Jack D. Welsh, *Medical Histories of Union Generals* (Kent, OH: Kent State University Press, 1996), 363.

27. Testimony of Maj-Gen. Godfrey Weitzel, *Report of the Joint Committee on the Conduct of the War, at the Second Session, Thirty-Eighth Congress*, 7 February 1865.

28. Ibid.

29. Ibid.

30. Ibid.

31. Ibid.

32. Ibid.

33. Ulysses S. Grant, *Personal Memoirs of U. S. Grant*, vol. 2 (New York: Webster, 1885), 334.

34. Weitzel testimony (see note 27 above).

35. Sumner, *Diary*, 291.

36. Ibid., 291, 292.

37. Ibid., 293.

38. Bob Blaisdell, ed., *The Civil War: A Book of Quotations* (Mineola, NY: Dover, 2004), 153.

Chapter 16: Fort Fisher and Ben Butler's Powder Boat

1. Benjamin F. Butler, *Butler's Book: Autobiography and Personal Reminiscences of Major-General Benjamin F. Butler* (Boston: Thayer, 1892), 813 (hereafter cited in text as *BB*).

2. Ulysses S. Grant, *Personal Memoirs of U. S. Grant*, vol. 2 (New York: Webster, 1885), 387.

3. Robert S. Henry, *The Story of the Confederacy* (New York: Grosset and Dunlap, 1931), 437.

4. William Lamb, "Defence of Fort Fisher, North Carolina," in *Operations on the Atlantic Coast, 1861–1865; Virginia, 1862, 1864; Vicksburg*, vol. 9, ed. Theodore F. Dwight (Boston: Military Historical Society of Massachusetts, 1912), 358 (hereafter cited in text as DFF).

5. O.R., Ser. 1, Vol. 42, pp. 837–38.

6. Richard S. West Jr., *Lincoln's Scapegoat General: A Life of Benjamin F. Butler, 1818–1893* (Boston: Houghton Mifflin, 1965), 281.

7. Ibid.

8. O.R., Ser. 1, Vol. 42, p. 799.

9. Ibid.

10. West, *Lincoln's Scapegoat General*, 283.

11. Maj. Gen. Godfrey Weitzel testimony, *Report of the Joint Committee on the Conduct of the War, at the Second Session, Thirty-Eighth Congress*, 7 February 1865.

12. Report of Maj.-Gen. Godfrey Weitzel, 25th Army Corps, 31 December 1864, O.R., Ser. 1, Vol. 42, pp. 985–87.

13. Ibid.

14. Ibid.

15. Merlin E. Sumner, ed., *The Diary of Cyrus B. Comstock* (Dayton, OH: Morningside House, 1987), 297.

16. Ibid.

17. Weitzel report (see note 12 above).

18. Sumner, *Diary*, 298.

19. Weitzel report (see note 12 above).

20. West, *Lincoln's Scapegoat General*, 285.

21. Ibid., 284.

22. Weitzel report (see note 12 above).

Chapter 17: Christmas Day, 1864: Attack on Fort Fisher

1. William Lamb, "Defence of Fort Fisher, North Carolina," in *Operations on the Atlantic Coast, 1861–1865; Virginia, 1862, 1864; Vicksburg*, vol. 9, ed. Theodore F. Dwight (Boston: Military Historical Society of Massachusetts, 1912), 361 (hereafter cited in text as DFF).

2. Scott W. Stucky, "Joint Operations in the Civil War," *Joint Force Quarterly* 6 (Autumn–Winter 1994–95): 10.

3. Report of Maj-Gen. Godfrey Weitzel, 31 December 1864, O.R., Ser. I, vol. 42, pp. 985-987.

4. Richard S. West, Jr., *Lincoln's Scapegoat General: A Life of Benjamin F. Butler, 1818–1893* (Boston: Houghton Mifflin, 1965), 287; Weitzel report (see note 3 above).

5. Testimony of Maj-Gen. Benjamin F. Butler, *Report of the Joint Committee on the Conduct of the War, at the Second Session, Thirty-Eighth Congress*, 17 January 1865.

6. Testimony of Maj-Gen. Godfrey Weitzel, *Report of the Joint Committee on the Conduct of the War, at the Second Session, Thirty-Eighth Congress*, 7 February 1865.

7. Ibid.

8. Merlin E. Sumner, ed., *The Diary of Cyrus B. Comstock* (Dayton, OH: Morningside House, 1987), 298.

9. Ibid., 299.

10. Ibid.

11. Weitzel report (see note 3 above).

12. Benjamin F. Butler, Butler's Book: *Autobiography and Personal Reminiscences of Major-General Benjamin F. Butler* (Boston: Thayer, 1892), 790–91 (hereafter cited in text as *BB*).

13. Weitzel report (see note 3 above).

14. Butler testimony (see note 5 above).

15. Ibid.

16. Ibid.

17. West, *Lincoln's Scapegoat General*, 287.

18. Weitzel testimony, p. 72 (see note 6 above).

19. Weitzel report (see note 3 above).

20. Butler testimony (see note 5 above).

21. Ibid.

22. Ibid.

23. Ibid.

24. Ibid., p. 23.

25. West, *Lincoln's Scapegoat General*, 289.

26. Butler testimony, p. 24 (see note 5 above).

27. West, *Lincoln's Scapegoat General*, 289.

28. Weitzel report (see note 3 above).

29. Ibid.

30. Sumner, *Diary*, 299.

31. Comstock testimony, *Report of the Joint Committee on the Conduct of the War, at the Second Session, Thirty-Eighth Congress*, pp. 84–85.

32. Ibid.

33. West, *Lincoln's Scapegoat General*, 288.

34. Weitzel report (see note 3 above).

35. Weitzel testimony (see note 6 above).

36. Hans L. Trefousse, *Ben Butler: The South Called Him Beast!* (New York: Twayne, 1957), 172.

37. Weitzel report (see note 3 above).

38. Ulysses S. Grant, *Personal Memoirs of U. S. Grant*, vol. 2 (New York: Webster, 1885), 395.

39. Ibid.

Chapter 18: The Trial of Benjamin F. Butler

1. Benjamin F. Butler, *Butler's Book: Autobiography and Personal Reminiscences of Major-General Benjamin F. Butler* (Boston: Thayer, 1892), 829.

2. Thomas P. Lowry, *The Story the Soldiers Wouldn't Tell: Sex in the Civil War* (Mechanicsburg, PA: Stackpole Books, 1994), 170.

3. Shelby D. Foote, *The Civil War: A Narrative*, vol. 3, *Red River to Appomattox* (New York: Random House, 1974), 743.

4. Ibid., 741–42; Rod Gragg, *Confederate Goliath: The Battle of Fort Fisher* (New York: HarperCollins, 1991), 114.

5. Foote, *Civil War*, 742.

6. Ibid., 746.

7. National Academy of Sciences, *Biographical Memoirs*, vol. 2, *Cyrus Ballou Comstock* (Washington, DC, 1911), 199.

8. "Testimony of Maj-Gen. Benjamin F. Butler," in *Report of the Joint Committee on the Conduct of the War, at the Second Session, Thirty-Eighth Congress*, 17 January 1865.

9. Ibid.

10. Ibid.

11. Ibid.

12. Testimony of Maj-Gen. Godfrey Weitzel, *Report of the Joint Committee on the Conduct of the War, at the Second Session, Thirty-Eighth Congress*, 7 February 1865.

13. Comstock Testimony, *Report of the Joint Committee on the Conduct of the War, at the Second Session, Thirty-Eighth Congress Joint Committee*.

14. Ibid.

15. Ibid.

16. *Report of the Joint Committee on the Conduct of the War, at the Second Session, Thirty-Eighth Congress*, 17 January 1865.

17. Porter testimony in ibid.

18. Butler, *Butler's Book*, 821.

19. Ibid., 822.

20. Ibid.

21. Library of Congress, *A Century of Lawmaking for a New Nation: U.S. Congressional Documents and Debates, 1774–1875* (Washington, DC: U.S. Library of Congress), http://memory.loc.gov/ammem/amlaw/lawhome.html.

Chapter 19: Final Days of War

1. O.R., Ser. 1, Vol. 51, pp. 1201–2.

2. Ibid.

3. Ulysses S. Grant, *Personal Memoirs of U. S. Grant*, vol. 2 (New York: Webster, 1885), 618.

4. O.R., Ser. 1, Vol. 46, Part 3, p. 51.

5. Grant, *Personal Memoirs*, 411.

6. Report of Col. James Shaw, Jr., 7th U.S. Colored Troops, April 26, 1865; O.R., Ser. I, Vol. 43, p. 1234.

7. Godfrey Weitzel, "Entry of the United States Forces into Richmond, April 3, 1865," in *Letter Book of Gen. G. Weitzel*, vol. 1, 1881, Cincinnati Historical Society Library.

8. Ibid.

9. Grant, *Personal Memoirs*, 439.

10. Captain Paul A. Oliver to Maj. Theodore S. Bowers, 31 March 1865, Reel 94, Abraham Lincoln Papers, Library of Congress.

11. Pres. A. Lincoln to Maj.-Gen. G. Weitzel, 29 March 1865, Reel 94, Abraham Lincoln Papers, Library of Congress.

12. Grant, *Personal Memoirs*, 439.

13. Ibid., 447.

14. Captain Paul A. Oliver to Maj. Theodore S. Bowers, 31 March 1865, Reel 94, Abraham Lincoln Papers, Library of Congress.

15. Ibid.

16. Ibid.

17. Grant, *Personal Memoirs*, 450.

18. Weitzel, "Entry of the United States Forces."

19. Report of Maj.-Gen. Godfrey Weitzel, 17 April 1865; O.R., Ser. I, Vol. 43, p. 1227.

20. Weitzel, "Entry of the United States Forces."

21. Weitzel report (see note 19 above).

22. Weitzel, "Entry of the United States Forces."

23. George F. Shepley, "Incidents of the Capture of Richmond," *Atlantic Monthly* 46, no. 273 (July 1880): 19.

24. Ibid.

25. Ibid.

26. Ibid.

27. Ibid.

28. Edward H. Ripley, "Final Scenes at the Capture and Occupation of Richmond, April 3, 1865," in *Personal Recollections of the War of the Rebellion: Addresses Delivered before the Commandery of the State of New York, Military Order of the Loyal Legion of the United States*, ed. A. Noel Blakeman (New York: Putnam, 1907), 474.

29. Ibid.

30. Richard S. West, Jr., *Lincoln's Scapegoat General: A Life of Benjamin F. Butler, 1818–1893* (Boston: Houghton Mifflin, 1965), 114.

31. Shepley, "Incidents of the Capture," 20.

32. Ibid.

33. Ibid.

34. Ripley, "Final Scenes."

35. Weitzel report (see note 19 above).

36. Raphael Semmes, *Memoirs of Service Afloat during the War Between the States* (Baltimore, MD: Kelly, Piet, 1869), 810.

37. O.R., Ser. 1, Vol. 46, Pt. 3, p. 496.

38. Joan E. Cashin, *First Lady of the Confederacy: Varina Davis's Civil War* (Cambridge, MA: Harvard University Press, 2006), 157.

39. O.R., Ser. 1, Vol. 46, Pt. 3, p. 1264.

40. Grant, *Personal Memoirs*, 452.

41. Ripley, "Final Scenes," 475.

42. Semmes, *Memoirs of Service Afloat*, 811.

43. O.R., Ser. 1, Vol. 46, Pt. 3, p. 1227.

44. Godfrey Weitzel, *Richmond Occupied: Entry of the United States Forces into Richmond, Virginia, April 3, 1865*, ed. Louis H. Manarin (Richmond, VA: Civil War Centennial Committee, 1965), 9.

45. Clement Sulivane, "The Evacuation," in *Battles and Leaders of the Civil War*, ed. Robert U. Johnson and Clarence C. Buel (New York: Century, 1884, 1887–88), 4:725.

46. Lyrics by Robbie Robertson, "The Night They Drove Old Dixie Down," copyright Canaan Music, Inc., 1969.

Chapter 20: The Fall of the Confederacy

1. Edward H. Ripley, "Final Scenes at the Capture and Occupation of Richmond, April 3, 1865," in *Personal Recollections of the War of the Rebellion: Addresses Delivered before the Commandery of the State of New York, Military Order of the Loyal Legion of the United States*, ed. A. Noel Blakeman (New York: Putnam, 1907), 475.

2. George F. Shepley, "Incidents of the Capture of Richmond," *Atlantic Monthly* 46, no. 273 (July 1880): 22.

3. Ibid.

4. Ibid.

5. Ibid.

6. Ibid.

7. Godfrey Weitzel, "Entry of the United States Forces into Richmond, April 3, 1865," in *Letter Book of Gen. G. Weitzel*, vol. 1, 1881, Cincinnati Historical Society Library.

8. Ibid.

9. Shepley, "Incidents of the Capture," 22.

10. Weitzel, "Entry of the United States Forces."

11. Ibid.

12. Ibid.

13. Thomas L. Johnson, *Twenty-Eight Years a Slave; or, the Story of My Life in Three Continents* (London: Mate, 1909), 31.

14. Ripley, "Final Scenes," 475.

15. Shepley, "Incidents of the Capture," 23.

16. Ibid.

17. Ibid., 22.

18. Clement Sulivane, "The Evacuation," in *Battles and Leaders of the Civil War*, ed. Robert U. Johnson and Clarence C. Buel (New York: Century, 1884, 1887–88), 4:725–26.

19. *Richmond Whig*, 4 April 1865.

20. Thomas T. Graves, "The Occupation," in Johnson and Buel, *Battles and Leaders of the Civil War*, 4:725–26.

21. O.R., Ser. 1, Vol. 43, p. 1227.

22. Report of Maj.-Gen. Godfrey Weitzel, 17 April 1865; O.R., Ser. 1, Vol. 43, p. 1227.

23. Michael Golay, *A Ruined Land: The End of the Civil War* (New York: Wiley, 1999), 152.

24. Weitzel, "Entry of the United States Forces."

25. Shepley, "Incidents of the Capture," 23.

26. Ibid.

27. Ripley, "Final Scenes," 476.

28. Weitzel, "Entry of the United States Forces."

29. Ripley, "Final Scenes," 476–77.

30. Golay, *Ruined Land*, 152.

31. Ripley, "Final Scenes."

32. Ibid., 477.

33. Graves, "Occupation," 725–26.

34. Weitzel, "Entry of the United States Forces."

35. *Newark (OH) Advocate*, 9 November 1960.

36. *Evening Whig*, 6 April 1865.

37. *Richmond Dispatch*, 10 February 1893.

38. Weitzel report (see note 22 above).

39. *Richmond Dispatch*, 10 February 1893.

Chapter 21: Entry into Richmond

1. Edward H. Ripley, "Final Scenes at the Capture and Occupation of Richmond, April 3, 1865," in *Personal Recollections of the War of the Rebellion: Addresses Delivered before the Commandery of the State of New York, Military Order of the Loyal Legion of the United States*, ed. A. Noel Blakeman (New York: Putnam, 1907), 479.

2. Abstract from address of Dr. J. R. Gildersleeve, President of the Association of Medical Officers of the Army and Navy of the Confederacy, at Nashville, TN (14 June 1904).

3. Ripley, "Final Scenes," 478.

4. Report of Maj.-Gen. Godfrey Weitzel, April 17, 1865; O.R., Ser. 1, Vol. 43, p. 1227.

5. Godfrey Weitzel, "Entry of the United States Forces into Richmond, April 3, 1865," in *Letter Book of Gen. G. Weitzel*, vol. 1, 1881, Cincinnati Historical Society Library.

6. Charles A. Dana, *Recollections of the Civil War: With the Leaders at Washington and in the Field in the Sixties* (New York: Appleton, 1898), 265.

7. Ripley, "Final Scenes," 480.

8. Ibid.

9. Weitzel, "Entry of the United States Forces."

10. Ripley, "Final Scenes."

11. Thomas T. Graves, "The Occupation," in *Battles and Leaders of the Civil War*, ed. Robert U. Johnson and Clarence C. Buel (New York: Century, 1884, 1887–88), 4:725–26.

12. Weitzel, "Entry of the United States Forces."

13. George F. Shepley, "Incidents of the Capture of Richmond," *Atlantic Monthly* 46, no. 273 (July 1880): 24.

14. Ripley, "Final Scenes," 480, 481.

15. Ibid.

16. Ibid., 481, 482.

17. Major General Godfrey Weitzel's handwritten draft of telegraph message to Lieutenant General Ulysses S. Grant, 3 April 1865. Courtesy of the Museum of the Confederacy, Richmond, Virginia. See figure 21.1.

18. Weitzel reports that the book from which he learned this information was General Adam Badeau's book, *Military History of Ulysses S. Grant* (Beford, MA: Applewood, 1881).

19. Shepley, "Incidents of the Capture," 25.

20. Weitzel, "Entry of the United States Forces."

21. Graves, "Occupation," 725–26.

22. *Richmond Whig*, 4 April 1865.

23. Weitzel, "Entry of the United States Forces."

24. Michael Golay, *A Ruined Land: The End of the Civil War* (New York: Wiley, 1999), 153.

25. Graves, "Occupation," 725–26.

26. Weitzel, "Entry of the United States Forces."

27. Ibid.

28. Shepley, "Incidents of the Capture," 24.

29. Ibid.

30. Weitzel, "Entry of the United States Forces."

31. Shepley, "Incidents of the Capture," 26.

Chapter 22: Lincoln in Richmond

1. Michael Golay, *A Ruined Land: The End of the Civil War* (New York: Wiley, 1999), 158.

2. O.R., Ser. 1, Vol. 46, Pt. 3, p. 566.

3. O.R., Ser. 1, Vol. 46, Pt. 3, p. 545.

4. Report of Maj.-Gen. Godfrey Weitzel, 17 April 1865; O.R., Ser. 1, Vol. 43, p. 1227.

5. Godfrey Weitzel, "Entry of the United States Forces into Richmond, April 3, 1865," in *Letter Book of Gen. G. Weitzel*, vol. 1, 1881, Cincinnati Historical Society Library.

6. Ibid.

7. O.R., Ser. 1, Vol. 51, pp. 1210–11.

8. Ibid.

9. James M. McPherson, *Tried by War: Abraham Lincoln as Commander in Chief* (New York: Penguin, 2008), 261.

10. O.R., Ser. 1, Vol. 12, pp. 173–76.

11. Henry De Garrs, "Mr. Lincoln's Visit to Richmond: Memoranda on the Life of Lincoln," *Century* 40 (1890): 307.

12. David D. Porter, *Incidents and Anecdotes of the Civil War* (New York: Appleton, 1885), 295.

13. Another publication places Lincoln's landing spot at Seventeenth and Dock Streets, quite a way from Rockett's Landing. But this appears to be in the minority. See Harry Kollatz, Jr., "Lincoln in Richmond," *Richmond Magazine* (April 2009).

14. Thomas T. Graves, "The Occupation," in *Battles and Leaders of the Civil War*, ed. Robert U. Johnson and Clarence C. Buel (New York: Century, 1884, 1887–88), 4:725–26.

15. William H. Crook, *Through Five Administrations: Reminiscences of Colonel William H. Crook, Body-Guard to President Lincoln*, comp. and ed. Margarita Spalding Gerry (Whitefish, MT: Kessinger, 2004), 52–53.

16. Marshall W. Fishwick, *Lee after the War* (New York: Dodd, Mead, 1963), 11.

17. Robert Saunders, Jr., *John Archibald Campbell: Southern Moderate, 1811–1889* (Tuscaloosa: University of Alabama Press, 1997), 179.

18. Graves, "Occupation," 725–26.

19. Porter, *Incidents and Anecdotes*, 299.

20. George F. Shepley, "Incidents of the Capture of Richmond," *Atlantic Monthly* 46, no. 273 (July 1880): 26 (hereafter cited in text as ICR).

21. Fishwick, *Lee after the War*, 11.

22. Graves, "Occupation," 725–26.

23. Ibid.

24. Ibid.

25. *New York Herald*, 9 April 1865.

26. *York & Cumberland Railroad Co. v. Myers*, 59 U.S. 246, 18 How. 246, 1855 WL 8195, 15 L.Ed. 380 (Dec. Term 1855).

27. William Gillette, "Benjamin R. Curtis," in *The Justices of the United States Supreme Court, 1789–1969: Their Lives and Major Opinions*, vol. 2, ed. Leon Friedman and Fred L. Israel (New York: Chelsea House, 1969), 937.

28. Charles A. Dana, *Recollections of the Civil War: With the Leaders at Washington and in the Field in the Sixties* (New York: Appleton, 1898), 268.

29. Weitzel, "Entry of the United States Forces."

30. Ibid.

31. Ibid.

32. Saunders, *John Archibald Campbell*, 180.

33. O.R., Ser. 1, Vol. 46, Pt. 3, p. 575.

34. Weitzel, "Entry of the United States Forces."

35. *New York Times*, 23 September 1899.

36. O.R., Ser. 1, Vol. 12, pp. 173–76.

37. Saunders, *John Archibald Campbell*, 180.

38. Ibid., 184.

39. John A. Campbell, *Recollections of the Evacuation of Richmond, April 2, 1865* (Baltimore, MD: Murphy, 1880).

40. Saunders, *John Archibald Campbell*, 180.

41. Roy P. Basler, ed., *The Collected Works of Abraham Lincoln*, vol. 8 (New Brunswick, NJ: Rutgers University Press, 1953), 408.

42. Campbell, *Recollections*.

43. Weitzel, "Entry of the United States Forces."

44. O.R., Ser. 1, Vol. 12, pp. 173–76.

45. Ibid.

Chapter 23: Political Troubles

1. Godfrey Weitzel, "Entry of the United States Forces into Richmond, April 3, 1865." In *Letter Book of Gen. G. Weitzel.* Vol. 1, 1881. Cincinnati Historical Society Library.

2. Ibid.

3. John A. Campbell, *Recollections of the Evacuation of Richmond, April 2, 1865* (Baltimore, MD: Murphy, 1880).

4. A. Lincoln to U. S. Grant, 6 April 1865, in Roy P. Basler, *The Collected Works of Abraham Lincoln*, vol. 8 (New Brunswick, NJ: Rutgers University Press, 1953), 388.

5. George F. Shepley, "Incidents of the Capture of Richmond," *Atlantic Monthly* 46, no. 273 (July 1880): 28.

6. Weitzel, "Entry of the United States Forces."

7. O.R., Ser. 1, Vol. 46, Pt. 3, p. 593.

8. Jacob D. Cox, *Military Reminiscences of the Civil War* (New York: Scribner, 1900).

9. Campbell, *Recollections of the Evacuation*.

10. Ibid., 23.

11. James A. Woodburn, ed., "George W. Julian's Journal: The Assassination of Lincoln," *Indiana Magazine of History* 11, no. 4 (December 1915): 333.

12. Ulysses S. Grant, *Personal Memoirs of U. S. Grant*, 2 vols. (New York: Webster, 1885).

13. Michael Golay, *A Ruined Land: The End of the Civil War* (New York: Wiley, 1999), 165.

14. Shepley, "Incidents of the Capture," 28.

15. Ibid., 27.

16. U. S. Grant to A. Lincoln, 6 April 1865, Reel 94, Lincoln Papers.

17. O.R., Ser. 1, Vol. 46, Pt. 3, p. 610.

18. Campbell, *Recollections of the Evacuation*.

19. Ibid.

20. Robert Saunders, Jr., *John Archibald Campbell: Southern Moderate, 1811–1889* (Tuscaloosa: University of Alabama Press, 1997), 182.

21. Campbell, *Recollections of the Evacuation*.

22. Dana, *Recollections*, 267.

23. O.R., Ser. 1, Vol. 46, Pt. 3, p. 677.

24. Dana, *Recollections*, 267.

25. Ibid., 268.

26. *A Prayer for the President of the Confederate States, and all in Civil Authority,* The Order for Daily Morning and Evening Prayer, Protestant Episcopal Church in the Confederate States of America (Atlanta: R. J. Maynard, 1863).

27. Charles A. Dana, *Recollections of the Civil War: With the Leaders at Washington and in the Field in the Sixties* (New York: Appleton, 1898), 270.

28. Godfrey Weitzel, "Entry of the United States Forces into Richmond, April 3, 1865," in *Letter Book of Gen. G. Weitzel,* vol. 1, 188, Cincinnati Historical Society Library.

29. O.R., Ser. 1, Vol. 46, Pt. 3, p. 678.

30. Ibid.

31. Dana, *Recollections of the Civil War,* 269.

32. Weitzel, "Entry of the United States Forces."

33. Bob Blaisdell, ed., *The Civil War: A Book of Quotations* (Mineola, NY: Dover, 2004), 169.

34. Carol K. Bleser and Lesley J. Gordon, eds., *Intimate Strategies of the Civil War: Military Commanders and Their Wives* (New York: Oxford University Press, 2001), 193.

35. O.R., Ser. 1, Vol. 12, pp. 173–76.

36. Dana, *Recollections of the Civil War,* 271.

37. Benjamin P. Thomas and Harold M. Hyman, *Stanton: The Life and Times of Lincoln's Secretary of War* (New York: Knopf, 1962), 354.

38. Weitzel, "Entry of the United States Forces."

39. Ibid.

40. O.R., Ser. 1, Vol. 46, Pt. 3, pp. 696–97.

41. Weitzel, "Entry of the United States Forces."

42. O.R., Ser. 1, Vol. 46, Pt. 3, pp. 696–97, 724.

43. Weitzel, "Entry of the United States Forces."

44. O.R., Ser. 1, Vol. 46, Pt. 3, p. 724.

45. Campbell, *Recollections of the Evacuation.*

46. O.R., Ser. 1, Vol. 46, Pt. 3, p. 573.

47. O.R., Ser. 1, Vol. 58, p. 573.

48. Weitzel, "Entry of the United States Forces."

49. Ibid.

Chapter 24: Good Friday—Black Friday

1. "Change of Commanders," *Richmond Whig,* 14 April 1865.

2. Godfrey Weitzel, "Entry of the United States Forces into Richmond, April 3, 1865," in *Letter Book of Gen. G. Weitzel,* vol. 1, 1881, Cincinnati Historical Society Library.

3. Ibid.

4. Ibid.

5. Ibid.

6. Timothy S. Good, *We Saw Lincoln Shot: One Hundred Eyewitness Accounts* (Jackson: University Press of Mississippi, 1995), 10.

7. Thomas T. Graves, "The Occupation," in *Battles and Leaders of the Civil War*, ed. Robert U. Johnson and Clarence C. Buel (New York: Century, 1884, 1887–88), 4:725–26.

8. Ibid.

9. Ibid.

10. G. Weitzel to Judge B. Storer, 27 April 1865, Bellamy Storer Papers, Folder No. 14, Cincinnati Historical Society Library.

11. Ibid.

12. Ibid.

13. Ibid.

14. *New York Times*, 15 April 1865.

15. Robert Saunders Jr., *John Archibald Campbell: Southern Moderate, 1811–1889* (Tuscaloosa: University of Alabama Press, 1997), 185.

16. John A. Campbell, *Recollections of the Evacuation of Richmond, April 2, 1865* (Baltimore, MD: Murphy, 1880).

17. Saunders, *John Archibald Campbell*, 187.

18. William Gillette, "Benjamin R. Curtis," in *The Justices of the United States Supreme Court 1789–1969: Their Lives and Major Opinions*, vol. 2, ed. Leon Friedman and Fred L. Israel (New York: Chelsea House, 1969), 938.

19. Campbell, *Recollections of the Evacuation of Richmond*.

Chapter 25: Postwar Life of the Young General

1. Maj.-Gen. G. Weitzel to Capt. J. F. Lacey, 23 June 1865.

2. Godfrey Weitzel, "Entry of the United States Forces into Richmond, April 3, 1865," in *Letter Book of Gen. G. Weitzel*, vol. 1, 1881, Cincinnati Historical Society Library.

3. G. Weitzel to Rep. T. L. Young, 28 April 1882, *Letter Press Volumes of Gen. G. Weitzel*, vol. 1, Archives of the Cincinnati Historical Society Library.

4. *Journal of the Executive Proceedings of the Senate*, 9 December 1867.

5. G. Weitzel to Judge Alfred Yaple, 25 April 1878, *Letter Press Volumes of Gen. G. Weitzel*, vol. 1, p. 72, Archives of the Cincinnati Historical Society Library.

6. John W. Ward and Christian Warren, *Silent Victories: The History and Practice of Public Health in Twentieth-Century America* (New York: Oxford University Press, 2007), 70.

7. *New York Times*, 19 March 1873.

8. *New York Times*, 12 April 1876.

9. Joseph P. Smith, *History of the Republican Party in Ohio*, vol. 1 (Chicago: Lewis Publishing, 1898), 450.

10. G. Weitzel telegram to Pres. R. B. Hayes, 14 May 1878, *Letter Press Volumes of Gen. G. Weitzel*, vol. 1, p. 115, Archives of the Cincinnati Historical Society Library.

11. Smith, *History of the Republican Party*.

12. Leland R. Johnson, *The Falls City Engineers: A History of the Louisville District, Corps of Engineers, United States Army, 1970–1983* (Louisville, KY: U.S. Army Corps of Engineers, 1975), 122.

13. Ibid., 123.

14. Ibid., 128.

15. G. Weitzel personal biographical sketch, undated, U.S. Military Academy.

16. *Second Treatise on the Decrease of Water, G. Wax*, trans. G. Weitzel, U.S. Printing Office (1880); see also G. Weitzel letter to Brig.-Gen. H. Wright, 17 October 1881, *Letter Press Volumes of Gen. G. Weitzel*, vol. 1, p. 713, Archives of the Cincinnati Historical Society Library.

17. G. Weitzel personal biographical sketch, undated, U.S. Military Academy.

18. G. Weitzel to Brig.-Gen. H. Wright, 4 October 1881, *Letter Press Volumes of Gen. G. Weitzel*, vol. 1, p. 704, Archives of the Cincinnati Historical Society Library.

19. Merlin E. Sumner, ed., *The Diary of Cyrus B. Comstock* (Dayton, OH: Morningside House, 1987), vii.

20. G. Weitzel to Brig.-Gen. A. A. Humphreys, 28 February 1878, *Letter Press Volumes of Gen. G. Weitzel*, vol. 1, pp. 26–27, Archives of the Cincinnati Historical Society Library.

21. G. Weitzel to Sec. Wm. M. Evarts , 12 March 1878; and G. Weitzel to Brig.-Gen. A.A. Humphreys, 14 March 1878, *Letter Press Volumes of Gen. G. Weitzel*, vol. 1, pp. 37, 40, Archives of the Cincinnati Historical Society Library.

22. G. Weitzel personal biographical sketch, undated, U.S. Military Academy.

23. G. Weitzel to Gen. C. Crasse, 31 March 1882, *Letter Press Volumes of Gen. G. Weitzel*, vol. 1, p. 793, Archives of the Cincinnati Historical Society Library.

24. Jack D. Welsh, *Medical Histories of Union Generals* (Kent, OH: Kent State University Press, 1996), 363.

25. G. Weitzel to Rep. T. L. Young, 28 April 1882, *Letter Press Volumes of Gen. G. Weitzel*, vol. 1, Archives of the Cincinnati Historical Society Library.

26. *Chester (PA) Times*, 4 August 1882.

27. Welsh, *Medical Histories*.

28. Buried alongside Godfrey are his second wife, Louise (Bogen) Weitzel, who was born in 1842 in Cincinnati, Ohio, and died of senility on 18 August 1927 in St. Paul, Minnesota; and their daughter, Irene (Weitzel) Nye, born on 11 April 1876 in Detroit, Michigan; died of respiratory failure on 11 October 1936 in St. Paul, Minnesota.

Glossary

abatis: A line of heavy trees laid down or cut around a fort, the tops or upper portions of which are sharpened to a point, often interlaced so that men cannot easily crawl through them.

battalion: A unit of soldiers consisting of approximately 500 men or one-half the strength of a 1,000-man infantry **regiment**. Occasionally two **companies** (100–200 men) were referred to as a battalion.

bivouac: A temporary encampment for one or more nights consisting of hastily constructed shelter from the elements in the form of tents or by using branches or other types of available natural cover.

bombproof: A reinforced structure built of wood and covered with earth that could withstand artillery fire.

breastwork: A constructed parapet that was breast-high to the average soldier.

brigade: A military unit, most often comprising four **regiments**, or approximately 4,000 soldiers, though actual numbers varied. Brigades were commanded by brigadier generals.

cheval-de-frise: From the French for "horse from Friesland," this term was used to describe a defensive barbed entanglement. During the Civil War, these obstacles were made of a wooden shaft from which wood projections or spears radiated in four directions. Chevaux-de-frise were used to obstruct passages, protect a breach in the line, or form an impediment to cavalry.

Columbiad: A large-caliber, smoothbore, muzzle-loading cannon that was able to fire heavy projectiles using both high and low trajectories.

company: The smallest military unit of soldiers, usually containing 50 to 100 men, commanded by a captain.

corduroy road: A type of road made by placing sand-covered logs close together and perpendicular to the direction of the road over a low or swampy area. The result improved passage for troops, horses, and wagons over impassable mud or dirt roads.

corps: An army unit of two to four divisions, commanded by a major general in the Union armies or by a lieutenant general in the Confederate armies.

earthworks: A generic term applied to fortifications that were built of soil for temporary use. Mostly hand-dug, these earthen mounds provided protection against enemy fire and varied in height and configuration.

entrenchment: A type of fortification created by hand-digging the earth to create a passageway or protective structure.

ironclad: A steam-propelled wooden warship protected by iron or steel armor plates of varying thickness.

magazine: A **bombproof** compartment designed to safely store and contain gunpowder and other types of ammunition.

palisade: A wooden fence or wall of variable height used as a defensive structure; often made from logs with pointed tips.

parapet: A wall-like barrier on the top of a defensive barrier such as an **earthwork** or other fortification.

pontoon bridge: A bridge that floated on water, supported by wooden barges or using boatlike pontoons to support the bridge deck.

ram: A ship or boat equipped with an armored prow for ramming another ship.

rampart: A type of defensive wall or embankment forming the main body of a fortification and consisting of an **earthwork** and a **parapet**.

redoubt: An **earthwork** that was enclosed on all sides. The overall configuration may have been square, polygonal, or circular.

regiment: A military unit composed of ten or more **companies**, usually a total of about 1,000 men. Regiments were commonly thought to consist of two **battalions**. Over the course of the Civil War, regiments were often undermanned, containing considerably less than 1,000 men.

skirmishers: Armed foot soldiers used in advance of the main body of advancing troops. When formed into a line of battle, a **regiment** might send one or more **companies** forward as a "skirmish line." Skirmish lines were often positioned 400 to 500 yards ahead of the main troop formation.

Bibliography

Badeau, Adam. *Military History of Ulysses S. Grant.* Bedford, MA: Applewood, 1881.

Baker, Jean H. *Mary Todd Lincoln: A Biography.* New York: Norton, 1989.

Barnes, William H. *The Fortieth Congress of the United States: Historical and Biographical.* Vol. 2. New York: Perine, 1870.

Bartlett, Asa W. *History of the Twelfth Regiment: New Hampshire Volunteers in the War of the Rebellion.* Concord, NH: Evans, 1897.

Bartlett, Napier. *A Soldier's Story of the War: Including the Marches and Battles of the Washington Artillery, and of Other Louisiana Troops.* New Orleans: Clark and Hofeline, 1874.

Basler, Roy P., ed. *The Collected Works of Abraham Lincoln.* New Brunswick, NJ: Rutgers University Press, 1953.

Blaisdell, Bob, ed. *The Civil War: A Book of Quotations.* Mineola, NY: Dover, 2004.

Bleser, Carol K., and Lesley J. Gordon, eds. *Intimate Strategies of the Civil War: Military Commanders and Their Wives.* New York: Oxford University Press, 2001.

Butler, Benjamin F. *Butler's Book: Autobiography and Personal Reminiscences of Major-General Benjamin F. Butler.* Boston: Thayer, 1892.

Campbell, John A. *Recollections of the Evacuation of Richmond, April 2, 1865.* Baltimore, MD: Murphy, 1880.

Carpenter, George N. *History of the Eighth Regiment Vermont Volunteers, 1861–1865.* Boston: Deland and Barta, 1886.

Cashin, Joan E. *First Lady of the Confederacy: Varina Davis's Civil War.* Cambridge, MA: Harvard University Press, 2006.

Casso, Evans J. *Francis T. Nicholls: A Biographical Tribute.* Thibodaux, LA: Nicholls College Foundation, 1987.

Cornish, Dudley Taylor. *The Sable Arm: Negro Troops in the Union Army, 1861–1865.* New York: Norton, 1966.

Cotham, Edward T., Jr. *Sabine Pass: The Confederacy's Thermopylae.* Austin: University of Texas Press, 2004.

Cowley, H. Robert, and Thomas Guinzburg, eds. *West Point: Two Centuries of Honor and Tradition.* New York: Warner, 2002.

Cox, Jacob D. *Military Reminiscences of the Civil War.* New York: Scribner, 1900.

Crook, William H. *Through Five Administrations: Reminiscences of Colonel William H. Crook, Body-Guard to President Lincoln*. Compiled and ed. Margarita Spalding Gerry. Whitefish, MT: Kessinger, 2004. Originally published 1910.

Cunningham, Edward. *The Port Hudson Campaign, 1862–1863*. Baton Rouge: Louisiana State University Press, 1963.

Custer, George A. "War Memoirs." *Galaxy* 21, no. 4 (April 1876): 448–60.

Dana, Charles A. *Recollections of the Civil War: With the Leaders at Washington and in the Field in the Sixties*. New York: Appleton, 1898.

De Forest, John W. *A Volunteer's Adventures: A Union Captain's Record of the Civil War*. Edited by James H. Croushore. New Haven, CT: Yale University Press, 1946.

De Garrs, Henry. "Mr. Lincoln's Visit to Richmond: Memoranda on the Life of Lincoln." *Century* 40 (1890).

Doyle, Elizabeth J. "Civilian Life in Occupied New Orleans, 1862–65." PhD Diss., Louisiana State University, 1955.

Duffy, James P. *Lincoln's Admiral: The Civil War Campaigns of David Farragut*. Hoboken, NJ: Wiley, 1997.

Fishwick, Marshall W. *Lee after the War*. New York: Dodd, Mead, 1963.

Fleetwood, Christian A. *The Negro as a Soldier*. Washington, DC: Cook, 1895.

Foote, Shelby D. *The Civil War: A Narrative*. Vol. 3, *Red River to Appomattox*. New York: Random House, 1974.

Gillette, William. "Benjamin R. Curtis." In *The Justices of the United States Supreme Court, 1789–1969: Their Lives and Major Opinions*. Vol. 2, edited by Leon Friedman and Fred L. Israel, 895–926. New York: Chelsea House, 1969.

Glatthaar, Joseph T. *Forged in Battle: The Civil War Alliance of Black Soldiers and White Officers*. Baton Rouge: Louisiana State University Press, 1990.

Golay, Michael. *A Ruined Land: The End of the Civil War*. New York: Wiley, 1999.

Good, Timothy S. *We Saw Lincoln Shot: One Hundred Eyewitness Accounts*. Jackson: University Press of Mississippi, 1995.

Gragg, Rod. *Confederate Goliath: The Battle of Fort Fisher*. New York: HarperCollins, 1991.

Grant, John, James Lynch, and Ronald Bailey. *West Point: The First 200 Years*. Guilford, CT: Globe Pequot Press, 2002.

Grant, Ulysses S. *Personal Memoirs of U. S. Grant*. 2 vols. New York: Webster, 1885.

Graves, Thomas T. "The Occupation." In Johnson and Buel, *Battles and Leaders of the Civil War*, 4:726–28.

Hearn, Chester G. *When the Devil Came Down to Dixie: Ben Butler in New Orleans*. Baton Rouge: Louisiana State University Press, 1997.

Henry, Robert S. *The Story of the Confederacy*. New York: Grosset and Dunlap, 1931.

Howard, S. E. "Eighth Vermont Infantry Regimental History." VermontCivilWar. Org Database. http://vermontcivilwar.org/units/8/history.php.

Irwin, Richard B. *History of the Nineteenth Army Corps*. Fairford: Echo Library, 2009.

Johnson, Leland R. *The Falls City Engineers: A History of the Louisville District, Corps of Engineers, United States Army, 1970–1983*. Louisville, KY: U.S. Army Corps of Engineers, 1975.

Johnson, Robert U., and Clarence C. Buel, eds. *Battles and Leaders of the Civil War.* 4 vols. New York: Century, 1884, 1887–88.

Johnson, Thomas L. *Twenty-Eight Years a Slave; or, the Story of My Life in Three Continents.* London: Mate, 1909.

Keller, Christian B. *Chancellorsville and the Germans: Nativism, Ethnicity, and Civil War Memory.* New York: Fordham University Press, 2007.

Keyes, Frances P. *Madame Castel's Lodger.* New York: Farrar, Straus, 1962.

Kollatz, Harry, Jr. "Lincoln in Richmond." *Richmond Magazine* (April 2009).

Lamb, William. "Defence of Fort Fisher, North Carolina." In *Operations on the Atlantic Coast, 1861–1865; Virginia, 1862, 1864; Vicksburg.* Vol. 9, edited by Theodore F. Dwight, 347–88. Boston: Military Historical Society of Massachusetts, 1912.

Landry, James. *Cincinnati Past and Present: Its Industrial History, as Exhibited in the Life-Labours of Its Leading Men.* Cincinnati: Joblin, 1872.

Library of Congress. *A Century of Lawmaking for a New Nation: U.S. Congressional Documents and Debates, 1774–1875.* Washington, DC: U.S. Library of Congress. http://memory.loc.gov/ammem/amlaw/lawhome.html.

Lowry, Thomas P. *The Story the Soldiers Wouldn't Tell: Sex in the Civil War.* Mechanicsburg, PA: Stackpole Books, 1994.

Marshall, Jessie A., ed. *Private and Official Correspondence of Gen. Benjamin F. Butler.* Norwood, MA: Plimpton Press, 1917.

McPherson, James M. *Tried by War: Abraham Lincoln as Commander in Chief.* New York: Penguin, 2008.

Morrison, James L. *"The Best School": West Point, 1833–1866.* Kent, OH: Kent State University Press, 1998.

National Academy of Sciences. *Biographical Memoirs.* Vol. 2, *Cyrus Ballou Comstock.* Washington, DC, 1911.

Porter, David D. *Incidents and Anecdotes of the Civil War.* New York: Appleton, 1885.

———. *The Naval History of the Civil War.* Mineola, NY: Dover, 1998.

———. *The Opening of the Lower Mississippi.* New York: Yoseloff, 1956.

Reinhart, Joseph R. Kentucky's German-Americans in the Civil War. http://kygermanscw.yolasite.com.

Ripley, Edward H. "Final Scenes at the Capture and Occupation of Richmond, April 3, 1865." In *Personal Recollections of the War of the Rebellion: Addresses Delivered before the Commandery of the State of New York, Military Order of the Loyal Legion of the United States,* edited by A. Noel Blakeman, 472–502. New York: Putnam, 1907.

Robbins, James S. *Last in Their Class: Custer, Pickett and the Goats of West Point.* New York: Encounter Books, 2006.

Ryan, David D., ed. *A Yankee Spy in Richmond: The Civil War Diary of "Crazy Bet" Van Lew.* Mechanicsburg, PA: Stackpole Books, 2001.

Saunders, Robert, Jr. *John Archibald Campbell: Southern Moderate, 1811–1889.* Tuscaloosa: University of Alabama Press, 1997.

Semmes, Raphael. *Memoirs of Service Afloat during the War Between the States.* Baltimore, MD: Kelly, Piet, 1869.

Shepley, George F. "Incidents of the Capture of Richmond." *Atlantic Monthly* 46, no. 273 (July 1880): 18–28.

Smith, Joseph P., ed. *History of the Republican Party in Ohio.* Vol. 1. Chicago: Lewis Publishing, 1898.

Soley, James R. "Early Operations in the Gulf." In Johnson and Buel, *Battles and Leaders of the Civil War,* 2:13.

Sprague, Homer B. *History of the Thirteenth Infantry Regiment of Connecticut Volunteers during the Great Rebellion.* Hartford, CT: Lockwood, 1867.

Steckel, Richard H. "A History of the Standard of Living in the United States."EH. Net Encyclopedia, edited by Robert Whaples. July 22, 2002. http://eh.net/encyclopedia/?article=steckel.standard.living.us.

Storke, Elliot G. *History of Cayuga County, New York.* Syracuse, NY: Mason, 1879.

Strong, George C. *Cadet Life at West Point: By an Officer of the United States Army.* Boston: Burnham, 1862.

Stucky, Scott W. "Joint Operations in the Civil War." *Joint Force Quarterly* 6 (Autumn–Winter 1994–95).

Sulivane, Clement. "The Evacuation." In Johnson and Buel, *Battles and Leaders of the Civil War,* 4:725.

Sumner, Merlin E., ed. *The Diary of Cyrus B. Comstock.* Dayton, OH: Morningside House, 1987.

Sun-tzu. *The Art of War.* New York: Barnes and Noble, 2003.

Thomas, Benjamin P., and Harold M. Hyman. *Stanton: The Life and Times of Lincoln's Secretary of War.* New York: Knopf, 1962.

Trefousse, Hans L. *Ben Butler: The South Called Him Beast!* New York: Twayne, 1957.

Ward, John W., and Christian Warren. *Silent Victories: The History and Practice of Public Health in Twentieth-Century America.* New York: Oxford University Press, 2007.

Waugh, John C. *The Class of 1846: From West Point to Appomattox; Stonewall Jackson, George McClellan and Their Brothers.* New York: Random House, 1994.

Weitzel, Godfrey. "Entry of the United States Forces into Richmond, April 3, 1865." In *Letter Book of Gen. G. Weitzel.* Vol. 1, 1881. Cincinnati Historical Society Library.

———. *Richmond Occupied: Entry of the United States Forces into Richmond, Virginia, April 3, 1865.* Edited by Louis H. Manarin. Richmond, VA: Civil War Centennial Committee, 1965.

Welsh, Jack D. *Medical Histories of Union Generals.* Kent, OH: Kent State University Press, 1996.

West, Richard S., Jr. *Lincoln's Scapegoat General: A Life of Benjamin F. Butler, 1818–1893.* Boston: Houghton Mifflin, 1965.

Williams, C. S. *Williams' Cincinnati Directory, City Guide and Business Mirror.* Cincinnati, OH: C. S. Williams, 1853.

Winters, John D. *The Civil War in Louisiana.* Baton Rouge: Louisiana State University Press, 1991.

Woodburn, James A., ed. "George W. Julian's Journal: The Assassination of Lincoln." *Indiana Magazine of History* 11, no. 4 (December 1915).

Index

About the Author

G. William Quatman is the great-grandson of Jacob Louis Weitzel, an emigrant from Alsace-Lorraine who the family believed was the nephew of Godfrey Weitzel. Despite efforts to connect the dots, the link between Jacob and Godfrey has not been established. This fascination resulted in years of research into the life of Major General Godfrey Weitzel. Mr. Quatman is a licensed architect and an attorney, as well as a historian and lecturer. He has been a partner in a major Kansas City law firm and since 2008 general counsel to a large international design and construction company. Bill Quatman has taught courses at the University of Kansas and is a published author of numerous legal books and articles.

When not engaged in law or architecture, Mr. Quatman is an avid reader of Civil War history. He and his family live in a house on the battlefield of the October 1864 conflict known as the "Battle of Westport," and Bill is a member of the Civil War Roundtable of Kansas City. The Quatmans have three grown children, and despite his Union leanings, Bill's youngest daughter attended the University of Mississippi, home to the "Rebels." Quatman and his wife are both graduates of the University of Kansas in Lawrence, Kansas—the town burned by Confederate guerrilla William Quantrill and his band of bushwhackers in August 1863—and whose school mascot is named for the local abolitionists, the "Jayhawks."

Quatman also serves on the board of directors of the American Society of Ephesus, Inc., and the Ephesus Foundation, Inc. (USA), and is engaged in archaeological restoration of the ancient city of Ephesus, in modern-day Turkey. He is also involved in making a film related to the history of ancient Ephesus and its role in forming the Christian church worldwide.